D0147629

Marketing – the Retro Revolution

STEPHEN BROWN

SAGE Publications
London • Thousand Oaks • New Delhi

First published 2001

 SAGE Publications Ltd
6 Bonhill Street
London EC2A 4PU

SAGE Publications Inc.
2455 Teller Road
Thousand Oaks, California 91320

SAGE Publications India Pvt Ltd
32, M-Block Market
Greater Kailash – I
New Delhi 110 048

British Library Cataloguing in Publication data

A catalogue record for this book is available
from the British Library

ISBN 0 7619 6850 4
ISBN 0 7619 6851 2 (pbk)

Library of Congress Control Number available

Typeset by Mayhew Typesetting, Rhayader, Powys
Printed and bound in Great Britain by Athenaeum Press,
Gateshead

Contents

Recuperating Marketing: On Commencing a Course of Retro Shock Treatment

Many years ago, when I was a pustular and malodorous adolescent, I had a deeply disgusting habit. Despite what you might think, this trait did not entail libidinal fantasies, anorakish obsessions or proficiency on the air guitar, though my virtuoso interpretation of 'Stairway to Heaven' was something to behold.

It still is.

My teenage fixation, rather, revolved around advertising. Sad, simple-minded sociopath that I was – and remain – I used to concoct imaginary advertising slogans for equally imaginary products.[1] Most of these were predicated on bad puns or atrocious wordplay and, fortuitously, I forgot to found an archive. The only one that I can remember was for a brand of bananas called 'No'. The campaign, as you've probably already guessed, was based on the old song, 'Yes, we have No bananas'. The twist, however, was that I adapted it to specific consumer segments – Noel bananas for the Christmas market, Noh bananas for stage struck aesthetes, Nob bananas for the aspirant upper classes, Now bananas for time-pressed executives, Noah bananas for fundamentalists, apocalyptics and ark-building seafarers, etc. Modesty forbids, you understand, but I like to think that my yellow-packs anticipated the no-brand, own-label bonanza of the late seventies, albeit my elaborate plans for celebrity endorsement involving the then big-time rock band, Yes, weren't so much ahead of their time as a banana skin to oblivion.[2]

Suitably emboldened by my big bananas campaign, I decided that instead of going to university, I'd make my name in copywriting. So, I rang up a marketing agency on spec. to see if they'd give a long-haired, wispy-bearded, painfully shy teenager some much-needed careers advice, which they kindly agreed to do.[3] Ever astute, I arrived at their offices wearing my best biker jacket, adhesive tattoos, gold-plated earrings and Black Sabbath-emblazoned crash helmet. (I didn't actually own a motorbike, of course, just the leathers and accessories, but that is by the by.) After trying and failing to engage me in polysyllabic conversation, they decided to test me out. They told me about a client who was planning to open a chain of carry-out pizza parlours, selling single slices like they did in the States. I don't know whether it was a real or a hypothetical client – probably the latter – but I beavered away on the campaign over the weekend.

What I came up with was a concept called *Pizza in our Time*, based on a Second World War theme. The television ads used the famous footage of Neville Chamberlain returning from Munich: 'I have in my hand a piece of pizza.' The menu included items like Blitzkrieg Pizzas, Bismarck Pizzas, Panzer Pizzas, Vichy Pizzas, Pizzas on the River Kwai, the Sands of Pizza Jima, Pizzola Gay. There were utility pizzas, iron ration pizzas, spam and powdered egg pizzas, Battle of the Bulge pizzas. American-style pizzas were over spiced, over priced and over here. Japanese pizzas had bamboo shoots under the crust. Italian pizzas came with extra-runny sauce. Home deliveries were made by von Ryan's Express Pizza; take-aways comprised the Pizza Escape; and those with extra, chilli-peppered toppings became Where Pizzas Dare. I seriously considered a concentration camp design for the retail outlets, but because the ovens might put some people off, I opted for an operations room scenario (bandit pizzas at two o'clock, kind of thing). I also suggested future diversification options into sandwiches – wolf pack submarines, naturally – and foreign cuisine. Careless tacos cost lives. I even offered a number of alternative advertising slogans: 'Your pizza needs you'; 'We shall eat them on the beaches'; 'Never in the field of pizza baking has so much been sold, to so many, by so few . . . at only 45 pence a slice!'

When I went back to the agency on Monday morning, they were appalled. Truly appalled. The head honcho gave me a stern lecture about the need for preparatory market research, the preferences of consumers, the importance of marketing planning, budgeting, floorspace-to-sales ratios, customer throughput indices, the differing economics of cafeteria-style versus carry-out catering operations, the principles of targeting, positioning, outlet location and on and on and on. I think I even heard the word 'Kotler' for the first time, though maybe I've introjected it in retrospect. Suffice it to say, I was completely traumatized by this reaction. I now realize that it was done for my own good, to encourage me to study, to go to university, to get a proper grounding in marketing before trying again. But it didn't feel like that at the time.

I also now realize that the concept I came up with – juvenile though it was – is an example of retromarketing, as is this act of recalling and re-presenting it. Retro, indeed, seems to be everywhere these days. Old-style styling is *de rigueur* in numerous product categories: motorcycles, coffee makers, cameras, radios, refrigerators, telephones, toasters, perfumes and promos for Pentium processors, to name but a few. Retro is apparent across the various components of the marketing mix, from pseudo-antique packaging and repro retail stores to on-line auctions, which represent a hi-tech throwback to pre modern pricing practices. In addition to the cyber-souk, the recent rapid rise of heritage centres, mega-brand museums and festival shopping malls suggests that retroscapes are taking their place in the marketing pantheon alongside brandscapes, servicescapes, mindscapes and more besides.[4]

Retro, however, is not confined to 'mainstream' marketing endeavour. As I write this preface, ABBA, Tom Jones and Santana – seventies icons one and all – dominate the popular music industry. Meanwhile, the soundtrack from *Gladiator*, a sword and sandals epic, is defeating all comers in the classical charts. *Harry Potter and the Goblet of Fire*, a twenty-first-century take on *Tom Brown's Schooldays*, is Britain's best-selling hardback book; *Angela's Ashes*, Frank McCourt's memories of the good old, bad old days in 1930s Limerick, ranks high in the paperback listings; *Mission Impossible 2*, a remake of a remake of a seventies television series, is packing them in at the multiplexes; *The Thomas Crown Affair*, Brosnan and Russo's update of McQueen and Dunaway's 1970 classic, occupies prime slot in the sell-through video market; Lara Croft's archaeological adventures in *Tomb Raider II, the Final Conflict* are leading the charge at the nation's Playstations; and, those classics of children's television, *Pinky and Perky*, *Bill & Ben* and *The Woodentops*, are all set for a merchandise-spinning return to our screens.

In Milan and Paris, moreover, this year's look is remarkable, not simply because it is retro (as it was last year and the year before that), but because it pick 'n' mixes several time periods at once. Seventh Avenue follows suit, as does the remainder of 'Neo' York. *Kiss Me Kate* is the Emmy-winning toast of Broadway; the nostalgia of Norman Rockwell and Walker Evans is on show in the art galleries of SoHo; Wall Street is wallowing in a dotcom bubble bath, while the ghost of panics past (class of 1929) prepares to pull the plug. On the other side of the Great Divide, Seattle is rocked by '68-style retro riots, groups of anti-capitalist protesters bound together by the Internet, as are downtown Davos and central London. Even the suburban sticks are not exempt, since south-east England's projected population growth is set to be met by the abandonment of mock-Tudor executive estates, with their faux-Victorian interiors, and the building of neo-Georgian terraces instead, complete with retro-stucco decorative detailing. Sixties-style regional planning, to be sure, is only to be expected from retro politicians, such as Tony I'm-Backing-Britain Blair, though he is not alone. Wild Bill Clinton rebuilt JFK's Camelot, concupiscence included; his putative successors squabble over the Reagan mantle; Jörg Haider brings a hint of National Socialism to Austria; Vladimir Putin is a cold war warrior of old; and, as rapidly escalating petrol prices testify, the Middle Eastern oil czars are doing a 1973 on the western world.

Retro, then, is all around. Retro religious beliefs abound, both new age and bible belt. Retro diseases, such as leprosy, malaria, polio and TB, are back with an anti-antibiotic vengeance. Retro feminists reclaim Barbie, Miss World and romantic fiction, whilst complaining of retro sexism in retro auto commercials. Retro traditions and identities are invented anew (e.g. the Ulster-Scots) and ancient rights of ethnic self-determination duly demanded. Retro consumerists are hijacking bill-boards, subverting advertising slogans and boycotting twenty-first-century sweatshop operators. Barter, we are told, is back. Dead celebrities hawk heritage brands. Shopping channels are postmodern medicine shows. Store loyalty cards are latter-day Green Shield stamps. Grocery retailers reintroduce home deliveries (postmodern equivalents of the boy on a bicycle), and good old-fashioned imperial measures (for those who haven't had sufficient time to come to terms with decimalization). Ford produces a special edition Ka, in 'any colour as long as it's black'. Oil of Olay claims to combat the 'seven signs of ageing', a Rosser Reevesque slogan if ever there was one (he must be turning five ways in his grave). The for-mash-get-Smash Martians are reanimated in light of their high placing in a 'Greatest Adverts of all Time' opinion poll. *The Onion*, an American satirical magazine, reports that retromarketers are running out of pasts: retro rationing a possibility! The *Guardian* publishes a retro hit parade, where the seventies still top the charts, though the eighties are about to be re-released. Art Nouveau, evidently, is the next big thing – coming soon to bed linen, place mats and fridge magnets near you – just the way it was in the 1970s (as neo-Art Nouveau), the 1930s (as Art Deco) and the 1890s (as a revival of the Pre-Raphaelites' medieval revival). Maybe we should call it neo-neo-neo-neo-Art Nouveau. Or, Mart Nouveau, come to think of it.

Thirty years on from Alvin Toffler's *Future Shock*, it seems that we are not only living in a time of *Retro Shock* – retro schlock, rather – but retro retroism is also in fashion. That is to say, we are engaged in a reflexive retro debate about the roots of today's retro marketing revival.[5] We are told, for example, that *la mode retro* was big in France during the 1970s; ten years later, nostalgia swept all before it in Japan; and Australia surfed the nostalgia tsunami in the decade just past. In Britain, the turning point came in 1985, when Levi's 'Laundrette' – a retro ad. for the company's classic 501s, featuring Nik Kamen's retro boxer shorts and Marvin Gaye's immortal 'I Heard it Through the Grapevine' – was broadcast for the first time and sent sales rocketing by 800%. In the United States, the epochal shift also occurred during the mid-1980s, largely on account of the New Coke débâcle. When the world's biggest brand was forced to bring back the original, the classic, the once and future Coke – and sell it with a retro message[6] – it became clear that heritage was building up a head of steam. Fifteen years later, the retro loco is still clattering through the station, whilst new-and-improved marketers wait patiently at the crossroads, hoping it will pass.

In this regard, the pessimists amongst us might be inclined to conclude that today's retromarketing mindset is indicative of inertia, intellectual bankruptcy and the waning of creativity. Certainly, it is very much in keeping with marketing's so-called 'mid life crisis', a widespread sense that our subject has ground to a halt and is being bypassed by newer, sexier concepts.[7] It is my belief, however, that the complete opposite is the case. Retro is a harbinger of revolutionary change, a long overdue return to the roots of the discipline, to a time before the 'modern' marketing paradigm held insidious, invidious sway. This argument will be elaborated as the present exercise unfolds, but for the meantime it is sufficient to refer, in suitably retro research fashion, to Karl Marx's *Eighteenth Brumaire of Louis Bonaparte*. Now, everyone is familiar with the essay's famous opening line, that history repeats itself, the first time as tragedy, the second time as farce, and its oft recycled aphorism about men who make history, 'but not under circumstances of their own choosing'. The latter remark, however, is followed by the hirsute one's claim that:

> The tradition of all the dead generations weighs like a nightmare on the brain of the living. And just when they seem engaged in revolutionizing themselves and things, in creating something entirely new, precisely in such epochs of revolutionary crisis they anxiously conjure up the spirits of the past to their service and borrow from them names, battle slogans and costumes in order to present the new scene of world history in this time honoured disguise and this borrowed language. Thus Luther donned the mask of Apostle Paul, the Revolution of 1789 to 1814 draped itself alternately as the Roman Republic and the Roman Empire, and the Revolution of 1848 knew nothing better than to parody, in turn, 1789 and the revolutionary tradition of 1793 to 1795. In like manner, the beginner who has learnt a new language always translates it back into his mother tongue.[8]

This book, in a nutshell, is about the mother tongue of marketing. It is predicated on the simple premise that the future of marketing lies in its past. It contends that just as today's retromarketing practitioners are looking over their shoulders for inspiration, so too students, consultants and academics should seek to do likewise. It maintains that marketing's history contains practices, precepts and pointers that can help us plot a new, twenty-first-century course for our field. Lest there is any misunderstanding, however, it must be stressed that this book is not a how-to-do-it manual for prospective retromarketers, although historically minded managers might find some of it of interest. Nor does it claim to be encyclopaedic, though the text contains copious examples of retromarketing practices, principles, postulates and pursuits. Nor, for that matter, does the book pretend to be marketing *à la mode*, since its cutting-edge retro exemplars are sure to be superseded by the time this volume is published (albeit that should imbue them with an appropriately antiquated patina).

In keeping, rather, with its resolutely retro ethos, the present book consists of a root, a rummage, a riffle (who said ransack?) through the hidden records, dusty archives and secret files of the marketing discipline. It relies upon retro-research procedures of the pre-scientific era; principally, aphorism, anecdote, aside and autobiography, all wrapped up in extended essay format. As such, it comprises a kind of New Historicist hypertext,[9] a past times grab-bag, where proper historical method is less important than improper historical accident, 'fancy that' and strange-but-true. It is written in retro rococo, the exaggerated, hyperbolic, totally over-the-top literary style that characterized marketing discourse before 'scientific' discretion dominated the discipline (for that reason alone, the book is best read in small doses). It is predominantly Anglo-American in emphasis, partly on account of my personal peregrinations in recent years, but mainly because of the basic, if curiously overlooked, fact that marketing is quintessentially American.[10] (And don't let relationship marketers tell you otherwise.) It focuses on people – renowned practitioners of times past – rather than impersonal environmental or organizational forces, the escape clauses that have served marketers so well in the past ('the environment changed'; 'organizational barriers to implementation' and so on). It tries to appeal to general readers, while providing nourishment for postmodern theorists (in the notes) and marketing students (pedagogic appendix) alike. It engages with most of the topics contained in mainstream marketing textbooks – concept, strategy, mix, etc. – but in a deliberately provocative and hopefully challenging manner. It aims to antagonize and entertain in equal measure. The intense irritation and occasional outrage you'll feel are deliberately induced. Well, that's my excuse and I'm sticking to it (until such times as I can think of a better one).

Above all, this book contends that there is an alternative to the 'modern' marketing concept, an alternative that has always been there but has been consistently ignored in marketing's headlong, headstrong, headless-chickenesque flight into the future. The future, as we shall see, is history and, if nothing else, retromarketing reminds us of Marshall McLuhan's mid-sixties truism, that it is sometimes necessary to look back in order to see ahead.[11] Whether this academic imperative represents a Revolution, in the 'capital letter' sense of the word, is not for me to decide. What I can say, after Benjamin,[12] is that 'revolution' originally carried commercial connotations. The word was coined by medieval furriers to describe the process of turning over and examining the underside of a pelt, prior to purchase. This book examines the underside of modern marketing's moth-eaten hide and discovers that we have been preoccupied with the wrong side, the back side, the reverse side for fortysomething years. It is time, I firmly believe, to turn the pelt again, to shake marketing's magnificent mane and take pride in our brightly coloured covering.

Is there a taxidermist in the house?

However, as I look back on writing a book about looking back – the book that lies ahead of you – I appreciate that it couldn't have been composed without extensive back-up and unstinting encouragement. Rosemary Nixon of Sage supported this venture at every stage, as did her esteemed colleague Kiren Shoman. Thank you both. I'm also deeply indebted to Hope Schau (Temple University, Philadelphia) and Anthony Patterson (University of Ulster) who helped gather some of the retro raw material contained herein, though the innumerable stylistic infelicities are my own, my very own. Once again, Sharon Malcolm prepared the excellent diagrams, for which I am very grateful. Last but not least, I appreciate the (im)patience and (mis)understanding I've received from my wife, Linda, and daughters, Madison, Holly and Sophie, who suffered while I struggled to write in an academic yet accessible style. Maybe next time.

Stephen Brown
August 2000

INTRODUCTION

LOOKING BACK TO SEE AHEAD

1

Remembering Marketing: The Future is History

If, as has often been suggested, blue is this season's black and comedy the new rock 'n' roll, then the past is this season's present and old the new 'new'. For marketers, at least. As the merest glance across today's marketing landscape reveals, retro is *de rigueur*, the venerable is venerated, up-to-date is out-of-date and *démodé*'s the *dernier cri*. The new Jaguar S-Type, for example, looks remarkably like the immortal Mark II, beloved by 1960s police officers and getaway drivers alike, and the accompanying retro advertising campaign is equally evocative.[1] The television commercial boasts a bygone backing track – 1960s torch singer Shirley Bassey's 'just a little bit of history repeating' – while the print version is endowed with the time-steeped strapline, 'The style of the last generation, the excitement of the next'.

Not to be outdone by Jaguar's retro positioning, Mercedes is promoting itself by means of a monochromatic televisual take on an old Janis Joplin number ('Oh Lord, won't you buy me a Mercedes Benz . . .'). The Ford Puma brilliantly reprises Steve McQueen's timeless car chase in *Bullitt*, with a passing nod to *The Great Escape*, and exploits Dennis Hooper's *Easy Rider* excesses to telling contemporary effect. The VW Golf offers a montage of motoring motivations to the soundtrack of *Badlands*, Terrence Malick's twenty-five-year-old retro road movie, which was set in the 1950s. The Fiat Cinquecento interpellates ageing Slade fans with 1973 chart-topper 'Cum On Feel the Noize'; Audi resurrects its twenty-year-old strapline, *Vorsprung durch Technik*; and Jeep Wrangler proudly advertises its fifty-year heritage of off-road experience, a 'record of exploration that's as long as your sun-tanned, weather-beaten arm'.

Quite.

Mars Confectionery, meantime, has relaunched Spangles; Angel Delight is as delicious-deeelightful as ever; Bird's Custard has made a

gratifyingly lump-free comeback; and Spam, of all products, is reappear-
ing on the menus of fashionably old-fashioned restaurants. The latest
theme pubs sport a traditional English 'look'; Babycham is bubbling
under once more; Red Barrel, believe it or not, was rolled out for a
while, only to be rapidly rolled back in again; Rémy Martin exhorts
cognac imbibers to 'drink the past, celebrate the future' (what, all of the
past, or just the last hundred years?); and J. Lyons coffee bars, last
sighted in the middle to late 1950s, are getting set to do battle with
Starbucks, Coffee Republic, Aroma and analogous operators of retro
bistros.[2]

Flared trousers, furthermore, are flapping on the catwalks of Paris
and, like the button-flies of chaos theory, causing hurricanes on Kensing-
ton High Street. Lee Jeans have recently reissued their septuagenarian
101Zs, the first ever zip-fly denims, along with the 101J jacket, as worn
by Marilyn Monroe in *The Misfits*. Pringle cashmeres and twin-sets are
back on retailers' display racks, thanks to the company's Vintage Collection of replica 1950s designs. Platform shoes are striking fear into the
soles of unsuspecting feet everywhere, especially those that still bear the
bunions of the previous seventies revival. Twenty years on from Brooke
Shields' Lolitaesque revelation, Calvin Klein Originals have been revived,
as has the original 'nothing comes between' advertising campaign. And
Yardley's abortive attempt at modernization, which catapulted the cash-
strapped cosmetics giant into the welcoming arms of Wella, has been
thrown into reverse by the reactivation of English Lavender, its most
traditional range.[3]

On the opposite side of the gender divide, Dockers K-1 khakis, created
in 1932 as regulation pants for the US Army Air Force, are poised to
reinvade the beaches of western Europe, not to mention the bars, clubs,
discos, over-the-top nightspots and fashionable foxholes. Hai-Karate
aftershave has been exhumed, heaven help us; Brylcreem is bouncing as
never before; armies of anoraks are playing with Retro Force, the latest
computer game to evoke the old Space Invaders, zap-em-up, amusement
arcade experience; and, lager-lout throwbacks can knock back the
outback with cans of Castlemaine, which is reviving its fifteen-year-old
slogan, 'Australians don't give a XXXX for anything else'.[4]

These days, in sum, nostalgia is not what it used to be – since it is no
longer a thing of the past – and consumers don't so much keep up with
the Joneses, as with the Joneses' parents. From neo-steam trains and retro
motorcycles to artfully aged sales brochures and Habitat's recently
announced policy of reproducing 1960s design classics, it seems that then-
and-there is here-and-now.[5] So ubiquitous is retromarketing, indeed, that
it is quite difficult to think of an unaffected product category. Today's
refrigerators, kettles, mixers, ovens, toasters and kitsch kitchen imple-
ments look like go-faster reminders of space age sitcoms; the classic
Adidas sneaker has been re-released to greater acclaim than the somewhat

unsuccessful original; banks, insurers, stockbrokers, estate agents and similar stipendiary parasites proudly advertise their illustrious commercial heritage (Scottish Widows, Clerical Medical, Merrill-Lynch, Dean Witter), as do no less reputable retail brands (Thornton's – 'Chocolate Heaven since 1911'; Ellesse – 'Forty Years in the Making'; Eddie Bauer – 'Est. 1920, Seattle, USA'); and, in a meta-marketing *mise en abyme*, Millennium Collectibles Ltd. has produced a limited edition of eight classic trade characters, including the Guinness Toucan, the Milky Bar Kid and the rather less than politically correct Robertson's Golly. It is even rumoured that certain retromarketing professors are so committed to the concept that they have started recycling their lecture notes.

Again.

Although Coke's decision to bring back the moulded glass bottle perfectly symbolizes today's past times obsession, the old can easily be created anew, as in the case of Caffrey's Irish Ale.[6] Launched on St Patrick's Day 1994, Caffrey's is one of the most remarkable marketing triumphs of recent years. A winning combination of the best features of lager (light, cool, refreshing) and more traditional Irish beers (mellow flavour, creamy head, slow to settle), the product integrates old and new in a strikingly original manner. To complement its retro-product attributes, Caffrey's has also been provided with an instant Irish heritage, which draws inspiration from an ostentatious amalgam of Yeats's *Celtic Twilight*, Ford's *Quiet Man* and Flatley's *Lord of the Dance*. The brand name, to be sure, dates from 1897; there may well have been an actual Irish brewer called Thomas R. Caffrey; and the unforgettable television ads feature free-floating images of a forgotten Emerald Isle – lakes, mountains, bogs, scudding clouds, flame-haired colleens and that ever-present stallion galloping down a picturesque inner-city street adjacent to the gasworks – but the product is completely new, a triumph of cutting-edge brewing technology, an alcoholic beverage that is produced in computer-controlled vats in a dedicated brewhouse in industrial west Belfast.

Sláinte.

Now, it almost goes without saying that the rise of retro has not been lost on the legions of marketing gurus, pundits and spokespersons. The trade press is littered with bite-sized retrospections, though a number of commentators have cogitated at length on marketing's reproduction orientation.[7] Most of the latter meditations, understandably enough, are aimed at practising managers and deal with the retro advertising campaigns that accompany the latest retro products to hit the newly retroed shelves of fashionably retro retail stores. Nostalgia, however, has also attracted the attention of several prominent marketing scholars, cultural theorists and quick-buck-seeking consultants.[8] Suggestive though such studies are, they fail to engage with the fact that many revived goods and services are bang up to date, despite the old-fashioned styling, and thus there's more to retro than maudlin memories for time-was. What's more, the conceptual implications of today's retro revolution have been completely ignored to date. Hence, it is necessary to reminisce in advance on the *categories*, *causes*, *cultural characteristics* and *consequences* of marketing's present preoccupation with the past, if only for old times' sake.

Without doubt, the principal difficulty facing students of retro-marketing is its sheer amorphousness. No definitions of retro are extant – 'yesterday's tomorrows, today!' is as good as any – and marketing's past record on the definitions front suggests that scholarly consensus is unlikely in any event.[9] Yet despite the definitional difficulties, it is evident that there are several different forms or manifestations of the retro phenomenon, though these are not clear cut. For the purposes of the present argument, nevertheless, three major categories can be distinguished: *Repro*, *Repro Nova* and *Repro de Luxe*. *Repro* pertains to reproducing the old pretty much as it was, albeit meanings may have changed in the meantime. *Repro Nova* refers to combining the old with the new, usually in the form of old-style styling with hi-tech technology. *Repro de Luxe*, on the other hand, involves second helpings of the past, insofar as it revives or reproduces something that traded on nostalgia to start with. Neo-nostalgia, in other words.

All things considered, *Repro* is probably the most common variant of retromarketing, if only because it is the least demanding from an organizational resources standpoint. Rebroadcasting an old black and white advertisement (e.g. Shell petrol, PG Tips tea, Colgate toothpaste, Pal dog food, Cadbury's Flake) is a fairly low-cost way of emphasizing the distinguished lineage of a product or service, whilst intimating that the company doesn't take itself too seriously. Old ads, after all, are inherently amusing, especially those that boast the 'latest' technology or new and improved reformulations of the then futuristic (now Palaeozoic) product. Anheuser-Busch achieves much the same effect with its recent colour photo-spread of historic Budweiser cans, from 1936 to 1991, an advertisement which also carries competitor-crushing connotations of evolution, Darwinianism and the survival of the fittest. The ascent of can.

Occasionally, however, Repro is more than a straightforward attempt to cash in on the nostalgia boom. Past Times is an interesting case in point. Established in 1986 as the Historic Collections Group PLC, Past Times is a chain of retro gift shops. It sells all manner of reproduction knick-knacks and decorative home furnishings from seventy retail outlets in the United Kingdom and supplies items by mail order to 180 countries worldwide.[10] As a rule, the stores are situated in near-prime locations in prestigious shopping areas (Regent Street, Knightsbridge, Covent Garden), major regional malls (Bluewater, Meadowhall, Trafford Park) and historic cities with heavy concentrations of tourists (Chester, Cambridge, York, Stratford-upon-Avon). More to the point, the store interiors are themed by various historical eras – Medieval, Regency, Victorian, Edwardian, etc. – and museum shop atmospherics are further evoked by extensive use of display cases, pseudo-curatorial labelling and apposite period music playing perpetually in the background. True, the eras are somewhat loosely defined (what epoch, pray, is Cottage Garden, The Library or Other Lands?), and the bulk of the 'authentic replica' products are 'inspired by', 'reminiscent of', 'derived from', 'based on' or a 'contemporary interpretation' of the originals, where there are any. Nevertheless, Past Times's range of *Repro* reproductions, from medieval glass bowls to Art Nouveau lamps, seems to have struck a late twentieth-century chord. Sales rose from £23 million in 1994 to £74 million by 2000, and international expansion plans are afoot. As its Victorian toilet roll holders, gargoyle soap-on-a-ropes and Lord Nelson ('England Expects') Y-fronts amply testify, anachronism sells!

Repro Nova, by contrast, judiciously combines past and present. The TAG Heuer watch may look like the 1930s original, but where there was once a mechanical escapement there is now a solar-powered microchip.[11] The reproduction Bush transistor radio is blessed with the massive tuning dial of its 1950s progenitor, but the station settings are contemporary, a socket for headphones is provided and double cassette decks are available as optional extras. The Gap's television advertisements for khaki retro chic may employ pseudo psychedelia, swing and country as toe-tapping, finger-clicking, line-dancing musical accompaniments, but their production quality and special stop-action effects are state of the video art. Dyson vacuum cleaners, similarly, are the early seventies incarnate – they look like a cross between lava lamps and iffy installation art – but the suction technology is cutting edge and the bagless collecting receptacle brilliantly original.[12]

Without doubt, however, the apotheosis of *Repro Nova* is the 'new' Volkswagen Beetle, which was premièred at the Detroit Motor Show in January 1998. Designed by leading automotive imagineer, J. Mays, and manufactured at a hi-tech plant in Puebla, Mexico, the new Beetle combines the distinctive bubble shape of the old VW Bug with the latest automotive technology to produce a futuristic car with anachronistic styling.[13] It may look, as Stodghill aptly observes, like a 'motorised monument to Flower Power' – thanks, in no small measure, to the accompanying retroadvertising campaign – but it also boasts an adjustable steering column, CD player, air conditioning, six-speaker stereo system, air bags front and side, an 115 horsepower engine and a top speed of 120 miles per hour (compared to the 53 horsepower and 78 m.p.h. of the 1967 model). What's more, a four-cylinder, two-litre, turbo-charged sports version, the 1.8T, has just been launched, with a V6, dual-turbo, burn-em-up Bug to follow.

Brilliant as the Beetle nouveau undoubtedly is, it is not unsurpassable. On the contrary, there is another, even more superlative, twist in the retro tale. In classic postmodern fashion, *Repro de Luxe* comprises revived revivals, nostalgia for nostalgia itself and state of the art reproductions of past state of the art reproductions of the past.[14] For example, the tenth birthday of the retro-auto prototype, the Mazda Miata, has recently been celebrated by a special, bang-up-to-date anniversary edition.[15] Currently on tour, the *Happy Days* and *Grease* stage shows are contemporary revivals of 1970s originals, set in the 1950s. Amazon.com advertises its book search facility with a nostalgic nod to J.R. Hartley, the fictional subject of a 1983 television ad for 'good old Yellow Pages' (which nostalgically featured an aged author's search for the last copy of his life's work, *Fly Fishing*).[16] And *Dr Finlay*, a 1960s television series set in the 1920s, has not only been remade, but also updated to the more fashionable 1940s. Trendies!

Nevertheless, when it comes to *Repro de Luxe* there is only one contender for the all-comers title: the *Star Wars* franchise.[17] At one level, the current movie cycle simply trades on consumers' fond memories of the original trilogy. The kids who were taken to the first episodes now have their own kids to take. However, the special effects remain on the cutting edge of DFX technology. In fact, just as the original movies pushed back the frontier of special effects, so too *The Phantom Menace* and its sequels are effectively required to do the same, since anything less would fail to evoke the nostalgic magic of the futuristic originals. At another level, it is necessary to remind ourselves that the originals were themselves retro movies, deliberate attempts to update and revitalize the 'Saturday morning serial of the Buck Rogers type'.[18] What's more, whereas *Star Wars*, *The Empire Strikes Back* and *Return of the Jedi* were retro movies set in technologically advanced worlds, some time in the distant past ('A long time ago, in a galaxy far, far away', etc.), the current trilogy are prequels, futuristic precursors of the futuristic first-born and its two futuristic siblings. They are nostalgia movies that nostalgically trade on nostalgia for Lucas's nostalgic classics. Or something like that.

The sheer scale of Lukewalkonwater's success suggests that retro, in its various manifestations, is more of a Ubiquitous than a Unique Selling Proposition. It is thus incumbent upon marketers to try to account for today's past times preoccupation. To this end, it may be helpful to distinguish between *company*-led and *customer*-orientated explanations. Clearly, the pervasiveness of retromarketing has something to do with the companies that are promulgating it, since it doesn't happen all by itself. From an organizational standpoint, indeed, it makes eminent sense to play the heritage card when there is a heritage to play with. In a world where top-notch performance is industry standard in countless product categories – cars, cameras, colas, cornflakes, chinos, computers, cellular phones – the length of one's lineage remains a meaningful dimension of differentiation and, at the same time, a means of portraying the competition as less trustworthy, less reputable, less knowledgeable than the original (and best!). As Wolfgang Reitzle, the brains behind the neo-Jaguar S-Type, cogently observes, 'The products are operating increasingly at a similar level of quality. There are almost no bad cars on the market; even for mass produced products, quality is now a given, not a matter for differentiation'.[19] When it comes to retro positioning, then, a kind of postmodern primogeniture obtains.

At the same time, few would deny that retro sells – George Lucas especially. Hence, it follows that the current retrobubble is attributable, at least in part, to marketers' me-too mentality. Like the lemmings of legend, twenty-first-century marketers are throwing themselves off the cliff of the contemporary into the ravine of retrobsession. Past Times, for instance, is a slightly lower-price version of the manifold museum stores that line countless US fashion malls (MMA Store, The Museum Store, etc.) and its success has encouraged the National Trust to accelerate its own shop refurbishment programme. The Volkswagen Beetle has stimulated a dramatic about-turn in the automobile industry, with most major manufacturers announcing variations on the retro-auto theme. Examples include the Chrysler PT Cruiser, a pastiche of the upright sedans of the 1940s; the BMW Z8, which evokes the two-seater Ferraris of the 1950s; and the 'new' Ford T-Bird, an affectionate nod to the style, if not the under-braked, over-powered performance, of the 1954 original.[20] Caffrey's Ale, furthermore, spawned a host of Oirish imitators – Kilkenny being the most successful – all of which trade on the retro-republican myths and legends of the neo-Celtic revival. So crowded did the market become that Caffrey's recently relinquished its retro *go bragh* positioning in search of a Paddy-free constituency.[21]

To be sure, to be sure, Caffrey's attempted repositioning may prove unsuccessful and, should this be the case, it is liable to revert to its original retro stance. The same is true of troubled retailer Laura Ashley, which has struggled to recapture its initial image of engagingly anti-quarian Englishness. British Airways, moreover, is slowly returning to its traditional union flag livery after a singularly unsuccessful foray into multiculturalism. Penguin Books reissued a selection of its classic back catalogue, in the original bright orange covers, at a time when it was under threat from an American publishing conglomerate. Coca-Cola's resurrection of the quintessential glass bottle just might have something to do with the Belgian contamination scare of mid-June 1999 and the associated PR disaster.[22] McDonald's retro commercial for Lamb McSpicy came hot on the heels of a spectacularly shambolic two-Big-Macs-for-the-price-of-one promotion, as we shall see in Chapter 5. And cynics may surmise that George Lucas's admittedly lucrative decision to revive his inter-galactic soap opera was precipitated by a post-*Return of the Jedi* sequence of cinematic flops, most notably *Howard the Duck*.

Now, this is not to suggest that reversion to retro is an admission of marketing defeat, though it sometimes looks that way. Just as rock bands are inclined to go back to basics when their 'new direction' falls flat on its face, so too organizations in difficulty are prone to resurrect the marketing strategies that proved successful in the past. Sainsbury's disastrous attempt to dumb down in search of a less stuffy image, courtesy of John Cleese, has been followed by a disorganized retreat to its middle-class redoubt and the appointment of a retro CEO, former employee Sir Peter Davis.[23] Marks & Spencer, likewise, has latterly launched the 'classics' lifeboat, as has one-time own-label cereal-killer, Kellogg's ('have you forgotten how good they taste?'). Indeed, companies and brands that were retro to start with, such as Crabtree and Evelyn, Phileas Fogg and Christopher Wray Lighting, may be particularly prone to revert to their retro roots at the first sign of trouble. It would be a mistake, however, to conclude that retro is a sign of marketing desperation. On the contrary, there is evidence to suggest that retro is a very successful way of softening the hard sell. Rip-offs don't seem quite so rapacious when they are seen through the rose-tinted, soft-focus lens of nostalgia. Retro advertising, as Samuel notes, utilizes heritage in order to humanize the present, a lesson that has not been lost on strip-changing football clubs (retro soccer tops are all the rage, to say nothing of those fifties-style long shorts) and more-power computer manufacturers (consider the psychedelia of Apple's Powerbook or Pentium's protective-suited, disco dancing operatives).[24] The past, *pace* L.P. Hartley, is a familiar country.

It is, of course, common knowledge that soccer clubs and the cyber-barons of Silicon Valley are not exactly concert pitch performers of the noble marketing arts. Marketing, as everyone knows from day one, class one, case study one, is customer orientated and it therefore follows that the rise of retro is a direct reflection of customer preferences. As consumers age, they are more inclined to retrospect and marketers are simply responding to the demand. End of story. Certainly, this hypothesis has been expounded by analysts of nostalgic advertising treatments, commentators on the proliferation of heritage centres and students of the retromarketing condition generally.[25] Retro, in other words, is largely due to the demographic *longue durée*. The greying of the baby boom generation has prompted a psychic return to the comforts, certainties and conflict-free times of childhood or early adolescence, when people were polite, picket fences pearly white and Mom's apple pie sat cooling in the kitchen. Like the golden age of the ancients, this sepia-hued retroscape never actually existed (outside of Hollywood studio back-lots), but the image undoubtedly does and it is expropriated, exaggerated and artfully exploited by the hucksters of heritage. QED.

It is interesting in this regard that many adult-orientated retro products seem to have adopted a tiny-tots aesthetic.[26] The Dyson vacuum cleaner, for example, looks like relic from a Brobdingnagian dolls' house. BT uses ET to sell its latest telecommunications equipment. Most retro autos have a decidedly Noddy and Big Ears aspect, with just a hint of Postmodern Pat, and seem absolutely perfect for cruising the not-so-mean streets of Toytown, hurtling down the Trumpton turnpike and negotiating the one way system of Camberwick Green. It is surely no accident that the founder of Past Times, John Beale, made his first fortune with the Early Learning Centres, a chain of educational toy shops. And countless customer surveys show that the bulk of visitors to heritage parks are multi-generational extended families or groups of schoolchildren, who are expected to benefit from their encounters with the past, if in a punitive, take-your-medicine-it's-good-for-you sense.[27] By seeing at first hand the drudgery, deprivation and sheer destitution of life in times past, today's youth may be induced to appreciate their good fortune and treat their elders and betters with due respect thereafter.

That'll be the day.

In a similar vein, present-day consumers' preoccupation with the past is sometimes explained in terms of long-term migration patterns. The rise of urbanism in the nineteenth century and its acceleration in the twentieth has transformed much of the western world from a settled agrarian society into an itinerant urban one, with the consequent loss of rural rootedness, community spirit and sense of place.[28] Retro products and services, many of which come ready-wrapped in the ersatz rusticity of 'country gardens', 'kitchen gardens', 'market gardens' and suchlike, thus offer a welcome glimpse of *Gemeinschaft* for agitated, alienated, asphyxiated city slickers. The milk and dairy cabinets of contemporary supermarkets, for instance, are an overflowing cornucopia of haystacks, water meadows, plough teams, grazing cattle, gnarled olive groves and analogous celebrations of package design pastoral. Likewise, health and beauty counters groan under the weight of mass-produced natural essences, herbal extracts, arboreal unguents and Edenic evocations of a pre-lapsarian marketing paradise where pimples are prohibited, bikini lines wax lyrical, free-range fragrances gambol gleefully and oxters remain odourless in perpetuity.

At the same time, it is not unreasonable to surmise that there are considerable variations on consumers' bucolicity, if there is such a word. One doesn't need a logit, probit or conjoint model to demonstrate that not all shoppers are back-to-nature wannabes or are equally susceptible to the wallet-opening wiles of retromarketers. Surveys show that there are marked differences in people's attitude to the past, as portrayed in museums and equivalent retroscapes.[29] Holbrook has developed and empirically validated a 20-item attitude scale of US consumers' nostalgia-proneness.[30] The gay community is reputed to be particularly retro-friendly, possibly on account of the slightly kitsch, somewhat campish tone of many retromarketing campaigns.[31] Samuel, moreover, maintains that women are much more inclined to retro-shop than men and, extrapolating from this basic premise, he explains the advent of retro in terms of female emancipation, the spending power of working women and marketers' use of gender-based segmentation strategies.[32] This may well be the case, but an empirical study of Caffrey's Irish Ale reveals that men, if anything, are more enamoured of its ersatz Emerald Isle-isms than women.[33] It follows that consumers' retro-proneness may have less to do with gender than the extent of their involvement with the product category concerned.

More research, as they say, is necessary . . .

Micro-retro research is all very well, since marketing wouldn't be marketing without a typology or two of retrophiles, retrophobes and retropococurantes, be they companies or consumers. However, macro-retro considerations also have their place. In truth, some of the most suggestive accounts of our present past times preoccupation are predicated on broader socio-cultural considerations. According to Davis, a nostalgic ethos is particularly characteristic of societies in turmoil, those experiencing troubles, turbulence and transformation.[34] Thus, the dramatic collapse of communism, the Gulf War, the 1992 European integration imbroglio and subsequent societal eruptions have created conditions conducive to the advent of a retro, some would say recidivist, mindset.[35] Likewise, the latter-day emergence of ecological concerns – a consequence of all sorts of environmental catastrophes – has led to a renewed emphasis on conserving, restoring and protecting the past. The sheer pace of contemporary technological change, what is more, may well have stimulated a yearning for simpler, less stressful times amongst those required to keep up, keep moving, keep ahead of the globalized game.[36]

Equally global, at least in an explanatory sense, is postmodernism. Now, postmodernism is one of those irritatingly ubiquitous terms that is always prefaced by an apologia about its inherent indefinability and the futility of definitions *per se*. Much like retro, in point of fact. The parallels, to be sure, are not accidental, because postmodernism is characterized by a retro orientation. One of its key presuppositions is that stylistic innovation is impossible, that everything has already been done and dusted, and all that remains is to mix, match and play with the pieces of the past.[37] Not everyone would accept this PoMo pen-portrait – countless figures, metaphors and tropes are deemed symptomatic of postmodernism – however, most would agree that it is associated with nostalgic inclinations, historical bricolage, a marked loss of faith in progressivist ideologies and, all things considered, by a preference for the tried-and-tested over the new-and-improved.

On this reading, PoMo and retro are, if not exactly kith and kin, certainly the kissing cousins of the conceptual gene pool. This is hardly the place to hurl accusations of intellectual in-breeding, nor do we have time for a 'Duelling Banjos' interlude. Perhaps the most meaningful genetic marker, however, is good old-fashioned irony. It is well known that the four Ps of postmodernism are parody, persiflage, pastiche and playfulness, with just a dash of plagiarism and dollop of pasquinade. The same is true of retro. Indeed, one of the most characteristic features of retromarketing is its irreverence, insouciance and hopeless addiction to irony. The new VW Beetle, for instance, playfully alludes to its hippie-wagon heritage by means of a plastic flower-holder on the dashboard. Budweiser's ascent of can sequence is wryly interrupted by a crushed reminder of 1957, the year Sputnik's flight gave the US a fright. British Airways re-flew the flag with the aid of self-deprecating commercials featuring Brit-bashing humorist, P.J. O'Rourke. Spam was successfully relaunched with the aid of an ironic cookery book, *Tasty Meals in Minutes*, featuring such celebrated gourmet dishes as Spam Carbonara, Deep Spam Pizza and Spicy Spam Rigatoni. Past Times sensibly under-cuts its own self-importance with reproductions of medieval mouse mats and laptop-toting gargoyles, to name but a few. And McDonald's wormed its way back into Britain's Big-Mac-denied affections with a sublime parody of 1960s-vintage cinema commercials – abysmally edited, atrocious puns, asynchronous soundtrack, wooden acting and so on – for no-need-to-book, greasy-spoon restaurants 'a few minutes from this theatre'. Not only did McDonald's ad receive the ultimate accolade of a favourable review in the *Sunday Times* television column, by the invariably acid-penned A.A. Gill, but it proved enormously popular with the public, entering *Marketing* magazine's Adwatch chart at Number 1, and it remained in the Top 10 throughout the entire campaign.[38]

Although many marketing purists may be horrified by retro's incorrigible refusal to take itself seriously, it is arguable that without the leavening effect of irony and camp, retromarketing is doomed to fail. Even though *The Phantom Menace*, the first slice of Lucas's second Star Wars cycle, proved to be a staggering commercial success, it was rather less successful than many originally anticipated. The principal reason for this (undeniably impressive) under-performance was the simple fact that the film treated itself and the whole inter-galactic epic with far too much respect, not to say excruciating pomposity.[39] In this regard, it is entirely appropriate that the movie was deposed from the top of the US box office, after only four weeks, by *Austin Powers: The Spy Who Shagged Me*, an irony-replete remake of a retro spoof of 1960s James Bondesque blockbusters (which featured a parody of the *Star Wars* credit sequence and a time-travelling neo-Beetle, for good measure). Analogously,

Caffrey's stab at portentous mythopoeticism, in the shape of its retro-Hiberno advertising campaign, is regarded ironically by its target market. This does not mean that consumers dislike Caffrey's advertising, or are unmoved by its O'Topian images of the Celtic sublime. Quite the opposite. It's just that it's very difficult to take something seriously when it has been parodied to telling effect (by Denis Leary, in the case of Caffrey's, and *South Park*, amongst many others, for *Star Wars*). *The Phantom Menace* might have been better served by a touch of farce in the Force – presumably they'll get it right next time round – and, if the storm brewing around Caffrey's persuades the brand to return to its original Quiet Pint positioning, it may be prudent to parody its perceived self-importance. As CIM spokesperson, Vanessa Moon, perspicaciously notes, 'relaunches that work need to address the audience in a quirky, tongue-in-cheek way'.[40]

Irrespective of ironic inflections, the essential point about retro and PoMo is that they are both predicated on recapitulation and thus rest upon cyclical rather than linear models of time. Indeed, this self-evident truism underpins one of the most frequently posited causes of retro-mania: the *fin-de-siècle* effect.[41] At the turn of centuries, humanity is inclined to cast backward glances on its successes, failures, lucky escapes and catastrophic decisions during the preceding epochs. The terminus of the twentieth century, what is more, was extra significant on the logarithmic scale of remembrance, since a thousand years of triumph and disaster were on parade instead of a paltry one hundred. The only problem with the *fin-de-siècle* thesis, however, is that it doesn't withstand close scrutiny.[42] While there is no doubt that the twentieth/twenty-first centuries' cusp is characterized by retromarketing mania, a neo-romantic preference for the past over the present, such commercial nostalgicity is not confined to centuries' ends. On the contrary, it is ever-present. Five years ago, for example, Schweppes revived its veteran 'Sssch' campaign and the future of Habitat rested on recapturing its past. Ten years ago, the GM Saturn represented a return to the good old days when motoring was fun, and Coca-Cola updated its celebrated 'hilltop' commercial of the 1970s, the current decade *du jour*.[43] Indeed, the recent seventies revival conveniently overlooks the fact that the seventies themselves were a remarkably retro-orientated era. Many historic preservation societies and environmental protection regulations date from that epoch. It was in the seventies that the postmodern revolt against modern architecture first materialized and the vernacular-minded Robert Venturi exhorted city planners to learn from Las Vegas.[44] It was in the 1970s that several of the most successful retro movies of all time were made (*The Last Picture Show, American Graffiti, The Sting, The Godfather, Parts I* and *II*) and *Brideshead Revisited* revitalized the British heritage industry. Similarly, it was in the seventies that Ridley Scott's sublime sepia-hued advertisement (sepiad?) for Hovis was first broadcast,[45] the Laura Ashley 'look' swept all before it and the Hard Rock Café made its mark as a museum *manqué*, with a side order of fries.

The 1930s were equally nostalgia prone, all the way from Frank Lloyd Wright's Broadacre City, a futuristic attempt to evoke Thomas Jefferson's fantasy of self-sustaining villages, through consumers' propensity to decorate their dwellings with pewter tankards, spinning wheels and pseudo-Colonial artefacts, to the Maxfield-Parrish-inspired, cod-mythic architecture of Howard Johnson's restaurants and motels. Part of a broader recovery of rapidly disappearing folk and small town traditions (cf. Frank Capra movies, Aaron Copland's music, Greenfield Village, WPA murals), Depression-era marketers bent over backwards to associate their products with the past. In the words of eminent advertising historian, Jackson Lears:

> By mid-decade, 'emancipated modernism' was out according to the conventional wisdom, and 'old-fashioned convention' in; trade journals advised advertisers to address 'Grandma Jones, Buyer', who was more concerned with 'comfortable living' than with fashion. Corporate food processors shifted their emphasis from purity to 'home cooked flavour'; Hurff's Soup, for example, took consumers into the enveloping warmth of the rural hearthside rather than the sterility of the scientifically managed kitchen. Other advertisers linked mass-produced goods with preindustrial craftsmanship and family solidarity. By 1936, *Fortune* magazine was marvelling at the tendency of national advertising to 'bury its alert head in the sands of the past'. Advertisers, like other symbol makers in the 1930s, had turned to a mythic version of the American past to validate their present identity.[46]

Naturally, it is tempting to explain such periodic past times predilections in terms of a Kondratieff-style cycle of socio-economic turbulence (the Great Depression of the 1930s, the Oil Crises of the 1970s, the Tiger Economies turmoil-cum-dotcom bubble of the 1990s). However, as the Frankfurt School tradition repeatedly informs us, it is unwise to regard developments in the superstructure as a direct outcome of developments in the socio-economic base. It may, in fact, be much simpler to acknowledge that *retro is the normal state of affairs*. If anything, as Lowenthal observes, the progressive, forward-looking, things-can-only-get-better mindset is the exception rather than the rule of western culture.[47] Much-lauded literary critic, Jacques Barzun, makes a similar point in his monumental review of the west's cultural history, where various forms of *anachronism* (Antiquarianism, Romanticism, even Modernism) are a principal defining feature.[48] It seems that, akin to Molière's *bourgeois gentilhomme*, who had been speaking prose for forty years without knowing it, retro is nothing less than the *lingua franca* of modernity.

The recuperation of retro is doubtless long overdue, but what are the implications for marketing? This is a very difficult question to answer since it demands a present-day assessment of the future of the past. The dawning of a new millennium, moreover, might incline us to adopt an eyes-front outlook and thereby dismiss retro as the latest passing fad in a particularly fad-prone field. But the present omnipresence of past-ness suggests that retrospection might be around for some time to come. Indeed, if the Lowenthal/Barzun line of argument is accepted, perhaps the progressivist, gung-ho, we-have-the-technology ethos of the modern marketing era is itself an aberration and retromarketing is – *and should be* – the norm. Like Dorothy Gale in *The Wizard of Oz*, who eventually realized she already possessed what she'd been looking for all along, maybe it is time to recognize that the wonderful wizard of marketing is in the buy-gones business.

In this regard, it is noteworthy that Josiah Wedgwood, the oft-cited prototype of marketing orientation, was himself a retromarketer. Many of his best-selling styles were replicas or 'contemporary' interpretations of classical themes.[49] The present-day popularity of William Morris's *fin-de-siècle* designs makes it easy to forget that they were irredeemably retro to start with, valiant Victorian attempts to recapture the golden age of medieval craftsmanship.[50] Coca-Cola, the biggest brand in the world, has always been steeped in nostalgia, as its celebrated copper-plate script – a late nineteenth-century attempt to evoke an earlier, elevated, pre-patent medicine show era – bears literate witness.[51] The Marlboro cowboy was retro from day one and, since his departure to the great roll-up in the sky, the brand has continued to advertise itself with retrotopian images of the West that never was. The single most celebrated television commercial of all time, Apple Computer's '1984', was an evocation of the 1980s as viewed through a 1950s Cold War lens (what Jameson, after Lyotard, terms the 'future anterior').[52] The centrepiece of Disneyland, Main Street USA, is an admittedly bogus homage to the downtown of Marceline, Missouri, as it was at the start of the twentieth century when Walt was knee-high to Jiminy Cricket.[53] The Body Shop is a latter-day commercial paean to Rousseau's non-existent noble savage, as is The Nature Store, and Kentucky Fried Chicken not only continues to intimate that its finger lickin' achievements rest upon a 'traditional' recipe, but they have recently resurrected the Colonel as a necro-celebrity spokesperson. When it comes, moreover, to the most successful movies of all time – *The Phantom Menace, Titanic, Jurassic Park, Gone With the Wind, Birth of a Nation* – what more need be said?

These examples, to be sure, are chosen for effect and no one would claim that retro is the only show in town. Few would deny, furthermore, that just as there is an element of cyclicity in retro revivalism, so too *retrouvé* becomes *passé* in the fullness of time. The key point about retro orientation is not that it is the primal form of marketing, but that it acts as a foil or counterpoint to 'modern' marketing. It enables us to step outside the Analysis, Planning, Implementation and Control (APIC) paradigm that has held sway for fortysomething years and view it as an

historical artefact. Perhaps the clearest indication that something fundamental has changed is that the word modern, as in 'modern marketing',
now strikes us as curiously old-fashioned. Likewise, the nomenclature
new, as in 'new product', is increasingly attached to line extensions of
long-established brand names, whether it be chunky Kit-Kat, Levi's
sta-pressed jeans, Virgin Personal Pensions, Manchester United's
television channel or Dove, Palmolive, Nivea, Vaseline or – I ask you
– Harley-Davidson deodorant. The flavour may be 'new', the packaging
may be 'new', the market itself may be 'new'. But, in keeping with retro's
I-have-seen-the-past-and-it-works ethic, the product or service itself
remains reassuringly old.

It doesn't take a Lincoln Steffens to see that this state of affairs has
serious implications for marketing scholarship.[54] If the modern marketing
paradigm is suspect, possibly obsolete, what is there to replace it with?
Interestingly, the academic community has already (inadvertently)
articulated a retro response to this question, insofar as the relationship
marketing paradigm is inherently retrospective.[55] Like today's toothpaste
and washing powder manufacturers, who promise to *restore* the natural
whiteness of our teeth and *protect* the colour of our clothes, relationship
marketers attempt to retain existing customers rather than create them
anew. The adepts of relationship marketing, furthermore, unfailingly
position the paradigm with reference to the past, the good old days of
mom and pop stores, living above the shop and what have you. This was a
time when marketers knew each and every one of their customers
personally and ministered to their individual needs. It's a time that has
long gone but one which relationship marketing, thanks to modern
technology and the dedicated database, is capable of recapturing.
Relationship marketing, according to this rose-tinted interpretation, is
the embryonic form of marketing that sadly fell by the wayside in the
1960s, when modern marketing came to the fore and a round-em-up,
stick-a-brand-on-em, milk-em-dry spirit of cowboy marketing held
unfortunate sway. Today's customers, admittedly, are no more convinced
by marketing's good-ole-boy bonhomie than they were with the new-and-
improved rhetoric that previously prevailed, but that hasn't stopped
relationship marketing sweeping all before it, academically at least.

Although the relationship marketing paradigm shift is the most
striking manifestation of retromarketing scholarship, it is not the only
one. A retroactive creeper seems to be wrapping itself around the ivied
walls of marketing's ivory tower.[56] Apart from the compendious mid-
life crisis literature – academic marketers' hair-shirted ruminations on
where the discipline went disastrously wrong and why – the journals are
replete with reflections on the state of scholarly play. Even special issues
devoted to the future of marketing are dominated by backward-looking
contributions (the ongoing series in *JAMS*, for example). What's more,
there have been many calls to re-think, re-invent or re-imagine marketing;

some of the discipline's fundamental principles have been given the retrospective treatment; pre- or proto-modern marketers are being resurrected and reclaimed from intellectual obscurity; numerous scholars are turning their backs on marketing science and espousing the sorts of artistic approaches once deemed dead and buried; the academic avant-garde are increasingly drawing upon inter-war thinkers – Bakhtin, Bataille, Bloch, Benjamin and so on – or intellectual alumni of the 1960s like Lacan, Derrida, Barthes, Foucault and Debord (their ideas may be new to marketing but they have been around for thirty-odd years); and, casual observation suggests that 'readers' and analogous greatest hits packages are more popular with publishers than original contributions to knowledge (not that I'm jealous or anything). Most tellingly perhaps, the titans of the modern marketing era are getting in on the retroactive act, as Kotler's recently published *summa* clearly indicates.[57]

These developments, I grant you, are relatively easily explained away: as mere backward glances brought about by the millennial transition; as a result of the retirement of the post-war generation of marketing theorists; as a consequence of the protracted, verging on glacial, academic diffusion process; or, as an outcome of developments in the pedagogic environment (semesterization breeds readers, anthologies and the like). However, an ironic undercurrent indicates that retro is also involved. Marketing, let's be frank, is not exactly renowned for its ability to laugh at itself. Possibly on account of its carnivalesque, snake-oil-selling, bunco-artist origins, 'modern' marketing has consistently emphasized its seriousness, its rectitude, its out-and-out professionalism. Although this prim and proper propensity is still very strongly marked – as exemplified by the recent name change of the principal academic association in the UK (from the cheap and cheerful Marketing Education Group to the suitably scholarly Academy of Marketing) – irony, parody and playfulness are beginning to creep into the mainstream journals and textbooks.[58] Smithee has scandalously declared that Kotler is Dead; Holbrook offers a hilarious parody of the interpretive research tradition; Belk brings down the house with a brilliant think-piece on a proposed theme park called Hell, thereby sealing his own fate; Piercy takes perverse pleasure in profaning practitioner-orientated pundits-cum-pontificators, such as himself; light-hearted intertextual allusions to various forms of popular culture – movies, rock music and suchlike – are now something of a commonplace in academic literature reviews; and, appropriately enough, relationship marketers have been known to raise a titter or two at transactional marketing's expense, though the joke is on them, as we shall see.

Such attempts to put the con into concept remain few and far between, I grant you. There is a world of difference, furthermore, between arguing for alternative approaches to marketing endeavour – irony included – and actually delivering the parodic goods. The disciplinary mechanisms of the discipline also serve to control any outbreaks of irony, usually by means of the mainstream's deliberately staged misunderstanding, misconstrual and marginalization. Ironically, indeed, by far the most effective weapon against irony is allowing it to flourish; what the critical theorists of the Frankfurt School used to call 'repressive tolerance'.[59] Whereas censorship, hostility or strong-arm tactics simply provide the oppressed minority with a sense of purpose, permissiveness serves to neutralize their negativity by making the radicals' arguments appear strange, ridiculous or, as in the case of the toleration-equals-intolerance contention, contrary to common sense.

There are, however, two ultimate ironies about the rise of retro-marketing and the threat it poses to modernist marketing perspectives enshrined in primers and principles textbooks. The first of these is that mainstream marketing of Kotlerite stripe is implicated in the discipline's growing retro orientation. After all, one of the most frequently voiced complaints about marketing in general and marketing research in parti-cular is that it tends to stifle innovation.[60] True, most marketing enthusiasts, zealots and fully paid up members of its professional bodies don't exactly see things that way. As is well known, the merest hint that marketing is less than progressive, let alone regressive, is instantly dismissed as ignorant, incompetent or indicative of insufficient commit-ment to the marketing cause. Nevertheless, studies show that inter-rogating customers about new product concepts invariably leads to the perpetuation of the old, the established, the tried and tested, the me-too marketing that is all around us. By complete contrast, 'proper' marketing, 'breakthrough' marketing, genuinely 'innovative' marketing are the work of creative, combative iconoclasts rather than focus groupies and vox pop prognosticators. Or so the story goes. The latter-day triumph of the marketing concept, in short, is one of the principal causes of today's retromarketing revolution.

The second and even more ironic outcome of the current outbreak of retro is that it may stimulate a revival of the modern marketing paradigm itself! Just as architectural, artistic and literary Modernism is in the throes of being revived, re-evaluated and re-canonized (high-rise tower blocks are back in fashion, as is Jackson Pollock, and Samuel Beckett has recently been reclaimed as a pre-postmodern ironist), so too modern marketing is ripe for redemption. The APIC paradigm, lest we forget, is a child of the sixties and, minor modifications aside, it is still sporting a tie-dye T-shirt, making love not war and patiently awaiting the Age of Aquarius. Retromarketers, then, are in the possibly unique intellectual position of being able to institute a revival before the expiry of the original. But, as the original concept begat its pre-demise revival, a renaissance of retromarketing might well occur before the initial idea takes hold.

And, if you believe that, let alone understand it, you've been reading too many books about postmodern marketing . . .

PART I

PUTTING THE 'CON' INTO CONCEPT

2

Reviewing Marketing: The Defective Vision of Theodore Levitt

It is a truth universally acknowledged that 'It is a truth universally acknowledged' is the most compelling opening line in English Literature. Some bookworms, admittedly, might plump for 'It was the best of times, it was the worst of times' and others doubtless set great store by 'Call me Ishmael', 'A spectre is stalking Europe' or 'It was a bright cold day in April and the clocks were striking thirteen'.[1] But few would deny that Jane Austen's opening salvo in *Pride and Prejudice* is extremely hard to beat. So much so, that the unspeakable people who pontificate on matters of literary style invariably introduce their self-important thoughts with a contrived variation on Austen's incomparable inaugural sentence.[2]

Have they no originality?

If, of course, an analogous Rhetorical Assessment Exercise were performed on the marketing literature, it is a truth universally acknowledged that there'd be very few contenders for the 'it is a truth universally acknowledged' title. Marketers, after all, are not exactly renowned for their literary acumen, nor do they claim to be. Most scholarly publications start with those sturdy, albeit less than stirring, words 'This paper' or, when they're really pushing the philosophical boat out, 'The purpose of this paper'. Writers targeting the practitioner market, furthermore, consistently commence with a corporate parable of the 'Joe Doe faced a difficult situation' variety. Happily, the organization – sometimes real, often fictional, always stricken – is unfailingly saved thanks to the wonder-working power of the modern marketing concept. Praise the Lord and pass the mess of 4Ps potage.[3]

Regrettably ubiquitous though such introductory banalities, barbarities and bromides undoubtedly are, marketing possesses at least one opening line of real literary merit. It is 'Every major industry was once a growth industry' by the superlative Ted Levitt, stalwart of Harvard Business School and one of the greatest marketing gurus of all time.[4]

Although Levitt produced many other arresting pipe-openers and textual throat-clearers in the course of his glittering career – 'Greed is boring', 'Never leave well enough alone' and 'There is no such thing as a commodity' spring immediately to mind – none quite attain the sublimity of 'Every major industry'. It is succinct (eight words, many monosyllabic). It is bold (a statement of ostensible fact). It is aphoristic (easily remembered, eminently quotable). It is intriguing (curiously downbeat, the antithesis of marketing boosterism). It is anthropomorphic (imputes fallible human qualities to an inanimate object). It is allusive (shades of Arnold Toynbee, Oswald Spengler, Henry George and Edward Gibbon on the rise and fall of civilizations). It is almost biblical in its inalienability (in the beginning was the word, as it were). Most importantly of all, it is retro. It combines past and present to brilliant stylistic effect and, as the very first line of a 12-page paper, it intimates that a major statement about the future of marketing is about to unfold. Like Nietzsche, that most literary of philosophers, Levitt grabs his readers by the metaphorical lapels, shakes them vigorously and dares them not to read the rest of 'Marketing Myopia'.

Few, it appears, have refused to take the Ted Levitt challenge, since 'Marketing Myopia' is perhaps the most famous paper in the entire marketing literature.[5] It has been anthologized on numerous occasions, cited on countless more, dissected in virtually every principles of marketing seminar and, akin to directors' cuts of influential Hollywood movies, it has even been reflected on and added to by the author himself.[6] It was recognized as an instant classic at the time of publication (lead article in a leading journal, given the special this-is-sure-to-prove-controversial-read-it-at-your-peril editorial treatment,[7] winner of the prestigious McKinsey Award for the best paper in *Harvard Business Review* that year) and subsequent decades have only served to increase its standing. At more than half a million copies sold, 'Marketing Myopia' is by far the best-selling *HBR* reprint *of all time*. What's more, it launched Levitt's career as marketing's foremost spokesperson, a position he continues to hold notwithstanding the competitive onslaughts of Philip Kotler, Tom Peters and all the rest. Certainly, he is the only marketing person, alongside Kotler, routinely referred to in management primers, synopses and anthologies.[8] To many non-marketers, he represents the voice, the personification, the embodiment of the modern marketing concept. To many marketers, moreover, he is the field's foremost thinker of the century just past and most would agree that 'Marketing Myopia' is his greatest thought.

This does not mean, of course, that Theodore Levitt is some kind of intellectual one-hit wonder. On the contrary, his 1986 volume *The Marketing Imagination* has been translated into no fewer than eleven languages and was recently reprinted with the addition – naturally – of 'Marketing Myopia'.[9] Another anthology, *Innovation in Marketing*, won the annual Academy of Management award for best business book (again, it included his greatest hit)[10] and he has had more papers published in *HBR* than any other management guru, acquiring four McKinsey Awards along the way.[11] At the same time, however, it is true to say that the sheer brilliance of 'Marketing Myopia' tends to overshadow the remainder of Levitt's literary *oeuvre*. Just as western philosophy is often described as a series of footnotes to Plato, so too modern marketing is a series of errata slips inserted into Ted's bravura contribution. It is salutary to think that it has probably been read, inwardly digested and acted upon by more practitioners, academicians and students alike than any other article in the history of our field. The so-called 'modern' marketing concept effectively began with 'Marketing Myopia' and one suspects that the paper will continue to occupy pride of place until such time as it is tackled head-on and treated as a work of historical literature, rather than a compelling call to marketing arms.

When Levitt's masterpiece *is* examined from a historiographic perspective, several interesting issues arise. The first of these is that he got it completely wrong. Apart from outright factual errors in the historical overview, such as his misrepresentation of railroads marketing,[12] Theo's confident predictions concerning rocket-powered cars, ultrasonics, fuel cells, the end of the oil industry by 1985, etc., all proved sadly mistaken.[13] It is, of course, the easiest thing in the world to take past futurologists to task, since hindsight – unlike marketing – is not myopic. In theory at least. Yet it says much for Levitt's literary ability that neither his historical misrepresentations nor his failings on the futurology front seem to have affected readers' acceptance of the accompanying conceptual contentions. True, he has received a bit of a pasting in the strategic management literature,[14] and at least one indigenous cynic has pounced on Levitt's flawed forecasts to dismiss the paper as a whole, describing them as 'the buggy-whip manufacturers, the railroad companies, the Hollywood studios of marketing discourse'.[15] Such is Levitt's rhetorical brilliance, nevertheless, that most readers seem content to overlook the article's errors of fact and method, or simply fail to infer that his conceptual argument might be as suspect as his prognostications. Levitt may not be much of a medium, but his message transcends space and time. Almost.

Another intriguing feature of 'Marketing Myopia' is that it is mistitled. So much so, the paper is well nigh prosecutable under the Trade Descriptions Act. Now, this is not to suggest that it is *badly* titled. On the contrary, the root metaphor of 'Marketing Myopia' is undeniably arresting. Not only is it based on the oracular trope that has characterized western philosophy since Descartes,[16] if not before, but by suggesting that organizational failure is attributable to visual impairment, to an inability to see clearly, to a short-sighted focus on the product offer rather than the customer benefits thereby obtained, Levitt

coined a conceptual conceit that calls down the years like none other.
Myopia, indeed, has become the ultimate term of abuse within marketing discourse – a six-letter four-letter word, as it were – since being
described as 'myopic' is tantamount to being deemed anti-marketing,
anti-business, anti-American. Nevertheless, the merest glance at
'Marketing Myopia' reveals that the visual metaphor barely features in
the body of the paper itself. Despite its admittedly brilliant title, there is
a complete lack of visual imagery in 'Marketing Myopia'. Incredible as it
sounds, the piece is primarily predicated on aural analogies ('If you had
told them sixty years ago', 'a nation of production-orientated business
managers refuses to hear the great lesson he taught', 'it was not a
discussible subject, or an askable question', 'yet the automobile companies do not seem to listen'.) So marked is the aural metaphor that it
should really be called 'Marketing Misheard'.

Metaphor, as the prominent literary critic Roman Jakobson reminds
us, may be a very powerful figure of speech, but it is not the only one.
Metonymy, where the part stands for the whole, is equally important.[17]
In this respect, it is striking that Levitt's article is best known for its
myopia metaphor yet the paper itself is predominantly metonymical.
That is to say, the author presents each of his highly specific, historically
contingent company vignettes as exemplars for businesses and managers
as a whole. What's more, he considers the idiosyncratic contents of a
single issue of a single trade magazine, the *American Petroleum Institute
Quarterly*, to be indicative of the production-orientation ethos of an
entire industry and, by metonymical extension, of industry *per se*.[18] He
contends that his three calamitous case studies contain lessons for all
companies, in all places, at all times (by any stretch of the imagination,
this is an incredible stretch of the imagination). Levitt himself, moreover,
performs in an essentially metonymic capacity insofar as 'Marketing
Myopia' is the epitome of his entire literary corpus. As all of his signature textual stratagems – wordplay, hyperbole, humour, etc. – are on
display in the paper, 'Marketing Myopia' is to Theodore Levitt what
Theodore Levitt is to marketing as a whole.

Après myopia le déluge.

Whatever its metonymical merits, the (metaphorical) bottom line is
that the root metaphor of 'Marketing Myopia' is itself astigmatic, not to
say dangerously defective. For Levitt, the fundamental mistake of
Hollywood studios was that they considered themselves to be in the
movie business rather than the entertainment business. The railroads,
likewise, ran into the buffers because they failed to appreciate that they
were in transportation, not tracks. The oil companies, similarly, didn't
supply petrol but power, consumers wanted quarter-inch holes not
electric drills, perfumers sold hope not fragrance, coffee drinkers quaffed

liquid refreshment not dilute-to-taste caffeine and, last but not least, 'the organisation must learn to think of itself not as producing goods and services but as *buying customers*'.[19]

While few would deny that it is senior management's duty to think about strategic issues – about what business their business is in – Levitt's laudable desire to avoid myopia brings with it the dangers of long-sightedness, of marketing hyperopia.[20] These include excessive diversification, unnecessary acquisitions, corporate sclerosis and the ruinous consequences of not 'sticking to the knitting', as Levitt's latter-day *bête noire* once described it.[21] The rise of specialist coffee vendors like Starbucks and Aroma suggests that many people require something more specific than liquid refreshment. It is by no means certain that any fragrance will do – anyone for Old Spice? – or any power tool, or sneakers, or blue jeans, or hamburger, or hi-fi, or automobile, or whatever. Indeed, if any motor car suffices why aren't we all driving rejected-by-focus-groups Rover 75s, or Ford any-colour-you-want Kas, or Neo what-colour-do-you-dream-in Beetles? Hollywood survived, surely, as much by its renewed commitment to making good movies, improving customer service (multiplexes, Dolby stereo, catering) and exploiting ancillary markets (videos, memorabilia, soundtracks), as it did by considering itself to be in the entertainment business, whatever that is exactly. To put it another way, is attending a performance of *Taming of the Shrew* really analogous, as Levitt would have us believe, to sitting at home watching *Ten Things I Hate About You* on DVD? The plots are identical, I grant you, but *Ten Things* has scene selection, soundtrack excerpts, the theatrical trailer and a blissful lack of talking, coughing, sweet-sucking people, whose heads always get in the way.[22]

Little, admittedly, is gained by lacerating Levitt for his short-sightedness – in truth, there is much to be said for myopia, the narrowness of vision that is oft-times necessary for commercial success – since the real astigmatism surrounding 'Marketing Myopia' is not Levitt's. It's ours. We, the cockeyed readership, have either failed to see, or simply overlooked, the infirmities of Theo's argument. In the kingdom of the blind the myopic marketing man may be king, but we must bear some responsibility for preferring not to see our emperor's intellectual nakedness (pardon my parable plundering promiscuity). The brutal truth is that we choose not to notice Levitt's conceptual *décolletage* because he tells us what we want to hear, what we want to believe. Principally, that marketing is the be all and end all of management, that companies *must* be marketing orientated otherwise failure is certain, that marketing is a universal verity, relevant to all places, all times, all organizations. Levitt may not have been the first to portray marketing as the philosopher's stone of management but his unparalleled powers of persuasion – his scholarly salesmanship, his cerebral chutzpah, his retro rhetoric, if you will – guaranteed that future generations of marketers would apply his prescription to the discipline itself. Marketing must not be myopic. Marketing must not be blinkered, bound, bashful, bettered. Marketing must.

Forty years have now passed since Levitt's inextinguishable exegesis and, as marketing stumbles around trying desperately to orient itself in a world where everyone is marketing-led, or claims to be, and there aren't any organizational apostates who have yet to see the light, it is clear that the discipline has been completely blinded by Father Ted's stylistic brilliance. Indeed, the ultimate achievement of 'Marketing Myopia' is that it conveys the impression of timelessness, that it is speaking the truth, the whole truth and nothing but the truth. It is nothing less than the gospel according to St Theodore, which if truly believed in and acted upon, will not only ensure worldly success but a much-prized place in the paradisal marketing hereafter. The concluding paragraphs in particular read like a cross between the imprecations of an Old Testament prophet, the histrionics of a hellfire-and-brimstone evangelist and, not least, neo-Nietzschean bombast of the God-is-dead-long-live-God variety.

Although 'Marketing Myopia' continues to give the impression of imperishability, the philologists, hermeneuts and archaeologists of knowledge amongst us will readily appreciate that it was very much an artefact of its time. Just as the abstruse post-structuralist theorist, Paul de Man, maintains that blindness affords insight, since what we ignore is as important as what we examine,[23] so too the ultimate form of marketing myopia concerns 'Marketing Myopia'. Generally speaking, we have been so mesmerized by its gratifyingly flattering message that we've failed to see that it was written at a particular point in time, in a specific historical setting and dealt with important issues of immediate concern. In order to grasp the contemporary significance of 'Marketing Myopia', it is necessary to appreciate its historical context.

It is no exaggeration to state that the 1950s have acquired a kind of *Pleasantville*que lustre. They are regarded as an Edenic era, a bygone black and white age when the world was young, the burbs were burgeoning, tail-finned autos cut the motoring mustard and the future was something to look forward to. It was a time when marketing became the new commercial credo; a time when sales- and product-orientated companies confessed to their sins of omission and 25% commission; a time when marketing doctrine was reformulated thanks to a series of stunning theoretical developments, theoretical developments that still occupy pride of place in principles textbooks. Amongst others, the marketing mix, the PLC, STP, the wheel of retailing, the hierarchy of advertising effects and the marketing concept itself were added to our roll of academic honour during this remarkably fecund period. Granted, many of these principles had extensive antecedents but such precursors have only become important retrospectively, after they were articulated, circulated and canonized during Levitt's golden years.[24]

Attractive though this image of a post-war marketing paradise undoubtedly is, not least because it counterpoints the contemporary rhetoric of crisis (whither marketing?), decline (marketing is dead!) and recovery (long live marketing!), it is largely a figment of our febrile marketing imaginations. While there is no doubt that marketing transformed itself in the late 1950s, this process of intellectual transmogrification transpired through necessity, not choice. Far from being a Golden Age, when the great chain of corporate being finally begat *Homo marketus*, it was a time of marked anti-marketing sentiment. Truth to tell, the standing of marketing has never been lower than when Ted Levitt and his Herculean ilk were toiling in the Augean academic stables. Indeed, the sheer scale of their achievements may well be attributable to the total and unremitting hostility that marketers then endured.[25]

This extreme antipathy is nowhere better illustrated than in *The Hucksters*, Frederick Wakeman's thinly disguised *roman à clef*,[26] which was made into a movie in 1948. Based upon the author's experiences in the Foote, Cone and Belding agency, best known for handling the Lucky Strike cigarette account, the film painted a picture of the advertising industry that was almost entirely negative. It was a picture of fawning account executives, of duplicitous company chairmen, of back-scratching, hard-selling, three martini lunching, damn the customer double dealing, all of which were hidden behind a façade of sanctimonious, pseudo-scientific professionalism and unctuous, client-relationship-sustaining 'sincerity'. It was, in fact, nothing less than a commercial dystopia from which the protagonist, Victor Norman, eventually escaped by the skin of his Pepsodent-polished teeth and with his moral compass miraculously intact. More to the point perhaps, the book spawned a series of negative media portrayals, such as *The Man in the Gray Flannel Suit*, *Twelve Angry Men*, *Death of a Salesman*, *Organisation Man*, *Please Send Me Absolutely Free* and *The Space Merchants* – to say nothing of *Mad* magazine – all of which excoriated the marketing system in general and the advertising industry in particular.[27] Just as the stock villains of today's movies unerringly speak with an English accent, so too the classic 1950s bad guy was a Madison Avenue madman.

Egregious though they were, such media representations cannot be dismissed as blind prejudice, as yet another manifestation of the hate-marketing mentality that has been around since time immemorial.[28] On the contrary, this early post-war commercial jeremiad was almost entirely justified. In a series of landmark investigations, for example, the Federal Trade Commission revealed that all manner of dubious practices were rampant in the distribution sector, ranging from the organized crime-infested Teamsters, and price-colluding automobile dealers, to the attempts by shopping centre developers to minimize competition through restrictive leases, radius agreements and tenant mix manipulation.[29] Bribery was rife in the then burgeoning popular music industry, where radio station disc jockeys were paid handsomely to play the hottest sounds, as determined by the marketing departments of ambitious record companies.[30] And television game shows, which attracted huge audiences for their corporate sponsors-cum-producers, were exposed as an elaborate fraud. The questions were rigged and answers provided to attractive, audience-building contestants, such as the infamous Charles van Doren, scion of New England's finest family.[31] In the ensuing fracas, which commenced in late 1958 and culminated in the congressional investigations of 1959, the television network owners disingenuously denied all knowledge of the deceitful practices of quiz-show sponsoring corporations, such as Geritol, though they vowed to purge the networks thereafter (hence the decline of sponsor-produced programmes and the advent of modern spot advertising).

Above and beyond its questionable, verging on criminal activities, the marketing industry was held responsible for all manner of fads, fashions, frivolities and failures, which further undermined what little standing it had.[32] These heavily promoted and (usually) short-lived crazes included the Barbie Doll in 1959, the Hula-Hoop in 1958, Frisbees in 1957, Ant Farms in 1956 and, thanks to Disney's successful TV series, the fleeting fashion for Davy Crockett coonskin caps in 1955. Attempts to manu-facture fads, furthermore, often ended in failure – who now remembers Speedee, McDonald's pre-1960 mascot? – as did me-too attempts to cash in on a pre-existing passing fancy. Davy Crockett, for example, begat pseudo-history series on Texas John Slaughter and General Francis Marion (who they?); the Ant Farm, a transparent, sand-filled tank containing a colony of Harvester Ants, spawned the rather less successful Sea Monkeys (heavily advertised as aquatic, semi-humanoid 'pets' but in fact tiny brine shrimp in minuscule plastic bowls); and the countless Hula-Hoop spin-offs comprised Wiggle-a-Hoop, Hoop-Zing, Hooper-Dooper and Whoop-de-Do, amongst others.

Whatever happened to Barbie, by the way?[33]

The failure of all failures, of course, was the Ford Edsel, perhaps the most extensively researched and pre-tested new product calamity in marketing history.[34] All sorts of explanations have since been posited for the Edsel episode – mechanical failings, gimmicky gadgetry, 1957's mini-economic recession, excessive pre-launch hoopla, which raised expecta-tions to an intolerable level, etc., etc. – but the fact of the matter is that the product was presented as the epitome of modern marketing and its instantaneous failure only served to further reveal our field's feet of clay. In many ways, the Edsel became a symbol of – arguably a scapegoat for – the shortcomings of America *per se*, since it took place in the very same year as Sputnik. Strange though it now seems, the launch of the Russian satellites in October and November 1957 shocked America to the core. So much so, that it precipitated a purge of the nation's further and higher education system. Thanks to the National Defense Education Act, the Conant Report on high schools, and the devastating Ford and Carnegie analyses of business schools,[35] the American education system adopted a scientific imperative, an imperative that led directly to the founding of the Marketing Science Institute in 1963. You know, it is staggering to think that marketing science – a legacy of the thermo-nuclear 1950s – still holds our field in thrall, even though the Cold War has long been tossed into the trashcan of history. MAD, or what?

Tarred as it was by the brushes of finagling, faddishness, frivolity and failure, the final blow to marketing's post-war credibility came when the industry turned on itself in a ruinous civil war. The insurrection was led by Bill Bernbach, ace copywriter for Doyle Dane Bernbach, and the first shots were fired in his agency's much-lauded 1959 campaign for the Volkswagen Beetle. Although this campaign is routinely cited as the high water mark of post-war marketing creativity – indeed, it is still alluded to, albeit with a knowing postmodern wink – its success rested on a root and branch critique of extant marketing practices. In rendering virtuous the VW's ostensible vices, the two-toned, tail-finned, chrome-crammed extravagances of American automobile manufacturers were mercilessly lampooned in DDB's immortal critique.

The conventions of marketing research, what is more, were given equally short shrift by advertising's *enfant terrible*. Anticipating the cele-brated 'two cultures' debate,[36] Bernbach declared that advertising was an art, not a science and no amount of copy-testing, test marketing and test-retest reliability measures could compensate for the all-important creative spark. Excessive and unnecessary research, in fact, was largely responsible for the slough of mediocrity into which mid-fifties marketing had sunk. 'There are a lot of technicians in advertising,' he observed. 'And unfor-tunately they talk the best game. They know all the rules. They can tell you that [pictures of] people in an ad will get you greater readership. They can tell you that a sentence should be this short or that long. They can tell you that body copy should be broken up for easier and more inviting reading. They can give you fact after fact after fact. They are the scientists of advertising. But there's one little rub. Advertising is fundamentally persuasion and persuasion happens to be not a science, but an art.'[37]

In retrospect, these heresies are regarded as the beginning of the so-called Creative Revolution which swept all before it in the 1960s and 1970s. Premised on a determination to 'tell it like it is' in colloquial, straight-talking, non-exclusionary language, and embraced by every major agency come the end of the decade – even JWT succumbed – the Bernbachian revolt did much to transform popular perceptions of adver-tising and marketing. The somewhat dull, servile, conformist, condes-cending, elitist, time-serving, grey-suited, middle-aged image of the 1950s was cast aside and replaced by the cool, chic, cheeky, sexy, streetwise, insouciant, teenage-rebel-of-the-week character that it enjoyed until the no-logo outbreak of recent years. At the time, however, Bernbach's campaigning reinforced the then prevalent notion that there was something rotten in the state of marketing. His was a lone voice, a Jewish prophet in the WASP wilderness, who profited from his prophecies and the philistinism of the east-coast advertising establishment.[38]

Be that as it may, by far the most damning late-fifties indictment of marketing (apart, possibly, from Galbraith's *Affluent Society*, which lambasted the tub-thumping, billboard-erecting, want-creating, desire-inducing strategies of marketers and advertisers),[39] came from a decidedly unexpected source: an unemployed newspaperman and aspirant social commentator. Vance Packard was a Pennsylvania farm boy at heart, someone who believed that the American character, predicated on thrift, self-reliance and an infinite capacity for hard work, was being compromised by the iniquitous side-effects of success. Materialism, urbanism, hedonism and over-indulgence in the sybaritic achievements of consumer society had led the country astray, rendered it flabby, made it unfit for global leadership and placed it in very real danger of being deposed by the thrifty, self-reliant and hard-working Soviet Union.

The chief architects of this potentially disastrous state of affairs, according to Packard, were the devious denizens of Madison Avenue, who employed a battery of brain-washing techniques to persuade unsuspecting consumers to do their maleficent bidding. Big Brother was not only watching the American public, he was making it buy, buy and buy again. Motivation Research, as practised by the suspiciously East European Ernest Dichter, was by far the blackest of marketing's black arts, though subliminal stimulation was also on standby, as were psychobiology, psycholinguistics, psychometrics, psychographics and other opprobrious procedures too psycho to mention.[40]

Although the 'disgraceful' depth psychologies it so lovingly describes now strike us as insufficiently deep, *The Hidden Persuaders* undoubtedly struck a chord with the American public.[41] It pandered to the Cold War paranoia that was then pervasive (ads under the bed, as it were) and chimed with widespread concerns about bureaucratization, conformity, mass society and the unintended consequences of affluence. Indeed, as it provided a clearly identifiable target for puritanical, non-conformist, anti-bureaucratic, true-blue, back-to-nature, God's-own-country American ire, the book quickly became a Number 1 best-seller. It topped the non-fiction list for 1957–8, had almost three million copies in print by 1975 and inevitably spawned a couple of equally successful, if less well remembered sequels, both of which boasted mendacious marketing men as the bad guys.[42]

Predictably, the advertising industry returned immediate fire, arguing that marketing was predicated upon rigour, objectivity and professionalism, that it was a force for the good, working in the consumer's best interest, that motivation research was only practised by occupants of the lunatic fringe. Packard, moreover, was accused of indulging in the very thing he condemned by exploiting the selfsame unconscious motivations – such as the fear of being exploited – that the book took great pains to disparage. None other than Ernest Dichter described Packard as a 'morality huckster', who pounded his royalty-stuffed chest and wept bitter tears over tailfins, only to step into a sports car and drive off to his mansion in Connecticut. Van the Man, however, revelled in the industry's outrage, especially when the front cover of *Printer's Ink* was given over to an anti-Packard diatribe, believing that advertising's antagonism was the best advertisement he could possibly have. 'The best thing for an author, next to being banned in Boston, is to be blasted on Madison Avenue,' he quipped.[43]

The ironies of Packard's bull run in marketing's china shop don't end there, of course. Although he occupies pride of place as our field's favourite hate figure – the person who misrepresented marketing to the world at large – his critique probably did more to promote the discipline than any number of affronted protestations concerning marketing's well-meaning, caring-sharing, hug-a-customer-any-customer credentials. Packard, apparently, was flooded with letters asking for further information on motivation research. Most of his correspondents, mind you, intended to employ the techniques in their own promotional strategies! Numerous advertisers developed campaigns premised on the hidden persuaders motif; several creatives congratulated him on his copywriting skills, which they hoped to emulate in future; and, a sociology professor informed Packard that although 10% of his class were horrified by what they had read, 60% had plans to pursue a career in motivation research (the remaining 30%, presumably, were insufficiently persuaded by the persuaders, hidden or otherwise).

What's more, by implying that Madison Avenue medicine men had the power to prise open customers' pocket-books, whether they liked it or not, VP unwittingly endowed marketers with abilities that they simply didn't possess. 'The most tangible result of Packard's book,' his official biographer openly acknowledges, 'was an increased and unrealistic demand for motivation research . . . [It] allowed advertising agencies to complain bitterly about what he wrote and then call on people like Dichter to help them take advantage of the authority that *Hidden Persuaders* had given them.'[44] Indeed, Dirty Dr Dichter actually wrote to thank him – tongue in cheek, surely – for the extra work that had come his way as a result of the book.[45]

In addition to Packard's inadvertent endorsement of Madison Avenue, and the approach-avoidance appeal he unwittingly bestowed upon the advertising industry,[46] VP accidentally perpetuated the single biggest hoax in the history of marketing research. True, *The Hidden Persuaders* mentions subliminal advertising only in passing – interestingly

Vany doesn't employ the actual term, preferring to call it 'subthreshold effects' – but the book's ringing condemnation of this particularly disreputable practice both publicized and effectively legitimized an otherwise suspect technique. So effective was Packard's exposé that the federal government stepped in to curb the use of subliminal stimulation, as did policymakers in Australia, Holland and Great Britain. Yet, it is now recognized that the subliminal scare of 1957–8 was a complete and utter con, the mischievous concoction of an unemployed marketing researcher, James M. Vicary.[47]

Charlatan nonpareil, Vicary claimed that he had conducted extensive experiments, in an unidentified movie theatre, on 45,699 anonymous subjects, at some unspecified time in the not too distant past. While watching the nameless movie, his unsuspecting subjects were exposed to two hidden messages – 'Eat Popcorn' and 'Drink Coke' – which purportedly increased sales of the latter by 18.1% and the former by an incredible 57.4%. Sensibly, this Svengali of subliminal advertising refused to reveal further details of his proprietary procedures, or discuss them with journalists, though he declared himself ever-ready to instruct marketers and advertisers on their implementation. For a suitably modest retainer. Indeed, like the public-spirited citizen he was, Vicary claimed that subliminal advertising would eventually replace inter-programme inserts, thereby eliminating unnecessary interruptions and enhancing the enjoyment of television viewers, while fulfilling the station's commercial obligations.

The feds were not so sure, however, and they insisted on a public demonstration of Vicary's subliminal acumen. This duly took place in January 1958 and, as one might expect, when the attendees didn't see something they weren't supposed to see in the first place, they went away completely satisfied with the veracity of the method. Ever ahead of the game, learned academics lined up to replicate the experiments and signally failed to find support for Vicary's findings (the results, rather, were mixed). But by that stage the hoaxer had long since disappeared, without a forwarding address, his pockets stuffed with hard-earned consultancy dollars. Unfortunately, he forgot to file a patent, or trademark his terminology, since it is used to this day in spoof, spot-the-naked-lady-in-the-ice-cubes advertising campaigns (for Cutty Sark, Absolut, Seagrams and Sprite, amongst others) and surveys show that no less than 62% of the general public believe embedding is an everyday advertising practice.[48] At least one eccentric academic, what is more, has made a career out of the subliminal threat to truth, justice and the American marketing way.[49]

Subliminal advertising may have entered the pantheon of urban legend, alongside microwaveable cats, psychotic hitchhikers and venomous spiders beneath the toilet seat, but it did wonders for Van the Man. As he openly acknowledges in the second (1981) edition of his best-seller,

The Hidden Persuaders only really took off thanks to the controversy surrounding Vicary's 'experiments'. It transpires, moreover, that Vicary was one of Packard's principal informants, perhaps *the* principal informant. It is difficult to be sure, since VP's own research procedures are not clearly laid out, which is somewhat ironic given his castigation of motivation researchers' questionable practices. But he does note that, in a particularly tight-lipped industry, Vicary is an 'ingratiating and genial' exception to the norm. Vance, indeed, was so taken by his voluble (and invaluable) insider that he felt moved to rhapsodize: 'In appearance he is handsome; in fact he might well have stepped out of a clothing ad'.[50]

Like many rogues, then, Vicary must have been a bit of a charmer and, in light of the obvious gullibility of our penurious, sensation-seeking author, who was desperate to produce a blockbuster, it is unsurprising that several of the juiciest stories in *The Hidden Persuaders* come courtesy of this commercial con-artist. These include such memorable items as the purported relationship between baking a cake and giving birth; the 'hypnoidal trance' that housewives fall into in supermarkets; the precise dates of 'psychological' spring and winter; and, in an imaginative extrapolation of anal fixation, the fact that prune eaters are parsimonious. Many other anecdotes may have come from the same source but Packard carefully covers his tracks – and thereby avoids giving the impression that he relied too much on a single informant – by referring to 'a well-known motivation researcher' or pleading confidentiality constraints. Be that as it may, Vicary's findings purportedly derived from 'rigorous', 'carefully controlled' trials and experiments, albeit Vany doesn't provide any additional details (and only a cynic would infer that there were no additional details to give).

It is difficult not to be amused by the thought of Vance Packard, ace investigator of Motivation Research gallimaufry, being gulled by a fast-talking MR mountebank. Perhaps we shouldn't laugh too soon, however. On re-reading *The Hidden Persuaders*, one cannot help but notice that a number of Ted Levitt's best lines came straight from Packard's shock-horror showstopper! A leading executive, for example, informed Van the Man that 'cosmetic manufacturers are not selling lanolin, they are selling hope . . . We no longer buy oranges, we buy vitality. We do not buy just an auto, we buy prestige.' 'Don't sell shoes,' another exhorted, 'sell lovely feet.' 'Sell the sizzle, not the meat,' yet another volunteered (presumably the prosaic informant had been informed that he was in the meat business not the steak business).[51] And yet another – I like to think it was Vicary – asserted that the secret of marketing success was not to sell goods but to buy customers.

Yes, that's right, Father Ted's discipline-defining aphorism in 'Marketing Myopia' was pre-dated by *The Hidden Persuaders*.[52] Perhaps his paper should really be called 'Marketing Misappropriated'.

Now, far be it for me to suggest that Father Ted plagiarized Packard for his own self-serving purposes. However, it has to be said that 'Marketing Myopia' – a paper, remember, based entirely on secondary information – is somewhat parsimonious with the citations. Insufficient intellectual prunes are probably to blame, but the fact of the matter is that Levitt fails to acknowledge his reliance on Schumpeter's notion of 'creative destruction'. What's more, he is condescendingly dismissive of the few sources that are referred to (Barzun's work on the railroads, Galbraith's 'affluent society' thesis, the special issue of *American Petroleum Institute Quarterly*, etc). And, as for his conceptual predecessors in marketing, they don't even warrant a mention, though he makes extravagant amends in his fulsome, tantamount to false-modest, 'postscript' of 1975. The amateur psychologists among us might be inclined to explain Levitt's almost pathological hatred of motivation researchers – variously described as 'imprecise and artless', 'astrologers', 'untrustworthy' and 'blind guessers' – in terms of his own dependence on their Packard-refracted pronouncements.[53] Doubtless this influence was subliminal, but it is fascinating to think that the modern marketing concept may well be predicated on the tall-tale-telling capacity of conceptual snake-oil salespersons.

The ultimate snake-oil salesperson, of course, is Ted Levitt himself. Unlike Vicary, however, he has never been exposed for the scholarly cozener he is. Forty years on from his intellectual apotheosis, marketing academics and practitioners continue to swallow his textual elixirs, smear themselves in his conceptual embrocations and write I-was-lost-but-now-I'm-found testimonials to Levitt's life-enhancing efficacy. Yet the evidence against Harvard's finest is compelling. As his most famous publication and, truth to tell, his entire literary corpus perfectly illustrates, Theo exhibits all the characteristics, hallmarks, qualities – call them what you will – of academic quackery. He has a. brass neck;[54] he is blessed with considerable personal charm;[55] he has a truly wonderful way with words;[56] and, like many mountebanks, he is an outsider with something to prove and a determination to prove it.[57]

However, before you jump to the wrong conclusion and accuse me of disrespect towards the immortal beloved of modern marketing, let me make it absolutely clear that *there's nothing wrong with mountebanks*. Quackery, in my opinion, is an integral part of marketing, as the rest of this text will attest. In fact, Levitt's single greatest achievement was quintessential quackery. At a time when the entire marketing system was under attack and its exponents widely regarded as the spawn of the devil, he gave marketers something to believe in. Namely, customer sovereignty. Marketers, according to our prestidigitator-in-chief, are only doing customers' bidding, responding to their needs and giving them what they want. Marketers aren't in the business of customer exploitation, nor do they wish to pick shoppers' pockets or participate in

disreputable behaviour of any kind. Such activities undoubtedly go on –
sometimes in the name of marketing – but they are most definitely *not* the
actions of 'genuine' marketers. They are the actions of production-
orientated or sales-orientated organizations, those that are unaware of or
have failed to adopt the customer-orientated marketing concept.

So there.

Although the centrality of the consumer is a commonplace today –
something labelled 'the consumer' is slap bang in the middle of almost
every diagram in almost every marketing textbook – it most certainly
wasn't in the late-1950s. Premodern marketing, if it can be called that, was
not characterized by total customer orientation, curious though this
notion now seems. As Sheth et al. have shown,[58] institutional, functional,
regional and various other schools of marketing thought held sway before
the advent of the 'modern' (or 'managerial') paradigm, which was effectively launched by Levitt's landmark endeavours. Although consumers
featured prominently in prior representations of the field, they were
positioned at the *end* of the marketing process, not at the beginning. Ted
Levitt's intellectual acumen lay in inverting the traditional schema,
implying that his was the proper interpretation of our discipline's domain,
and blaming all marketing misdemeanours on those who were unaware of
this basic truth. He actually went out of his way to attack the 'tricks and
techniques' of selling- and production-orientated organizations.

In this regard, perhaps the most striking thing about 'Marketing
Myopia', as a work of literature, is that it is deliberately downbeat,
verging on flagrantly counterintuitive. For example, it focuses on the
inevitability of failure, it demolishes four 'myths' about marketing, it
makes a case for Henry any-colour Ford as a marketing man supreme
and it undermines the then triumphant petrochemical industry by intimating that it survived despite a catalogue of elementary marketing
errors. In adopting this rhetorical stance, Levitt skilfully aligned himself
with, and benefited from, the then virulent critiques of marketing life,
whilst offering an untainted alternative vision – or, rather, re-vision – of
the same. His enthusiasm for customer orientation, it must be stressed,
was not new. Consumer sovereignty had been a basic precept of neo-
classical and classical economics, since Adam Smith at least. However,
he repackaged and represented it at a time when marketing was being
accused of manufacturing customers, creating unnecessary demands and
fomenting hidden desires, and when marketers themselves had descended
into self-defeating civil warfare.

Ted Levitt, in short, was a retro rhetorician of the first rank. He
completely rewrote the history of marketing and reinvented the field as a
consequence; he combined past and present, thereby setting a course for
the future; and he persuaded people, by means of his compelling myopic

metaphor, to see things from a different perspective. It is arguable, then, that the real lesson of 'Marketing Myopia' – the twenty-first-century lesson – lies less in its content than its incomparable style. At a time when marketing is under systematic attack by the no-logo contingent and anti-capitalist protesters; at a time when marketing is once more the subject of innumerable books, movies, newspaper columns and television programmes; at a time when Hidden Persuaders are reputed to be rearing their ugly heads yet again; at a time when marketers themselves are embroiled in self-destructive bouts of internecine strife; at a time when marketing is being tarred with the brush of finagling (Rip-Off Britain), fad-mongering (Beanie Babies, Pokémon, Re-engineering) and calamitous failure (the Rover 75 is not only retro, it is the Edsel reborn),[59] it is astonishing that our field continues to rehearse the hoary customer-orientated story, continues to adopt servile, we-are-not-worthy mannerisms and continues to cleave to the calcified credo of marketing science. Surely it is time to reconsider Levitt's legacy of marketing megalomania, marketing myopia and consumer mindedness. If ever the time was ripe for a neo-Ted Levitt, another conceptual charlatan, someone capable of pulling the rhetorical wool over our purblind eyes – or should that be P-blind? – that time is surely now.

Dig for Vicary.

3

Redeeming Marketing: The Spiritual Side of Trade

Not many books about marketing make the top of the best-sellers' list, systematic critiques like *The Hidden Persuaders* and *The Hucksters* possibly excepted. Yet, seventy-five years ago, a stirring endorsement of modern marketing, *The Man Nobody Knows*, became a Number 1 best-seller, racking up 250,000 sales and going through twenty-two reprints in less than eighteen months.[1] What's more, it was translated into eighteen languages and, thanks to occasional reissues, went on to sell more than one million copies in the United States alone.

The Man Nobody Knows was written by Bruce Barton, forty-year-old founder of Barton Durstine & Osborn, an up-and-coming advertising agency with an impressive client list that included General Electric, General Motors, Dunlop Tires and Lever Bros. Catapulted to instant fame by the media attention his runaway best-seller attracted, Barton used it to launch an illustrious and remarkably eclectic career.[2] He dabbled in the movies, where he served as consultant to Cecil B. de Mille's (1926) biblical epic, *King of Kings*; became a semi-official national spokesperson on marketing-related matters, thanks to his syndicated columns in various mass circulation magazines; and, despite a scandalous court case that comprised an intoxicating mix of blackmail, religious rectitude and marital infidelity, he ended up as a congressman for Manhattan's fashion district, which he served with considerable distinction and not a little aplomb. So much so, that at one stage he was considered a serious vice-presidential possibility.

Although Barton was widely regarded as an advertising industry 'outsider', he not only succeeded in establishing what became BBDO as a powerhouse agency, which was vying with the mighty JWT at the time of his death in 1967, but he also did much to contest marketing's decidedly *déclassé* image.[3] Previously considered the domain of scalpers, shysters, snake-oil salespeople and chips off the P.T. Barnum block – a reputation, as we have seen, regained in the early post-war era – marketing was transformed into an acceptable, if not exactly admirable, professional calling, thanks in no small measure to Barton's celebrity status. Only two years after the publication of his surprise best-seller, marketing attained the pinnacle of socio-political respectability when President Coolidge described it as the single most potent influence on the day-to-day lives of American people and nothing less than 'the spiritual side of trade' (albeit his speech was ghost-written by none other than Bruce Barton!).[4]

At this remove in time, it is almost impossible to imagine the impact, or appreciate the extent, of Barton's literary triumph, not least because of present-day marketers' widespread if ahistorical belief that the marketing concept was 'invented' some time in the 1950s.[5] While few would gainsay the astonishing accomplishments of Levitt, Keith, Kotler and analogous post-war thinkers, the production-era/sales-era/marketing-era stereotype that continues to be recycled in mainstream textbooks bears *no resemblance whatsoever* to the actual state of commercial affairs before the Second World War. As numerous commentators on popular culture have made clear, marketing was very firmly established in the pre-Depression era.[6] In fact, it was during this precise period that mass marketing really came to the fore. New products proliferated, advertising budgets burgeoned, copywriters' creativity reached remarkable heights and the sheer merchandise-moving power of the marketing system was recognized for the first time. This is not to suggest that marketing was universally admired or that advertising had successfully shed its hucksterish heritage. The enormous popularity of Sinclair Lewis's *Babbitt*, a best-selling 1922 satire on business boosterism, go-getting and catch-phraseology, clearly indicates otherwise.[7] There is no doubt, however, that Barton's brilliant book helped deodorize, at least temporarily, a notoriously noisome industry.

To be sure, *The Man Nobody Knows* hardly constituted a conventional work of marketing scholarship. On the contrary, it was essentially a marketing-inflected reinterpretation of the Life of Christ, an attempt to reappropriate, reanimate and rearticulate the then languishing spirit of liberal Protestantism. The book, in essence, portrayed Jesus Christ as the very model of a modern businessman, as the greatest marketer on earth, as someone incomparably blessed with innate advertising, promotional and interpersonal skills. A master self-publicist, who created 'big stories' by healing the sick and courting controversy, Jesus's parables were presented as exemplars of effective advertising copy – simple, succinct, stirring, sincere – and Jesus himself deemed a consummate adman, forever persuading, cajoling, generating interest, stimulating desire, recruiting followers and generally spreading the Word. More to the point perhaps, just as Jesus was a marketing man *avant la lettre* – according to Barton, the story of the Good Samaritan was 'the greatest advertisement of all time'[8] – so too Lost Generation marketers continued to do the good Lord's work. The archangels of Madison Avenue were merely writing updated versions of biblical parables, with the same exalted purpose and anticipated outcome. For Barton at least, the most effective advertisements were 'written by men who have an abiding respect for the intelligence of their readers and a deep sincerity regarding the merits of the goods they sell'.[9] It was surely no accident, claimed the peerless wordsmith, that *credit*, the very basis of modern business, was derived from *credo*: I believe.

Needless to say, Barton's fanciful take on JC, as a proto-captain of consciousness, *bon mot* disbursing bon-viveur and mountain-man *manqué*, attracted a modicum of derision at the time and continues so to do. Part of this disdain is due to his debased, all too easily lampooned interpretation of the Son of God, variously summarized as 'a glad-handling host, nature-lover and canny businessman', 'an extroverted general practitioner who liked camping' and 'a Babbitt, Rotarian and suitcase-carrying drummer'.[10] It is also attributable to the self-serving purpose behind Barton's polemic; namely, his attempt to redeem Jesus for materialistic times while exorcizing his own doubts about the merits of advertising. God was a marketing man, he argued, therefore marketing men were doing God's work. They were not exploiting customers, stimulating unnecessary wants, commending over-consumption of comestibles and puffing the not-so-good things in life – the very goods that made it easier for a camel to pass through the eye of a needle than for a rich man to enter the kingdom of Heaven – but going about their father's business.[11]

Literally.

Now, it doesn't take a doctorate in psychotherapy to appreciate that Barton's uncertainty about his calling cannot be separated from his own family circumstances. Like many pious pioneers of Madison Avenue – prior to the 'creative revolution' of the 1960s, that is[12] – Bruce Barton was cut from a man of the cloth. His father, the Reverend William E. Barton, was a very distinguished cleric, public figure and champion of liberal Protestantism, who wrote the (then) definitive biography of Abraham Lincoln, as well as a series of best-selling religious primers under the provocatively pagan pseudonym Safed the Sage. These advocated a life of self-denial and community service, whereby the strength of one's beliefs was demonstrated, judged, and salvation ultimately ensured through personal accomplishment, material success and willingness to help the less fortunate.

Barton thus laboured in the long shadow of celebrity and at one stage endeavoured to follow in his father's footsteps by enrolling in theological college. Although he was an excellent student – President of the Christian Association, voted person most likely to succeed, etc. – he experienced a severe crisis of faith and, on graduation, effectively dropped out. He rode the rails, worked as a lumberjack in Montana, edited a women's magazine (as lapsed lumberjacks are wont to do) and eventually ended up in New York as sales manager for a publishing house. Here, he wrote his first famous advertisement for Collier's Five-Foot Shelf of Harvard Classics ('the essentials of a liberal education in only fifteen minutes a day') and formulated his notion that preachers were marketing men in dog-collared disguise. Akin to his father, furthermore, Bruce Barton maintained that businesspeople should seek to combine profit-making with personal probity, public service and a paternalistic outlook. With this in mind, he employed his not inconsiderable promotional talents to further the (First World) War effort, the YMCA and the Salvation Army, for whom he coined his most celebrated slogan, 'A man may be down but he's never out'. He also founded his 'ethical' advertising agency in 1919, arguing that marketing and advertising were not merely an integral part of the modern economy but helped keep the wheels turning by providing new objects of desire. What many Christians considered a vice – the creation, stimulation and exploitation of wants – Barton regarded as a virtue, because the prospect of acquiring something new raised consumer expectations, spurred individual ambition and encouraged people to better themselves.

The want that Bruce Barton best stimulated, however, was the want for his works of literature. Although *The Man Nobody Knows* remained on the best-sellers' list for two years and led non-fiction titles in 1926 – despite generally hostile reviews – the favourable public response was not entirely spontaneous. Thousands of copies were distributed by businesses as promotional tie-ins. It was brilliantly merchandized thanks to window displays consisting of two lighted candles, a bible and, naturally, Barton's gooder-than-good book. Encouraged, what is more, by his partners, who regarded it as an excellent advertisement for their agency, the celebrated copywriter quickly produced a series of follow-up texts, *The Book Nobody Knows* (1926), *The Man from Galilee* (1926), and *What Can a Man Believe?* (1927). Like all good sequels, these lightly rehashed the original, contending that the precipitous decline of Protestantism could be reversed by the use of modern business methods and that the Bible, concomitantly, was full of premodern businessmen. The sizzle, nevertheless, belied the steak because Barton's ever-present doubts about *his* father's business, coupled with professional concerns (not least the revival of hard-sell hucksterism as the Great Depression unfolded) and personal problems (perpetual insomnia, the much-publicized court case, a paralysed daughter, the death of his father) led to a series of nervous breakdowns, hospitalizations and, eventually, a second career as Congressional spear carrier.

Barton's moment in the political sun wasn't to last, however. Partly, one suspects, on account of his high-profile pacifism – famously denounced by President Roosevelt in October 1940[13] – the great communicator's reputation didn't have a particularly good war. By the

Eisenhower era, the people's judgement on the man everybody knew was that, for all his fine words, he was sadly typical of his duplicitous breed. Akin to most marketing men, commercial travellers and Elmer Gantryesque evangelists, he was a complete hypocrite, who said one thing but did another. And there was ample evidence to that effect. When Barton was sales manager for *Collier's* magazine, he routinely praised salesmen who duped housewives into taking out unnecessary subscriptions, sanctimoniously adding that maybe the swindlers will 'grow into the habit of being square with themselves'. He played the part of an aw-shucks, straw-chewing, hill-billy farm boy – Barton was born in rural Tennessee – even though he was a Boston Brahmin through and through. (When he was seven, his father was appointed to one of the most prestigious pulpits in New England, having earned his spurs in a lowly circuit-riding ministry, as theological high-fliers were then expected to do.) He ceaselessly pontificated on the joys of matrimony and Christian marriage, only to be publicly exposed as a womanizing philanderer when he foolishly instituted legal proceedings against a former lover and employee of BBDO, who was attempting to blackmail him.

Most perniciously perhaps, he consistently maintained that marketers were ethical, do-gooding, God-fearing, whiter-than-white defenders of the faith. This contention may have carried a modicum of conviction in the Roaring Twenties, but the malevolent machinations of wartime propagandists, coupled with the Cold War atmosphere of Stalinist conspiracies abroad, communist conspirators at home and the dubious behaviour of brain-washing admen on brain-washed consumers, ensured that marketing rapidly lost what little inter-war lustre it enjoyed. So degraded did marketing's reputation become that when *The Man Nobody Knows* was republished in 1960, in an attempt to cash in on the religious revivalism that was then sweeping the country, thanks to Billy Graham, Norman Vincent Peale and several others,[14] all references to the advertising industry were excised from the text.[15] Barton had become the marketing man nobody knew, or wanted to know.

Although the advertising agency he founded is alive, well and continues to ride high in the billings rankings, Bruce Barton is now largely forgotten, dismissed as a regrettably typical representative of go-getting, Jazz Age vulgarity, who traded in boosterism, bombast and bible-thumping banalities. Yet few would deny that he was a staggeringly brilliant marketing man. Apart from his astonishing professional accomplishments (such as his work with Norman Rockwell on the Mazda Lamps account or his ads for the Alexander Hamilton Institute, which regularly feature on all-time-best lists), he was the first fully paid up marketer to examine the spiritual side of trade, the relationship between God and goods, sanctity and selling, communion and consumption, marketing and mammon. What's more, he was totally committed to truth in advertising, to exorcizing the demons of charlatanry, to raising marketing's moral and ethical standards, and to shedding the constrictive skin of snake-oil salesmanship which was – and to some extent still is – tenaciously attached to the commercial body. In this regard, he contended that marketers should avoid pitched battles between rival brands, settle for reasonable shares of the market, refrain from promoting defective goods and treat each advertising campaign as an 'act of faith'. As the man himself knowingly put it:

> Faith in business, faith in the country, faith in one's self, faith in other people – this is the power that moves the world. And why is it unreasonable to believe that this power, which is so much stronger than any other, is merely a fragment of the Great Power which operates in the universe.[16]

Far be it for me to foment faithlessness, or find fault with the fundamentals of our field.[17] However, for those of us brought up to believe that Levitt, Kotler and analogous academic prophets descended from the marketing mount in the 1960s, armed with the tablets of scholarly stone, Bruce Barton cuts a fascinating figure. Duplicitous undoubtedly, the epitome of marketing mendaciousness possibly, but he is proof that giants walked the earth before the so-called 'modern' marketing era. More to the point perhaps, his stature was achieved by, and his rhetorical revolution predicated upon, a diet of retro. Barton's reinvention of marketing, like that of Theodore the Incomparable, involved an historical rewrite which not only combined old and new – Jesus was a marketing man, as were Napoleon Bonaparte, George Washington, Robert E. Lee and several others besides – but offered an alternative future for the field based on faith, spirituality and sincerity rather than hard sell, humbug, Babbittry and Barnumism. What's more, just as Levitt wrapped himself in the flag of American industrial history, so too Barton's believe-in-business, business-as-belief credo drew inspiration from a long-established intellectual tradition, known as the Mind Cure movement, which emerged in New England around the middle of the nineteenth century.[18]

Mind Cure, to put it in a nutshell, was a form of auto-suggestion. It was based on the belief that belief itself can bring about change for the better, that the mind can cure itself by willing it to be so, that self-improvement is possible if the self wishes to be improved, that heaven can be created on earth by thinking heavenly thoughts here on earth. It was, admittedly, a flagrantly optimistic credo which banished negativity, regarded pessimism as pernicious and simply refused to countenance failure. As such, it stood in marked contrast to the morbidity of Puritanism – humanity's fallen state, innate wickedness, eternal damnation in prospect, etc. – that held sway in the early Colonial period and was slowly being ousted by the less despondent ethos of Unitarianism, Latitudinarianism and emergent forms of liberal Protestantism.

Granted, the doctrinal origins of the mind cure movement actually resided in the decidedly murky depths of Anton Mesmer's animal magnetism, the mystic ruminations of Emmanuel Swedenborg and Jakob Boehme, as well as the alchemic concoctions of Paracelsus, the-artist-formerly-known-as-Bombastus, who practised a form of mind cure in the early sixteenth century.[19] What's more, it flourished in the far from unyielding intellectual soil of the north-eastern United States, already prepared by the fake spiritualism of the infamous Fox sisters, aerated by the transcendentalism of Emerson and Whitman, enriched by the evolutionary theories of Darwin and Spencer, and fertilized by the religious ferment – the so-called 'Great Awakening' – of the 1860s and 1870s.[20]

Nevertheless, it is generally accepted that the mind cure movement commenced with the missionary endeavours of Phineas Parkhurst Quimby, an illiterate handyman-cum-clockmaker from Belfast, Maine. Impressed by the hypnotherapy of Charles Poyen, an acolyte of Anton Mesmer's, Quimby decided to dabble in the hypnotic arts, promptly cured himself of mysterious ailments, and by the early 1860s had established something of a local reputation for his miraculous healing abilities (he actually issued a disclaimer concerning unseemly comparisons with Jesus Christ!). Efficacious though hypnotism was proving, Phineas surmised that it was not the actual therapy but his patients' *belief* in the therapy that played the decisive role.[21] The mind cured itself. This prompted him to abandon hypnosis, head rubbing and the laying on of hands, in favour of telepathic treatments, which had the decided advantage (given the state of the roads) of working at a distance. Unfortunately, Quimby was denied full credit for his clairvoyance, due to the seer's unforeseen death in 1866 and it was left to two ambitious pupils to hammer his ideas into a coherent system.

And hammer they did.

In 1869, the Reverend Warren Evans of Boston published *The Mental Cure*, the first testament of the mind cure religion, which combined crypto-Swedenborgian notions of 'divine influx' with Quimbyesque concepts. This was soon followed by fellow New Englander Mary Baker Eddy's *Science and Health* and the subsequent formation of her Church of Christ, Science (i.e. Christian Science) in 1879. Variously accused of plagiarism, promiscuity, perfidy, parsimony, profligacy, prevarication and parental shortcomings, to name but a few, the prodigiously gifted Mary Baker Eddy proved to be a marketing genius, who turned the much reviled Christian Science movement into one of the most successful religious denominations of our time.[22] To be sure, hers was only one version – admittedly a hard-line version – of mind cure and many others, more or less distant from evangelical Protestantism, emerged in the second half of the nineteenth century. These included the Unity School and the New Thought Alliance, as well as more exotic cults like the Vedanta of Swami Vivekananda and the Theosophy of Madame Blavatsky, whose bare-faced charlatanism and all-round roguery put the shamelessness of Mary Baker Eddy to shame.[23]

However, it wasn't necessary to be a fully paid up member of a mind cure cult to be affected by its premises. In an era of rapid economic expansion prior to the First World War, it clearly struck a chord with the American people. It was cheerful, optimistic, self-confident, wish-orientated and totally devoid of disillusion, darkness or despair. It eschewed gloomy self-denial in favour of a sunny credo of self-absorption, living for today and revelling in the materialistic rewards of one's hard labour. It reflected, indeed inculcated, the characteristic American conviction that people could shape their own destinies, find total happiness and be what they wanted to be. It was all-pervasive.

Much more pertinently perhaps, it was actively promulgated by marketers and advertisers.[24] Not only did legions of businessmen enrol in courses on positive thinking but the trade press carried regular reports on the latest outpourings of mind cure gurus. The market was flooded with quasi-mind cure manuals and self-help texts. And all manner of tie-in products were marketed in association with mind cure's much-vaunted 'happiness machine'. The most successful of these was the Billikins 'no worry' doll – and variations thereof, such as 'Billycan and Billycant' figurines – which precipitated the 'doll craze' of the early 1900s and did much to engender the habit of buying gifts for children at Christmas-time, birthdays and on other ceremonial occasions.[25]

The *fin-de-siècle* fetish for mind cure was not, of course, confined to the lower orders – advertisers, businessmen, Yankee bunco artists and petty bourgeois social climbers – although the trading classes comprised a very strong constituency. It was also endorsed from on intellectual high, most notably by America's foremost philosopher, William James, and a now largely forgotten but at the time titanic economist, Simon Patten. The former, to be frank, was in need of a little mind cure himself.[26] Possibly on account of his father's extreme Swedenborgianism or simply as a result of spending too much time in Barnum's American Museum as a child, William James was prone to nervous disorders, as was Henry, his equally eccentric if rather more literary younger brother. At the age of twenty-eight, however, William made a classic take-up-thy-bed-and-walk decision, when he willed himself to believe in free will and acted on it. He put his lassitude, melancholy, physical afflictions and occupational failings behind him, rapidly established himself as the philosophical lion of Harvard Yard and thereafter enjoyed a long, extremely distinguished career as the epitome of Gilded Age scholarship.

Best known for his philosophy of Pragmatism – an essentially pluralist position, which is open to all perspectives and attempts to combine the best of continental idealism (abstract theory) with Anglo-American empiricism (lived experience), and which is still very much with us in the neo-Pragmatism of postmodern plenipotentiary, Richard Rorty – William James also published a series of philosophical essays on issues of popular concern. In the most famous of these, 'The Will to Believe', he posited that the very existence of certain transhuman realities, such as love, beauty and God, depends *entirely* upon human will to believe in them and act as if they existed.[27] Likewise, the acclaimed fourth chapter of *Varieties of Religious Experience*, 'The Religion of Healthy Mindedness', unequivocally endorsed the mind cure movement, concluding that this semi-secularized belief system represented America's 'only decidedly original contribution to the systematic philosophy of life'.[28]

Although his celebrated 'mystical' encounter prior to delivering the prestigious Gifford Lectures in 1901–2 ('a state of spiritual awareness of the most vital description', etc.) has latterly been explained in much more down-to-earth terms,[29] there is no doubt that William James was several psalms short of a hymnbook. He was a model of mental stability, however, compared to the so-called 'prophet of abundance', Simon Nelson Patten.[30] Born in Cossumyuna, New York, the son of emigrating New Englanders who traced their roots back to the Pilgrim Fathers, Patten was a mass of contradictions. One of the greatest intellects of his day, he dropped out of the University of Chicago, though he eventually found a niche in an obscure Pennsylvania institution now known as the Wharton School of Business. He was struck blind for three years by a bizarre psychosomatic condition brought on, apparently, by youthful sexual excesses.[31] He was raised in a strict Calvinist household and expressed lifelong distaste for the pleasurable, hedonistic, indulgent, concupiscent side of life. His wife, what is more, left him for a younger man and compounded the humiliation by publicizing Patten's sexual shortcomings. He lived a monastic existence, cared not for aesthetic matters, or indeed his personal appearance, and routinely gave all his money away to impecunious students. Yet he espoused a happy-smiley, getting and spending, immoderate verging on profligate economistic version of Mind Cure, aptly described as 'a disembodied vision of abundance that has pervaded corporate advertising, and American thought generally, throughout most of the twentieth century'.[32]

According to Patten, America had passed from an era of penury to an era of plenty.[33] A never-ending stream of mass-produced goods and services had rendered redundant established economic concepts predicated on assumptions of scarcity and limited resources. In order to keep the engine of the 'superlative machine' ticking over, however, it was necessary to pay workers adequate wages and encourage them to consume, to enjoy themselves, to take pleasure in indulgence, to luxuriate in industrialization's illimitable largesse. Not only was this good for the economy, insofar as the multiplication of wants increased demand, stimulated production and created additional jobs, but it was good for workers as well. Consumption raised expectations, promoted ambition, engendered the desire for self-improvement and comprised an integral part of the civilizing process. Materialism, possessions and 'inconspicuous' consumption – incremental acquisition by the masses rather than the Veblenesque excesses of social elites – thus served as a marker of progress, of modernization, of democracy, of America's manifest destiny. For Patten, it was nothing less than a new basis of consumption-led civilization, a complete rejection of the ascetic Puritan ethos of self-denial, self-sacrifice and self-inflicted suffering. Pleasure, leisure, fulfilment, spending, self-indulgence and suchlike were no longer signifiers of immorality but a right, a duty, a norm, an ethic, an expectation, an act of patriotism. An act of fealty. An act of fraternity. An act of faith, in fact.

Viewed from the perspective of the late twentieth century – a century stricken by war, waste, barbarity and environmental degradation – the mind cure movement strikes us as somewhat quaint, incredibly naïve, touchingly trusting and almost impossibly optimistic. However, its combination of sanctity and shopping, its contention that spending is spiritual, its devotion to a credo of consumption, does at least help place Bruce Barton in the broader scheme of things. Granted, his post-First-World-War version of mind cure was somewhat darker and more ambivalent than the unalloyed optimism of Progressive Era enthusiasts, let alone the bumptious boosterism of certain post-Armistice proselytes, such as the celebrated sloganeer, Emile Coué ('every day, in every way, I'm getting better and better').[34] What's more, he treated mind cure from a meso-level organizational standpoint – the way to better business – rather than the micro-level individualism of Christian Science or the macro-level societal visions of Simon Patten. Barton's basic message, nevertheless, was not off the wall. He was speaking to the converted.

Barton *still* speaks to the converted, because his interest in the spirituality of commerce and the commerce of spirituality is back with a bang. True, it never really went away, as innumerable mind cure mutations – Dale Carnegie in the 1930s and 1940s, Norman Vincent Peale in the 1950s and 1960s, and Tom Peters, Stephen Covey, Kenneth Blanchard, Anthony Robbins et al. in recent decades[35] – bear perpetual witness. At the same time, however, the current millennial transition has seen an extraordinary upsurge in corporate faith-professing. Retro religiosity, so we are told, is the management fad of the moment and spirituality now comprises the 'ultimate competitive advantage'.[36] In corporations throughout God's own country it seems that the landlord is taking his place behind boardroom tables. According to Reed, 'All sorts of companies, from the Fortune 500 to medium-size firms and small businesses, are hiring chaplains, starting departmental meetings with prayer, permitting services, posting slogans and biblical quotations, and allowing employees to discuss religion'.[37] A veritable host of evangelical pressure groups and management consultancies, such as Marketplace Ministries, the Churches' Advertising Network and the Fellowship of Companies for Christ International, is spreading the gospel that God is good for business. And the management self-help shelves of most good bookstores are groaning under the weight of how-to texts like *God Owns My Business*, *Moses on Management* and – holy moly – *Jesus CEO*. Can a reissue of Barton's blockbuster be far away?[38]

This proliferation of corporate piety, it must be emphasized, is not confined to right-wing, neo-fundamentalist, Bible-belted and braced businesses. In our nothing if not New Aged era, all sorts of spiritual apparitions are apparent in the organizational ether. From feng-shuied high streets and astrologically informed shopper typologies (Arians are particularly impatient, don't you know) to Successories screensavers and graphology tests for putative executives, non-Christian belief systems are making their managerial mark.[39] Marketers and advertisers, moreover, are appropriating the full spectrum of neo-pagan esoterica to anoint products and services with magical or supernatural powers. Camel filters are sold with the assistance of ouija boards and voodoo dolls. The 'messy burger' campaign of Carl's Junior incorporates a subway sooth-sayer who tells the future from splashes of ketchup.[40] Commercials for Kit-Kat variously portray chocolate-bar-shaped crop circles, mesmer-ized, chicken-imitating canines and a reincarnated Elvis, complete with blue suede shoes. The Peugeot now-you-see-it-now-you-don't 206 makes its point with the aid of a street-smart card sharp. Finlandia vodka announces that in a past life it used to be pure, glacial spring water. The Greek gods swore by olive oil or Carlsberg Special Brew, depending on which commercial you consult. And, of course, an unheavenly host of diabolically possessed products – motor cars, ice-cream bars, toilet ducks, dotcom demons – is attempting to tempt us astray.

Management savants and spokespersons, similarly, have not been slow to read the religiosity runes, whether it be Deepak Chopra's 'seven spiritual laws of success', Charles Handy's recent conversion to 'alchemy', Kunde's advocacy of 'corporate religion', Scott's 'seven seminal paths to corporate greatness', Firth and Campbell's adaptation of Native American lore to the windswept prairies of Middle England; Weinreich's eleven steps to 'brand heaven' (plus a twelfth, presumably, for the markaholics amongst us), Pringle and Thompson's successful relaunch of Cause Related Marketing as 'Brand Spirit', Ben and Jerry's discovery of the Infinite in a bucket of low-fat Cherry Garcia, or, indeed, the semi-divine powers that are being imputed to the Internet, that perfect yet intangible place where all good gurus and E-vangelists eventually end up.[41] The E-ternal city, no less. When it comes, what is more, to *The Little Book of Cash* (sorry, *Calm*), I get agitated just thinking about it.[42] Not that I begrudge them their royalty cheques, or anything.

It is, admittedly, easy to scoff at such shameless spiritual seques-
tration,[43] but the marketing academy is no less implicated in twenty-first-
century supernaturalism. One group of market researchers, for example,
has considered how religious beliefs affect consumer behaviour and, to
this end, the acquisitional idiosyncrasies of Jews, WASPs, Mormons and
evangelical Protestants, amongst others, have been studied in some
depth.[44] The distinctive repertoires of marketing-related activities associated with significant religious festivals, such as Easter, Thanksgiving,
Hanukkah and, above all, Christmas, have also been carefully investi-
gated.[45] A second group of scholars, meanwhile, prefers to ponder the
spirituality of consumption and the consumption of spirituality. Just as
televangelists rank among the foremost marketing practitioners of our
time, what with their cable television shows, radio stations, newsletters,
direct mail operations and diverse array of tie-in products from T-shirts
to diet books (*More of Jesus, Less of Me*), so too consumption is
increasingly imbued with a spiritual cast.[46] Shopping, they tell us, has
become sanctified; consuming is an act of consecration; hallowed be thy
brand name. And the things once regarded as unalterably profane,
unspeakably sinful, veritable one-way tickets to the gates of Gehenna –
indulgence, extravagance, luxury, usury, hedonism, materialism, money,
greed, covetousness, fashion consciousness and consumption in all its
maleficent manifestations – are now deemed, if not quite next to godliness, certainly within spitting distance of devotional.[47]

Above and beyond the ostensible religiosity of contemporary consumer behaviour or marketers' devout desire to don the money-spinning
spiritual mantle, there is a third academic dimension to messianic
marketing. Namely, the inherently spiritual character of the marketing
concept itself.[48] For this group of researchers, the spirit of marketing
scholarship is embedded in faith: faith in the efficacy of its preachings;
faith in the catechisms of its teachings; faith in the textbooks of marketing doctrine; faith in the rituals of marketing planning, situations analyses, research reports and alliterative benedictions, preferably beginning
with the letter 'P'.[49] Marketing, moreover, has its celestial city of customer orientation; its four commandments of analysis, planning, implementation and control; and its pantheon of priests, prophets, apostles,
apostates and the-Inquisition-is-too-good-for-them heretics of postmodern persuasion.[50]

According to its adepts, remember, marketing is the one true way of
looking at, organizing and understanding the world. It is a world where
disbelievers are damned as 'production' or 'sales' orientated and back-
sliders denounced as 'myopic' or as preoccupied with the 'trappings' of
marketing rather than its 'substance' (or should that be transubstantia-
tion?). Indeed, like members of any other religious persuasion, marketers
are quite content to take credit for marketing successes, yet absolve
themselves of any responsibility for its failures. Thus, businesspeople

who have specifically eschewed marketing, such as Anita Roddick of the Body Shop, are rapturously anointed as 'intuitive' or 'innate' marketers (until such times as things start to fall apart and the 'need' for formal marketing becomes apparent), whereas any hint of failure in the marketplace, even by organizations that have followed marketing dogma to the letter, automatically translates into sinful deviation from the straight and narrow ('you've only yourself to blame', 'try harder', 'get it right next time').

There is, of course, a major problem with spiritual interpretations of marketing phenomena. But it is not that the messianic metaphor is hackneyed, inappropriate or overstretched, albeit the shopping mall as cathedral of consumption is perhaps the most clichéd commonplace of our time. The real problem is that it is *not* a metaphor. Marketing *really is* spiritual. It is nothing more or less than corporate mind cure. Like mind cure, marketing promises health, wealth and perpetual organizational plenitude. Like mind cure, it is unfailingly optimistic, progressive, forward-looking, some would say utopian. Like mind cure, it emphasizes becoming over being, the unending quest for customer orientation, general theories and what have you. Like mind cure, it prescribes a complete way of life, with codified forms of behaviour and ritual which must be adhered to or enacted. Like mind cure, marketing quickly wrapped itself in the honorific mantle of science. Like mind cure, marketing is obsessed with what it is not (cheating, unscrupulous, hucksterism, selling). Like mind cure, marketing repeatedly asserts that it is *true*, that truth, trust and professionalism are an essential aspect of marketing orientation (as Barton exemplified). Like mind cure, marketing is preoccupied with establishing and maintaining relationships (the troika of God, prophet and sinner is paralleled by that of producer, marketer and consumer). Like mind cure, marketing has steadily lost its evangelical fire and become increasingly obsessed with technique, procedure and method, as the academic journals bear illiterate witness. Like mind cure, marketing is ineradicably feminized, notwithstanding its mucho macho, tantamount to androcentric, affectations, aspirations and applications.[51]

Like mind cure, moreover, *marketing works*. As William James rightly observed about the astonishing success of mind cure, 'the plain fact remains that the spread of the movement has been due to practical fruits'.[52] Just as people rose from their sick-beds thanks to mind cure therapists, so too marketing can perform organizational miracles. Granted, in our degraded postmodern times, marketing has been, and is being, attacked from all sides. It is in crisis; it is exhausted; it has limitations; it is ending; a new paradigm is necessary. Elaborate attempts to 'prove' that it works by suitably rigorous procedures only serve to highlight its shortcomings and reveal that it is inappropriate to today's supposedly turbulent, chaotic, globalized, ever-accelerating business environment.[53] Or so we are repeatedly informed. But the all too easily forgotten fact is that, as with mind-cured invalids, marketing orientated companies *really do* get better, *actually are* more healthy and *genuinely enjoy* the life-enhancing benefits of marketing's emollient embrocation. Unlike many management fads that have had their fifteen minutes of fame, marketing has stayed the course. And it has stayed the course because it works. It doesn't work all the time, admittedly, but the failures merely reinforce the successes, as was the case with mind cure ('they did it properly', 'they truly believed', 'you too can be healed if you really want to be'). Marketing, in fact, needs failures as much as it needs successes, true believers and organizational parables-cum-case-studies of the I-was-lost-now-I'm-found variety. Without evidence of sinfulness – or, increasingly, backsliding – marketing can't present itself as the answer to an organization's prayers. And that would never do.

Many, of course, may be dismayed to discover that marketing is a belief system, similar to mind cure, since the latter is suspiciously propinquitous to superstition, paranormality, telekinesis, UFOlogy and the like. Marketing, they maintain, is a science with a capital S.[54] It may not be a very exact science, to be sure, but it is a science or proto-science all the same. If, however, belief comprises a 'set of ideas, more or less integrated by reason, but held with a conviction that they are true, that they are meaningful in relation to reality',[55] then science is also a belief system (as the SSK literature repeatedly reminds us). It follows, therefore, that oft-expressed fears for marketing's scientific 'integrity' are not only misplaced but are themselves premised on faith in marketing's faith-free premises.

Others, especially those hailing from the 'critical' end of the intellectual spectrum, may be reluctant to recognize marketing's status as a belief system, since they consider it to be an ideology, defined as a manner of thinking characteristic of certain groups, classes or individuals.[56] This is true to some extent but ideologies are normally regarded as intangible, imperceptible, essentially incontestable, much like the air that we breathe or the behaviours we unthinkingly engage in (like flicking through *Marketing Science* in the vain hope of finding something worth reading). If that is the case, then marketing can't be an ideology, because the marketing concept has to be actively embraced, accepted, entered into and, not least, practised by its devotees. Marketing demands, as do all secular or sacred belief systems, a quasi-Kierkegaardian 'leap of faith', a conversion experience, some kind of life-changing, light-seeing transformation.

A hallelujah moment, in short.

And yet others, perhaps the majority, consider marketing to be a technology, a soft technology, a body of tools, techniques and procedures which can be used to solve marketing problems, applied or adapted to diverse marketing-related decisions and, naturally, successfully trans-ferred to hitherto deprived organizations, industries and domains.[57] Again this is incontestable since countless marketing plans, situations analyses, scenario-building programmes and so forth are undertaken day and daily by marketing departments worldwide. But the tools and techniques of marketing are unimportant in and of themselves. They are the equivalent of communion, prayer, baptism, crucifixes, rosaries, voodoo dolls and the hypnotist's swinging watch fob. They are tangible symbols that the believer is 'doing', performing and taking part in the ritualized practices of the requisite belief system. To cite a single example: useful though the STP process undoubtedly is (not least as a means of demonstrating the neophyte's familiarity with a fundamental tenet of marketing doctrine),[58] the outcome of the actual analysis is immaterial in many respects. It is the *belief* in segmentation, targeting and position-ing *per se*, not the process itself, that renders the exercise efficacious. Conversely, it is perfectly possible to adopt the marketing 'trappings' by performing all manner of marketing-related activities – product portfolio planning, GAPS analyses, market research, etc. – and yet still fail to make a substantial difference to an organization's competitive situation.

The key point, then, is that it is necessary to believe in marketing, otherwise it won't work. And the reason it doesn't work, as is often the case, is due to insufficient faith. To those brought up in the Analysis, Planning, Implementation and Control tradition, this statement may seem dangerously recondite, but it is nothing to be embarrassed about or, indeed, fudged with pseudo-intellectual scholarly justification or pretentious postmodern obfuscation. The power of auto-suggestion is well established in the medical, sociological and anthropological literature.[59] The placebo effect – the P nobody knows – is not inconse-quential. People *really do* get better because they will it. People *really do* curl up and die because of the sorcerer's evil eye. People *really do* get cured at Lourdes, Lisieux and other places of pilgrimage. In this regard, the Calvinist tradition of the north-eastern American seaboard, from which mind cure, Bruce Barton and marketing itself ultimately derive, makes a crucial distinction between *faith*, the belief in God, and *works*, the good deeds believers perform. Just as salvation cannot be attained on the basis of works alone, so too the secret of marketing success boils down to faith in marketing's salvific power. As a couple of pre-postmodern marketing heretics pointed out some time ago, 'marketing is not what marketers do, marketing is what marketers believe it to be'.[60]

The APIC paradigm, in conclusion, is a secularized version of Norman Vincent Peale's positive thinking apophthegm, 'picturize, prayerize and actualize' (he wasn't called 'God's salesman' for nothing). Relationship Marketing is an organizational rerun of Dale Carnegie's 'how to win friends and influence people' (DC served his time as a travelling salesman before he started selling selling). Marketing Science, with its onward and upward mentality, is merely Emile Coué in a white lab coat and suitably studious mien (all together now, 'Every marketing day, in every marketing way, I get better and better'). Postmodern Marketing boils down to Bruce Barton in inverted commas, a belief in not believing (or, for post-structuralist sceptics, a belief in not believing in not believing . . .). Even the retro revolution rests on the belief that, at a time when people find it hard to believe in modern marketing, we can go back to our roots, we can renew our increasingly shaky faith, we can rediscover the beliefs we once believed in.

Repeat after me: *I believe in Ted the Father Almighty, Maker of modern marketing: And in Philip Kotler, his only son, who was conceived in the 1960s, Born of the Virgin Packard, Suffered under Postmodern Pilates, Was crucified, dead and buried, He descended into hell, And on the third day he rose again. . .as a retromarketing Messiah.*[61]

For thine is the Kotler; Ted's power and the glory; for Barton and Bernbach.

Our men.

4

Reconfiguring Marketing: The Greatest Sham on Earth

One hundred and fifty years ago, a small businessman faced the biggest decision of his career. Despite a degree of success in his chosen specialism, he was firmly stuck at the bottom of the market, with a reputation to match. On various occasions, he had been run out of town by disgruntled, pistol-packing customers, reduced to penury by potentially lucrative but spectacularly unsuccessful products and mercilessly ripped off by ill-chosen, fly-by-night partners. Of late, admittedly, things had improved somewhat. His early grounding in dead-end marketing jobs – store manager, advertising copywriter and door-to-door mousetrap salesman, amongst others – stood him in good stead as he made his way in the market for miniatures, maritime exhibitions and museum requisites. By 1849, he had built up his business, possessed a palatial residence in an exclusive suburb and his name was pretty well known, if held in very low esteem. Although he often boasted that notoriety was necessary in his particular line of work, the bankers, financiers and investors he desperately needed didn't quite see things that way . . .

Redemption, however, was at hand. Potentially. But it carried an enormous risk. It would take every penny he possessed and some he didn't. It involved a top-of-the-range product that was extremely fragile and difficult to handle. It was a product he had never seen, in a product category he had never sold. Although it had been very successful in sophisticated foreign markets, the merchandise was totally untested in the rough and ready territory he'd be entering, where no one had even heard of it. What's more, there were several competitors vying for the agency, all of whom were held in much higher regard, were better connected and financed, and had more sector-specific experience than the upstart. Indeed, even if he struck lucky and acquired the rights, chances were he'd only break even at best, albeit with his reputation considerably enhanced. Set against this, there was a very real possibility of ruinous failure, ignominious failure, failure that would make him a standing joke and ensure he'd never be able to show his face again.

Tough call. Very tough call. The toughest. Yet he went ahead. He risked everything and the rest is history. The small businessman was P.T. Barnum, then a well-known but decidedly disreputable huckster, freak-show operative and 'museum' proprietor. The product was Jenny Lind, a capricious opera singer who had conquered the capitals of Europe. And the untested market was the United States of America, less than seventy-five years after independence.

Although sceptics, rivals and troublemakers surmised that Barnum was planning to exhibit the so-called 'Swedish Nightingale' in a cage, he still managed to sign the superlative soprano, largely because she liked the logo on his headed stationery (an engraving of his retro-rococo mansion, Iranistan). Closing the deal was the least of his problems, however. He had less than seven months to plan a 150-date itinerary and stimulate sufficient interest to fill the auditoria he was booking. What's more, a chance encounter with a railway guard, who wondered just who on earth Jenny Lind was – 'Is she a dancer?' – revealed the sheer depths of the showman's marketing dilemma.

Ever energetic, Barnum set to work and thanks to a torrent of advertising, promotions and publicity stunts, Jenny Lind hysteria was steadily stirred up. Reputable newspapers carried regular stories of the Nightingale's European triumphs (the conscientious hacks were suitably rewarded by Barnum); the market was flooded with Jenny Lind tie-in merchandise (hats, shawls, stoves, candy, cigars, buggy whips and mule bridles, to name but a few); a song-writing competition was held, the winning entry to be sung at the close of her opening concert (more than 700 were submitted); the best seats in the theatres were auctioned for mind-boggling sums, making the bidders national celebrities (the impresario, naturally, apprised interested parties of the possible commercial benefits beforehand); and Barnum even delayed the docking of Lind's transatlantic schooner to ensure that it arrived on a Sunday, when a large crowd of well-dressed admirers – many in the pay of the show-man – would be on hand to witness the diva's disembarkation. In the event, 30,000 turned up. Jenny Lind entranced them. Reviewers waxed lyrical. The tour was a triumph. Barnum made a fortune and his reputation reached an all-time high.[1]

Only to plummet less than five years later . . .

As the Swedish Nightingale extravaganza illustrates, P.T. Barnum (1810–91) was an exceptionally astute marketing man. He launched an unknown product in a difficult market and succeeded beyond his wildest dreams. The launch was carefully organized and orchestrated, at least until Barnum withdrew after ninety-one dates (thereafter, Lind was completely mystified when the official receptions, packed railway stations and public relations frenzy suddenly evaporated). The product was

superbly promoted, skilfully priced, carefully packaged, artfully positioned and judiciously placed in the most promising markets. He conducted admittedly primitive marketing research with his railway porter
sample of one; he understood the importance of visual identity, thanks to
his Lind-catching logo; and he recognized the strategic significance of his
decision to risk all on the reputation-enhancing, high-end European
import. For all his faults – and they were many – there is no doubt that
P.T. Barnum was a magnificent marketer.

Yet he is very rarely, if ever, mentioned in the marketing literature. A
content analysis of today's top-selling principles textbooks reveals that
precisely *none* refer to the marketing capabilities of P.T. Barnum, let
alone consider him a master of the art.[2] This neglect is doubtless partly
attributable to the fact that he died before our field took formal shape at
the start of the twentieth century. It is also fair to say that advertising,
promotion and the like were always secondary to his main business of
circuses, museums, menageries, freak shows *et alia*. By far the most
important reason for the oversight, however, is that Barnum's basic
commercial credo – encapsulated in his infamous dictum of customer
exploitation, 'There's one born every minute' – represents the complete
antithesis of contemporary marketing philosophy, predicated as it is
upon customer satisfaction, orientation, care and consideration.[3]

P.T. Barnum, in point of fact, can reasonably be considered a perfect
example – *the* perfect example – of what 'modern' marketing is *not*. It is
not a rip-off. It is *not* exploitative. It is *not* the sales patter of patent
medicine men wrapped in a pseudo-scientific package. Today's marketers love their customers; they don't cheat on them; they believe in long-
term, monogamous relationships; they aim to captivate, entrance and,
ideally, delight their customer co-evals, though they expect commitment
in return (or a show of loyalty at least).[4] But only if it's warranted and
truly deserved.

Barnum, then, represents a form of anti-marketing marketing, characterized by an exploitative ethic, a non-PC (philosophically correct)
business philosophy, a couldn't-care-less concept of customer care and
an undying devotion to the 4Ds of deception, dishonesty, duplicity and
double-dealing.

There are, to be sure, plenty of apologists for Barnum. As an
exemplar of robber-baron, *fin-de-sièclesque* outrageousness, and totally
over-the-top showmanship, there is a mini-industry in P.T. Barnum
scholarship.[5] Historians of advertising and sales promotion also unfailingly refer to his Promethean pioneering spirit, if in a backwoodsmanish,
how-the-west-was-won, settling-the-uncivilized-frontier-now-thankfully-
behind-us sense of the expression.[6] However, it is arguably his archetypal
Horatio Alger qualities that continue to guarantee Barnum's place
among the US immortals, thereby ensuring regular appearances in
everything from children's books and Broadway musicals to made-for-

TV movies and ice-skating routines.[7] Despite the latter-day demise of the 'great man' hypothesis, P.T. Barnum is and remains an embodiment of the American Dream. True, this dream may be somewhat tarnished today, thanks to self-destructive debates on dumbing down, imperial decline and presidential degeneracy, amongst others, but it continues to compel for all that. Indeed, Barnum's incredible rags to riches to rags to riches story (yes, he did it twice) is an exemplar of the genre.[8]

Named after his paternal grandfather, a renowned prankster and practical joker, Phineas Taylor Barnum was born in Bethel, Connecticut, the eldest child of a large but impoverished family. PTB's childhood idyll, however, was rudely interrupted by the untimely death of his feckless father, which swiftly led to the fifteen-year-old's early exposure to the unprincipled principles of nineteenth-century business. He ran a country store, peddled lottery tickets on the side, became hopelessly addicted to printer's ink (though his scurrilous newspaper, *The Herald of Freedom*, foundered in a storm of litigation whipped up by libelled local worthies) and, after secretly marrying his childhood sweetheart, Charity Hallett, ventured forth to make his fortune in New York City.

The economic climate of the early 1830s, unfortunately, was far from equable and the entrepreneur struggled until he found his true vocation as showman and impresario. For several years he travelled the length and breadth of America, with various variety acts and varying degrees of success. In 1840, however, the opportunity of a lifetime came a-knocking when Scudder's American Museum was put on the market and, ever resourceful, Phineas T. blustered his way into sole proprietorship, despite a complete absence of capital or collateral. Situated in a prime location on Broadway, this musty but marketable museum provided the launching pad for Barnum's seemingly unstoppable ascent, unparalleled notoriety, unimaginable wealth and, as his self-promoting autobiography of 1855 perfectly attests, unbearable arrogance.[9]

Hubris, inevitably, took a hand and ill-advised investments rapidly brought the egotistical titan to his knees. Declared bankrupt in 1856, the social leper eventually repaid his debts, reacquired the museum and, almost unbelievably, went on to greater things, most notably 'The Greatest Show on Earth'. Although he dallied with politics, publishing and property development in his later years, it was the peripatetic three-ring circuses of the 1880s that P.T. Barnum is best remembered for. They not only made him one of the richest men of his time – and there was no shortage of Gilded Age competitors – but unequivocally established his position as 'the most widely known American that has ever lived'.[10] Such was his worldwide celebrity that letters addressed to 'Barnum, America' were delivered as a matter of course. What's more, his *New York Times* obituary was published in advance so that the fabulous showman could enjoy it before he expired, to an extraordinary outpouring of international lamentation, on 7 April 1891.[11] Even *Printer's Ink*, the principal organ of the marketing industry, got in on the obit. act when it recorded that he was 'one of the shining examples of success attained through judicious advertising'.[12]

These days, of course, he rarely gets a mention in the management literature, except in a derogatory sense. Not everyone, however, ranks Barnum among the untouchables of modern marketing. Joe Vitale, a consultant based in Plano, Texas, contends that Barnum's hyperbolic business principles are eminently applicable to today's competitive marketing environment and he has written a self-help management text-book to prove it.[13] He stoutly maintains, moreover, that the Barnum-equals-Bunkum equation is incorrect, a complete misrepresentation, a grotesque caricature of the truth. Barnum may have been a larger than life showman, impresario, museum curator and circus ringmaster, but he wasn't the chiseller of legend who never gave a sucker an even break or fooled some of the people all of the time, all of the people some of the time and, almost but not quite, all of the people all of the time.

In truth, one doesn't need to be a revisionist researcher to make a compelling case for Barnum. On the contrary, he can quite legitimately be portrayed as an important precursor of many current marketing and promotional practices. He was one of the founders of franchising, when he leased his name to manifold itinerant circuses and menageries; he helped institute celebrity endorsement, when he exploited Queen Victoria's patronage to promote the not inconsiderable talents of General Tom Thumb, a vertically challenged variety artiste; he prefigured product demonstrations – beloved by vacuum cleaner salespersons and Tupperware party animals in the 1950s – when he jumped through a harmless flaming hoop to confound his critics in the American Society for the Prevention of Cruelty to Animals; he recognized the importance of the pre-teen market long before Walt Disney, when he reinvented himself as the 'Children's Friend' in the twilight of his career; and, he anticipated the Pepsi Challenge, when he persuaded rival performers – jugglers, giants, magicians, dancers – to battle it out on stage. Meta-phorically, you must appreciate.

More specifically, Barnum invented promotional competitions of the bouncing baby, bathing beauty, coin-a-catchy-slogan variety; the com-plex logistics of his travelling circuses directly influenced the assembly-line approach of Henry Ford; he was an early exponent of international marketing, employing agents to scour the globe for oddities, exhibits, exotica and collectables of all kinds; and he personally changed the character of advertising by, firstly, utilizing vivid vernacular language instead of the elevated mode of commercial discourse that had pre-viously prevailed, secondly, by the sheer amount of space he gleefully filled in the course of his blitzkrieg promotional campaigns and, thirdly, by his attendant promotional innovations like free sheets, mobile billboards and public holiday tie-ins (St Patrick's Day, in particular).[14]

The Promethean PR man was also an absolute master of product repositioning, such as the theatre which he single-handedly transformed from a den of iniquity into an acceptable middle-class pastime (to say nothing of grand opera which he sold to the masses thanks to the exquisite strains of the Swedish Nightingale). Likewise, his creation of the three-ring circus, with its multiphrenic, everything-at-once qualities, was an important precursor of today's channel-hopping, web-surfing, MTV-watching, multi-tasking, couch-potato mindset. Few, furthermore, would deny that his now rightly reviled freak shows live on in the form of emaciated, catwalk-stalking supermodels, self-mutilating, body-piercing performance artists and surgically enhanced celebrity grotesques like Cher, Michael Jackson and Lolo Ferrari.[15]

As if that weren't enough, Barnum's remarkable climb out of bank-ruptcy and social disapprobation was almost entirely achieved on the back of his staggering oratorical abilities. The contrite showman used to go on lucrative speaking tours of the United States and Europe, where he expatiated – believe it or not – on the principles of marketing. Granted, his keynote speeches were entitled 'The Art of Making Money' and, understandably, 'The Art of Losing Money', but they dealt with what today would be deemed the principles of marketing. (This was in the 1850s, remember, long before there were any marketing courses, degrees, textbooks, professors and the like.)[16] These Barnumarketing axioms included: drive ahead; don't spare the steam; select the right location; make as much noise as possible; be systematic; keep expenses down; use lots of light; and, something he signally failed to practise, don't get above your business. His oft-repeated philosophy of advertising, furthermore, rested on repetition, repetition, repetition, as brought to fruition in the 1950s by advertising agencies of the Ted Bates/Rosser Reeves persuasion. The first time an advertisement appears, said Barnum, 'a man does not see it; the second time he notices it; the third time he reads it; the fourth he thinks about it; the fifth he speaks to his wife about it; and the sixth or seventh he is ready to purchase'.[17]

Above and beyond the astonishing advertising acumen of our ante-bellum Bruce Barton, who periodically proselytized on behalf of good causes, the temperance movement especially, P.T. Barnum was an inveterate retro marketer. His success was based, as much as anything else, on creatively rewriting history by judiciously combining old and new. This amalgam was particularly strongly marked in the Great Showman's reanimation of the American Museum, which introduced the latest technology – gaslight, running water, photography, dioramas, telegraphy, hot air balloons and the like – to display his historical artefacts, tableaux, re-enactments and outright inventions to spectacular effect. He tried to buy Shakespeare's cottage during a visit to Stratford; he erected an 'exact' replica of Lincoln's birthplace in the aftermath of the statesman's assassination (in preference, interestingly, to the actual contents of the scene of the crime, which were offered to him); he furnished General Tom Thumb with a miniature eighteenth-century carriage, complete with petite horses and footmen, and trained the tiny titan to reanimate a cavalcade of immortals, from Romulus to Napoleon, in the course of his act; and he recreated the Ancient Rome of Nero – fiddles, flames, Christians, lions, chariots, gladiators, you name it! – in his unprecedented 'Greatest Show on Earth'.[18] The last of these, however, was only possible thanks to his application of new technology to the traditional travelling circus. By abandoning horse-drawn wagons, the then accepted mode of inter-city travel, in favour of flatbed railroad carriages, Barnum was able to reduce big top pitching, breaking and travelling times. This enabled him to concentrate on the major cities, which in turn supported more extravagant shows and historical spectaculars, with their casts of thousands.[19]

Although it is perfectly possible to make a plausible case for P.T. Barnum, to portray him as a misunderstood pioneer of modern market-ing, to regard him – as he regarded himself – as the Shakespeare of Advertising,[20] it is both unnecessary and erroneous to do so. Soft-soaping Barnum in such a manner only serves to massage the facts and misrepresent the nature of the beast. By doing so, indeed, one is merely aping the great man himself, who valiantly strove to distance himself from the chicanery that characterized the early part of his career. He *literally* rewrote history – in numerous reworkings of his autobiography and in a book which distinguished between legitimate and illegitimate forms of chicanery[21] – to intimate that he was actually a respectable citizen all along. Towards the end of his life, moreover, when he was a much-loved philanthropist and confidant of princes and presidents alike, Barnum brazenly denied that he had ever sought to bamboozle the public. The fact that he succeeded in bamboozling the public into believing that he had never bamboozled the public speaks volumes for his bamboozling abilities.

Make no mistake, Barnum believed in ripping his customers off. He revelled in it. He regarded himself as the Prince of Humbugs, the Plato of puffery, a Yankee prankster nonpareil. He openly bragged about his duplicity, chicanery and incomparable customer-duping capacities. As the reviewers of the notorious first edition of his autobiography rightly noted, Barnum considered himself a hoaxmaster general, an abominable showman, the veritable Grand Canyon of con-men, the Cagliostro of commercial casuistry.[22] According to one of the book's more charitable critics, 'it has inspired us with nothing but sensations of disgust for the frauds which it narrates, amazement at its audacity, loathing for its hypocrisy, abhorrence for the moral obliquity which it betrays and sincere pity for the wretched man who complied it'. The *New York Times* thundered that 'his success has been achieved – his wealth acquired – his reputation and consideration established, by the systematic, adroit and persevering plan of obtaining money under false pretences . . . he takes an evident pride in the boldness and enormity of the impositions by which he has amassed his fortune.' Another supporter concluded that Barnum 'will ultimately take his stand in the social rank . . . among the swindlers, blacklegs, blackguards, pickpockets and thimble-riggers of his day'.[23]

Strong stuff. Very strong stuff. The strongest. But the evidence against Barnum is irrefutable. His catalogue of con-tricks and anti-customer conniving is nothing if not compendious. Consider the Joice Heth hoax. She was the purported 161-year-old 'nanny' of George Washington, who was exhibited around the country to huge crowds keen to hear tales of the founding father's childhood, only to be exposed as a mere eighty-year-old impostor. Then there was the Fejee Mermaid fake of 1842, which comprised the tail of a fish and the body of an orang-utan. (Barnum wrote anonymous letters to the newspapers 'denouncing' it as a fix, thereby attracting even more punters determined to check for themselves.) Then there was the 'free' buffalo hunt in Hoboken, New Jersey, where Barnum negotiated a secret cut from the Hudson River ferry operators, massive crowds of New Yorkers made the day trip, and, it almost goes without saying, the four forlorn buffaloes failed to stampede on cue. Then there was the infamous working model of Niagara Falls – with real water! – which he publicized by gigantic, nearly Niagara-sized advertising hoardings. The 'great' model itself was all of 12 inches high and utilized a single pail of recyclable water in its awe-inspiring cascade. Then there was the celebrated White Elephant episode of 1884. Disappointed with the less than albino hue of his expensive acquisition, the great man gave it a couple of clandestine coats of whitewash (and when informed that the 'white' elephant of a rival circus had died, Barnum famously retorted 'It was dyed already'). Mind you, this was a last resort. He had previously darkened the rest of the herd!

And then, of course, there's the sublime, some would say unsurpassable, Jumbo the Giant Elephant saga.[24] In 1881, Barnum purchased this truly prodigious pachyderm from the Royal Zoological Gardens in London; engineered an enormous public outcry about its imminent departure to the Colonies (newspaper campaigns, protest songs, parliamentary debates, pleading letters from the royal family, etc.); brilliantly exploited the recalcitrant beast's recumbent refusal to enter its tastefully appointed transporter cabinet ('Let him lie there for a week if he wants to,' Barnum wired, 'it's the best advertisement in the world'); organized a 'victory parade' through the streets of New York from the docks to Madison Square Garden (where Barnum's circus was just about to open, conveniently enough); and not only made a fortune from Jumbo memorabilia but recouped his entire investment within three weeks of the gala opening night (the word 'jumbo' also entered common parlance at this point). Even the circumstances of the creature's tragic demise, several years later, were dramatized to peerless promotional effect. When it was accidentally struck by a passing goods train, the lachrymose showman let it be known that the self-sacrificing tusker charged the onrushing express in order to protect its infant companion, as copious death-of-a-hero newspaper headlines gratifyingly recorded. Still unsatisfied, Barnum brought in a female elephant, Alice, which he bathetically billed as Jumbo's 'widow', and posed her next to the fallen mastodon. A taxidermist, what is more, quickly set to work and before long both Jumbo's skeleton and amply stuffed hide (stretched, naturally, to exaggerate its height) were on permanent, profitable display.

Few would deny that P.T. Barnum was a commercial con-artiste of the first water; the epitome, the Everest, the Einstein, the Edison of customer exploitation; the *primus inter pares* of rip-offs, swindles, shenanigans and good old-fashioned confidence tricks. How, then, can marketers account for his staggering success? Clearly, the principles of modern, APIC marketing, as presented in mainstream textbooks and regurgitated to generations of grateful managers, can't explain Barnum's triumphs, let alone his stupendous profits. Conventional marketing theory, after all, repudiates customer maltreatment, regards offending consumers as the height of offensiveness and constantly reiterates that customer dissatisfaction is disastrous, certainly in the long term. If anything, indeed, the premises of modern marketing have become *increasingly* consumer orientated with the passage of time, as the recent, rapid rise of Relationship Marketing readily testifies.

Yet Barnum espoused an egregiously anti-customer orientation. He deliberately duped his far from affluent clientele. He affronted, offended, deceived and generally pulled the wool over the eyes of his patrons, his prospects, his patsies, his rubes, his hayseeds, his suckers. What's more, he revelled in it, he boasted about it, he considered himself the very best in the bamboozling business, which is true. Most importantly perhaps, he did it repeatedly, he did it without respite, he did it over the entire course of a long, successful and exceptionally remunerative career. With Barnum it was not a case of once bitten, twice shy. He persuaded a veritable shoal of saps to bite again and again, to put their money where their ever-gullible mouths were, and he laughed uproariously as he reeled them in. To cap it all, he then told them how he'd done it. How he'd done them!

In attempting to account for Barnummarketing, perhaps the most 'obvious' explanation is that it was an artefact of its unsophisticated time, an epiphenomenon of the crude, rude and rambunctious nineteenth century. Hoaxes, japes, practical jokes, faith healers, quack medicines, mesmerists and spiritualists, as well as omnipresent peddlers, pitchers, barkers, drummers and diddlers of diverse stripe, undoubtedly loomed large in the Victorian social psyche. The oft-recounted fabrications of Washington Irvine, Edgar Allan Poe and Mark Twain – not forgetting the exquisite Moon Hoax of 1834[25] – represent a mere fraction of the tom-foolery that erupted as the restrictive 'blue laws' and Calvinistic mores of the early Colonial period slowly ceased to compel. For a long time, in fact, practical jokes were almost the only socially sanctioned source of amusement, though the proximity of the frontier, with its associated tall tales, and a pervasive progressivist ethos, which was predisposed towards new discoveries and technological breakthroughs, created conditions conducive to large-scale scamming.[26] However, as the long and illustrious history of humbugs makes clear, commercial chicanery was by no means confined to the nineteenth century, nor to the United States, nor indeed to P.T. Barnum. While the Barnum years may have been more prone to pranksterism than other periods, the fact of the matter is that scallywags, scoundrels and shysters have always been around, are still around and, unless human nature changes radically as the twenty-first-century unfolds, are likely to be around for the foreseeable future.[27]

Truth to tell, Barnum himself was ripped off on a number of occasions, most notably by the unscrupulous proprietors of the Jerome Clock Company, investment in which precipitated the showman's cataclysmic pecuniary collapse. Having said that, he also hoaxed the hoaxers and hoaxed his own hoaxes. The latter is exemplified by the 'death of Heth' imbroglio, whereby Barnum convinced a newspaper proprietor – someone who had previously extolled the exhibit and then denounced the showman's chicanery – that George Washington's nanny was alive, well and treading the boards in Boston. The hapless printer went to press with his 'Heth Lives' exclusive, only to find that he had been fooled and, as every other newspaper eagerly publicized his predicament, that he'd become a national laughing stock for good measure. The hoaxer-hoaxed variant is typified by the timeless Cardiff Giant double-bluff of 1869. When a fossilized colossus was discovered in a field in upper New York State, the enterprising landowner exhibited the remarkable find at 50 cents a peep (as one does).[28] Barnum attempted to buy the petrified relic, and when his offer was contemptuously spurned, opted to put a perfect replica on display (seems reasonable). The affronted landowner sought immediate reparation through ever-good-for-business legal redress (nice one). However, the trial dramatically uncovered that the original was a fake and thus Barnum's fake fake was declared perfectly legitimate (Holy Kotler!). More astonishing still, the fake fake managed to attract substantially more paying customers than the original fake and this fact, in turn, further enhanced its appeal (now, that's what I call marketing).

Compelling as it is, the Cardiff Giant contretemps suggests another possible 'explanation' of the Barnumarketing phenomenon. Namely, that his accomplishments were industrial sector specific. After all, it has often been argued that arts marketing is markedly different from the FMCG or B2B norm, albeit the necessary conceptual adjustments are usually limited to the elite, art-for-art's-sake, damn-the-paying-customers-and-pass-the-subsidy end of the entertainment spectrum.[29] Popular culture, as the term implies, has always been commercially minded and, consequently, disdained for its make-em-laugh, money-grubbing, soul-selling philistinism. Granted, Barnum probably had no soul to sell – or, if he had, would assuredly have attempted to swindle Mephistopheles on the fine print of their Faustian pact – but it is important to appreciate that the great showman operated in an exceptionally competitive environment. The second half of the nineteenth century was literally chock-a-block with travelling circuses, freak shows, penny-ante museums, amusement arcades and step-right-up attractions, most of which have faded into merciful obscurity.[30] Barnum, moreover, didn't attempt to undercut the competition thanks to his economies of scale, low cost base or proto-franchising system. On the contrary, he charged substantially *more* than the going rate – typically a quarter rather than the then standard dime. His marks, in short, paid premium prices to be marked by marketing's master marker.

More to the point, Barnum was not an originator, as is so often the case with supremely creative people.[31] Many of his best-known and most notorious exhibits were already on show prior to the irrepressible impresario's involvement. Joice Heth, Jumbo, the Fejee Mermaid, the woolly horse,[32] Chang and Eng (the original Siamese twins) and countless others were all working the freak show circuit *before* Barnum sprinkled them – or close substitutes in the case of the Cardiff Giant – with marketing magic-dust, thereby transforming them into punter-pulling, money-spinning, bill-topping attractions. Likewise, when the maestro's personal participation ceased, the magic quickly dissipated. Receipts at the American Museum fell off rapidly during the post-bankruptcy hiatus, though they never quite descended to pre-Barnum levels. After the showman and Jenny Lind parted company, furthermore, the box office takings of her hitherto triumphant American tour immediately plummeted and she was playing to less than packed houses by the end of her stint. Even Tom Thumb, the carriage-trade Pinocchio of the 1840s, couldn't quite recapture his glory days when Barnum wasn't pulling the promotional strings.

Interestingly, the only time Barnum really met his match was on the one and only occasion he crossed swords with James A. Bailey, forty years his junior. When a female elephant in Allied Shows, Bailey's rival circus, produced the first calf to be born in captivity, Barnum attempted to acquire the much-publicized infant. Bailey not only spurned the titan's $100,000 offer and boldly reproduced his bid on all of Allied's advertising, but also impertinently announced that he had the elephant Barnum desperately wanted, thereby enjoying the fabulous showman's endorsement *in absentia*. Instantly recognizing that he had finally found someone 'worthy of his mettle', Barnum joined forces with the young pretender and their alliance is the stuff of showbiz legend. If ever a partnership was made in heaven, it was surely that of P.T. Barnum and J.A. Bailey. A shy, modest and retiring man, who abhorred personal publicity and hated seeing his face on promotional material, Bailey was essentially an administrator, organizer, fixer and arranger, the efficiency expert behind the scenes. Barnum was the marketing magician. The pinnacle of their joint endeavour, the 1889–90 'Greatest Show on Earth' in London's Olympia Auditorium, illustrates this perfectly:

> The logistics for the journey were staggering – it would take a small fleet to cross the Atlantic with a menagerie, car-fulls of equipment and gear, band-wagons, an enormous herd of horses, Roman chariots, costumes galore, eight tons of posters and ads, and 1,240 performers. But that was Bailey's job, exactly the kind of complex management he was skilled at. It was Bailey's task to construct slings that would lift elephants and camels aboard, to measure every cage and wagon so all would fit snugly, to dream up the idea of freezing the meat for all the flesh-eating animals. It was the job of Bailey's 79-year-old, white-haired partner to make sure that for three months a man named Barnum was on the tip of every last Britisher's tongue.[33]

Although Barnum's marketing skills are blindingly obvious to all but the most myopic observers, many scholarly traditionalists might be tempted – as a last resort – to reach for the ultimate 'explanatory' option. That is, to account for our customer-cozening conundrum by simply denying that he is a marketer. Marketing is defined as being customer orientated and, whatever his achievements, Barnum was *not* customer orientated. Therefore he is not a marketer. End of story. While all too typical of hidebound academicians, such hair-splitting pedantry is (to continue the corporeal conceit) a classic case of cutting off one's nose to spite one's face. For marketers to belittle Barnum's accomplishments because he never signed the customer care pledge – just think how successful he *might* have been if only he'd been truly marketing orientated! – merely serves to make our field look foolish and, indeed, says more about the principles than the practitioner.

Slightly more subtle is the closely associated contention that some kind of strange customer need is met, desire is satisfied, utility is served or fulfilment derived from being unceremoniously fleeced. Thus Barnum can claim to be a marketer of sorts. This is certainly plausible – insofar as John Locke, the no-nonsense empiricist, noted that 'men love to deceive and be deceived'[34] – but it requires marketing scholars to perform all sorts of conceptual contortions pertaining to the satisfaction that comes from dissatisfaction, the character of careless customer care, the limits of inoffensive offensiveness, the responsibilities of irresponsibility and rendering the unacceptable acceptable, not to mention establishing rules of 'good' bad marketing, honest dishonesty, fair cheating, true lies and the like. A deconstructionist would be proud of these axiological aporias, epistemological implausibles and seemingly illogical syllogistical circumlocutions.

Even here, however, Barnum managed to pre-empt postmodern marketing and beat the boa-deconstructors at their own convoluted game. If, as Hartman maintains, deconstruction is regarded as a refusal to accept that the presence of the word is equivalent to the presence of meaning,[35] then Barnum must be regarded as a premodernist postmodernist. He frequently exploited the disjunction between word and world, signifier and signified, connotation and denotation, inscription and intent, between what-you-see and what-you-get. His exotic Circassian Beauties were born in deepest Brooklyn; his 'missing link' was an encephalitic African-American from New Jersey; his bearded ladies were often decidedly deficient in the X-chromosome department; his wild men of Borneo were neither wild nor from Borneo (though the Bowery could get pretty hairy at times); and, naturally, his Native American war-dancers were just off the banana boat from Ireland, although few saw through their Michael Flatley-esque footwork or understood their incomprehensible dialect. He once displayed, to a jam-packed auditorium, the celebrated cat that was let out of the bag, which consisted (what else?) of an empty bag! And then, of course, there was Barnum's inventive approach to controlling the crowds – and coincidentally increasing customer throughput – at the American Museum. Close to the main entrance he erected a large sign, 'To the Egress', which led lexically challenged clients not to the *outré* exhibit they expected but to a side alley, the back of the line and another 25 cents outlay on re-entry. One is indeed born every minute, as the marketing magus rightly observed.

Rather than try to account for Barnum in conventional marketing terms or portray him as a premodern apostle of postmodern marketing, it may be preferable to think the unthinkable and accept that Barnum knew more about marketing than marketers do.[36] Much more. In this regard, perhaps it is time to recognize that Barnum's marketing record is considerably better than those who cavort at the feet of Kotler, follow Levitt to the letter or believe in Barton's (preached rather than practised) belief in probity, integrity, sincerity and all the oleaginous rest. Maybe the brutal fact of the matter is that Barnum built a better marketing mousetrap and it is high time marketing 'thinkers' beat a path to his door. At least he had practical experience of the mousetrap marketing business, which is more than can be said for most academic marketers, theorists and researchers.

Such a suggestion, to be sure, comprises the most heinous marketing heresy, insofar as it involves abandoning customer orientation – or customer adoration in the case of Relationship Marketing – as the touchstone of the field. Tough decision. Very tough decision. The toughest. Indeed, killing off customer orientation is almost Oedipal in its intellectual elementalism. However, if there is one lesson to be learned from this retro root around modern marketing's prehistory, it is that customers aren't the be all and end all of marketing, that one can still claim to be a bona fide marketer *without* being consumer-orientated, -focused, -led or whatever. Customer-centred marketing, as we have seen, dates from Levitt, from the 1950s, from the 'modern' period.[37] It is an historical artefact, not a tablet of stone, both in its early (APIC) and latter-day (RM) manifestations.[38]

Proposing to cut marketing off from consumers, of course, is almost certain to induce acute castration anxiety – possibly a complete nervous breakdown – amongst its adepts, proponents and proselytizers. Conceptually speaking anyhow. The trauma can be lessened slightly by noting that it does not mean that customers are unimportant or that ripping them off is the way to go. ('Attention shoppers. It's hate-the-customer day, today. Make your way to the back of the store where you will be abused, disdained, short-changed and misinformed about our disloyalty scheme. Have a nasty one.') It merely means that consumers are no longer the centre of marketing's solar system, the sun around which 4P planets revolve.

More significantly perhaps, Barnumarketing presents a meaningful alternative to customer-centricity. But in order to appreciate it, it is necessary to comprehend the psychology of deceit. Although marketers and advertisers in the post-Barnum era have gone to great pains to distance themselves from chicanery, by emphasizing the truthfulness, honesty and trustworthiness of their calling,[39] the truth is that truth, honesty and suchlike are extremely rare commodities in everyday life. On the contrary, lies, fibs, deceptions, fabrications, exaggerations and mis-representations of various kinds are the norm. These range from the lies told to lubricate social relationships ('nice dress'), through the lies told to help or comfort other people ('he didn't suffer'), to the lies we constantly tell ourselves ('I coulda been a contender'). It is widely accepted that the ability to dissimulate is an integral aspect of the child development process, being fully formed by the age of eight or so. Falsehoods are found in every society, every social class and every walk of life from politics to the physical sciences, though the predominant forms of deceit differ from domain to domain. Some fanatics, furthermore, contend that the very evolution of the human brain and everything that this entails – the Pyramids, the *Principia Mathematica*, the Mona Lisa, the moon landings and the Big Mac – is attributable to an ability to tell fibs. Lying, so we're told, is the secret of worldly success.[40]

Unless of course they're kidding.

In this regard, it is striking that the extant academic literature on lies, deceit and disinformation invariably mentions marketing and advertising as prime examples of deception in action.[41] Ford, for instance, puts forward a four-category typology of marketer disingenuousness: *blatant misrepresentation*, such as pushing products that purport to 'increase the size of one's penis or breasts, restore virility, or provide rapid weight loss without effort'; *exaggeration*, the constant use of superlatives of the best-a-man-can-get variety; *bait and switch techniques*, where merchandise is advertised at inconceivably low prices only to be 'out of stock' when customers turn up to take advantage of the offer; and, perhaps the most insidious of all, *subtle implication*, which intimates that possession or use of a product will bestow certain desired characteristics on the purchaser.[42] The lying literature, what is more, unfailingly observes how advertising's regulatory bodies, such as the ASA or FTC, are careful to police literal truth claims (cures constipation, contains 100% beef, etc.). However, they are fairly lax when it comes to controlling puffery, 'because of the assumption that people expect advertisements to exaggerate and therefore astute consumers discount them'.[43]

It follows, therefore, that when marketers maintain they tell the truth, the whole truth and nothing but the truth, or claim that they really, really care for their customers, or assert that they have the consumer's best interests at heart, they are on a hiding to nothing, since such assertions are tainted at source, even if they are sincerely meant. Customer-loving protestations, endearments, entreaties and emollients, especially those emanating from relationship marketers and their hug-a-shopper epigones, are instantly dismissed as just another rip-off and a less than subtle one at that. Marketers may believe their customer-led self-deceptions but no one else is deceived by them, as survey after survey attests.[44] What's more, marketing's attempt to counteract this negative image by levitating Levitt (i.e. emphasizing that it truly is about customer orientation, that commercial con-artists aren't proper marketers, that everything would be okay if only the cowboys were reined in), merely serves to reinforce the extant perception by adding a 'doth protest too much' dimension. By contrast, the celebrated Joe Isuzu advertising campaign, which accepted, exaggerated and successfully exploited the hucksterish stereotype, is much more believable, much more Barnumesque.[45] It is the sheer unbelievablility of Joe Isuzu that makes him believable.

The fundamental principle of Barnumarketing, it must be stressed, has nothing to do with brazen acts of customer exploitation. Outright rip-offs are quickly recognized and their perpetrators avoided thereafter. Nor does Barnumarketing simply involve eschewing traditional approaches of the truth, justice and consumer care way. The customer still features in the marketing scheme of things, if in a less venerated place. Nor, for that matter, does it necessitate naked honesty about marketing's commercial intent – we don't love you, we just want to do business – since this supposed honesty is automatically suspect and immediately discounted.[46]

The essence of Barnumarketing is making the unbelievable believable, making the impossible possible, making the incredible credible, making the extraordinary ordinary, making the supernatural natural, making the illogical logical, making the magical mundane. It is about making people believe, albeit temporarily, that they are better looking, more attractive and generally healthier, wealthier and wiser than they ordinarily are. Or, rather, that they'll be thus blessed once they buy the wares that provide a passport to this marketing-mediated wonderland. And even if this never transpires – as it never does – the experience of believing in, working towards and imaginatively pre-figuring post-purchase possibilities is sufficient reward in itself.[47]

The major reason Barnum managed to get away with his humbugs – and people kept coming back for more – was because they were so elaborate, so excessive, so cleverly executed that the humbugged unfailingly appreciated the effort that had been expended to exploit them, the sheer imagination that the rip-offs entailed, the twisted genius of the person who had fooled them (and it would take a genius, naturally enough, to fool them). For all their savvy, for all their worldliness, for all their scepticism, for all their common-sense, intelligence, hard-headedness and suchlike, someone had got the better of them. They had been tricked by a master trickster, a notorious trickster, a trickster who informed them beforehand that they were going to be tricked and, despite their determination not to fall for any trickery, the trickster supreme still managed to pull it off. It seems, then, that consumers really can get satisfaction from dissatisfaction, pleasure from displeasure, comfort from discomfort, enchantment from disenchantment and find the disagreeable agreeable, the distasteful tasteful, the discouraging encouraging and the dissonant consonant. They want to believe the unbelievable.

Rendering the unbelievable believable is not, of course, limited to marketing. On the contrary, it is part and parcel of everyday existence, an integral part of the human condition.[48] Our disbelief is suspended when we read a novel, watch a movie or wonder how the stage magician makes the rabbit disappear. We believe in unbelievables like chance, fate, coincidence, serendipity, good luck, bad luck and, in some cases, astrology, aliens and the Loch Ness Monster. We firmly believe that the vitamins, herbal remedies and New Age health drinks we consume in vast quantities are doing something for us, besides emptying our pocketbooks to the tune of $6 billion per year.[49] We believe, hope and pray that God and his angels are watching over us, care for us, have more of our good deeds on file than bad and, not least, that our faith will be suitably rewarded in the fullness of time. We even believe that we don't believe in politicians, realtors, advertisers and con-artists, yet we still fall for their platitudes, patter, pitches and pretence. But only if they're good at it, only if they make us believe what we would ordinarily deem dubious, improbable, impossible, preposterous. As Braudy astutely observes about Barnum's audiences,

> They revelled in the all-embracing if momentary belief compelled by the show itself. For Barnum to be exposed as a fraud could never undermine, only enhance, his showmanship. Coleridge thought that art required a 'willing suspension of disbelief'. But nothing so static would satisfy Barnum, who interwove belief and disbelief in an unceasing dialectic . . . He put his audience on their mettle as people of sophistication and insight into what was true and what wasn't – and charged them admission for the chance to prove it.[50]

Indeed, it is one of those delicious academic ironies that at the very time the customer-focused paradigm shift took place in marketing – with Levitt and his ilk in the late 1950s – social psychologists identified the so-called 'Barnum Effect'.[51] This refers to people's propensity to believe unbelievable statements about themselves, usually the kinds of banalities, trivialities and generalizations found in horoscopes, palm readings, magazine surveys, personality tests and, arguably, advertising appeals (because you're 'special', 'different', 'smart', 'thrifty', 'beautiful', 'elegant', 'better', 'generous', 'desirable', 'do what's right', 'have impeccable taste', or whatever). The Effect, furthermore, is remarkably robust, having been demonstrated on countless occasions, in countless settings and with countless kinds of experimental subject.[52] Doubtless these studies can be critiqued on points of methodological and operational detail, as is always the case. Post-structuralists, moreover, are likely to be appalled by their imputations of essentialism, but if you believe post-structuralist unbelievables you really are in trouble. Many possible 'explanations' of the phenomenon have also been posited including gullibility, insecurity, social desirability and situation-specific factors. Nevertheless, the evidence suggests that humankind has some kind of need or propensity to believe the unbelievable. And, if that is the case, then it can be contended that the Barnumarketing Effect concerns making the unbelievable believable in commercial contexts, broadly defined.

Marketing, in conclusion, has nothing to do with customer satisfaction, though that may be a side-effect of the process. It has nothing to do with reciprocity, since marketers should always give more than they bargained for, or the appearance of it at least. It is not about precision, specification, control or identifying the legendary half of advertising that 'works' (in fact, it is the imprecise, indefinable, uncontrollable half of advertising that does all the real work). It is not about propriety, responsibility and do-gooding as much as impropriety, irresponsibility and do-badding. It has nothing to do with profitability, efficiency, accountability and suchlike because it is predicated upon excess, extravagance and exaggeration. Marketing is the potlatch of post-industrial society. The more the merrier. A little ain't enough and too much is impossible. It is the *son et lumière* of capitalism, what P.T. Barnum aptly described as a 'skyrocket'.

Marketing, the imperishable impresario would surely agree, is the greatest sham on earth.

PART II
DOWNSIZING STRATEGY

5

Repositioning Marketing: Ballyhoo's Who

Wild Bill Shakespeare is hot, hot, hot, these days. From the Oscar-adorned *Shakespeare in Love* to the BBC's 'Man of the Millennium', the Swan of Avon is set fair for twenty-first-century flight.[1] True, the recently reconstructed Globe Theatre is a perfect replica of an entirely imagined original; Harold Bloom's claim that Willy invented humanity is inventive, to say the least; and the Simpsons' interpretation of *Macbeth* – *MacHomer* – dares d'oh all that may become a man.[2] But, there is no doubt whatsoever about it: the Bard is back in town.

So much so, that even management theorists are getting in on the Shakespearean act.[3] Having plundered the pantheon for the leadership secrets of Niccolò Machiavelli, Marcel Proust, Attila the Hun, Stonewall Jackson and Winnie the Pooh, amongst others (can Harry Potter be far behind?), the slings and arrows of outrageous fortune have taken arms against a sea of middle managers. Cranfield University, no less, is in the process of developing short courses predicated upon the Bard's greatest hits: *Henry V* for leadership, *Julius Caesar* for office politics, *A Winter's Tale* for organizational change and, doubtless, *The Merchant of Venice* for mendacious marketing types. As Ashworth observes:

> It is easy to imagine what *Titus Andronicus* might teach those facing a City bloodbath, or *Love's Labour's Lost* to civil servants under the present Government. *Hamlet* could be useful for indecisive managers, *Macbeth* for those facing hostile takeovers, and *King Lear*, a warning to those tempted to break up a business empire. But for those who want to identify with their senior managers, there can be only one play – *A Comedy of Errors*.[4]

Be that as it may, the whirligig of time brings in its revenges to reveal that there is nothing new under the sun. Despite Cranfield's crowing, William Shakespeare has previously stepped into the retromarketing breach (though if you have tears, prepare to shed them now). In a curious volume published in 1942, an imaginative Midwesterner called

Bill Burruss culled the Bard's canon for commercial insights – scenes, situations or episodes that might be pertinent to top-flight insurance salespersons, such as himself.[5] Although the Avon caller often flunked Burruss's stop-me-and-buy-one test, he more than made up for it in Mark Antony's celebrated sales pitch to his friends, Romans and countrymen. The less than noblest Roman of them all not only managed to attract his prospects' attention (by asking to borrow their ears), he skilfully steered them through every phase of the personal selling process, from arousing interest to closing the sale. Antony's only fault, according to our Prairie pitchman in excelsis, was his inexplicable lack of musical accompaniment. The presentation would have been perfect, the Bard of the Boondocks concluded, if MA had had a PA, a backing band and a show-stopping, sing-along, song 'n' dance finale.

Mark(eting) Antony may have been a bit lax on the soft soap shuffle, but he can hardly be described as 'the triple pillar of the world transform'd/Into a salesman fool'. Indeed, compared to some of the incompetents that have strutted across the marketing stage, mewling and puking, he bestrides the commercial world like a Colossus. As losers go, for example, Mark Antony is not in the same league as those responsible for (say) the Ford Edsel fiasco, the New Coke débâcle, the Hoover free-flights catastrophe or, to cite a fairly recent embarrassment, McDonald's two-Big-Macs-for-the-price-of-one disaster.[6] Designed to celebrate the organization's silver anniversary in Britain, as well as dispel some of the negative publicity that had surrounded the corporation since its pyrrhic court victory over two penniless eco-warriors,[7] the McShambles commenced with X-Filesque commercials informing consumers of the mysterious Big Mac. Buy one and another appeared . . . as if by magic.

Yet, despite their purported paranormal capabilities, the clairvoyants in McDonald's marketing department failed to foresee that four million McMulders and McScullys would immediately descend upon the organization's emporia, demanding empirical proof of this promotional apparition. Like UFO-logists of legend, most were disappointed, since the company couldn't cope with the demand, which was eight times the McForecaster's best guess. Hordes of disillusioned psychics, sceptics and new age nutritionists had to make do with hastily printed Big Mac vouchers (allegedly tastier than the real thing, your Honour), coupled with abject apologies in all the national newspapers. Ever sympathetic, Burger King took out ads stuffed with supportive knocking copy; journalists had a field day with the marketing-orientated organization that had bitten off more than it could chew; and, needless to say, the company mascot – a clown – was veritable McManna from headline writers' heaven. Just as well all publicity is good publicity.

Only the most hard-hearted manager would fail to be moved to tears by McDonald's maladroit marketing. Tears of laughter, let it be said. It is never less than gratifying to see the mighty falling, especially when their marketing is to blame. Such corporate shambolics combine the relief of there-but-for-the-grace-of-God with a *frisson* of holier-than-thou self-righteousness. Some conspiracy theorists, admittedly, might surmise that the company's manoeuvres were a deliberate double-bluff, a faux failure designed to tweak McDonald's disconcertingly efficient, tantamount to draconian, image (look folks, we get it wrong too!). But, rather than conclude that their Big Mac débâcle was a cunning corporate plan to endear the organization to the burger-buying public, it might be simpler to accept the fiasco for what it was. Unless, of course, the conspiracy theorists are conspiring against us.

No doubt there are many contenders for the 'worst marketer of all time' accolade and debating their demerits – working out the best worst, as it were – is likely to prove an unending, if highly enjoyable, exercise. I would submit, however, that one of the best representations of sub-standard marketing is provided by Bob Hope in his 1948 smash-hit film, *The Paleface*.[8] Released in the same year as *The Hucksters*, the movie based on Wakeman's devastating critique of maleficent Madison Avenue, *The Paleface* presented the opposite side of the pernicious marketing coin. In what is unquestionably his finest comic hour, Hope plays 'Painless' Potter, a hapless quack dentist travelling the Wild West in a covered wagon. Notwithstanding the ready market for his services and coloratura sales patter, Potter fails to pull a single incisor or sell a single bottle of cures-all-ills elixir. That said, he *does* succeed in beating the baddies, saving the townsfolk and dispatching one or two dozen pesky redskins (thanks largely to the redoubtable assistance of Jane Russell, as Calamity Jane), but when it comes to unloading his wares, Potter finds that marketing is far from painless.

Some may dismiss Hope's sublime performance – brilliantly reprised four years later in *Son of Paleface*[9] – as 'only a movie' or, worse, 'only a comedy'. However, this is not the place to rehearse hackneyed arguments concerning academic marketers' continuing antagonism to works of art, even though brute scientism still has a very strong following in our field.[10] It is sufficient to note that Bob Hope's bravura portrayal of a cack-handed marketing man remains instructive on two main counts.

First, it was based on a real person, someone whose commercial adventures were more remarkable, if anything, than those represented in *The Paleface*. Painless Parker, the 'tooth tycoon' of the 1920s, commenced his professional career as a dental pitcher in a peripatetic medicine show.[11] Such was his wisdom-extracting expertise that he built up a chain of seventy-five dental depots – tooth-pulling franchises, in effect – which he publicized by spectacular promotional stunts. These included human flies, who swarmed up and over Manhattan's sky-scrapers sporting suitably inscribed sandwich boards; a three-ring circus, where Potter not only put his head in the lion's mouth but whipped out a couple of carious choppers, for good measure; and, last but not least, hyper-humungous advertising hoardings. Twenty-five feet high and 110 feet long, these ran around the first storeys of prominent urban landmarks, modestly announcing, 'Painless Parker – I am positively IT in painless dentistry'. Each 'IT' was a full four floors high and, reputedly, visible from several miles away. Parker's real skill, however, was apparent at the interpersonal level. Apart from countless sexual conquests on the operating chair, he had the ability to convince his patients that the excruciating pain they felt when he set to work on their unanaesthetized molars was a figment of their fevered imaginations.

Now that's what I call making the unbelievable believable.

A second pedagogic point about *The Paleface* pertains to its prepostmodern reflexivity. Above and beyond Hope's knowing winks to the audience – in 1948 Painless Parker's tooth-pulling factories were within living memory and the crown prince himself was still going strong – the subtext of the movie was profoundly ironic. It alluded to the early days of the film industry itself, with its less than exalted reputation. Silent pictures and dioramas were often incorporated into itinerant medicine shows – as an essential ingredient of snake oil, so to speak – and until the 1940s movie marketing was dominated by OTT promotional escapades organized by the 'ballyhoo' brigade.[12] These spin doctors of show business, the Painless Parkers of the silver screen, were paid to concoct outrageous publicity stunts that would place posteriors on the plush and not so plush seats of nickelodeons, fleapits and proto-picture palaces. In fact, a satirical magazine called *Ballyhoo*, which parodied the pretensions of advertisers in general and movie press agents in particular, commenced publication in 1929.[13]

The uncrowned king of ballyhoo, at least until Russell Birdwell conned the country into searching for someone to play Scarlett O'Hara in *Gone With the Wind* (long after Vivien Leigh had been given the part), was Harry Reichenbach.[14] An artful dodger extraordinaire, Reichenbach was born in 1882, on a farm near Frostburg, Maryland. His deeply religious parents ran a combination grocery store and saloon, but at the tender age of eleven Harry saw something that persuaded him to forgo the slow, steady and stultifyingly scrupulous family business. A tall stranger arrived in town, carrying two building bricks and a large roll of paper, and proceeded to perform the (retro) routine that Barnum frequently used to fill the American Museum on slow show days.[15] He stopped in the main street, placed one of the bricks on the sidewalk, took ten carefully measured steps and set down the second brick. He then retrieved the first brick, took another ten carefully calculated paces from the second and positioned the first one again. This process continued, in total silence until a substantial crowd of intrigued onlookers had assembled. The stranger then unrolled the piece of paper, a publicity poster for a forthcoming minstrel show, and started selling tickets to the curious, clamouring hordes.

There and then, Reichenbach decided to go into show business and, when a travelling medicine show – starring 'Professor' Harry Helms – passed through town, he took the phoney scholar's counterfeit shilling. Reichenbach was a precocious pupil and ere long he was well versed in the professor's perfidies: short-changing customers, striking up the scream-drowning band when the professor pulled teeth and generally acting the shill (an audience confederate who volunteered impromptu testimonials to the miraculous healing powers of whatever fraudulent potion the learned one happened to be peddling). After a few years on the road, Harry finished up in New York where he established a theatrical agency – his first client was The Great Raymond, a not so great escapologist whose career was cut short when a buried-alive stunt went awry – and rapidly made a name for himself in motion picture promotions. Reichenbach's cinematic triumphs are too numerous to mention but the one that set the ball(yhoo) rolling was for a meretricious film of George du Maurier's melodramatic novel, *Trilby*. Fortunately, it featured a scene in which the eponymous heroine was hypnotized by the dastardly villain, Svengali.[16] As, indeed, were several female members of the audience, who just happened to be on Harry's payroll. Newspapers devoured the pseudo-spellbound story and for several weeks thereafter debated the hypnotic power of motion pictures in general and *Trilby* in particular.

A little obviously went a long way in the early days of the cinema and, in addition to his manifold promotional escapades, Harry acted as press agent for Rudolph Valentino (he got Rudi to grow a beard and engineered howls of protest from the Master Barbers Association, fearful of the fashion leader's influence on their stubbled clientele); advised the US government on its wartime propaganda campaigns (he recommended dropping doctored bibles, where passages from the good book were interlarded with anti-Kaiser sentiments, behind enemy lines); and, in a *tour de force* of FMCG marketing, established tuna fish as a credible suppertime alternative to salmon by claiming that it was 'guaranteed not to turn pink in the cans' (which preyed on people's unfounded fears concerning contamination through canning).

Reichenbach's ultimate achievement, however, involved convincing *himself* that a malarial swamp in Boca Raton, which he had been promoting for a couple of shady property dealers, was worth investing in. A nationwide advertising campaign, masterminded by the master of ballyhoo, portrayed Boca Raton as a Floridian arcadia, a residential Shangri La, where yachts anchored at the front doors of palatial estates and everything in the garden was rosier than rosy. So compelling was this representation – the architectural models alone were works of art – that Harry sank his life savings into the fly-by-night operation and lost every penny when the investment bubble burst. He died a broken man in 1931.

Reichenbach, as his biographer suggests (not without a touch of ballyhoo),[17] may have been personally responsible for elevating motion pictures into an important industry – alongside nonentities like D.W. Griffith and Cecil B. de Mille! – but he was very much a product of the medicine show tradition. Now almost forgotten, the great American medicine show was the primordial ooze from which modern marketing originated.[18] Between 1870 and 1930, literally thousands of performance artistes traversed the highways and byways of the United States purveying patent medicines with brand names almost as colourful as the water they contained: Dr Duponco's Golden Periodical, Dr Sappington's Vegetable Febrifuge, Dr Hembold's Genuine Preparation of Highly Concentrated Compound Fluid Extract of Buchnu, and many more besides. Good and bad, large and small, undercover and alfresco, medicine shows comprised a compelling mix of popular entertainments, interspersed with proto-commercial-breaks for sundry potions, palliatives, purges and panaceas. Although there were many variations on the medicine show theme, the concept can be summarized in terms of the, er, 4Rs: *remedial, recreational, recherché* and *roguish.*

It almost goes without saying that the principal purpose of such peripatetic extravaganzas was to sell *remedies* and restoratives. Admission charges were sometimes made but these were nominal. Many shows, in fact, were free or free-ish. And, although a great deal of profit accrued from the sale of ancillary items, such as soap and prize candy, the real money-spinners were the patent medicines themselves (mark-ups of several hundred per cent were not unusual). In the early days, indeed, the nostrums, tonics and emollients were manufactured in cauldrons or hotel bathtubs, as required, or purchased direct from wholesale druggists, who not only bottled the brew but labelled it according to the purchaser's specifications. Hence the proliferation of branded products – Hostetter's Bitters, Ayer's Cherry Pectoral, Dr Hooker's Cough & Croup Syrup, Louis Goelicke's Matchless Sanative – most of which were indistinguishable. By the early twentieth century, however, nationally advertised brands, like Lydia E. Pinkham's Vegetable Compound, Hamlin's Wizard Oil and Kickapoo Indian Sagwa, tended to predominate.[19] So much so, that the shows were essentially ambulatory advertising vehicles for the manufacturers.

Regardless of the source or the name on the label, these mixtures of camphor, ammonia, chloroform, sassafras, cloves, aloes and turpentine (to name but the most readily identifiable ingredients), were purportedly capable of curing anything and everything. When employed as a liniment, for example, Hamlin's Wizard Oil took care of rheumatism, sprains, bruises, lame back, frostbite, burns and scalds. When taken internally, which was no mean feat since it comprised between 55 and

70% alcohol, Wizard Oil conquered headache, neuralgia, diphtheria, pneumonia, hydrophobia and cancer. Other physics were targeted at more specific ailments including epilepsy, hysteria, croup, constipation, bad blood, unmentionable women's problems and, naturally, 'lost manhood'. Magnetic belts, moreover, were believed to be especially efficacious for renal problems, though they only contained capsicum (red pepper), which generated a therapeutic tingle when triggered by the wearer's body heat. Most medicines, however, claimed to cure 'every disease, human or inhuman, from a broken finger-nail to natural death of two weeks' standing'.[20]

Retailing remedial requisites may have been the ultimate object of the exercise, but the show was the essence of the elixir-selling business. Just as the prime purpose of television programmes and newspaper articles is to deliver an audience to advertisers, so too the patent medicine sales pitches were surrounded by a *recreational* wrapper. A very substantial recreational wrapper, it has to be said, consisting of approximately three-quarters of the total running time, typically 2–4 hours. The shows themselves were an extremely eclectic combination of whatever happened to be popular at the time, the only unifying theme being that the individual acts had very little, if anything, to do with patent medicine. Itinerant medicine extravaganzas thus comprised an admixture of vaudeville, burlesque, pantomime, minstrelsy, magic, menageries, mesmerism, acrobatics, ventriloquism, dog and pony turns, Punch and Judy performances, pie-eating contests and suchlike. Musical acts and comedy routines were a particularly important part of the package, often bookending the show, as well as the individual 'commercial breaks'.

That said, the sales pitches were performances in their own right. By all accounts, the best pitchers were very skilled orators who 'never wearied an audience and were able to manipulate the emotions of a crowd like a good tent evangelist'.[21] They often dressed the part, what is more, or pressed suitably alarming props into affliction-inducing service (tape worms in a bottle, intimidating dental instruments, *trompe-l'oeil* diagrams of gruesome diseases, etc.). In order to sell his own-brand balm and painless tooth-pulling operation, for instance, Dr Andrew Dupré dressed in the uniform of a French chasseur, complete with doeskin breeches and an oversized horsehair helmet. The hilt of his sabre contained forceps which he used to extract teeth whilst gripping his patient by the throat (thereby conveniently cutting off any agonized screams). Diamond Kit, meanwhile, modelled a natty outfit that boasted coat buttons set with rhinestones, a gigantic zircon tiepin and a glittering crown of glass diamonds. Lest people failed to notice him, he commenced his performances by galloping through the crowd in a huge chariot attached, after a fashion, to four frisky stallions.

Such singular salesmanship may strike today's precision marketers, with their computer programmes, personalized mail-shots and points-disbursing loyalty schemes, as somewhat naïve, not to say hopelessly amateurish, yet they were considered fairly *recherché* at the time. Indeed, much of the appeal of the medicine show was attributable to its out-of-the-ordinary qualities. In the days before television, radio and film, roving medicine shows were nothing if not exotic and sheer exoticism was an aspect they unfailingly emphasized. Perhaps the best examples of this propensity were the so-called Indian medicine shows, which comprised scaled-down versions of the then popular Wild West shows (with a dash of vaudeville and blackface minstrelry thrown in for good measure), and Oriental medicine shows, which provided the 'whistlers, whittlers and spitters' of rural America with a taste of the Orient, or rather the Orient of an enterprising impresario's imagination. The two concepts were sometimes ingeniously combined, as in Nevada Ned's Hindoo Patalka show, which featured the proprietor – sporting an elaborate buckskin frontier outfit – two Syrians hired from a rug store, a Hindu hypnotist, and a dipsomaniac elephant which once imbibed too much Wizard Oil and leapt off a bridge in New Jersey (but, sadly, failed to take flight).

The patent medicine pitchers, moreover, set great store by their products' extraordinary qualities, whether it be in terms of their miraculous healing powers – Wizard Oil claimed to be 'magical' in its effects, as Dumbo's prototype would surely attest – or their 'secret' ingredients, as in the case of Kikapoo Indian Sagwa, or simply that they came from a distant or unusual source. The medicine show itself, of course, is unusual today but way back then 'the exotic' was seen in terms of Native Americana, the Far East and parts of Western Europe, Germany in particular. With their reputation for methodical methods (tried and tested), implicit authoritarianism (take this, it's good for you) and linguistic incomprehensibility (lots of unpronounceable technical terms), the scientific German, Herr Doktor stereotype was especially popular, as were products with suitably teu-tonic brand names like Bavarian Malt Extract, Westphalia Bitters, Hoofland's German Tonic, Schiffman's German Asthma Cure, Teutonia Liniment, Germania Oil and the Berlin Corn and Bunion Cure. All made in Cincinnati by the German Medicine Company.

To be sure, the recherché character of the great American medicine show cannot be divorced from its very itinerancy – strange tradespeople who appeared and disappeared in short order – nor indeed can its reputation for *roguery*. Deception, duplicity, hyperbole and humbuggery were an integral aspect of the medicine show business and recognized as such by the audience. Far from being simple rustics bamboozled by fast-talking out-of-towners (showmen often described their clients as dupes, gulls or rubes), it is clear that a considerable amount of pleasure was provided in return for Barnumesque chicanery. The fact that most medicine shows played for at least a fortnight in every reasonably sized town on the annual circuit – with crowds increasing throughout the run – suggests that grand larceny or mass fraud was not taking place.[22] It seems that free entry, coupled with the admittedly remote chance of a cure, or even something from the prize candy draw, was more than sufficient for most patrons. Indeed, as most of the tonics were intoxicant cocktails, a snifter or two of the restorer, refresher or chest-hair provider was enough to quell all but the most querulous consumer.

Set against this, there is no doubt that double-dealing went on in the environs of medicine shows: confidence tricks, short-changing, pickpocketing, sharp practices at the sideshows and so forth. However, this did not inhibit impresarios' attempts to occupy the high moral ground. The rectitude, honesty and honourable reputations of the operators were repeatedly stressed. Testimonials to the ameliorative abilities of their products were routinely paraded, the more celebrated the endorser the better. And, in truth, the employees of some of the larger, manufacturer-sponsored shows, such as Hamlin's Wizard Oil and Kikapoo Indian Sagwa, were expected to behave decorously, on pain of instant dismissal. But for every Kickapoo, there were at least a dozen quack Quaker shows, strolling players that sported porridge-coloured Puritan uniforms, interspersed their pitches with 'thou', 'thee', 'brother' and analogous anachronisms, blessed customers at the close of every sale, and, despite trading on the Quakers' reputation for honest dealing, had nothing whatsoever to do with the Society of Friends. Likewise, Wizard Oil, Kikapoo Indian Sagwa and several other widely promoted brands were plagued by cheap-and-cheerful imitations – Magic Oil, Lightning Oil, Sagwah, Awaga and so on – which piggy-backed on the reputation of the original. At least one snake-oil salesperson, furthermore, was forced to advertise the fact that he sold 'genuine' snake oil (acquired, naturally, from an authentic Indian source) which was guaranteed to alleviate arthritis, rheumatism and painful piles. However, as he had no idea what the grog actually contained, this ever-ethical marketing man slapped a skull and crossbones on the label and intimated that it was not to be taken internally.[23]

The late great American medicine show, of course, was not confined to the United States and Canada. Just as Barnum, Bailey and Buffalo Bill toured the capitals of Europe, so too some of the more adventurous medicine show artists made transatlantic trips. By far the most swashbuckling of these was William Henry Hartley (1857–1924), an alumnus of the Kickapoo campus who operated under the striking (if derivative) stage name, Sequah.[24] Aptly described as 'the most flamboyant quack ever to traverse England',[25] Hartley was the snake-oil salesman's snake-oil salesman. Born and bred in Yorkshire, of all places, he purported to be an American frontiersman, akin to Kit Carson, Davy Crockett or Wild Bill Hickock. Having acquired the ancient pharmaceutical lore of the Apaches and blessed with a burning desire to heal the sick in

'civilized' society, Hartley travelled around the UK selling his proprietary patent medicines, Prairie Flower, Indian Oil and Indian Denti-
frice. In keeping with accepted medicine show practice, what is more,
Sequah dressed like something out of Fenimore Cooper, talked in an
ostensible American accent and came equipped with a colossal golden
carriage, six-piece brass band, tribe of Native American assistants (in full
feathered headgear) and a fearsome collection of bloodcurdling medical
instruments. He materialized on the south coast in or around September
1887 and managed to attract 30,000 people to his first *plein air* performance in Portsmouth. A high-speed demonstration of painless dentistry
(317 teeth extracted in 39 minutes) was swiftly followed by a series of
'miracle cures' for the local halt, lame and rheumatic (a vigorous rub
with Indian Oil and they were soon up and about) and, after recounting
the melodramatic story of how he came by his secrets, Sequah's wonder-
working medicines were made available for a philanthropic pittance to
all and sundry.

To say that his retro redskin remedies were staggeringly successful
hardly does justice to the scale of Hartley's triumph. His entourage
toured the country, attracting massive crowds wherever it went. Such
was the demand, that several additional 'Sequahs' had to be recruited
and trained. At one stage, more than thirty clones were on the road in
the British Isles, western Europe, South Africa and the Colonies, though
maintaining quality control was difficult, to say the least (they were
managed by James and Tom Norman, freak show operators and one-
time handlers of 'The Elephant Man'). In each locality, nevertheless,
much the same procedure was followed: generate advance publicity by
means of handbills, free sheets and extensive newspaper advertising;
recruit local worthies to lend their weight to the wares in return for
charitable donations or equivalent rewards; attract controversy by
denigrating the achievements of medical science and its know-nothing,
bill-padding practitioners; ensure that there is *insufficient* stock to meet
the likely demand, thereby increasing the gotta-get-em frenzy of would-
be purchasers; and persuade local agents to sell the merchandise after
demand has been drummed up and the medicine show has moved on.

This strategy was not without its drawbacks, admittedly, since trouble
seemed to follow in Sequah's wake. Riotous behaviour was not
uncommon, especially when belligerent anti-quack, pro-science medical
students attempted to disrupt the performances. Competitors and detrac-
tors spread malicious rumours about the undeniably dubious ingredients
of Prairie Flower and Indian Oil or parodied his distinctive advertising
appeals. All sorts of copy-cat, sound-alike operations – Rhuma, Lequah,
Pasqua, Sepoy, Sequa – emerged from the woodwork and forced Sequah
to take legal action against these quack quacks. The miraculously cured
were wont to complain when the miracle wore off and the rheumatism,
gout or whatever returned with a vengeance. Affiliated apothecaries were

unfailingly infuriated by the fact that Sequah undercut their prices when the show came to town, leaving his franchisees with nothing but a display window full of Prairie Flower promotional materials. Yet, despite the difficulties, Sequah's ruse was enormously successful; in the first year alone he sold more than 1.5 million bottles. So profitable did it prove, that the company was floated on the London Stock Exchange in March 1889 (at the same time as another, much smaller pharmaceutical organization, Boots the Chemist) and, thus fully capitalized, seemed set for even greater success. At one point, a Sequah show was actually touring the United States, though Healy and Bigelow, purveyors of the original-and-best Kickapoo Indian Sagwa, were quick to institute legal proceedings against the shameless sound-alike.

Tangling with Healy and Bigelow was a strategic mistake, because Kickapoo was by far the biggest, brashest, brook-no-opposition medicine show then extant.[26] Sadly, it wasn't Sequah's only strategic error of judgement. The authorities in Spain, South Africa, Argentina and the Low Countries took steps against the troublesome trickster and, even in Hartley's heartland, the medicine show's days were numbered. Behind the scenes lobbying by the much-maligned medical and dental professions, coupled with the complaints of disaffected retailers, whose businesses were plagued by cheapjack chain stores and the proliferation of question-able me-too products, precipitated an inevitable 'bury my Hartley at wounded knee' showdown. Antagonized, in addition, by Sequah's failure to pay sufficient stamp duty, the Inland Revenue acted decisively in 1890 when it passed legislation limiting the sale of patent medicines to 'licensed' premises. These premises specifically excluded the types of venue – wagons, tents, commons, parade grounds, waste land, etc. – utilized by medicine show operations. Hartley's company collapsed soon after and, although his customers wanted more, nothing remains of the Sequah phenomenon but a few mouldering newspaper clippings, brightly coloured posters and non-returnable bottles of Prairie Flower Oil.

Notwithstanding Sequah's ignominious failure, his incomparable commercial adventures contain an important lesson for today's market-ing community, as does the American medicine show generally. This lesson, it must be stressed, is not simply a question of retro, although the Indian shows were the *Repro de Luxe* of their day. [27] In many ways, they represented a *fin-de-siècle* revival of the mountebank tradition of western Europe and the perambulating quack doctor extravaganzas of the early modern period. What's more, they were predicated on the notion that Native Americans were late nineteenth-century noble savages, the fount of ancient lore, the source of natural remedies and endowed with the secret of good health, long life and spiritual contentment.[28] Nostalgia for the then rapidly closing American frontier, especially among eastern urbanites whose experience of the Wild West was limited to dime novels and the sub-Barnum spectaculars of Buffalo Bill, also contributed to the enormous popularity of these 'extinct tribes that never existed'.[29] That said, appeals to past ages were equally apparent in non-Native-American themed medicine shows, such as those that purveyed King David's Honey Coated Pills, Rameses II's Sarsaparilla, Druid Ointment ('handed down from mystic days when Stonehenge was a busy temple'),[30] or the ever popular purges, pectorals and palliatives produced from 'secret formulae', which were passed down from generation to generation.

Nor, for that matter, does the twenty-first-century lesson of the nineteenth-century medicine show refer to the latter-day renaissance of the nostrum business.[31] It stands to reason that the recent rapid rise of herbal medicine, coupled with the homeopathic challenge to the allopathic mainstream, contains much more than one part per million of snake oil.[32] At the turn of the century, it was daily doses of Bellingham's Onguent, Brandreth's Pills, Hostetter's Bitters, Hembold's Extract of Buchnu and what have you, whereas today the supplementary shots are called by Ginkgo Biloba, Ginseng, Echinacea, St John's Wort and all the rest. The contemporary boom in Chinese medicine is analogous, is it not, to the nineteenth-century fad for Dr Lin's Celestial Balm of China, Dr Drake's Cantonese Hair Cream and Carey's Chinese Catarrh Cure.[33] Our much-vaunted rediscovery of Ayurveda, a 5,000-year-old Indian restorative, is not a million miles removed from Persian Balm, Mecca Compound, Kennedy's East Indian Bitters or Osgood's Indian Cholagogue.[34] Magnets, moreover, are attracting the credulous once again, the way they did when medicine show pitchmen sang the praises of magnetic belts, bracelets, cravats, collars, combs, corsets, insoles, anklets, pillows, elbow pads and any number of Heath Robinsonesque contraptions.[35] Talking of contraptions, today's blackhead and pimple alleviating patches are not only contemporary variations on an old theme, but much less mortifying, since nineteenth-century pustules were blamed on 'bad blood' caused by excessive masturbation. (However, it may be some time before the then failsafe cure, electrical jolts to the unmentionables, makes a twenty-first-century comeback – short of a short from an Ann Summers sex toy.)

Nor, finally, is the let-that-be-a-lesson-to-you lesson metaphorical rather than literal, even though the patent medicine business is a singularly appropriate analogy for management consultancy *per se*.[36] The exceptionally high death rate of business organizations, coupled with a limitless supply of academic apothecaries and 'consultants', means that the aforementioned 4Rs are readily discernible in the management medicine show. Almost every intellectual huckster, for example, has a sure-fire proprietary *remedy*, whether it be a simple diagnostic model of market entry strategy, a gentle pick-me-up from the ever-popular relationships range or an heroic, kill-or-cure emetic like 're-engineering the corporation'.[37] *Recreation* is *de rigueur*, as many management commentators have come to realize that they are part of the entertainments industry. Tom (foolery) Peters, clearly, is the master of ceremonies, with Dilbert not far behind, but even workaday business pundits now recognize the importance of stage presence, cerebral soundbites and all-singing-all-dancing, bells-and-whistles, Powerpoint-assisted presentations.[38] *Recherché* research is also necessary, since replication and me-too remedies do little to establish one's brand name or guarantee shelf space in the conceptual dispensary. True, the reputation of the pharmacy itself helps sell some questionable nostrums (Wharton Magic Oil, Harvardia Boil & Bunion Cure, Insead Elixir, LBS Liniment) but the majority of management pharmacologists mix standard ingredients, according to established recipes, in imitation of top-selling brands: Painless Porter's Panacea, Drucker's Delicious Detoxicant, Levitt's Liver Pads, Kotlerpoo Indian Sagwa. (Anyone for Brown's Bombastic Balsam?) *Roguery*, finally, is not exactly unknown in the money-laundering laboratories of management science. Consider, if you will, the skulduggery of Treacy and Wiersema, who bought up thousands of copies of their book, *The Discipline of Market Leaders*, in an attempt to hype it on to the *New York Times* best-sellers list.[39] I, myself, am acquainted with a disreputable marketing academic who not only tried the same trick but actually press-ganged his aged mother into the book-buying scam. What is the world coming to?

Fin-de-siècle medicine shows may not be able to answer that particular imponderable, though they do at least help us reposition marketing in relation to its surrounding context. Our twenty-first-century lesson, then, refers to the marketing environment. If ever there was an institution that exemplified the functioning of the marketing environment, it is surely the great American medicine show. The Food and Drugs Act of 1906, which required all ingredients in patent medicines to be listed on the label, effectively killed off the core product.[40] Likewise, the muckraking journalism of *McCall's* magazine, which ran a series of shock-horror articles in 1904, did much to undermine public confidence in the industry and, at the same time, created conditions conducive to the passage of highly restrictive legislation (despite intense, well-funded lobbying by patent medicine producers).[41] Increased regulation of the medical and pharmaceutical professions also helped reduce the more overt manifestations of quackery, although down-and-out physicians were often taken on the road in an attempt to circumvent federal controls. More pertinently perhaps, improvements in transportation, rural–urban migration and the advent of alternative forms of entertainment – radio, cinema and eventually television – slowly but surely put paid to the patent medicine show.[42] By 1930, only a handful of operations remained and the passage of another round of anti-pectoral legislation in the late 1930s (the brainchild, incidentally, of Rexford Tugwell, an acolyte of our old friend Simon Nelson Patten),[43] hammered the final nail into the medicine show coffin.

Or did it?

When the history of the American medicine show is examined, perhaps the most interesting aspect of the itinerant institution is that it succeeded *despite* the marketing environment.[44] Environmental conditions were *consistently* inhospitable, whether it be the state of the roads in the early days, the legislative restrictions that were placed on the industry from the very outset, the unremitting antagonism of mainstream medical practitioners, neighbourhood pharmacies and local law enforcement officers, the ferociously competitive character of the febrifuge business (which forced Coca-Cola, no less, to pull out and reposition itself as a soft drink), or indeed the manifestly absurd claims of the panaceas, purges and pick-me-ups. Although it is easy, in retrospect, to regard patent medicine consumers as gulls and hayseeds, they were nothing of the sort, or no more so than contemporary purchasers of, say, Molitium 10, which claims to be a sure-fire remedy for 'dismotility' (the latest in a long line of marketer-invented ailments). Medicine shows succeeded, rather, because they persuaded their patrons to believe the unbelievable, *à la* Barnum. They succeeded because of their rebellious, rambunctious, larger than life commercial credo, a credo that characterizes both pre- and post-modern marketing, if not the epoch in between. Indeed, one suspects that people like Hartley, Harry Reichenbach and Painless Potter would be successful in any market, at any time, for any product or service, on account of their imagination, their determination and their downright effrontery.

This assertion is amply illustrated by the apotheosis of the American medicine show, the so-called Hadacol Caravan. Hadacol hit the road, not in the institution's 1890s heyday, but during the early 1950s, when the complete battery of restrictive legislation was in place, when a full range of entertainments alternatives was available, when the allopathic medical establishment was in its pomp and, as we have previously noted, when an anti-marketing ethos was abroad.[45] The brainwave of Dudley J. LeBlanc, a somewhat shady southern senator, Hadacol was third time lucky for this charismatic Cajun. His two previous attempts to break into the patent medicine business, with Happy Day Headache Powders and Dixie Dew Cough Syrup, were less than successful. Hadacol, however, was the bee's knees of bracers. Supposedly based on a stolen secret recipe, and tasting apparently of 'ripe bananas', Hadacol was a mixture of B vitamins and honey (hence the bee's knees) with a generous dollop of alcohol. LeBlanc, nevertheless, let it be known that, in addition to curing just about every ailment known to man and some that aren't, Hadacol was an extremely potent aphrodisiac. The poor man's monkey glands, in effect.[46] Word of mouth immediately took over, bawdy jokes abounded, dirty ditties were composed and, when combined with an intensive advertising campaign, there was simply no stopping the stimulant.

LeBlanc's *pièce de résistance*, however, was the humungous Hadacol 'caravan', which toured the southern states attracting enormous crowds wherever it went. His caravan, in certain respects, was retromarketing incarnate. It comprised a state-of-the-art revival of the classic medicine show concept and boasted the suitably futuristic byline 'Hadacol for a better tomorrow'. It not only pressed every one of the traditional medicine show buttons – extensive pre-publicity, bannered biplane bypasses, main street parade prior to the show, fireworks display afterwards, claques of clowns, jugglers, acrobats, magicians, bathing beauties, balloons, elephants, kangaroos etc., etc., etc. – but it pressed them much harder and for longer than ever before. In fact, the stage show featured a mind-boggling bill of blue-chip performers including Carmen Miranda, Mickey Rooney, Jack Benny, Jimmy Durante, George Burns, Groucho Marx, Judy Garland, Hank Williams and, naturally, the son of Paleface himself, Bob Hope. Most astonishingly of all, the price of admission was only one Hadacol box top for children and two for adults. As McNamara rightly notes, it was 'like nothing ever seen before in the world of the medicine show'.[47]

A better tomorrow, sadly, never came for LeBlanc, because he sold the Hadacol Corporation not long after the second season. Worse, the new owners quickly discovered that the books were not only cooked but strained, bottled and 'all sold out, professor'.[48] The Cajun con-man then disappeared from view, changed his name to James Vicary, set himself up as a motivation researcher and we all know what happened next.[49]

Be that as it may, the lasting legacy of LeBlanc – the aptly named Barnum of the Bayoux[50] – is that there is *no such thing as the marketing environment*. Now, this does not mean that the external environment doesn't exist.[51] Only the most rabid postmodern marketer would maintain that demographic, economic, legislative, technological and cultural changes have no impact on commercial endeavours (quick, pass the antidote). Of course they do. However, the problem with the APIC paradigm is that it sets *too much store* by environmental fluctuations, it posits that marketing practice is constrained by, subordinate to and a function of environmental forces, both external and internal. Textbook discussions of the subject typically comprise a catalogue of its component parts – sometimes 'the consumer environment' is included – followed by suitably sage advice to the effect that would-be marketers *must* take environmental factors into account when formulating marketing plans, strategies, new product launches and so forth.[52]

In fairness, many of these commentators acknowledge that marketing practitioners can shape the environment, to some extent at least, by lobbying legislators, staging media events, publishing promotional freesheets and funding 'disinterested' research by tame academics. It is undeniable, moreover, that 'unforeseen environmental circumstances' can provide a convenient excuse (for consultants, practitioners and researchers alike) when marketing goes awry, as the Ford Edsel, New Coke and McDonald's Big Mac give-away remind us. Nevertheless, the overwhelming impression that such excuses, explanations and attempted exculpations leave is of abject environmental determinism. Marketing is portrayed as a hopeless hostage to changing circumstances, a reed in the wind, a child of nature rather than nurture, not so much done to as done for. Marketing merely reflects consumer preferences; marketing is constrained by volatile environmental forces; marketing is a consequence not a cause; marketing is but a humble servant, the Uriah Heep of the academy. Granted, marketing is happy to affirm its all-important contribution when there's something it wants to take credit for – increased church attendance, reduced cigarette consumption, burgeoning profit margins or whatever – but for the most part marketing protests that it is not worthy, not responsible, not to blame, not top drawer. The milieu made us do it.

Maybe it's time to abandon the self-abnegating, self-exonerating, I-can't-believe-it's-not-Barton mentality that has held sway since Father Ted sampled the subversive sounds of Van the Man Packard, some forty years ago. In my view, twenty-first-century marketing needs a bit more devil may care, it needs to take more responsibility for its actions, it needs to act *as if* environmental constraints don't exist, it needs to stop kow-towing to the consumer, it needs to reposition itself in relation to the market for marketing, it needs to become a bit more production orientated.

What it needs above all else, however, is a shot of conceptual Hadacol. For a better tomorrow . . .

6

Representing Marketing: The Secret of the Black Magic Box

Everyone loves a good, old-fashioned put-down and few are better than the one attributed to the evolutionary biologist, J.B.S. Haldane. Deeply embroiled in the Darwinian 'monkey's uncle' controversy, he was accosted by a bunch of eager-beaver creationists, who believed that such were the wonders of nature, they must have been begat by a higher power. In an attempted trick question, the true believers inquired what one could infer about the Creator from careful study of his creation. Haldane famously replied that she exhibited 'an inordinate fondness for beetles'.[1]

As crushing rejoinders go, Haldane's can hardly be improved upon, though it was not for want of trying. Apparently, the *bon mot*-disbursing biologist was inordinately fond of his 'inordinately fond' remark and repeated it *ad nauseam*. When he was on song, Haldane allegedly added that God's countless attempts to create the perfect beetle stood in marked contrast to her one-shot, slip-shod effort at hominids. Hence, when we finally meet the Almighty face to face, she is much more likely to look like Coleoptera than Cleopatra.

High table talk has never been higher, I'm sure you agree, but it is clear in retrospect that Haldane failed to do justice to the full depth of her Highness's infatuation with the insect kingdom. At the time of his remark, there were an estimated 400,000 species of beetles on the planet, compared to only 10,000 species of mammals, and decades of biological research have since confirmed the latter total. More or less. As Coleoptera are hard to identify and enumerate, however, the former figure has been raised by a factor of forty to approximately 30 million species of beetle.[2]

A bug's life, some might say, but there's a scholarly corollary. If a bunch of Kotler-fixated marketing creationists were to approach a conceptual entomologist and inquire what we could infer about the Creator from His creation, the answer would have to be 'an inordinate fondness for boxes'. As a quick flick through *Marketing Management* –

or any of the Kotler-clone textbooks – readily demonstrates, the marketing discipline is knee-deep in boxes, matrices and minor variations thereof. There are boxes pertaining to new products, research methods, consumer types, brand choice, service quality, customer care, retail locations, pricing policies, marketing information systems, classifications of goods and many more besides. True, some Salvador Dalis of marketing scholarship have experimented with circles, triangles and things that look like strands of DNA having a bad hair day, but when it comes to portraying marketing phenomena diagrammatically, there's no doubt that grid squares, checkerboards and rhomboid-ish rectangles rule the representational roost.

Of the one hundred figures in Kotler, for instance, no less than 95% involve boxes of one kind or another. Somewhat disconcertingly, this is almost exactly the same ratio observed by Haldane in his beetles/humans comparison, which implies either a universal law of the Golden Mean variety or a cabbalistic conspiracy of the Golden Dawn variety. Worse, it intimates that there is a plethora of boxes out there – by a factor of forty, possibly – just waiting to be discovered, catalogued and displayed by the intellectual entomologists of marketing. I'd ask God to help us but she's probably an enthusiastic proponent of matrix management.

Ubiquitous though boxes are in the rogues' gallery of marketing misrepresentation, one sub-discipline is especially susceptible to receptacles. The strategists, let's be frank, suffer from a severe case of matrix-mania (or, boxes on the brain, as it's colloquially known). Ever since Ansoff broke into the box in 1957, when he concocted a 2×2 product-market matrix that ranks alongside Theodore Levitt's contemporaneous cogitations in terms of its long-term influence on our field,[3] boxes have been the hallmark of marketing strategists. Like Furbies, computer viruses and genetically modified soya beans, they are everywhere, they are unstoppable, they breed like rabbits on Viagra. Indeed, there are now so many mutant matrices running around that they are impossible to classify, let alone control, though there is talk of introducing a contagious disease – matrixmatosis – which should help reduce their numbers somewhat. Sounds cruel, I know, but until such times as they build a better matrixtrap,[4] we're stuck with extermination.

There is no alternative.

In-breeding, obviously, is to blame for the present parlous state of strategic affairs, though I'm pleased to report that conceptual diagnosticians are close to identifying the original locus of infestation. Apart from Ansoff, the ancestral sources are known to include the infamous General Electric matrix, which was once so ubiquitous that it was known as the National Grid; the BCG Box, with its rabid dogs, mad cows, shooting stars and questionable question marks; the PIMS cocktail of thirty strategic ingredients, that left countless organizations' market shares shaken rather than stirred; and Michael Porter's geriatric strategies of cost leadership, differentiation, focus and stuck-in-the-middle.[5] The last of these, admittedly, has comparatively few adherents – oh how I've longed to hear someone say 'We're stuck in the middle and proud of it' – but the rest of the cells in this prison house of representation are overflowing to the point of dirty protest.

Strategic slopping-out is not an attractive thought, I grant you. However, it is a calamitous consequence of congested conditions in the house of conceptual correction, which have deteriorated to such an extent that marketing textbooks can unblushingly include ninety cell matrices – repeat, *ninety* – for estimating market demand (six categories of product, by five geographical regions, by three time periods).[6] Fill that if you dare. Entire books, moreover, have been devoted to *Marketing by Matrix*, the appearance of which prompted one over-enthusiastic reviewer to respond in kind, if not kindness (Figure 6.1a).[7] An 'emergency matrix' is also available for untrained marketing practitioners who have been force-marched, at short notice, to the strategic front line (Figure 6.1b).[8] And none other than Painless Porter has extracted gold from lead fillings by doing the seemingly strategically impossible: turning a box into an arrow and vice versa (Figure 6.1c).[9]

In truth, the bloom is going off boxes. Although most large companies continue to cultivate the strategic marketing allotment, they are less like formal gardens than corporate window boxes these days. Even mainstream textbooks now acknowledge that strategic matrices, while useful for pedagogic purposes (translation: anything to avoid rewriting the 'strategy' chapter for the new edition), are decidedly reductive, downright dangerous and easy to formulate but difficult to fulfil. Predictably perhaps, their predictive abilities have also been questioned, though only time will tell whether predictions of their demise will come to pass.[10] In recent years, admittedly, a Microsoft aesthetic has been adopted by many matrix installation artists (tiled and multi-layered have superseded flat and non-overlapping). But this is more like a final stylistic flourish of a decadent artistic movement than an avant-garde aspiration to *épater la boite*. Such is the degeneracy of late period marketing boxwork that we seem to have entered an era of – pardon my French – postmodern matrices.

Postmodern matrices, as you've probably already guessed, are matrices about matrices. In the course of a recent 'strategy safari', to mention but one example, the indefatigable Henry Mintzberg positions the positioning school by a series of boxes about boxes.[11] True, he completely fails to foreground his own figure – the strategy of strategy as safari – with its connotations of exoticism, uncontrollability and latent threat (thereby rendering strategic management exciting once more, instead of safe and sorry). Nevertheless, his matrix matrices remain

Figure 6.1   Compassing the box

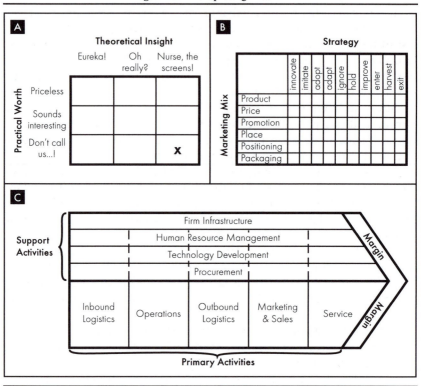

characteristically postmodern, inasmuch as they are simultaneously complicit with and seek to connive against conceptual convention, not to say compromised by the very thing they are seeking to contest.[12] To be sure, boxing the box that boxes you is a standard postmodern strategy, as is boxing the box-boxer, but from our present historical perspective it is apparent that a longer-term strategic process is at work.

Illustrated in Figure 6.2, this process involves two strategic strategies: using or not using matrices and approving or disapproving of marketing boxology. Tyro researchers, as a rule, fall into the bottom left-hand cell, in that they haven't concocted any matrices of their own but, thanks to Kotlerite textbooks, are fairly favourably disposed toward such constructions *per se*. Newly minted PhDs, desperate for publication, coupled with mainstream marketing academics of the clan McDonald, tend to be incarcerated in the top left-hand cell and remain committed to the Boxes-R-Us mindset. The top right-hand cell is the domain of windswept and interesting postmodern marketers, such as Morris Holbrook, who don't think much of modernist matrices yet continue to play the cubistic card, air-kissed by invisible inverted commas.[13] The final cell contains, in

Figure 6.2 Circle the boxes

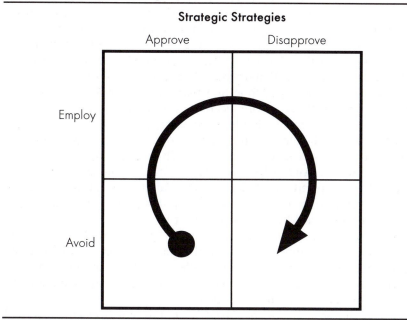

Strategic Strategies

classic P.T. Barnum cat-and-bag fashion, the boxologists who have finally broken out of the box, only to find themselves in the box box, the box box box, the box box box box, etc. As Clifford Geertz almost said, 'it's boxes all the way down'.

The real problem with boxes, of course, is not that they are mad, bad and dangerous to know, although they can indeed be that. The difficulty is that they are so damn attractive, intriguing and seductive, don't you know. I speak, let it be said, from considerable personal experience, since I've concocted one or two (by two) matrices in my time.[14] I am, in fact, a secret matrixomane, a backdoor boxaphile, a recovering typoholic on the 2 × 2 × 2 step programme. Indeed, as someone who has oft-times rolled in the gutter of gridlines, and spent a night or several in the cells, I'm only too well aware of the intoxicating appeal of conceptual receptacles. There's the sense of pixillated personal satisfaction, akin to completing a crossword or winning a game of Scrabble, that comes from their compilation. There's the inebriated feeling of spurious insightfulness that derives from imposing a coherent framework upon the hitherto inchoate. There's the intemperate anticipation, unfailingly unrealized, that this will prove to be the contribution that catapults its creator into the pantheon of marketing immortals, the one reproduced in textbooks, lauded in lectures and, naturally, named after its suitably modest, painfully self-effacing, shy and retiring inventor (the Brown Box has a ring to it, I'm sure you agree).

At the same time, I know from painful personal experience that the two or three 'key dimensions' are pretty arbitrary, having been whittled down from a much longer list of axiomatic axes and selected because they somehow seem to 'work' better than the others (all of which have been tinkered with at length). The conceptual distinction between adjoining cells is often infinitesimal, though a resonant name can help disguise the fact (dog, star, question mark and equivalent mixed metaphors preferred). What's more, a great deal of shoehorning, massaging and general matrix manipulation is usually necessary to ensure that the field fits neatly into a multidimensional mould (it's a bit like packing a parachute, tucking a tent into its container or trying to close an over-stuffed suitcase). And, when the framework is complete, there's the inevitable retrospective root through the literature in order to demonstrate its veracity, to find evidence to support the structure – gimcrack, jerry-built and decidedly rickety though it is.

Still, they look kinda neat on the page, students find them easy to remember at exam time and, as the theoretical Tonka toys of marketing's child minders, they provide endless hours of innocent fun for hyperactive executives on short courses, day release programmes and damn-the-expenses training weekends.

This infantile allusion may be trite but is not accidental, since I suspect that my love–hate relationship with matrices is upbringing related. One of my earliest childhood memories, alongside misappropriating my sister's bottle of Milupa, involves the box-rich ritual of shopping for shoes. After the incomparable pre-purchase experience of having my petite feet measured by the everyone-knows-what-it-is-but-no-one-knows-what-it's-called Brannock Device[15] – in all its chrome and black metal glory – my proud, if less than prudent, parents allowed their only son to carry the package containing his first pair of C. & J. Clark's finest. The silly boy, needless to say, absent-mindedly left it behind in Woolworth's cafeteria, where the family had paused to partake of a post-shopping sundae.

The horror, the horror . . .

As a raw recruit to the research regiment, what's more, my inaugural marketing patrol comprised a journey to the heart of shoe-shopping darkness. Amongst other fascinating footwear factoids, such as the infallibility of 'nice shoes' as a chat-up line,[16] this admittedly inept investigation revealed the enormous importance shoppers attach to shoe boxes. Now, everyone knows that shoes themselves are sexy, foxy and freighted with meaning,[17] but it transpires that the boxes are no less significant. Buying shoes without shoe boxes bespeaks cheapness of Scroogesque proportions. In fact, their absence is associated with ill-fitting, Day-Glo plastic trainers that are not only unbreakable, with all the associated agonies of chaffed heels, constricted toes and brutalized bunions, but when worn contrive to make one's feet look elephantine at best or Coco the Clownish at worst.

Shoe boxes, conversely, are redolent of superior taste, money well spent and, above all, *newness*, the fact that the shoes have never been worn by anyone else. The wisp of protective tissue paper is particularly important in this regard, since it connotes virginity, as does the pristineness of the leather behind the toe-cap (creasing or puckering are tell-tale signs of violation, penetration and other people's sweaty feet).[18] And, while few people are shoe box collectors or fetishists, many hold on to the receptacles after purchase, employ them as part of their wardrobe organizing system and, finally, use the containers, coffin-like, to dispose of old shoes when new ones arrive. This may strike some readers as a bit bizarre, not to say barking, but it is a fact that footwear manufacturers who have tried to eliminate boxes as a sop to environmental conservation have met with considerable consumer resistance.[19]

Boxes are not just for Christmas.

Singular though it is, this shoe box fixation is not unique. Many people, so it seems, have an inordinate fondness for boxes, all sorts of boxes.[20] A quick trawl through the Internet bags any number of box-buyers – antique biscuit tins are especially popular – and a visit to your friendly, neighbourhood electronic bookstore reveals countless volumes written for collectors of Chinese boxes, tenders of window boxes, installers of Windows boxes and manufacturers of cardboard boxes (anyone for the Proceedings of the Packaging Society?). Some enthusiasts have even published billets-doux to boxes, such as *Inconspicuous Consumption* by Paul Lukas.[21] This rhapsody to brandname reliquaries includes a paean to Pringles, a panegyric to the packaging for Glide dental floss and a lovestruck dithyramb to a disused safety-deposit box. In *Quintessence*, the cultural commentators Betty Cornfeld and Owen Edwards wax lyrical about the boxes for Ohio Blue Tip Kitchen Matches, Barnum's Animal Crackers and, inevitably, the timeless Tupperware caskets.[22] The history of 'best dressed' boxes, bottles and containers is covered in Ralph and Terry Kovel's compellingly titled *The Label Made Me Buy It!*[23] And the classic *Cult Objects*, by design guru Deyan Sudjic, includes a fulsome to the point of effusive tribute to cigar boxes.

'Inside the humidor,' Sudjic soliliquizes,[24] 'those colourful wooden boxes, decorated as gaudily as an ambassador's state uniform and sealed with documents that look as solemn as a blue chip share certificate, are piled up with all the loving care of bars of bullion. Once you breach that barrier, you find enough tissue paper inside the box to stock an entire counter at the average Comecon department store, along with slivers of wood to separate the ranks of cigars from each other. There may even be an individual aluminium torpedo tube as a further protective screen, followed by the *pièce de résistance*, the band around the cigar itself . . . Throughout this three act performance, a sense of quality and connoisseurship has been steadily built up from the expectations established by the teasingly slow process of discarding layer after layer of packaging. This, and not plain raw cost, is what makes a cigar a luxury, and a ritual not just a product.'

Box-buffery attains its pinnacle in *The Total Package*, a tribute to totemic commercial containers, from the flat box revolution in the 1850s to the recent 'long CD box' controversy amongst recorded-music retailers.[25] According to Hine, key container marketing milestones include: the first breakfast cereal box, introduced by Quaker Oats in 1884; the Uneeda biscuit box, which completely transformed the cracker-barrel business; Gerhard Mennen's tamper-proof talcum powder in 'the box that locks'; the Kleenex tissues box, which languished on the shelves of general stores until the pop-up, serv-a-tissue system was developed in the 1930s; the redesign of Marlboro cigarettes in 1955, with its revolutionary 'flip-top-box'; and the mesmeric concentric circles of the Tide detergent container, which was enthusiastically endorsed by many motivation researchers during the Hidden Persuaders heyday. Doubtless it was responsible for the in-store 'hypnoidal trance' reported by our old mucker, James Vicary.

This fascination with boxes, furthermore, extends far beyond the commercial sphere. When it comes to popular culture, one doesn't have to go too far before crashing into containers of all sorts. Apart from the aptly named 'box', with its attendant array of black-boxed attachments (video, satellite, DVD, etc.), television is replete with receptacles.[26] From the golden age of *Camberwick Green* (with its clockwork musical-box-based prelude), through the gone but not forgotten test card (with its noughts and crosses emblazoned blackboard), to gamy game shows like *Celebrity Squares* and the primordial *Take Your Pick* (with its avuncular compere, chronologically challenged contestants and recondite catchphrase, 'Take the Money or Open the Box'), containers have been a constant feature of our television sets.[27]

When it comes to movies, moreover, how can anyone forget the Coen Brothers' *Barton Fink*, where we are left in agonizing doubt about the contents of psycho-killer John Goodman's cardboard box? Or what about that little green box in *Still of the Night*, a sub-Hitchcockian (but still pretty scary) shocker starring Roy Scheider and Meryl Streep? Or, then again, there's the box at the end of *Seven*, which brought the wrath of Brad down on a deadly sinner. Or, if a fairly catholic interpretation of the phenomenon is permitted, consider the celebrated container in *The Cabinet of Dr. Caligari*, that much-cited if rarely watched celebration of 1920s German Expressionism; or *The Music Box*, Laurel and Hardy's finest comic incarnation as piano delivery persons; or the attaché case containing who knows what in *Pulp Fiction* (a Big Kahuna Burger, perhaps?); or, indeed, *The Matrix*, Keanu Reeves's religious allegory-cum-spiritual self-help guide.[28]

Can *Marketing by The Matrix* be far away?

Art and literature are no less bitten by the box bug. With regard to the former, one immediately thinks of Andy Warhol's Brillo boxes, Donald Judd's stainless steel containers, Corban Walker's neo-minimalist box-alikes, Joseph Cornell's creepy wooden coffins filled with photos of fake parrots, phials of pharmaceuticals and fading movie stars, Marcel Duchamp's *Boite-en-valise* ('Box in a suitcase'), each one containing an original artwork or *objet trouvé* of some kind, and that frankly box-fixated, Beuys-fixated, artistic collective known as Fluxus.[29] Literary examples include: *Granny Dan*, one of Danielle Steel's recent blockbusters, based upon the protagonist's discovery of a secret box belonging to her grandmother; B.S. Johnston's 1969 'novel in a box', which comes in 27 loose-leaf sections to be read in any order; Kurt Vonnegut's *Bagombo Snuff Box*, an anthology of the ex-marketing-man's early short stories; *The Trumpet-Major*, Thomas Hardy's veritable boxfest, a book literally chock-a-block-a-boxes; and, just in case you think I've forgotten, there's the plethora of biscuit tins which punctuate the Joycean corpus, from *A Portrait* to *Finnegan's Wake*.[30]

As for those desert island redoubtables, the Bible and Shakespeare's *Complete Works*, the good book is bunged with boxes, most notably the Ark of the Covenant, the sealed containers in Revelation, the carefully wrapped gifts of the three wise men, the five foolish virgins, who paid a very heavy price for their empty vessels and, naturally, Noah's Ark ('ark', as you know, being Hebrew for 'box' or 'chest'). Shakespeare, similarly, is stuffed with chalices, crucibles, cauldrons, crocks and compotes, not least in that Cranfield-certified monument to marketing, *The Merchant of Venice*, with its three – count 'em – casket scenes. Mind you, how anyone could fall for the gold or silver caskets, with their patently false inscriptions, is completely beyond me. It *had* to be the lead casket. Don't these people go to the movies, watch soap operas or read fairy tales?

Fairy stories and myths, now that you mention it, are society's secret vault of virtual vessels. Pandora's Box is perhaps the best-known mythical container and, indeed, is particularly pertinent to the marketing condition.[31] As every schoolkid and Greek geek knows, the multi-talented Pandora (meaning all-gifted) was offered to and accepted by Epimetheus, despite the advice of his brother Prometheus, who cautioned against gods bearing gifts. Charged with the task of constructing man and his world, Epimetheus stashed all the potentially noxious substances in a secret box, which the ever-curious Pandora proceeded to open without permission. A multitude of plagues, both physical (gout, colic, rheumatism, etc.) and psychic (envy, spite, revenge and the like), escaped before she could replace the lid, leaving only hope at the bottom of the box. And hope, as Father Ted constantly reminds us, is what marketers ultimately purvey, albeit in our postmodern, post-history, post-human, post-traumatic stress disordered world, hopeless hope is as close as we come.

Equally exemplary is 'The Tinder-box', Hans Christian Andersen's first and, if not exactly his most famous, certainly his fame-establishing, fairy tale.[32] In fact, it comprises a cornucopia of containers within containers and contains a moral about materialism, for good measure. Thus the eponymous tinderbox is contained within a hollow stump of an oak tree, which also contains a chamber illuminated by one hundred lamps and three ante-rooms containing boxes of brass, silver and gold coins respectively. Naturally, the soldier fills up every available receptacle – knapsack, boots, hat and what have you – with plunder and proceeds to squander it in the nearest town on clothing, entertainments, fine wines, palatial apartments and fair-weather friends ('who told him every day that he was an excellent creature, a perfect gentleman; and all this the soldier liked to hear'). It was only when he was down on his uppers, living in a grimy garret and all his new-found friends had long since taken flight ('for, of course, they could not go up so many pair of stairs for his sake') that he discovered the secret of the tinderbox . . . which of course you all remember.

Don't you?

Boxes are no less integral to the world of science, pseudo-science and magic. With regard to the hard sciences, one's heart goes out to Schrödinger's Cat, the metaphorical moggie placed inside a sealed box and exposed (or not, as the case may be) to a dose of radioactive-decay-triggered poison gas. The uncertainty surrounding kitty's condition – simultaneously dead and alive – is considered analogous to the Copenhagen interpretation of reality at the quantum level.[33] Similarly, the pseudo-science of psychology is knee deep in boxes – Thorndike's, Skinner's, Boden's etc. – as is the even more pseudo science of economics.[34] Think of all those black box models of pseudo-markets and pseudo-consumers, let alone the hubristic manoeuvrings of Prediction Company, who developed a black box model of Wall Street's workings, lost millions of dollars for their trouble and, when things went pear-shaped, treated the company's creditors to a philosophical shrug.[35]

While we're on the subject of philosophical shrugs, I suppose I should mention Wittgenstein's famous box-based brain-befuddler in the *Tractatus*.[36] As you'll recall, this was an attempt to illustrate the relativity of language by supposing that everyone possessed a box containing something called a 'beetle'. However, the rules of the language game prevent each participant from peeking into anyone else's box, which means that our only referent for all the presumed 'beetles' is the specimen in our own possession. Providing, of course, that our box really does contain a beetle, because we could well be bluffing each other . . .

Where's J.B.S. Haldane when you need him?

Moving swiftly on, boxes are also big in magical milieux, whether it be stage magicians akin to the Davenport Brothers, or good old-fashioned soothsayers like Joanna Southcott. The former were famous for their Victorian 'spirit cabinet', which produced all sorts of phantasmal apparitions, such as ringing bells, rattling tambourines and disembodied hands, while the brothers were securely tethered inside. Until, that is, a psychic from Liverpool tied the knots too tight, which produced the unforeseen circumstance of an audience angrily demanding its money back. Still, the Davenport cabinet has been a staple of stage magicians in the 150-odd years since the Brothers first devised it – Harry Houdini, for instance, openly acknowledged its influence on his work – though Penn and Teller have latterly made a career out of revealing the magic cabinet's secrets.[37]

At the prophetic, as opposed to the performing, end of the spectral spectrum, Joanna Southcott is best remembered for her false pregnancy (she claimed, at the age of sixty-four, to have been impregnated by the Messiah); her time-share in Paradise scam, whereby she sold salvation certificates, guaranteed to grant the holder a post-Second-Coming place at God's right hand (although the final trump signally failed to sound on the due date of 25 December 1814); and, not least, for the antics of her unhinged followers, principally the incomparable John Wroe. A bearded hunchback who made two well publicized attempts to walk on water, with predictable results, Wroe sought to restore his rapidly sinking reputation by the somewhat extreme expedient of public circumcision. More pertinently perhaps, Southcott also assembled a mysterious box containing the secret of world peace, the millennium and eternal happiness (not public circumcision, surely), which can only be opened in the presence of all twenty-four bishops of the Church of England.[38]

While we're waiting, it is worth noting that science, pseudo-science and magic are not entirely separate entities, at least not where boxes are concerned. To the contrary, all three come together in the weird and wonderful world of psychoanalysis. Reluctant as I am to subject modern marketing to a psychoanalytical reading, its fixation with boxes does suggest some sort of scholarly child abuse, possibly precipitated by its exposure to psychoanalytical constructs – courtesy of Dirty Doctor Dichter – in the early post-war period. Certainly, its marked reluctance to entertain psychoanalytical perspectives in the aftermath of Motivation

Research is suggestive of some kind of post-Packard neurosis or repression to the very depths of the commercial unconscious. But when one considers that Freud's own father was a marketing man (as indeed were Jacques Lacan's and Alfred Alder's), an Oedipal interpretation of our discipline's figural obsessions is very hard to resist.

In his breakthrough text, *The Interpretation of Dreams*, Sigmund Freud specifically deals with boxes and containers of various kinds, contending that they represent symbols of the female reproductive organs, as do all hollow objects such as ships, rooms, ovens, cupboards, wardrobes and what have you.[39] He expatiates, moreover, on the dream of a woman patient concerning the English word 'box' and the various ways in which it can be translated into German. These include *Schachtel* [case], *Loge* [box at the theatre], *Kasten* [chest], *Ohrfeige* [box on the ear] and *Buchse*, the last being a vulgar term for female genitalia, just as 'box' is in English. It is striking, however, that the box in his patient's dream was actually a coffin – again the colloquialism is apt – especially in light of Freud's later career, when the death drive (thanatos) superseded sexuality (eros) in his preferred conceptual schema.

To be sure, one doesn't need to subscribe to Freudian precepts to appreciate that boxes' traditional association with birth and death (however crudely expressed) is of considerable symbolic significance. Boxes occupy a highly salient place in most people's lives – how many residences in the western world don't have several decorative containers on display, I wonder? – associated as they are with traumatic events like moving house and joyous occasions like the giving and receiving of gifts. In this respect, it is noteworthy that the voluminous marketing and consumer research literature on gift-giving makes little or no mention of the important part played by packages and parcels (sex and death are also repressed by marketing researchers but that is neither here nor there).[40] This literary lack is highly suggestive from a psychoanalytical standpoint and indicates an obsessional side to marketing's personality. Most would agree, would they not, that Freud's obsessional 'type' is as good an encapsulation of the 'modern' marketing persona as one is likely to get – preoccupied with order, control, accuracy, neatness, reliability and precision. Obsessives, what is more, are particularly partial to system building (models, frameworks, general theories of marketing, etc.), dualistic or tripartite thinking (e.g. product/service, industrial/consumer, art/science, STP, three eras schema, three dichotomies model) and supreme self-confidence coupled with profound self-loathing (cf. the perennial dialectic of 'marketing is everything' versus 'marketing is dead').

An obsessive faux-Freudian might be tempted to wonder about marketing's inordinate fondness for figures containing boxes and arrows. Now, I'm not for a moment contending that the figurative practices of our field represent sublimated sexuality, although Sigmund did suggest

Figure 6.3   Victoria's Secret Box

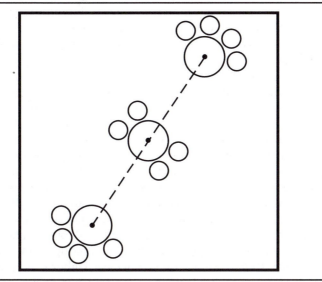

that unrequited libido was responsible for all art and literature. There is no doubt, however, that if marketing's signature illustrations were discovered daubed on the wall of a cave, any passing archaeologist would consider them fertility symbols of the resident, pre-literate society and indicative, possibly, of some kind of strange, upper Pleistocene sexual cult. Ridiculous you say, yet it is worth noting that very few female marketing scholars actually include boxes and arrows diagrams in their publications – formulaic marketing textbooks excepted – whereas symbols of engorgement, sometimes with spheres attached, are not unusual. Consider Figure 6.3 by Elizabeth C. Hirschman. Additional comment is superfluous, I'm sure you agree.

Tempting though it is to reduce everything to polymorphous perversity, there's more to psychoanalysis than the phallus (not much more, admittedly, but enough to be getting along with). As Carl Jung, that connoisseur of the collective unconscious and the occult, makes perfectly clear, boxes, squares, cubes, grids and all the rest possess considerable supernatural significance.[41] Rectangles resonate. In the esoteric tradition, boxes and squares are associated with reality, with the earth, with flesh and the body, with the maternal womb, with the here and now, as opposed to the circle which traditionally symbolizes the spirit, the cosmos, the heavenly father and the hereafter.[42] The four cardinal points, the four seasons, the four elements (fire, earth, air, water), the four humours (choleric, melancholic, sanguine, phlegmatic), the four bodily fluids (blood, gall, black gall, phlegm) and the four stages of life (childhood, youth, maturity, old age) are all predicated on the 2×2 matrix, as indeed are the 'quaternities' that characterize Jung's celebrated personality 'types' (sensation, thinking, feeling, intuition). His principal symbolic archetype, the mandala, is also rectangular, though its power primarily derives from an ability to square the circle by combining both primordial figures.

Higher-order matrices are no less pertinent to the esoteric tradition.[43] Known as 'magic squares', these are assigned to the planets in Chaldean order (3×3 = Saturn, 4×4 = Jupiter, 5×5 = Mars, 6×6 = the Sun, 7×7 = Venus, 8×8 = Mercury, 9×9 = the Moon) and, hence, are integral to various forms of astrological divination. More importantly perhaps, they exemplify the fundamental alchemical premise, *omnes in omnibus*. In other words, everything is in everything else; that the most profound metaphysical insights can be obtained from the merest grain of sand. As above, so below. This idea, first adumbrated by Hermes Trismegistos in the second century BCE, and subscribed to by countless premodern mystics, magicians, theologians and philosophers, such as Gregory the Great, Hildegard of Bingen, Agrippa von Nettesheim, Jakob Boehme, Robert Fludd, Emmanuel Swedenborg and the imperishable Paracelsus, is premised on the presumed parallelism of humanity and the heavens, the one and the many, the particular in the general, the part and the whole, the microcosm and the macrocosm. Thus, any individual (the microcosm) carries an entire universe (the macrocosm) within him or herself and is not only subject to planetary influence, but made up of the same four elements as the cosmos itself.[44]

It may surprise many would-be marketing scientists to discover that their matrixmania is actually based on magical precept, ancient wisdom and cogitations of pre-Christian seers. They may be shocked when they realize that casting a strategic grid over an individual organization is nothing less than a necromantic act of divination. They may be dismayed by their unwitting reliance on the primordial principle, *omnes in omnibus*, the purportedly congruent relationship of business organism and strategic universe. They may even be outraged when forced to recognize that their belief in the scientific rigour of strategic matrices is just as irrational as that of those who subscribe to the supernatural rationale of magic squares.

Such concerns, however, are unwarranted and, in certain respects, misplaced. Marketing and magic have always been closely related, as we noted in Chapter 3. The original Magi were a tribe of pre-Zoroastrian shamans whose descendants practised 'everyday' magic and marketed their spells, charms, amulets and occult concoctions on the peripheries of the ancient Athenian agora. Many premodern practitioners of the mantic arts were exceptionally able marketers, in the P.T. Barnum tradition.[45] What's more, the seminal twentieth-century text on non-western magical traditions, Sir James Frazer's *The Golden Bough*, has been aptly described as 'one of the best books ever on advertising'.[46] True, his tripartite model of historical development – magic, religion, science – has not stood the test of time (but then again neither has our own tripartite schema: production-orientated/sales-orientated/marketing-orientated), yet his distinction between contiguous and imitative magic is still evident in, respectively, celebrity endorsements, where the product benefits by its adjacency to the celebrity's charisma, and thaumaturgic marketing practices, where one thing symbolizes or stands in for another (company logos, brand names, the metonymy of 'Marketing Myopia', etc.).

In a similar vein, advertisers routinely inform us of the miraculous properties of products and services, often by means of a cavalcade of otherworldly characters (talking dogs, cartoon camels, jolly green giants et al.). Consumers buy the bewitching transformational capabilities of cosmetics, perfume, cigarettes, motor cars, clothing, multi-vitamins and so forth. The manifold magic kingdoms of hyperreal estate have held countless children (Disneyland) and adults (Las Vegas) spellbound by their amazing disappearing-dollar tricks. And we are regularly treated to 'fantastic', 'incredible', 'extraordinary' or 'superhuman' price reductions, which have to be seen to be believed. The marketing literature, furthermore, is replete with magic spells, incantations, hocus-pocus, abracadabras and intellectual hey prestos. We have 4Ps, five forces, 7 Ss and, Heaven help us, 30Rs. The principal journals are anthologies of numerological rumination – the numbers and equations don't actually 'mean' anything, though they signify a great deal to other adepts of academic alchemy – and we are all required to believe in the transmutational powers of the modern marketing concept, the philosopher's stone of commercial life.

Above all, however, we have our black magic boxes, white magic matrices and stage magic squares. The rectangular objects that adorn the pages of principles textbooks are not only representations in themselves, but they represent marketing in the round. They are a form of imitative magic, insofar as they symbolize or stand for 'marketing', as such. Thanks to generations of master matrix masons, we have constructed a Chartres of cubes, a Stonehenge of squares, a Babel of boxes, and one suspects that it is not going to be blown over by a puff of postmodern wind. Like the poor, like death, like taxes, like Levitt, like Kotler, like Baker, boxes will always be with us. *And so they should be.* Matrices *mean* marketing to the wider academic community and marketing matrices are freighted with meaning, the better-known ones especially. They are repositories of marketing significance, reliquaries of marketing research, reminders of marketing miracles.[47] For marketers, matrices are conceptual equivalents of the 'memory boxes' (mausoleums of family memories) and time capsules (mausoleums of future memories) that were all the rage at the recent millennial transition.[48] In many ways, they represent the acme of retromarketing – inasmuch as matrices collapse past, present and future into a convenient theoretical package. Just as the medieval heretic Cosmas Indicopleustes claimed that he possessed the universe in a box, so too the marketing universe is squeezed into an eclectic collection of containers.

Marketing may be the Tupperware of thought, but its manifold mantic matrices have a major problem. For all their ubiquity, for all their symbolic significance, for all their primordial power, no one really believes in them any more. Akin to the much-reviled 4Ps, they have become figures of fun, metaphors for old-fashioned modernist marketing and attendant APIC absurdities. Hence, the recent slew of ironic, knowing, playful, para-postmodern matrices, such as those by Piercy, Hackley and Mintzberg.[49] For some mainstream matrixomanes, admittedly, the postmodernists are largely to blame for this latter-day Boxer Rebellion. But the fact of the matter is that postmodernism is not opposed to matrices as such. Many leading postmodern lights, including Fredric Jameson, Michel Foucault and Roland Barthes, have employed boxes, grids, squares and suchlike for pedagogic purposes.[50] It follows, therefore, that marketing's recent crisis of representation is *not* directly related to postmodernism. The representations themselves are the root cause of the problem. No one takes matrices seriously, subscribes to them or constructs them without a self-conscious feeling of futility. Even the most earnest marketing scientists now look askance at some of the figures that were once put forward as the future of our field (Bagozzi's blizzard of boxes and arrows springs instantly to mind). The real difficulty facing today's rapidly diminishing stockpile of boxphiles is making marketers believe in matrices once again, of making the unbelievable believable. A Barnum of boxes, a Reichenbach of rectangles, a Sequah of grid squares is called for.

Disinclined as I am to don the mantle of matrix magus, or be held responsible for a revival of retro boxes and arrows diagrams, it may nevertheless be possible to unpack, dismantle and reconstruct them in an attempt to restore matrices' intellectual status. In order to do so, however, it is necessary to reveal the hidden secret of the black magic box. Obviously, it is not boxes *per se*. Boxes are so commonplace that they have lost their ability to entrance or enchant. Let's be honest, 2 × 2s are the 2 × 4s of marketing scholarship. One suspects, rather, that the secret of the black magic box is secrecy itself. Secrecy and its motivational shadow, curiosity, are very powerful forces, as any number of myths and legends inform us.[51] Apart from the unfortunate Pandora, noted earlier, Lot's unfortunate wife, Bluebeard's unfortunate wife, the *Pentamerone*'s unfortunate Princess Marchetta and the doubly unfortunate Psyche, who not only lost Cupid but opened the forbidden box containing Persephone's beauty, are just some of the cats killed, or almost killed, by curiosity.

What's more, we only have to peruse the representational practices of big-name marketing organizations to appreciate that intrigue, enigma and riddle-me-re are an important part of their success.[52] Consider the 'secret' recipes that help purvey all sorts of comestibles – Coca-Cola, Heinz Varieties, Kentucky Fried Chicken, Mrs Field's Cookies, Kellogg's Frosties, Grey Poupon Mustard, Brach's Chocolate Cherries, Campari, Carlsberg, Chartreuse, Benedictine, Angostura Bitters, Lee & Perrins Worcestershire Sauce, et al. – to say nothing of cosmetics companies (the secret of youthfulness), proprietary medicines manufacturers (the secret of longevity) and package tour operators (secret hide-aways a speciality). Consider the gift-giving business, which is predicated on secrets, surprises and eager anticipation, as is consumer desire. Period. Consider consumers' postmodern partiality for mazes, code-breaking and best-selling secrets of the ancients.[53] Consider the teaser campaigns, advertising soap operas and who'll-be-the-lucky-winner promotions that are launched day and daily by Machiavellian marketers. Consider the self-help marketing gurus, who claim to possess the secrets of success, leadership, efficiency, effectiveness, time management or corporate well-being. Consider the modern marketing paradigm, which owed much of its post-war appeal to the mistaken assumption that marketers could make people buy, despite themselves, and were blessed with all sorts of magical, manipulative, motivation-researched powers, the mysterious secrets of which were in the possession of the freemasons of Madison Avenue, the Kotlerite Knights Templar, the Levittite Illuminati.

Marketing's dirty secret, in sum, is secrecy itself and the fundamental problem with strategic marketing management is that its emblematic figures lack mystery, lack intrigue, lack inscrutability, lack the all-important peek-a-boo element. Everything is a bit too obvious, transparent, straightforward, unenigmatic, uninteresting. True, this excessive clarity is partly due to the two-dimensional nature of such representations. There is no 'inside', as it were, to arouse the onlooker's curiosity.[54] But it is also attributable to the banalities typically inscribed in the individual cells (cost/differentiation/focus or whatever). The ultimate undecidability of language leaves some scope for imaginative interpretation, admittedly, and it can be contended that the continuing appeal of the Boston matrix is related to its plurivalent, metaphorical contents (the descriptor 'dog', for example, carries all sorts of canine connotations). Yet there remains considerable scope for upping marketing's enigmatic ante. Mystifying matrices, baffling boxes, recondite receptacles, puzzling portrayals, furtive figures, deceptive diagrams and secret squares are sorely needed. As Chadwick rightly observes,

> The urge to discover secrets is deeply ingrained in human nature; even the least curious mind is roused by the promise of sharing knowledge withheld from others . . . Most of us are driven to sublimate this urge by the solving of artificial puzzles devised for our entertainment – detective stories or crossword puzzles cater for the majority – [but] some are fortunate enough to find a calling which consists in the [creation and] solution of mysteries.[55]

Figure 6.4   Stephen's Secret Strategic Square

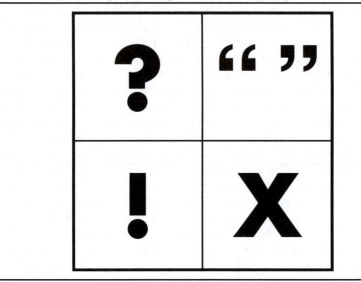

Figure 6.5   Brown's Boxbuster

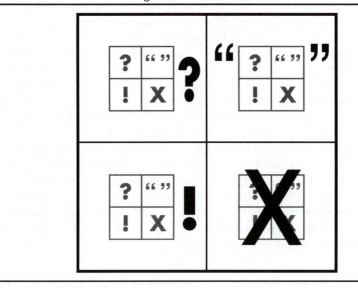

In an admittedly amateurish attempt to start the crystal ball rolling, I hereby give you Stephen's Secret Strategic Square, which can be applied to the positioning of each and every marketing artefact (Figure 6.4). It artfully, if I say so myself, combines intrigue (?) and the extraordinary (!) with irony ("") and doubt (X). What's more, it throws in a necessary touch of allusive, postmodern arcana (the cross, *sous rature*, Greimas, etc.) and is sufficiently vague (sorry, metaphorical) to prove meaningful in most marketing situations, especially when applied to strategic matrices themselves (! = BCG, ? = Ansoff, "" = Figure 6.1, X = SSSS). It can even be adapted to strategic matrix strategic matrices, as Figure 6.5 demonstrates.

Promise not to tell anyone, however. It's our little secret.

Replanning Marketing: If Ever a Whiz of a Swiz There Was

I have in my hand a piece of paper. It is, admittedly, a low-grade, badly printed, garishly coloured piece of paper. But it is an important piece of paper, for all that. I refer, of course, to the current *Innovations* catalogue. Now, for those of you who are unfamiliar with the ways of the marketing world, *Innovations* is the epitome of mail order art, the Sistine Chapel of specialogues, *The Night Watch* of newspaper inserts, *Les Demoiselles d'Avignon* of direct sales. It is nothing less than the ultimate referent of consumer society, a document that distils everything modern marketing stands for. As the zenith of new-and-improved, up-to-the-minute, I-have-seen-the-future-and-it-works, *Innovations* retails all manner of totally unnecessary, instantly obsolescent, cabinet-clogging, cupboard-cluttering, garage-filling gadgets.[1] These range from unsightly-hair removers ('banish unwanted hair – forever!) and tongue-scraping kits ('fresh breath guaranteed!') to automatic video rewinders ('protect your delicate recording heads!') and lawn-enhancing trainers ('with spiked soles to aerate as you mow!'). The sort of object, in short, that one should never have ordered in the first place but remain reluctant to throw out just-in-case. Doubly reluctant, since we know that the just-in-case scenario only ever arises once the wretched thing has finally been binned.

The historical document in my possession, however, demonstrates that the Innovations corporation, a hitherto impregnable citadel of *au courant* and *dernier cri* of the *à la mode*, has finally seen the retrospective light.[2] The company's latest offering respectfully invites browsers, buyers and sad bastards everywhere to 'preserve your past for future generations' by means of a personal time capsule hewn from the finest non-biodegradable polypropylene. Or, for more discerning archaeologists of the future, a top-of-the-range, Smithsonian Institution approved version is also available, at only £49.99 (delivery extra).

Create *your own* piece of Y2K History! This deluxe time capsule is engineered from solid brass made in the UK, with machined endpieces that seal it so efficiently it can be buried for years. But it is such a beautiful artefact in its own right, it's highly unlikely you'll want to bury this canister for the edification of a future archaeologist – far better to store it safely in your home! The 19cm (7½") tube comes with a set of scrolls, a traditional dip pen and calligraphy ink, enabling you to chronicle your personal profile, family tree and a diary of significant millennial events together with photos and other items of memorabilia. The completed scrolls slide into the capsule, neatly tied with a ribbon. After screwing in the ends, thread the leather tie and secure it with a wax seal bearing the imprint of the Millennium Seal (supplied). Gift boxed.

Innovations' conversion to the retro cause may well be a temporary aberration, an outbreak of *fin-de-siècle* fever brought on by the late millennial transition. Once-in-a-lifetime opportunities to offload mountains of memorabilia are just too good to miss, even if it means adopting a retrospective perspective until such times as the coast is clear and normal new-and-improved service can be resumed. True, some people might wonder whether millennium bug backpacks, slippers, corkscrews, toilet rolls, cocktail sausage sticks and limited edition refrigerator defrosting sprays are an entirely appropriate way of commemorating the 2000th anniversary of the birth of Christ,[3] but buylessness has never been next to godliness, as we noted in Chapter 3. Others might reasonably counter that as old is new to *Innovations*, cutting a slice of the time-was market is entirely in keeping with the company's progressive positioning and presumably forward-thinking mission statement, whatever that is. One suspects, however, that if the stuff sells in sufficient quantities, the mighty marketing machine that is Innovations Inc. will become a permanent player in the past times game. Can a *Retrovations* specialogue be far away?

While we await that happy day, it is worth reflecting on the principal problem *Retrovations* faces. Namely, predicting the size of the market for yesteryeuch. Granted, the demand for papyrus toilet roll, retro-refrigerator spray, solar-powered sundials and lawn-aerating sandals must be absolutely enormous. But, would you want to bet the company on it or remortgage the house to underwrite the retailing of retro tat? Prediction, however, is where modern marketing comes into its own. If Kotlerite marketing had to be summarized in a single word, that word would probably be 'futuristic'. Analysing emerging opportunities and threats, assessing corporate competencies and capabilities, envisioning alternative possibilities and scenarios, and developing customer-capturing and -retaining strategies comprise the gospel according to St Philip. Modern marketing is about pursuing the future, predicting the future, planning the future, precipitating the future. Marketing plans, in many respects, are the acme of the APIC paradigm. Granted, marketing planning only warrants a single chapter in most mainstream marketing textbooks – although many specialist tomes exist[4] – yet by intimating that the future is understandable, forecastable and, above all, manageable, marketing planning epitomizes the essential rationality that resides at the heart of the modern, scientific worldview.

Indeed, the briefest perusal of marketing planning primers reveals that they are more than mere microcosms of modernity, they are the Torah of our times, the Upanishads of consumer society, the twenty-first-century Septuagint. Consider the list of questions that marketing plans typically seek to address: where are we now and how did we get here? what is the future? where do we want to go? how do we get there? how much will it cost? how can progress be measured? These make 'what is the meaning of life?' seem like a starter question in *Who Wants to be a Millionaire?* What's more, the proponents of marketing planning claim that finding the answers to such imponderables is no big deal, a mere bagatelle, easy-peasy-tickle-my-kneesy. Marketing planning, we are repeatedly informed, is 'incredibly simple', 'straightforward in itself', 'simple common sense', 'logical and straightforward', 'a relatively straightforward matter' (would that all marketing matters were 'simple' or 'straightforward'). So much so, that the format of marketing plans is standardized to the point of formulaic. As Dibb et al. patiently explain to us, the perfect plan should contain precisely ten sections, plus appendices, ranging from 2–3 pages on product/market background, to a whopping 8–12 page SWOT analysis, not forgetting 1–2 pages on financial implications.[5] The planning process itself is no less stereotyped, though the number of 'stages' varies between seven and twelve, depending on the academic authority concerned. All, however, seek to set goals, review situations, formulate strategies, allocate resources and monitor outcomes.

This is all very commendable, I'm sure you agree, but it is complete moonshine. You know, it is nothing short of staggering that an academic discipline predicated on time-steeped principles of segmentation and differentiation should strive to pour each and every marketing plan into the same mechanistic mould. Given the stupendous differences in organizational structure, culture, size, history, technical sophistication and competitive circumstances, to say nothing of sectoral, regional, national and international variations, this one-size-fits-all model of marketing planning seems a mite ambitious, some might say totalitarian. Mass marketing may be dead and buried, boys and girls, but mass marketing planning is very much alive and kicking.

If you won't take my word for it, I suggest you peruse the fourth edition of Malcolm McDonald's *Marketing Plans*, a compendious volume that has tripled in size since the first 200-page edition of 1984.[6] In the preface, McDonald modestly admits that hundreds of thousands – millions, surely! – of marketing practitioners have followed his 12-step programme of marketing planning. What can I say except that the

McDonaldization of contemporary society truly knows no bounds. But, even Ronald McDonald modifies his Big Macs from time to time and place to place. Not so Brother Malcolm, whose proprietary planning process is 'universally applicable'. 'Exactly the same framework', he cautions, 'should be used in all circumstances'.[7] Yes, friends, McDonald is more McDonaldized than McDonald's.

Perhaps the most incredible thing of all, however, is that the promulgators of marketing planning place so little store by what is clearly a complex, convoluted and context-dependent process. The putative writers of marketing plans are advised, in no uncertain terms, to keep it simple, to keep it short, to keep it succinct. And why? Because *the marketing plan will not be read in any event.* CEOs, top management and the like are much too busy to wade through written marketing plans. Anything more than one side of A4 is unacceptably long-winded. By all means spend the best part of a year concocting the thing; by all means recruit specialist marketing planners to produce the facts and figures; by all means run the raw data through sophisticated off-the-peg (or bespoke, if you must) marketing planning software. Just don't expect anyone to read the document. As for acting on its recommendations, what planet do you come from? Surely you must realize that there are all sorts of insurmountable barriers to implementation: political issues, resource constraints, and intractable organizational inertia, companies' inability or unwillingness to take the necessary decisions or make the necessary changes. It requires at least three years to inculcate a planning-orientated mindset, I'll have you know. It needs the wholehearted commitment of the chief executive, let me tell you. It is hampered, may I remind you, by the attendant jargon, which can be confusing to neophytes (though if they know what 'neophyte' means, they're hardly likely to be baffled by 'scenario').

Plans, in short, are easy. Planning is impossible.

The impossibility of planning should not surprise us, I suppose, since the one thing we can predict for certain is that the future is unpredictable. All sorts of forecasting techniques are readily available – from simple moving averages and straight-line extrapolation to the iterations of Delphi and agonizing dilemmas of game theory – but forecasting, frankly, is failure waiting to happen. Several histories of prediction are extant and, without exception, these reveal that futurology is futile, augury is impossible and confident expectations are sure to prove erroneous.[8] To cite but a single example, *The Year 2000* was one of the best-selling books of 1967, a *tour de force* of forecasting by the single most respected futurist of the time, Herman Kahn.[9] Amongst his one hundred predictions for the final third of the twentieth century, Kahn sagaciously anticipated complete control over the weather, individual flying platforms and the jet-powered car, permanently manned lunar installations, artificial moons for illuminating large areas at night, human hibernation for months (or years) at a time, and technologies to let people choose their dreams before going to sleep. According to Schnaars, however, less than 10% of Kahn's predictions proved correct, with another 15% partially correct, providing a degree of leniency is exercised in their evaluation.[10] Even the predictions that proved accurate, furthermore, tended to transpire in an unanticipated manner. The oceans, for example, were widely regarded as a potentially important resource in the 1960s – and so they have proved – but Kahn's prediction of underwater hotels, deep-sea farming and strip-mining operations have not exactly come to fruition.

Kahn's mistaken prognostications, of course, can be dismissed as an unfortunate artefact of the get up and go-go 1960s. There is no doubt that forecasts are more a reflection of the society that produces them than the occurrences they attempt to anticipate.[11] Thus, the scientistic futurists of the 1960s were obsessed with the space race; the soothsayers of the oil-fired 1970s focused on energy issues; the diviners of the materialistic 1980s majored on maintaining the existing order; and the retrospective seers of the 1990s reflected on past futures, concluding that tomorrow is not what it used to be. It would be wrong, however, to dismiss Herman Kahn as a crank, wild-eyed proselyte or prophesying profiteer. On the contrary, his consultancy firm, the Hudson Institute, was very highly regarded; its predictions were considered eminently reasonable, pretty much in line with the norms of the time; and they were enthusiastically embraced by the business community, government think-tanks and the like. In fact, a follow-up survey of 1,433 scientists and engineers revealed that the consulted experts endorsed most of Kahn's predictions, deeming only four out of one hundred unlikely ever to occur (physically non-harmful ways to overindulge, 'true' artificial intelligence, modification of the solar system and major modifications of the human species).

The Kahn-do era may be long gone but there is no shortage of contemporary fortune sellers. Faith Popcorn, John Naisbitt and Francis Fukuyama are just some of the leading brand names in what is now a $200 million industry.[12] However, lest we imagine that accuracy has increased since the we-have-the-technology-whoops-wrong-again 1960s – think of all that extra computer power and trend-spotting capability – the currently available evidence indicates otherwise. Take Faith Plotkin, a.k.a. Popcorn.[13] Her much-lauded prediction that the 1990s would be the decade of 'cocooning', a stock-up-and-stay-at-home society (hey, hibernation! – come back Herman, all is forgiven), was wildly mistaken (on second thoughts, Herm . . .). Unfortunately for Faith, 'going out' proved to be one of the defining trends of the late twentieth century (movie admissions up, museum visits up, eating out up, etc.). Her equally confident anticipation of a 'Decency Decade', dedicated to the three critical Es of Environment, Education and Ethics, also failed to transpire (environmental consciousness waning, education spending down, ethics pretty much the same). Indeed, a recent assessment of Faith Popcorn's record led one commentator to conclude that 'she is an old-fashioned scam artist, hoodwinking corporations and journalists'.[14] Another surmised that her success was attributable more to her training as a method actress and her extensive advertising copywriting experience – snappy slogans a speciality – than to the accuracy of her forecasts. 'Popcorn and Nostradamus,' he contends, 'have much more in common than perhaps *Fortune* realized when it called her the "Nostradamus of Marketing". Like Popcorn, Nostradamus changed his name for marketing purposes, Latinizing his former name, Notre Dame, to give it more scientific authority. They both influenced the powerful: he the medieval court, she the executive suite. They both captivated their clients with their writing styles: he with mysterious prose, she with catchy sound bites. They both succeeded in selling a lot of baloney to the naïve elite.'[15]

Way to go, Faith!

Now, few would deny that Faith Popcorn is the James Vicary of our times, but many might maintain that the failings of such high-profile prophets are several steps removed from the practicalities of everyday marketing planning. I would submit, however, that they are nothing of the kind, because marketing planning exercises are predicated on expectations of what will come to pass. And the problem with planning exercises, like all trend-spotting and entrails-sifting experiments in futurology, is that they are likely to prove mistaken. Certain, in fact, if Popcorn's erroneous prognostications form part of the scenario-developing process, as they clearly do in many retainer-disbursing corporations. What's more, the all too predictable failure of even the most carefully calculated predictions is openly acknowledged by the foremost champions of the marketing planning process.[16] The question, then, has to be asked: if the predictions on which the plan is predicated are sure to prove mistaken, why bother with planning at all?

Suffice it to say, the answers to this poser are many and varied. Perhaps the most common defence is a variant of our discipline's favourite truism: you-must-be-marketing-orientated. The problem, so this argument goes, has nothing to do with marketing planning as such, but with those pesky practitioners who are congenitally incapable of doing it properly.[17] Certainly, the evidence on this point is overwhelming. There is no doubt that companies *do* have serious trouble with marketing planning,[18] though it never seems to occur to the planners that planning itself might be part of the problem. As far as plan-mongers are concerned, planning is self-evidently 'a good thing', like apple pie, motherhood and patriotism. Unfortunately, the available empirical evidence indicates otherwise.[19] There is no irrefutable proof that planning is better than not-planning. On the contrary, it can be contended that too much planning leads to organizational ossification, bureaucratization and an inability to respond to evolving competitive circumstances. The fact that radical innovations, in sector after sector, unfailingly come from entrepreneurial outsiders should give planners pause for thought. Surely with all that environmental scanning, competitor analysis and finely tuned, carefully calibrated forecasting, they should be in a position to know what's coming.

'Fraid not.

Of course, the counter to this anti-planning position is yet another statement of the obvious. Namely, that planning is the prudent, the sensible and, above all, the *rational* thing to do. Rationality, in fact, figures especially prominently in discussions of strategic planning in general and marketing planning in particular. Once again, however, this is little more than a restatement of conventional wisdom, the unquestioned and unquestionable premises of the planning paradigm. But, the obvious question still has to be posed: what's so good about rationality? The rationale for rationality is often rationalized – rationality is, like, *rational*, know-wot-I-mean – but never made explicit or demonstrated by its exponents. Consequently, the case for adoption must be considered unproven according to its own self-imposed criteria. Unless, that is, they expect us to espouse rationality on the basis of irrational argument. And that would never do.

Surely, if the postmodern revolution of recent years has taught us anything, it is that rationality is not the be all and end all of intellectual endeavour.[20] Intuition, inspiration and imagination are just as important as analysis, planning and control, possibly more so. The left brain may not know what the right brain is doing but the left brain isn't always in the right. The two, to be sure, aren't mutually incompatible. One of the most striking things about the planning literature is the enormous emphasis it places on creativity and insight. They even have boxes labelled 'creative input' and 'insightful reflections' in their flowcharts! It's comforting to know that planners plan rationally for irrationality, that they can programme unprogrammability, that they control the uncontrollable, analyse the unanalysable and implement the unimplementable. The fact that less than 10% of their anticipated outcomes actually come to pass – a figure Tom Peters considers 'wildly inflated' – is neither here nor there.

Such criticisms have often been levelled at the planning community and, to be fair to them, planners have responded robustly to the attacks, albeit in a less than dispassionate manner. They accept that second-guessing the future is impossible, even in stable competitive contexts, and admit that scenario planning's record is not much better. Yet they maintain, nonetheless, that the process itself is useful. Irrespective of the actual outcome of the plans, which are sure to go belly up in any event, the act of thinking systematically about the future of an organization is eminently worthwhile. Again, this is incontestable, as most managerial platitudes are. However, it does *not* follow that reflecting on the future requires formal marketing planning, let alone the technocratic, bureaucratic and meeting-generating apparatus that goes with it. A stiff drink and comfy armchair will serve just as well. Not only is this more enjoyable and much less expensive, but it also avoids all the unseemly politicking, intra-organizational anguish and interpersonal conflict that formal marketing plans inevitably spawn.

Planning, in other words, is part of the problem, not the solution to strategy development, articulation and implementation. It stifles innovation, sidelines imagination and gives rise to me-too generic approaches, usually the low-cost option (since quality, service and analogous intangibles are more difficult to quantify).[21] More to the point, successful strategies emerge *despite* the machinations of marketing planners and their number-crunching, risk-avoiding, competitor-obsessed ilk. Indeed, they are often knee-jerk reactions to an immediate, almost inconsequential problem. It is only in retrospect that they are reinscribed – *post hoc*, *propter hoc* – as 'strategic' decisions. Thus, even in the most forward-looking, future-orientated sphere of marketing activity, retro rears its ever-present head. Not only do most five-year plans involve straightforward extrapolations of past trends, but the strategies that are actually pursued get labelled as such with hindsight.

Retrospection excepted, I'm not suggesting anything particularly radical here, merely regurgitating the anti-planning prejudices of the anti-planning fraternity. Yet despite the manifest and well-publicized shortcomings of planning, the plan-producing business continues on its merry way, seemingly unaffected by the 'environmental turbulence' surrounding the plan-construction industry (doubtless the planners have contingency plans for planning in anti-planning conditions).[22] After a brief hiatus in the seventies, when Stalinesque strategic plans fell out of favour, the market for marketing plans and their organizational progeny – sales plans, pricing plans, advertising plans, distribution plans, planning plans and the like – seems as healthy as ever.[23] This vitality might strike some sceptics as profoundly paradoxical, but it is incontestable proof that plans are not simply about planning. Patently, they serve a deeper purpose. On the one hand, they clearly perform an *internal* political function, a means of exercising control over, encouraging co-operation between and enforcing compliance upon the fractious bailiwicks of corporate confederations. Marketing plans can be and are used as powerful political weapons, though planning is but one of many spheres of intra-organizational conflict (and inter- since plans can be used to coerce suppliers and suchlike). Politics is not confined to planning, nor is the planning process unusually political.

On the other hand, planning also has an important *external* purpose. Regardless of whether the plans themselves are implemented – or simply shelved, as so many plans are – the very fact that planning is undertaken speaks volumes about the organization concerned. It bespeaks order, objectivity, control, competence, rectitude, reliability, dedication, dependability and all sorts of equally commendable characteristics. It intimates that top management is on the ball, where it's at, hot to trot and up to date with the latest thinking. It suggests that the organization is staffed with battle-hardened veterans who wear their campaign ribbons with pride (MBAs, DMSs, CIM medallions, Steven Covey seminar name-tags, etc.) and are familiar with the prognostications of the management guru of the moment.

Most importantly, planning provides a means of convincing prospective investors, be they merchant bankers, stockbrokers, venture capitalists, government agencies or associated media influencers, that they can stump up with confidence. Or, to put it another way, what investor would dream of sinking funds into an organization that didn't have a meaningful marketing plan or had the temerity to announce that its strategies were formulated on the basis of intuition and gut-feel? Failure to plan implies irrationality, irresponsibility and irregularity (to the point of sharp practice) on the part of both investee and investor. Marketing plans, by contrast, serve to reassure an organization's disparate constituents, along with quality standards kitemarks, hi-tech facilities, spick and span factories, happy-clappy employees, community involvement audits and similar signifiers of managerial sagacity. Strategic planning, in effect, is the comfort blanket of commercial life, a teddy bear for would-be investors, a disposable diaper for incontinent executives, a bedtime story for insomniac marketing managers.[24]

Stories, to be sure, have always been part and parcel of management research.[25] One thinks, for example, of the copious case studies that punctuate the bullet-point bandoleered pages of our BFBAMs (big fat books about marketing). Then there's the get-up-and-go sub-genre that occupies so much cyber shelf space in our virtual mega-bookstores (Close-That-Sale!, Polish-Those-Shoes!, Get-Your-Hair-Cut!, Buy-This-Book!, you know the kind of thing), to say nothing of the self-help, made-easy, you-too-can-do-it business best-sellers (leadership-for-dummies, charisma-for-idiots, dynamism-for-indolents, personality-for-peanuts). And then again, there's the inexhaustible well of hoary, stop-me-if-you've-heard-it-before, Eddie-George-knew-my-father 'war-stories' that are regurgitated to generations of undergraduates by generations of guest lecturers.

In recent years, however, the advent of postmodern perspectives has helped shift storytelling from the margins to the centre of our field.[26]

Apart from studies of marketing phenomena portrayed in works of 'proper' literature, all manner of consumer, company and consultancy narratives have been analysed at length; advertising campaigns have been given the once-upon-a-time treatment; brand chronicles broken down into their morphological components; service encounter 'plots' poured over for performance-improving pointers; and management morality tales taken to textual task for fabulation beyond the call of duty.[27] What's more, the stories told by marketing researchers about the stories told by marketing managers have also been studied in detail.[28] Indeed, if irrefutable proof were needed that business stories are back in business, one need look no further than the management style-bible, *HBR*, which has not only made the case for strategic storytelling but regularly runs stirring tales of the marketplace.[29]

Bloodcurdling costs extra.

Somewhat surprisingly, marketing plans have never been examined from a narratological perspective.[30] 'Surprisingly', because marketing plans are by far the most manifestly literary artefacts in our field, bar none. They are the one telling tale that every marketer worth their yarn-spinning salt – practitioner, consultant and student alike – concocts at some stage. True, research reports, internal memos, work scheduling sheets, committee meeting minutes and the like all contain a storytelling component. But the marketing plan is the big one, the mother of all narratives, the work of fiction designed to suspend the disbelief of out-side investors, galvanize the organization's employees and help ensure that the company lives happily ever after.

This is not the place to proffer a Proppian, Greimasian, Todorovian, Brunerian, Bakhtinian or Barthesian analysis of the marketing planning process. Narratology is a very substantial sub-field of Cultural Studies, with its own fads, fashions, factions and research foci (poetry, novels, movies, jokes, daydreams, etc.).[31] For the purposes of explication, it is simpler to suggest that marketing plans are fairy tales *manqué* – works of fantasy with a pedagogic purpose – and that planners have much to learn from the foremost fairytale-teller-cum-marketing man of the twentieth century, L. Frank Baum. While there are many other no less gifted spinners of supernatural yarns – Hans Christian Andersen, Raymond Briggs, Lewis Carroll, Roald Dahl, Dr Seuss, J.K. Rowling, to name but a few – none has the practical marketing experience, or indeed marketing insight, of Lyman Frank Baum (1856–1919). A lifelong admirer of P.T. Barnum, who was taken to see the Cardiff Giant as a child, Baum not only was the Kotler, Levitt and Barton of his day, but his stories were also strikingly marketing orientated. Given the anti-capitalist bent of the literati generally, this alone makes the wonderful world of L. Frank Baum worthy of serious marketing consideration.

Baum may not have been born with ruby slippers on his feet, but a silver spoon was definitely *in situ*.[32] The youngest son of a Yankee wheeler-dealer, who made his fortune in the oil fields of Pennsylvania, Lyman was a very sickly sprog. Heart problems and a delicate constitution meant that much of his childhood was spent in splendid isolation, shuttling between secluded sanatoria and private tutors. Yet despite this distinct shortage of human companionship, Baum the bookworm found solace in a rich imaginary world of fairy stories, fantastic tales and fictional deeds of derring-do. As a rebellious teenager, he ran off to join the theatre, where his storytelling skills and vivid imagination could be exercised, expressed, extended. Indeed, Baum the Younger enjoyed considerable success as an impresario, but bookish to a fault, book-keeping proved to be a perennial problem. Frank lost money on the shows and, not long after he returned to the family business, the Baum Castorade Company went into financial free-fall and finally failed after Baum the Elder's fatal heart attack in 1887.

Inspired by the 'go west young man' ideology then prevalent, Baum and his young family settled in the cattle-ranching community of Aberdeen, South Dakota. They established a Woolworth's-style five and dime, Baum's Bazaar, which promptly flopped due to Frank's foolhardy custom of swapping stories with (and extending unsecured credit to) penurious customers, rather than running the business in a business-like manner. Journalism seemed the next natural step and, never one for half-measures, Baum set up his own local newspaper, the *Aberdeen Saturday Pioneer*. Essentially a one-man operation, insofar as Frank wrote much of the hard copy, penned countless op-ed columns (under a variety of pseudonyms), sold the advertising space and generally sought to increase circulation, the *Pioneer* eventually folded during the agricultural recession of 1891. Baum relocated to Chicago, where he worked as a stringer for the local *Evening News* and fell deeply into debt, before abandoning printer's ink for the wing-and-a-prayer world of salesmanship. Yarn spinning, to be sure, is one of the secrets of successful selling and Baum proved to be a brilliant exponent of the itinerant art. He consistently topped the annual sales rankings of his employers, Pitkin and Brook, though the constant travelling coupled with an abiding interest in the quasi-theatrical principles of window dressing (then coming into its own thanks to late nineteenth-century developments in department store retailing – plate glass, electric spotlighting and manikin manufacture) gave rise to yet another momentous career change. Baum became a nationally renowned, award-winning window dresser; he formed the National Association of Window Trimmers; he established and edited a trade magazine, the *Show Window*, which still exists under the title *Visual Merchandising*; and in 1900 he published *The Art of Decorating Dry Goods Windows*, his merchandising magnum opus.

In truth, 1900 was Baum's *annus mirabilis*. In addition to *The Art of Decorating Dry Goods Windows* – the *In Search of Excellence* of its day – he published his blockbuster fairy tale, *The Wonderful Wizard of Oz*. Although it wasn't his first story-book, *The Wizard* was an instant best-seller, partly because of its retro perspective (it contained echoes of traditional tales, whilst being indisputably up to date), partly on account of its American tenor (prior fairy tales had been stolidly central European), partly owing to its overwhelmingly optimistic ethos (which chimed with the mind-cured mentality of the Progressive Era), partly due to its truly wondrous production values (colour-coded pages, arresting illustrations by W.W. Denslow, etc.) and partly thanks to the spell-binding brilliance of Baum's simple, well-told, wryly humorous tale.

A marketing man through and through, Baum immediately recognized and moved to mobilize the money-spinning potential of his otherworldly invention. An enormously successful stage show, *The Wizard of Oz*, sent the cash registers rolling and a sequence of sequels, coupled with all sorts of Oz-affiliated collectables, continuously filled the LFB coffers like the magical, self-replenishing goblets of legend. A veritable Gilded Age George Lucas, Baum kept tight control on tie-in merchandise, astutely exploiting the brief national fad for the Woggle-bug, an insectoid character that featured in his first sequel, *The Marvelous Land of Oz*. He 'retired' Dorothy on several occasions, in order to stoke up demand for Sinatra-style comeback texts. He produced one book per year for several years and published it to coincide with the Christmas gift-giving season. He firmly believed in market development, insofar as the stage shows were written for adults rather than his core kiddie constituency, although a musical based on Professor Wogglebug failed miserably at the box office, as did his brief foray into movie-making. Baum, nevertheless, was always ready, willing and able to crank out another Oz-opus when his mountain of sheckles was sufficiently denuded. At one stage, he planned to open a proto-theme park, Ozland, on an island off the Californian coast. Forty years later, Walt Disney brought Baum's dream to fruition, after a fashion, though the Emerald City itself had to wait another forty years, until the MGM Grand Hotel was built in Las Vegas, which is just about as not-in-Kansas as it is possible to be.

There's no place like Vegas, as everyone knows. But, the power of Baum's fable extends far beyond built environments, media representations and occasional outbreaks of Ozmania, which range from the official International Wizard of Oz Club and its latter-day web-based affiliates, to the official ban slapped on Baum's books during the communist witch-hunts of the 1950s (Munchkins-under-the-bed, shock!).[33] It is arguable, however, that the chronicles of Oz are primarily a celebration of consumer society in general and a palimpsest for marketing planning in particular. One of the most striking things about Baum's books – which were fairly formulaic, comprising minor variants on recurring plot motifs – is their uncritical attitude to acquisitiveness, possessions, materialism and the good things of life.[34] As several critics have observed, the author *could* have used his fairy tales to draw attention to the injustices, iniquities, inequalities and indignities of late nineteenth-century American society (as did contemporary storytellers like Edward Bellamy, Harriet Beecher Stowe and Mark Twain). But he didn't.

Instead, the Oz books drip with precious stones, expensive clothes, attractive knick-knacks and tastefully appointed dwellings with well-stocked larders. When Dorothy first encounters the staggering opulence of the Emerald City, whose green-hued inhabitants 'seemed happy and contented and prosperous',[35] she is bowled over by the beautiful houses, bejewelled sidewalks and emerald-encrusted emporia selling green candy, green popcorn, green shoes, green hats, green clothes and green lemonade. Similarly, when she is installed in her sumptuous suite in the Palace of Oz, consisting of 'a beautiful sitting room, a dressing room, a dainty bedchamber and a big marble bathroom', the closets contain 'everything that heart could desire . . . lovely dresses of every description and suitable for every occasion . . . nothing so rich and beautiful could ever have been found in the biggest department stores in America'.[36]

Although 'Dorothy enjoyed all these luxuries', there is no doubt that she enjoyed eating even more. So much so, that contemporary readers cannot help but be struck by the sheer amount of ingestion that goes on – multi-course feasts, edible landscapes and, at a guess, seven square meals per day. At one particular point, Dorothy seems determined to devour an entire village and its residents, only to be fobbed off with a stale shortbread piano and a picket fence made of pancake mix. Such behaviour, to be sure, represents a primordial form of consumption that is found in many fairy tales and analogous poor man's paradises like the Land of Cockaigne and Big Rock Candy Mountain.[37] Some commentators, however, have sought to explain Baum's ostensible food fixation in terms of his support for the Populist Movement, a radical agrarian society opposed to the 'industrialization' of farming. Regardless of the reason, it is clear that Ozorexia was not a problem in Baum's high-calorie, extra-helping, all-you-can-eat wonderland, even if the gustatory excess is out of sync with today's low-fat, healthy-eating, Weightwatchers Anonymous ethic.

Be that as it may, *The Wonderful Wizard of Oz* can and has been interpreted as a nefarious apology for western capitalism and its attendant obscenity, conspicuous consumption. The basic plot, according to Culver, is an allegory for commodity fetishism, where the main characters – animated manikins, one and all – are driven by a desperate desire, a lack, an absence, an incomplete identity which they seek to satisfy through the marketing system.[38] Symbolized by the Wizard, who resides in the epicentre of the cornucopian Emerald City, a place of mixing and exchange between the blue land of the Munchkins and the yellow desert beyond, the marketing system makes false promises, offers false hope and foments false consciousness (since the things the protagonists desire, principally heart, brains, courage and the way home, they already possess). The Wizard, remember, turns out to be a Barnumish humbug,[39] a carnival barker from Omaha who has no magical powers, is incapable of granting wishes or delivering on promises made, and who tricks the inhabitants of Emerald City into believing in him, as well as building a precious stone-encrusted palace to his personal specification. At his insistence, what is more, the Ozites not only wear green-lensed, rose-tinted glasses (as it were), to enhance the illusion of prosperity but when his duplicity is finally revealed by Toto, they fail to utter a single word of protest. As Zipes observes, the wizard is an 'American con-man' who has 'colonised the city, duped its gentle and naïve inhabitants, and introduced American standards and norms based on salesmanship and deception'.[40]

Marketing redux.

At the same time, it is hard not to feel a certain degree of sympathy for the Wizard, especially when he poses the pointed question: 'How can I help being a humbug when all these people make me do things that everybody knows can't be done?' For Leach, in fact:

> Baum's portrait of the Wizard and the tale itself can be interpreted as a tribute to the modern ability to create magic, illusions and theatre, to do in effect what God and the Devil had done: to make people believe, in spite of themselves. For even though the Wizard is exposed as a charlatan or as a 'common man' without any magical powers in the true fairy-tale sense, nevertheless he is very powerful. He is powerful in the modern American capitalist sense, powerful because he is able to manipulate others to do his bidding, to make them *believe what is unbelievable*, to do what they might not want to do (or to buy what they might not want to buy) and to do it without realizing they are doing it. A superb confidence man, Oz excites a completely misplaced trust but 'the people' adore him anyway.[41]

The happiness he generates may be based on fantasy, fabrication, falsehoods and flim-flam, but it is happiness all the same. Like Barnum, like Baum, like marketing itself, the wiz is a swiz, a trickster, a dissembler, a possessor of magic-less magic and the illusion of control.

Not every literary critic, it should be acknowledged, accepts this interpretation of Oz. Baum's books have been subject to all sorts of allegorical readings, ranging from a political pastiche and cookbook for communism to a spoof on suffragettes and a theosophical tract.[42] In fairness, most of these interpretations are entirely plausible. Baum was actively involved in Bryan's presidential campaigns of 1896 and 1900; he was heavily influenced by the communistic visions of Edward Bellamy's *Looking Backward*; his mother-in-law was Susan B. Anthony, the lion of late nineteenth-century women's liberation; and he was a practising spiritualist, an adept of Madame Blatavsky's mystical sect, if not a member of her inner circle. The consumption-based interpretation is hard to resist, nevertheless, since Baum manifestly practised what he preached.[43] That said, however, there are several marketing-inflected ways of interpreting this consumption allegory. Some see it as perniciously pro-consumption; others read it as an anti-consumption critique and others, such as Zipes, posit a non-consumerist possibility predicated on potlatch, gift exchange and market-circumventing arrangements.[44]

The interpretive options, in a word, are limitless. Yet it is abundantly clear, to me at least, that *The Wizard of Oz* is nothing less than a marketing plan *manqué*. It is not simply an exordium to exchange, a monument to marketing, a call to consume. Though that is part of it. Nor is it a cabbalistic exercise in colour-coded marketing numerology, albeit Baum's frequent use of threesomes and foursomes (four companions, three trials, three wishes, four witches, etc.) is not dissimilar to our discipline's fixation with threes and fours (three eras, four Ps, four utilities, three dichotomies and so on).[45] Though that again is part of it. Nor, indeed, should we surmise that the oft-reprinted map of Oz, with its four separate kingdoms, focused on a consumption-orientated conurbation, surrounded by a hostile environment containing competitors and antagonists, is the progenitor of the here-be-marketing diagram found in the opening chapters of most principles textbooks. Though the parallels are striking.

It is arguable, rather, that the whole book is nothing less than a proto-marketing plan, as are its innumerable indistinguishable sequels. Like marketing plans, *The Wizard* is premised on an archetypal quest narrative, a search for something better, something seemingly unattainable, something different from, and superior to, the initial state of affairs.[46] In the former case, this comprises a successfully implemented marketing plan or marketing-orientated organization, whereas in the latter case it consists of courage, wisdom, compassion and the way back to Kansas. The journey, moreover, is made up of a series of steps or stages – twelve, according to McDonald's influential model of the marketing planning process; twelve, according to Vogler's celebrated structural analysis of *The Wizard of Oz*.[47] Such is the correspondence, indeed, that the classic marketing planning model can readily be applied to Baum's timeless fantasy. From the initial situation analysis of the travelling party's strengths, weaknesses, opportunities and threats; through the assembly of the marketing plan (arrival in the Emerald City); to its final implementation, despite powerful antagonists (the Wicked Witch of the West) and the myopia of top management (the Wizard), Baum's fairy tale is a *tour de force* of marketing planning. It describes a journey from the barren, windswept and threatening milieu of hand-to-mouth management (production orientation), to an unimaginably perfect, colour co-ordinated, carefully planned environment, where everyone knows their place, wants for nothing and works for the greater good of the Oz-anization. Who would want to go back to the unplanned, uncoordinated, all too unpredictable, black and white world of Kansas?

Well, Dorothy, for starters!

Despite Dorothy's retrograde recalcitrance,[48] the ultimate message of *The Wonderful Wizard of Oz* – that you already have what you're looking for – is the ultimate message of marketing planning. As the future is inherently unknowable and entirely unpredictable, it follows that marketing planning is a necessary fiction, a hair-raising but happy-ever-after tale to the effect that the environment *is* plannable, the future *is* manageable, that organizational survival *is* probable and prosperity possible. The purpose of marketing plans is not to predict the future, but to posit that the future is predictable. They comprise an organizational comforter, an amulet, a lucky charm, a much-needed assurance that, in today's uncertain world, the good guys always win in the end. The Wonderful Wizard of SWOT, what is more, tells us that organizations can only save themselves. Corporate salvation does not reside in a technique, a theory, a learned tome or the prognostications of the latest 'thinker' to top the best-sellers list. Like the Wizard, however, the witch doctors of management consultancy cannot help being humbugs when their clients expect them to do the impossible. It's hard to be humble, or so the old song goes, but humbuggery is harder still.

Some Kotlerites, Big Mac lovers and fabulous Baker boys may be grossly offended by my suggestion that marketing planning is parable-mongering. Fairy tales, so they say, are child's play and all very well for excitable youngsters or immature adolescents. But if marketing is to be taken seriously, as an adult academic discipline, then it's time to put away such childish things and act responsibly. The problems with this line of argument are fourfold. First, it can be contended that the dis-cipline has already tried to demonstrate that it is all growed up – laws, models, general theories and the pseudo-trappings of pseudo-science – to no avail. Its apologists attribute this lack of accomplishment to the comparative 'youth' of the subject area, an excuse that is starting to show its age.[49] However, if this really is the case perhaps marketing should act its youthful age, instead of trying to prove that it's an adult. What's worse: a youngster striving to be mature beyond its years or a youngster acting childishly?

Second, this grow-up-and-get-serious argument rests on the unstated assumption that childhood is an undesirable state, something to be swiftly abandoned for suitably serious, high-minded pursuits. Not so, I say. As the compendious literature on creativity reveals, pre-adulthood is a privileged condition where everything is possible, magic still prevails and imagination knows no bounds.[50] Marketing, remember, is not about rocket science, or curing cancer, or the meaning of life. It is about selling stuff. It is irredeemably childish, perpetually pre-teen, incorrigibly adolescent, except when it comes to our much-vaunted concepts, theories, principles and high-and-mighty textbooks. Perhaps it is time to preach what we practise.

Third, this I'm-a-man-I'm-a-real-man mentality presupposes that there's something demeaning about fairy tales. Again this is not the case, as the equally voluminous literature on their developmental, archetypal and pedagogical importance clearly demonstrates.[51] True, fairy tales occupy a fairly lowly place in the lit-crit firmament, just as marketing does in management studies. But the fact that fairy tales and marketing plans are functionally indistinguishable is nothing to be ashamed of, or embarrassed about. Quite the reverse. Fairy stories are fantastic adventures with a heuristic purpose – the moral of the story is to be good, generous, honest, respectful or whatever – as are marketing plans, the moral of which is the Boy-Scoutish 'Be prepared'. What's more, they both adhere to the classic narrative schema of once-upon-a-time (there was an unhappy organization) to happily ever after (and so the plan was perfectly implemented, the organization became marketing orientated and company profits increased exponentially). Preposterous perhaps, unattainable undoubtedly, yet happy endings have their place, because they encourage us to believe that somewhere over the rainbow wishes really do come true.

Fourth and finally, marketing plans may be fairy stories for middle management, but storytelling is fashionable these days. Whether it be *HBR*'s happy-clappy encomium to 3M's narrative-based corporate strategy, or the same journal's recent three-Kleenex weepie about J. Peterman, the failed mail order retromarketer, there is no doubt that strategic storytelling is back in business.[52] In this regard, consider Nigel Piercy's latest marketing-practitioner-targeted tome, *Tales from the Marketplace*.[53] Or what about the advice of noted futurist, Rolf Jensen, whose *Dream Society* best-seller espouses a storytelling approach to strategic management.[54] Mintzberg, moreover, recommends story-based scenarios in preference to boring boxes and arrows. The twenty-first-century fashion for fables is such that traditional, planning-orientated organizations are now regarded as rigid, doctrinaire, unimaginative and followers rather than leaders.[55] Corporate tale tellers, on the other hand, are considered cool, hip, creative, dynamic and modishly retro (insofar as they use the past – the extant organizational culture – to help narrate the future).

The future for marketing plans, then, does not depend on rationality, rigour and ever more computer power – a planning-by-numbers future.

It relies, rather, on our ability to tell mysterious tales, tell mirthful tales, tell marvellous tales, tell moving tales. It requires tales that are convincing, compelling, creative and capable of communicating a credible message to employees, investors, regulators or consumers. It needs narratives that are sufficiently imaginative to persuade 'readers' to suspend their disbelief, as Coleridge recommends, and buy into the author's vision of the future. It wants, finally, good old-fashioned storytellers, many of whom are incarcerated in the ivy-girt ivory tower.[56]

Marketers, marketers, let down your hair . . .

PART III

FIXING THE MIX

8

Replacing Marketing: Reading Retroscapes

When and if a Marketing Hall of Fame is finally established, the first inductees will doubtless include Ted Levitt, Philip Kotler, Shelby Hunt and our own, our very own, Malcolm McDonald. But a space, surely, should also be reserved for the one and only Donald Cameron, who departed to the great marketing department in the sky on 16 August 1998. The late, lamented Mr Cameron was not a household name, I grant you, nor did he stand shoulder to shoulder with the titans of marketing thought, such as the aforementioned Seer of Cranfield. In the annals of retromarketing, nevertheless, Donald Cameron deserves an honourable mention. A publican by trade, our redoubtable marketing martyr was informed by the absentee landlord, Bass Breweries PLC, that his establishment was about to be converted into a 1970s theme pub called Flares. Worse, he would have to wear seventies regalia – platform shoes, acrylic tank top, mega-collared shirt and matching kipper tie, not forgetting the eponymous flared trousers – while serving behind the bar. Such sartorial instructions would be enough to give anyone bell-bottom blues, I'm sure you agree, but DC was so shaken by the thought of sporting an Afro fright-wig, adhesive Zapata moustache and gold-plated plastic medallion, that he promptly committed suicide.[1]

Sadly, Mr Cameron was only thirty-nine years old when he decamped to the disco paradiso, with its retro seventies soundtrack of retro fifties rockers like Showaddywaddy, Suzi Quatro, Alvin Stardust and the like. Although all manner of male, mid-life anxieties may have contributed to his untimely demise, the crucial point is that DC was old enough to remember the dread decade in all its stack-heeled, keep-on-truckin', Where's Wally awfulness. As anyone who wore the timeless loon pants, toe-loop sandals and tie-dye T-shirt ensemble will readily testify, once was quite enough for most people. Being asked to relive one's worst teenage nightmares, even with tongue planted firmly in cheek, knowing winks all present and correct, and ironic smirk in carefully practised place, requires dedication above and beyond the call of marketing duty.

True, Generations X and Y might wonder what all the fuss is about (flares are cool, right?). Few would deny, furthermore, that it could have been a lot worse (had Bass opted for a New Romantics theme pub, the resultant mass suicide would have made Waco, Texas, look like a Mexican wave). But, when the restless retro spotlight finally falls on grunge or, indeed, the nineties' seventies revival, then they'll know exactly how we decrepit disco-ducks feel. A grunge-disco comeback has possibilities, mind you . . .

'Smells Like Saturday Night Fever' notwithstanding, if the Flares fiasco has an up side, then the silver lining is that it is just a place, a location, a somewhere which can quite easily be avoided. Its employees, admittedly, might not have too much choice in the matter – as the unfortunate Mr Cameron demonstrates – but the establishment's putative customers are perfectly free to embrace or evade its sham seventies kitsch. After all, there is no shortage of alternative retro venues, retro marts and retro destinations ready, willing and able to absorb our disposable retro dollars. Besides the benighted Flares, a veritable host of theme pubs, restaurants and commercial milieux lies in wait for retro-minded consumers.[2] There's hardly a high street in the country without its quota of refurbished Victorian pubs (complete with plastic horse brasses and electric gas fittings), pseudo thirties tea shoppes (white-collared waitresses and triple-decker cake stands akimbo), fake fifties diners (all chrome counter seating and red gingham tablecloths), sham seventies discotheques (glitterballs to you too!), and naff neo-nineties amusement arcades (featuring antique video games of the pre-Lara Croft epoch). The suburbs, similarly, are suffused with mock Tudor shopping malls (whose 'gallerias' convey a homeopathic one-part-per-million hint of Vittorio Emanuele's Milanese masterpiece), seen-one-seen-'em-all heritage centres (working smithy, weaving demonstrations, costumed attendants et al.) and Walt-Disney-ate-my-hamburger theme parks (turn left at the medieval log flume for the ancient Greek roller-coaster). Time was, indeed, that shoppers were judiciously divided into time-rich and time-poor.[3] Now they are time-seeking, time-travelling, time-ingesting, as well.

Time out.

The landscape may be awash with retro locales – from retro casinos and retro cruise liners to retro hotels and retro airports – but retroscapes are not confined to physical places, actual locations, tangibly themed environments. On the contrary, representations of retroscapes are all around us. In advertising, to cite but one example, the award-winning television commercial for Caffrey's Irish Ale climaxes in a sublime retro montage of scudding clouds, glistening lakes, miasmic bogs, heather-capped mountains, land-locked fishing boats, galloping horses, faithful greyhounds, ebullient hurley players, flame-haired colleens and equally evocative images of the Celtic pastoral.[4] Julian Barnes's recent novel *England, England,* describes the creation of a vast heritage park on the Isle of Wight, which so successfully captures the essence of Old England that it not only rivals but threatens to supersede the original:

> They had a half-size Big Ben; they had Shakespeare's grave and Princess Di's; they had Robin Hood (and his Band of Merrie Men), the White Cliffs of Dover, and beetle-black taxis shuttling through the London fog to Cotswold villages full of thatched cottages serving Devonshire cream teas; they had the Battle of Britain, cricket, pub skittles, *Alice in Wonderland, The Times* newspaper, and the One Hundred and One Dalmatians . . . They had failed to get any members of Parliament; but even half-trained, a bunch of resting actors were proving indistinguishable from the real thing. The National Gallery had been hung and varnished. They had Brontë country and Jane Austen's house, primeval forest and heritage animals; they had music-hall, marmalade, clog- and Morris-dancers, the Royal Shakespeare Company, Stonehenge, stiff upper lips, bowler hats, in-house TV classic serials, half-timbering, jolly red buses, eighty brands of warm beer, Sherlock Holmes and Nell Gwynn whose physique countered any possible whisper of paedophilia. But they did not have Buck House . . .[5]

Even the Internet, that vast, uncharted continent of cutting-edge computer technology, has a curiously retro feel. There's its general sense of steam-driven sluggishness. There's its somewhat old-fashioned but strictly observed rules of netiquette. There's its semi-literate, faux five-year-old syntax. There's its avalanche of retro billets-doux between love-lorn anoraks. There's its armies of amateur genealogists and tenders of family trees. There's its retrotopia of multi-player video games, unerringly set in sword 'n' sorcery netroscapes. There's its blatant appeals to nostalgia in manifold retro home pages, many of which are akin to overstuffed Victorian parlours, with their cybermacassars, E-spidistras and virtual trophy cabinets. And then, of course, there's E-commerce. The very term carries retro connotations, since 'commerce' is next to 'comestible', 'purveyor' and 'emporium' in the lexicon of ye-olde-shopping speak. In this regard, Amazon.com is blessed with the not unattractive atmospherics of a dusty filing cabinet; the colorized front cover of *The Virgin Internet Shopping Guide* depicts a forties shop assistant depressing the keys of a massive retro cash register; and Yahoo's advertising evokes the sheer abundance of the retronet by means of monochrome photos of the January sales in an overcrowded 1950s department store.[6]

In the immortal words of Samuel Beckett's little-known – cyberplay, *Waiting for Godotcom* (or was it *The Domainnamble*?; *Krapp's Last Download*, possibly?), 'I must go on-line, I can't go on-line, I'll go on-line'.

The discourse that surrounds the web, what is more, is like *déjà vu* all over again. The extravagant claim that E-commerce will destroy 'traditional' retailing has been made about every significant retail innovation since the nineteenth-century department store.[7] The massive paper fortunes being made by the new generation of cyberpreneurs is a virtual rerun of the Klondike – the silicondike – a retro gold rush by the '99ers.[8] Bluetooth, named after an obscure tenth-century Viking, promises to connect all our computerized domestic appliances, just like the 1950s house-of-the-future.[9] Cookies, the subsurface embeds that keep track of on-line purchases and illegal downloads from MP3 pirates, contain J. Edgar Hooverish hints of the Hidden Persuaders.[10] Cluetrain contends that the Internet represents a wholesale return to the ancient Athenian agora, where community, communitas and commerce combine, held together by conversations at the crossroads of connectivity.[11] And, when it comes to the Pacman's burden, is it not the case that the World Wide Web contains many threats to civilized society – pornography beyond de Sade's wildest dreams, hard-disk-drive destroying viruses and crack teams of ex-commie netcombers who scour the dotcomian steppes for unencrypted credit card numbers, like the cybercossacks they are.[12]

Be that as it may, the vast majority of retroscapes are fungible, if synthetic to the touch, and found at a variety of spatial scales: *individual outlet, flagship store, shopping complex* and *heritage park*. The first of these is exemplified by the 94th Aero Squadron Restaurant, which was developed by the Speciality Restaurant Corporation of Long Beach, California.[13] Modesty forbids, you understand, but the 94th is what *Pizza in our Time* would have been had it come to fruition. Except, of course, that the 94th doesn't sell pizza; nor is it based on a Second World War theme; nor, indeed, does it employ any of the marketing strategies referred to in my prefatorial remarks (apart from that I was spot on). Aptly described as 'a quintessential soul food outlet',[14] the Speciality Restaurant Corporation's signature retroscape looks like a French farmhouse that has been commandeered by a company of anally retentive airmen, somewhere on the Western Front. A French farmhouse, furthermore, that has been caught up in the fighting and received a direct hit from a howitzer loaded with mementoes instead of munitions.

Inside the sham shelled shell of a building, the walls of the 'Flight Room' foyer are lined with sepia photographs of air aces celebrating their deeds of derring-do, alongside bulletin boards, barrage balloon strafing instructions and fight-cum-flight kits of the brave souls slated for the next sortie (goggles, gas masks, trench coats, etc.). A sandbagged passageway leads to the hostess station (manned by a uniformed *maître d'*), the restrooms (picturesquely retitled 'Latrines'), and the dining area beyond. Here, a veritable Woolwich Arsenal hangs from every wall, the cocktail patio is fringed with razor wire, waitresses wear fetching 'French farm girl' outfits, and the background music comprises a jingoistic mix of period songs – 'Over There', 'Long Way to Tipperary' and so on – interspersed with snatches of ops-related conversation ('march to the sound of the buns, chaps!'). To cap it all, a bank of picture windows affords spectacular views, past the parked biplane and rustic hay-wagon, of an adjacent working aerodrome, the control tower of which can be listened to on complimentary headsets. Interestingly, the reverse anachronism of the situation, whereby historicized diners in their dug-out observe contemporary aircraft take off and land, appears to add to, rather than detract from, the sense of retro occasion. It somehow manages, as romantic novelist Judith Krantz rightly notes, 'not to feel fake, no matter how much it has to be'.[15]

This classic retro combination of old and new is typical of many well-known theme restaurants – Hard Rock Café, Planet Hollywood and TGI Friday spring immediately to mind – but it is also evident in the burgeoning number of *flagship stores* or, to be more precise, mega-brand 'museums'.[16] The World of Coca-Cola in downtown Atlanta, Volkswagen's Autostadt (or 'Car City') in Wolfsburg, the Heineken Reception Centre in Amsterdam, Cadbury's Chocolate World in Birmingham and Kellogg's Cereal City in Battle Creek, Michigan, are just some of the more elaborate instantiations of corporate glorification, though many not so mega-brands maintain mini shrines to themselves. Examples include Coleman's mustard museum in Norwich, Bewley's coffee-house museum in Dublin, the Sandeman Port Museum in Oporto, Wedgwood Visitors' Centre in Stoke-on-Trent and the Cointreau Museum in Angers.

Without doubt, however, the mother ship of these monuments to retromarketing is Niketown.[17] Although it wasn't the first musemporium, to coin a neologism, Niketown is perhaps the most prominent, with fourteen outlets worldwide at the time of writing. As befits one of the biggest brands on the planet, Niketown is a totemic tabernacle, a mind-blowing mélange of merchandise and memorabilia, retailing and religion, gallery and galleria, past and present. The façade of Nike's New York flagship is akin to an old-fashioned gymnasium, with an entrance modelled on traditional sports arena turnstiles. Inside, beyond the memento-lined foyer, lies a vast five-storey atrium, its futuristic feel tastefully offset by period detailing (aged bricks, wooden floors, wireglass windows) and suspended marblesque statues of Nike's Olympians, shod, clad and paid for by the magnificent marketer's munificence. At thirty-minute intervals, giant video screens descend into this retro-techno vestibule, extolling the virtues of the vestments on view in propinquitous 'pavilions', each dedicated to the past achievements, future prospects and 'just do it' Nikesperanto of the company's cadre of sport-bestriding superheroes. Variously described as 'one part nostalgia to two parts hi-tech',[18] 'a high-tech cross between a store, a museum and a media experience'[19] and 'part 1939 World's Fair, part theater',[20] this sporting expo is filigreed with transparent, stock-transporting, Plexiglas tubes, an amazing amalgam of Marshall Field, Fritz Lang, *The Jetsons* and *Back to the Future II*. Selling, however, is secondary to spectacle, to veneration, to reverence, to communion, to the company's awe-inducing combination of reach for the sky and the way we were.

It's logocentrism, Jacques, but not as Derrida knows it.

Niketown, to be sure, isn't the only retro show on the road. As the innumerable Old City, Old Town, Old Quarter, Old Tucson, Old Pasadena, Old New Orleans, Old (X marks the spot) appellations indicate, retro *shopping complexes* are two-a-penny these days.[21] Within the shopping centre industry, indeed, an entire sub-category of such developments is officially acknowledged, widely written about and regularly underwritten. Festival shopping malls, as they are known, have their origins in the ancient Greek agora – clearly, the commercial touchstone of choice – but the concept is usually dated to the 1976 redevelopment of Faneuil Hall, by James Rouse.[22] A former fish market in downtown Boston, the neo-classical building (itself an eighteenth-century monument to retro) was completely renovated, carefully reconfigured and ultimately re-leased to a judiciously managed selection of speciality stores and restaurants. Such was its success, that the Faneuil Hall experiment was repeated *ad nauseam* in countless downtown, dockside and dilapidated but interesting buildings throughout the world – Covent Garden (London), Princes Square (Glasgow), South Street Seaport (New York), Harborplace (Baltimore), The Rocks (Sydney) and many more besides.

A classic case of the festival mall concept is Dublin's Powerscourt Town House Centre, which opened in 1981.[23] Situated in a side street, immediately adjacent to the city's prime shopping thoroughfare, this retro centre occupies an elegant, seventeenth-century Georgian building, the former residence of Lord Powerscourt, avatar of Anglo-Irish Protestant Ascendancy. The original entrance hall of the town house, with its impressive fireplace and imposing family portrait, serves as a premodern portal to a postmodern paradise. Beyond its heavy wooden doors, the courtyard has been magically transformed – thanks to a simple architectural act of enclosure – into an airy, three-storey atrium, which is surrounded on all four sides by wrought-iron-balustraded, Victorian lamp-lit walkways, linked by serried ranks of sweeping staircases. Every nook and cranny, furthermore, is stuffed with idiosyncratic retail stores selling antiques, knick-knacks, collectables, artworks, designer-ware (and -wear), handicrafts, bibelots, gew-gaws and analogous evocations of other times, other places, other lives. Eating and entertainment are equally important, as evinced by the centrally located, bogus Beaux Arts restaurant and wooden-floored bandstand with open grand piano, ready to perform in the concert halls of consumer imagination. Nostalgia and cornucopia thus combine to convey the impression that everything, from the Alpha of alabaster figurines to the Omega of expensive timepieces, is available under the one retro roof. Or so it seems.

In truth, festival shopping malls have become a bit of a postmodern cliché, with their obligatory food courts, alfresco seating arrangements, studiously offbeat tenant mix (Skateboards-R-Us, Uneeda Tattoo, Ginseng-U-Like, etc.) and get-your-souvenir-T-shirt-here stalls. Compared to much maligned *heritage centres*, however, they represent the nearest thing to authenticity in an inauthentic age. An often uneasy admixture of traditional museum and theme park, heritage facilities typically comprise an array of replica, reconstructed or reproduction buildings on an historic site and, as often as not, are peopled with attendants in period costume who perform suitably antiquarian tasks (shoeing horses, baking bread, mining coal and suchlike).[24] There is, admittedly, considerable variation on the heritage theme 'theme'. At one extreme lies Disney's aborted Heritageland USA, with its money-spinning rides, restaurants and residential facilities. At the other extreme, there are 'authentic' heritage parks like Colonial Williamsburg, Virginia's eighteenth-century capital city and carefully preserved exemplar of the 'living museum' format. For all their variety, nonetheless, it is generally accepted that heritage parks 'epitomise the postmodern process whereby a past is nostalgically recreated as a form of substitute reality. Ex-miners are employed to inform the rest of us about mining in a time in which they did not live, while the need for "real" mining has all but disappeared'.[25] They represent, in short, the archetypal retroscape – consumer society stencilled in phoney stone – where the sanitized past meets the supercilious present.

Although the heritage park concept dates from 1891, when Artur Hazelius's Museum of Scandinavian Folklore opened on a 75-acre site just outside Stockholm, and owes much of its ubiquity to the world's fairs of the early twentieth century, most of which included egregious national tableaux,[26] it is only in the postmodern period that they have become a truly global phenomenon (e.g. the Polynesian Cultural Center, Hawaii; Kyongju World Tradition Folk Village, Seoul; Tjapukai Cultural Theme Park, Cairns; Museum of Welsh Life, Cardiff). Fairly typical in this regard is the Ulster-American Folk Park. Opened in July 1976, to coincide with the Bicentennial, it celebrates the historic links between Ireland and America by foregrounding the emigration experience. Situated in the rural hinterland of Northern Ireland, 40 miles west of Belfast, the park consists of two 'halves', one devoted to the Irish and the other to the American ends of the transatlantic journey. These are linked by a full-scale, part-replica of an early nineteenth-century sailing vessel, *The Brig Union*, which is abutted on either side by recreated Irish and American streetscapes. The emigrant experience is further evoked by the guiding thread of the Mellon family, who left Ulster in the early nineteenth century, settled in Pennsylvania, founded the famous banking dynasty and, to this day, remain part of the east-coast establishment. Thus, the Old World half of the park is centred on the original, if substantially rebuilt, Mellon farmhouse and the New World half consists of full-scale reconstructions of their first farmsteads in the United States. All told, the park consists of eighteen buildings, from weavers' cottage and working forge to refurbished public house and subterranean corn-crib, plus a museum shop, restaurant and Centre for Emigration Studies. In many ways, indeed, it exemplifies the heritage phenomenon, insofar as it combines authenticity (the original, *in situ* Mellon farm) and inauthenticity (the Disneyesque replica brig) to telling retromarketing effect.

Conceptually speaking, however, the Ulster-American Folk Park raises an important retro research matter. As its name implies, the heritage centre is just as much about *space* as it is about *time*. The same is true of festival shopping malls, which gather the world of goods under a single roof, and Niketown-style flagships, which exist to give global brands local representation. Theme restaurants, similarly, are characterized by spatial catholicism as well as temporal eclecticism. Our city centres and suburban shopping centres are suffused with gastronomic geographies, whether they come in the form of free-standing restaurants (Rainforest Café, Chicago Pizza Pie Factory, the Olive Garden), or the shared seating arrangements of all but omnipresent food courts (where Chinese crackers, Thai noodles, German sausages, Greek salads, American bagels and Japanese sushi seek a semblance of olfactory accord). Even the raw ingredients exhibit a cosmopolitan bent, as 'the Kenyan haricot beans, Californian celery, North African potatoes, Canadian apples, and Chilean grapes'[27] of the average British supermarket daily remind us.

A moment's reflection, nevertheless, reveals that these representations of space are situated in time. A time, furthermore, that is rarely, if ever, the present. Food courts and theme restaurants attempt to encapsulate the cuisine of specific locales, but it's the locale at some dim and distant point in the imagined past. After all, if the 'English' restaurant, with its roast beef, fruit scones, spotted dick and clotted cream, were truly contemporary, the menu would have to include hamburgers, samosas, pizzas and Marks and Spencer's boeuf stroganoff, for starters (well, okay, main courses). Analogously, the much-vaunted Irish pub, which is in the process of taking over the bibulous universe, bears only the remotest resemblance to 'the real thing', whatever that is.[28] Their garish green décor, pseudo-Gaelic invocations, thousand welcomes doormats, shamrock-inscribed fittings, peat burning fireplaces, freshly brewed stout, wide range of whiskeys, conspiratorial hints of under-the-counter poteen, traditional, *craic*-concocting, Aran sweater-wearing musicians and general air of to-be-sure, to-be-sure bonhomie, can hardly be considered representative of today's Ireland, yesterday's Ireland, or any other Ireland this side of *The Quiet Man*. They are, in fact, a commercially motivated commodification of the Celtic Revival of the late nineteenth century, which was itself a politically motivated commodification of half-baked Irish prehistory. Make no mistake, Scruffy Murphy's, Molly Malone's and the like are superb representations of the Irish imaginary. However, it is very much a retro-Hiberno imaginary, where archaic imbibing motifs meet hi-tech brewing technology.

Las Vegas, likewise, is often portrayed as a fantasy wonderland, with the world as its (fake Rolex) oyster.[29] New York, Paris, Egypt, Saudi-Arabia, Polynesia, Mexico and many more hyperreal hyperrealms, are all within easy reach, conveniently situated on either side of the Strip. 'Why' as one world-weary traveller seditiously confessed, 'go as far as Egypt, or even Mexico for that matter, and risk local insurrection and bilharzia when you can see it all, much more safely, right here?'[30] Why indeed? Once again, however, it is not today's Egypt, New York, Paris or Polynesia that is being re-created for consumer convenience, post-tourist approbation and high roller diversion. On the contrary, it is Pre-Dynastic Egypt, with its pseudo-sandstone Sphinx, larger-than-life pyramid and better-than-the-original Tut's tomb, not the high-risk, terrorist infested, panhandler ridden original, itself an imitation jewel of the Nile. It is the New York of huddled masses, *West Side Story* and *On the Town*, not the potholed, grid-locked, yellow-cabbed Gotham City that we know and love. It is gay Paree of *la belle époque*, Gustav Eiffel and the Impressionists, not the hamburger-chained Champs-Elysées, Arc de McTriomphe and tawdry, all-too-tawdry Follies of today. It is the pre-lapsarian Polynesia of free love, noble savagery, Kon Tiki rafting and Easter Island statuary, not the Levi's-wearing, Toyota-driving, pédalo-pushing, efflorescent-cocktails-in-a-split-coconut-serving pseudo-paradise that awaits latter-day travellers. When these are added to the Ancient Rome of Caesar's Palace, the medieval extravaganza of Excalibur, the golden age of Hollywood at MGM and the wild, Wild West of copious cowboy-themed casinos in Gamblers' Gulch (a.k.a. Fremont Street), then it is clear that Las Vegas is as much a retro resort as a space-based themeopolis.

In a similar vein, the wonderful world of Walt Disney World is a perfectly realized retroscape. Much discussed by cultural theorists, left-leaning critics and postmodern commentators,[31] Disney is widely regarded as the archetypal multinational corporation, the imagineer of globalization, the smiley face of late capitalism, the organizational embodiment of have-a-nice-one, show-me-the-money American cultural imperialism. Only McDonald's ranks higher on the charge sheet of neo-colonialism. This emphasis on geographic reach, representation and rapaciousness, however, belies the fact that Mickey's Magic Kingdom is retro writ large, nothing less than the *über*-retroscape. Main Street USA, as noted in Chapter 1, is fashioned on Walt's rose-coloured recollections of his turn-of-the-century childhood in Marceline, Missouri. Frontierland evokes America's early colonial experience, if under several glutinous layers of Davy Crockettesque ersatz. New Orleans Square comprises a creole concatenation of haunted mansions, mint juleps, plastic whippoorwills and antebellum-accented animatronics. Adventureland provides pseudo-echoes of pith-helmeted, scramble-for-Africa, the-natives-are-restless empire-building, thanks to the heart of demi-darkness jungle cruise. Toon Town based on *Who Framed Roger Rabbit?* a live-action cartoon set in a neo-noirish faux Prohibition Era of bootlegging, speakeasies and sub-Damon-Runyon dialogue. Fantasyland, furthermore, is a clingfilm-covered smorgasbord of *fin-de-siècle* fairy stories. Here lies Sleeping Beauty (of Brothers Grimm), there is Alice in Wonderland (of Lewis Carroll), over there soars Peter Pan (of J.M. Barrie), right next to Pinocchio (of Carlo Collodi), the Sword in the Stone (of T.H. White) and the Wind in the Willows (of Kenneth Grahame). Even EPCOT – and Tomorrowland generally – isn't so much futuristic as retroistic, insofar as it represents a fifties vision of the future, an Eisenhowerian paean to progress, a retro reminder of the optimistic, technocratic and supersonic attitudes that then prevailed. A pre-postmodern relic of what the future used to hold.

Now, this is not to suggest that such representations of space are *really* representations of time and, therefore, retromarketing is much more prevalent than it appears. Nor am I contending that theme restaurants, heritage parks and the like are characteristically postmodern fusions of space and time, brandbodiments, so to speak, of Harvey's 'time-space compression', Lash and Urry's 'economies of sign and space', or Baudrillard's America of implosive hyperrealized simulations.[32] My point is not that retro rules the millennial waves (though it does), nor that retromarketing has a significant spatial component (though it does). It is, rather, that *space* is of paramount importance. It is *space* that holds the key to marketing understanding and, more importantly, understanding marketing. Space is the air that marketers breathe (if you catch my drift), the water in the goldfish bowl of commercial life, the philosophical phlogiston of twenty-first-century marketing scholarship.[33]

Of course, you'd never realize from the armada of Kotler-clone textbooks that space has anything to do with marketing, let alone the wind that fills its sales. Despite their several hundred pages of non *bons mots*; and notwithstanding diagram after diagram of boxes-little-boxes-and-they're-all-made-out-of-ticky-tacky,[34] it seems that the Big Fat Books About Marketing have almost no space for space. True, they usually contain a single chapter on the fourth P of place (though it is very much the fourth out of four) and the obligatory 'international' chapter can be considered spatial, if you're feeling generous. The discussions therein, however, involve little more than a typology of distribution channels, an inventory of extant retail locations and a platitude or two about modifying the marketing mix in exogenous cultural contexts. There is, as Dorothy Parker famously observed about Oakland, no there there. The same shortcoming is evident in the specialist books on marketing places, which simply apply the classic APIC cookie-cutter to specific cities, countries and – I ask you – continents, irrespective of their individual social, historical, demographic, climatic and legislative circumstances.[35] When it comes, moreover, to 'Europeanized', 'Canadianized' and 'Far Easternized' versions of best-selling, American ghost-writers-in-the-sky marketing textbooks, I can only say that not only is there no there there, but there's no here there either.

In fairness, the marketing academy hasn't completely ignored the geography of exchange. Sheth et al.'s Whiggish history of marketing thought acknowledges the existence of a Regional School, which emerged in the 1930s with Reilly's 'Law of Retail Gravitation', climaxed in Grether 1950 analysis of America's inter-regional trade patterns, and has been revitalized of late, thanks to location-allocation modelling, all-singing-all-dancing geodemographics and the whole computer-driven, database-mining, address-list-assembling, hi-tech hunting and gathering of the micro-, maxi-, permission-, one-on-one marketing fraternity.[36] What's more, there is growing evidence of a spatial 'turn' in interpretive marketing research, as recent studies of flea markets, toy stores, hairdressing salons, ethnic neighbourhoods, suburban shopping malls, museum shops, brandfests, convenience stores and broadly similar servicescapes bear encouraging witness.[37] Indeed, it is arguable that the Retronet, perhaps the hottest marketing topic of our time, is fundamentally spatial, notwithstanding the webheads, netnerds and cyberfreaks' contentions that E-commerce has effectively eradicated geography.[38] As anyone who has bought anything on-line will confirm, spatial considerations still figure prominently in the purchasing decision, especially when consumer rights, customs regulations and delivery times are taken into consideration. In truth, it would require very little academic imagination to apply traditional location theories – the gravity model, intervening opportunities, cumulative attraction, etc. – in a cybersetting. As for the Wheel of E-tailing, I'm seriously tempted to give it a whirl, though there's only so much retro theorizing you can get away with . . .

Although the open cast mine of marketing scholarship contains a rich seam of spatial research, it remains nonetheless a very thin seam, deeply fractured and irritatingly intermittent. Welcome though it is, the recent rise of space-based research has done little more than raise the fourth P's profile, restore its standing and provide it with parity of P-steem, as it were. While this P-instatement is not unwarranted and long overdue, it doesn't quite go far enough. It fails to acknowledge the fundamentally, profoundly, ineradicably spatial nature of marketing. Place is not an aspect of marketing, a component part, an optional ingredient of the mix, to be included or excluded depending on the chef's personal preference. Marketing is *inherently* spatial, *relentlessly* geographical, *unavoidably* locational. Marketing, in fact, is a space, a place, a site, a situation, a locale, a region, a territory, a country, a continent, a world of its own.[39]

Acknowledging the spatial character of marketing is all very well, as is highlighting the pervasiveness of retroscapes. But alluding to their presence or positing pen portraits thereof doesn't aid comprehension or constitute an explanation. Although an entire book is necessary to do justice to time, space and the market – hey, there's a title to conjure with – some preliminary conceptual considerations can be gleaned from a Gilded Age retro theorist, who commented on the consuming excesses of America's east-coast establishment. Thorstein Veblen is often hailed as one of the greatest social critics of the twentieth century.[40] Yet for all his intellectual firepower, he ranks amongst the strangest ever incumbents of the academic asylum. Indeed, as scholarly eccentrics go, Veblen was much further gone than most. By all accounts, he was a hapless lecturer who muttered monotonously for his country; a taciturn verging on incommunicado conversationalist; a less than dedicated follower of fashion whose personal hygiene left a lot to be desired; a campus Casanova so committed to gross moral turpitude that his amorous escapades cost him several prestigious university appointments; an academic whose idea of pastoral duties involved making himself available from 10.00 to 10.05 every Monday morning and giving all class assignments a 'C', irrespective of their merits (when challenged by a disgruntled high achiever, he observed that 'my grades are like lightning, they can strike anywhere'); a national celebrity in the aftermath of the First World War who famously spurned the proffered presidency of the American Economic Association; and, not least, the coiner of the phrase 'conspicuous consumption', whose own consumption behaviour was inconspicuous to the point of invisibility (he lived in a remote cabin in California, surrounded by boxes of unpacked books and tottering piles of dirty dishes, which were lightly sprayed with the garden hose when a clean-up was unavoidable).

At the same time, Veblen's voluminous writings are brilliantly insightful, strikingly original, scathingly satirical and unerringly retro. Although this ironist of the Progressive Era wrote eleven books and 150 scholarly articles, including a root-and-branch critique of Marx's theory of labour value, he is best remembered for his 1899 *tour de force, The Theory of the Leisure Class.*[41] A bitingly sardonic dissection of the east-coast super-rich, who flaunted their status by means of offensively ostentatious exhibitions of wealth – houses, yachts, artworks, furnishings, extravagant balls and parties – the book can still be read with profit. For Veblen, consumption not production was the essence of capitalism and a combination of envy, emulation and exhibitionism comprised its principal driving force. The roots of this retro cupidity, he maintained, were found in potlatch, kula and the periodic seizure of property by marauding tribesmen. Nevertheless, it remained very much alive and well, and since the elite classes set behavioural standards for society as a whole, variants of conspicuous consumption were apparent in every social stratum, down to and including the most indigent. Emulation, furthermore, unfailingly gave rise to fraud, chicanery, predation, self-aggrandizement and the tantalizing obscenities of the marketing system. Against Marx, then, Veblen maintained that social revolution was unlikely to occur, since the labouring classes were envious of and aspired to the behavioural norms of the consuming elite. And, while his emulatory mechanism has since been heavily criticized,[42] many social commentators concede that the so-called Bard of Savagery succeeded in capturing much of the character of contemporary consumer society. According to Ritzer, indeed, conspicuous consumption is still readily apparent, alongside conspicuous leisure, conspicuous shopping and conspicuous inconspicuousness.[43]

Don't ask!

While the work of Thorstein Veblen can hardly be described as sadly neglected, he is widely, if erroneously, regarded as an intellectual one-hit wonder. Like his exact contemporary and alumnus of the 1893 Chicago Columbian Exhibition, L. Frank Baum, Veblen never quite managed to surpass his early endeavours, despite a steady stream of post-*Leisure Class* publications. Most of these dealt with the American economy, international relations and the continuing importance of workmanship in an industrialized age. It was only in his final book that he appended an analysis of 'salesmanship' to his initial studies of consumption and thereby closed the marketing circle.[44] Iconoclastic to the last, Veblen presciently argued that marketing was not only the key to long-term business success but that it was virtually unstoppable. Big spending, national advertising, market-share-grabbing organizations were sweeping all before them, thanks to their marketing acumen and ability to attract consumers. What's more, they would continue to sweep all before them, since increasing returns inevitably accompanied marketing expenditures and the companies that failed to keep up would be extinguished one by one. This was especially the case in product categories such as apparel, cosmetics and patent medicines, where consumer pride, poise, prestige and social position were involved. Marketing success, according to Veblen, did not rest upon rectitude, propriety or customer orientation. Marketing, rather, comprised the art of putting it over, getting something for nothing, promising much and delivering little. It was predicated on making the unbelievable believable, the implausible plausible, the incredible credible.

For Veblen, furthermore, the finest exponents of marketing were not the denizens of Madison Avenue, nor the purveyors of 'grave stones, lap dogs, parlour furniture, cosmetic pigments, fashion dress and equipage generally'.[45] As Bruce Barton was soon to demonstrate, *the church* more than any other marketing organization had perfected the art of promising everything, delivering nothing and rendering conceivable the inconceivable. The sellers of rubber heels, yeast cakes and restoratives of lost manhood were mere amateurs beside the publicity agents of the faith, whose relic-bedecked tents, temples and tabernacles were religious retroscapes *avant la lettre*.

> The Propaganda of the Faith is quite the largest, oldest, most magnificent, most unabashed, and most lucrative enterprise in sales publicity in all Christendom. Much is to be learned from it as regards media and suitable methods of approach, as well as due perseverance, tact, and effrontery. By contrast, the many secular adventures in salesmanship are no better than upstarts, raw recruits, late and slender capitalizations out of the ample fund of human credulity. It is only quite recently, and even yet only with a dawning realization of what may be achieved by consummate effrontery in the long run, that these others are beginning to take on anything like the same air of stately benevolence and menacing solemnity. No pronouncement on rubber heels, soap-powders, lip sticks, or yeast cakes, not even Sapphira Buncombe's Vegetative Compound, are yet able to ignore material facts with the same magisterial detachment, and none has yet commanded the same unreasoning assent or acclamation. None other have achieved that pitch of unabated assurance which has enabled the publicity agents of the Faith to debar human reason from scrutinizing their pronouncements. These others are doing well enough, no doubt; perhaps as well as might reasonably be expected under the circumstances, but they are a feeble thing in comparison. Saul has slain his thousands, perhaps; but David has slain his tens of thousands.[46]

How, then, can Thorstein Veblen help us make sense of latter-day retroscapes? Extrapolating a tad, it is clear that themed environments are sites of *consummate consumption*, insofar as they comprise the epitome, the essence, the (admittedly stereotyped) distillation of particular historical epochs, geographical locales, sporting accomplishments or whatever. Like movie trailers, news summaries, condensed encyclopaedias, greatest hits packages, political soundbites, compressed computer files, 'made simple' primers and (if you must) 'readers' on modern marketing theory, they function in an essentially meta-metonymical capacity, where the part not only stands for the whole but in certain respects *supersedes* the whole. After all, why waste your time wandering around the latest blockbuster exhibition, listening to the coolest bands, or reading the autobiographical novel of the moment, when it is expertly summarized in the potted 'pass notes' column of one's Sunday newspaper, filleted in the 'loafer's guide' of your favourite lifestyle magazine or distilled in the 'brief lives' section of the weekend supplement, alongside 'quotes of the week'?[47] Analogously, why wade through 800 pages of Kotler when *Bluff Your Way in Marketing* is substantially shorter and much less indigestible?[48] Why take two years formulating a marketing plan, as McDonald recommends, when it can be done in thirty minutes, with enough time left over to catch the soccer highlights?[49] Why spend a fortune studying for an MBA when a ten-day study-pack can be yours for £12.99 (or, if you're really pushed for time, what about the twelve-hour version)?[50] Why bother traipsing across western Europe, with its traffic jams, strange food and stranger people, when the acme of Italy, the essence of France, the kernel of Germany and the best bits of Great Britain are readily available in Busch Gardens Theme Park? The attendants speak English, the prices are in US dollars, the restrooms are immaculate, the funny food is made McPalatable and, if it all seems a bit too plastic, Colonial Williamsburg is right next door.

It is, of course, easy to mock and retroscapes are much maligned on account of their 'inauthenticity', 'artificiality' and 'stereotypicality', if there is such a word.[51] Set against this, however, many contemporary cultural commentators contend that there is no such thing as authenticity, only varying degrees of inauthenticity.[52] Thus, for all its painstaking reconstruction, Colonial Williamsburg is a *recreation* of America's pre-revolutionary past, a sanitized, whitewashed and politically correct version of invented history. As Sudjic rightly observes, Williamsburg is the 'township that the Rockefellers demolished so that they could rebuild it exactly as they thought it ought to have been'.[53] The same is true of Plimoth Plantation, the Parthenon, the Pyramids of Giza or any other staging post on the twenty-first-century tourist trail.[54] Granted, the Irish theme pub is several notches higher on the kitsch-o-meter than 'authentic' Irish pubs, but the beauty of such egregious fakes is that the conviviality, the communitas, the *craic* are certain to appear on cue. The 'character' holding court in the corner of an Irish bar on Sunset Boulevard may be an out of work actor, whose accent is closer to west Hollywood than west Cork, but at least he looks the part, knows the script and remembers to deliver the punchlines with gusto. The 'volcano' outside the Mirage Hotel in Las Vegas might well be made of non-biodegradable polystyrene, but it is timed to erupt at fifteen-minute intervals. The wildlife in Disney's Jungle Cruise may be animatronic, but thankfully the critters don't sleep all day or hide themselves away from paying tourists' prying eyes. The weavers, millers, miners, blacksmiths and farmhands down the local heritage centre may have acquired their 'traditional' skills all of two weeks beforehand (on the museum's rude mechanicks training course), but visitors seem content with their demonstrations of the art of work in an age of reproduction mechanicals.[55]

Inauthenticity is all very well, or dependable at least, but the question still has to be asked: what is the attraction of such establishments when they are patently fake, assembled from kits made on an industrial estate in Essex? The answer, at least in part, is *plentiude*.[56] As the imagineers of such milieux are unable to draw upon a discourse of reality, or originality, or veracity, or actuality, or antiquity, or authenticity of any kind, they are effectively forced to evoke a sense of real-ness, of past-ness, of place-ness. This is achieved, as Veblen surely meant to say, by *conspicuous production*, exaggerated attempts to capture 'everything' about the theme in question. *Fin-de-siècle* French-ness, Celtic Twilight Irishness, Prohibition Era American-ness, Battle of Britain blitz-ness, disco-dancing seventies-ness, neo-retro nineties-ness or whatever, is attained through the sheer proliferation of artefacts, objects, knick-knacks and memorabilia. Every available signifier and vaguely relevant referent is thrown into the mix and, while the result may strike many as a grotesque caricature, it is *ness*-essary to include 'everything' in order to convey a sense of (pseudo) plenitude and create a (counterfeit) cornucopia.

There remains, nevertheless, a major problem with such stereotypes and encapsulations. Namely, that no matter how brilliantly realized or semiotically rich they are, they remain one-dimensional caricatures and their appeal rapidly palls. For consummate consumers (as the term, with its connotations of one-off uniqueness, implies), boredom rather than emulation seems to be the basic motivating factor. Been there, done that, didn't buy the T-shirt, kind of thing.[57] The inevitable upshot is that developers of retroscapes are trapped on an extremely expensive treadmill of competitive conspicuousness, a constant and ever-accelerating cycle of re-creative deconstruction, where thematic signifiers are evoked, evaluated, evaded and evicted in rapid succession, only to be eclipsed by even more extravagant encapsulations. Veblen, admittedly, might well be appalled by such ostentatious waste, but as the nothing if not critical theorist Theodor Adorno pointed out in his cogent critique of *The Leisure Class*, it is only wasteful if one espouses a utilitarian perspective, an instrumentalist perspective, a pragmatic perspective, a Puritan perspective.[58] A perspective, in other words, that elevates waste-not-want-not over why-not-waste?

In summary, themed environments in general and retroscapes in particular are often described as imitations, as simulacra, as parodies, as superficial tissues of ill-chosen quotations, as preposterous monuments to postmodern artifice. *And so they are.* But they are also much more than that, insofar as the environments attempt to capture the core of the concept concerned. They are epitomizations not imitations, syntheses not simulacra, the pith rather than parodies, the quintessence rather than quotations. They are conspicuous productions for consummate consumers. They are spaces of superabundance, places of plenitude and persuasion. They make us want through waste. They should be admired for their exaggeration, their extravagance, their exorbitance, their sheer chutzpah. As William Blake, the great retro poet, rightly observed: 'The road of excess leads to the palace of wisdom.'

And so say all of us.

9

Rebranding Marketing: Yes, We Have No Bananaburgers

The paperback, *Yes We Have No*, was published in March 1999, at the height of Britain's pre-millennial musings.[1] Written by Nik Cohn, prominent rock music journalist and author of the immortal *Awopbopaloobop Alopbamboom*, it comprises a state-of-the-nation survey, a sort of end of century summary in the tradition of Beryl Bainbridge, George Orwell, J.B. Priestley and William Cobbett. True, this retro *Rural Rides* is closer in spirit to the innocents abroad genre of Bill Bryson, Mark Twain and P.T. Barnum (Cohn, an English Jew, grew up in Northern Ireland and spent most of his working life in the USA), but it perfectly evokes the nostalgic neurasthenia into which the disunited Kingdom is slowly sinking.

In the course of his peregrinations around the country, Cohn encounters scores of retro residents of our retro realm: an Odinist in King's Cross, neo-Beats from Bristol, peace-loving hippies in Hackney, an official CoE exorcist from Tunbridge Wells, and a litany of ageing ballroom dancers, penniless ex-footballers, born-again Christians who 'look like fifties pop stars', Long Good Friday-fied gangsters from the East End, and an obviously deeply disturbed anorak who writes imaginary advertising campaigns for long-dead megabrands. The book, what is more, abounds with dyspeptic reflections on UK retroscapes, all the way from Blackpool's 'pleasure beach', a postmodern parody of its stick-of-rock, kiss-me-quick, saucy-picture-postcard heyday, to the brown-signposted excrescences of the hi-di-heritage industry:

> As soon as morning comes, we hit the Robin Hood trail. First we go marauding in Sherwood Forest. What little remains of it is flush with car parks and souvenir shops, but that doesn't damp our ardour. We play the Automatic Outlaw machine and I draw the Sheriff of Nottingham. We buy a plastic bow, three arrows and a dagger for 99p at the Magical Medieval Shopping Experience. Friar Tuck's Café is closed, to let, but there's a week-long festival coming up soon, replete with banquets, skirmishing and

jousting, Outlaw Antics and Medieval Maniax. Mary sticks her head through the hollow trunk of a thousand-year-old oak, and I take her picture, and then it's off to Robin Hood World, where a well-upholstered lady done up as a character called Winnie Scarlett, complete with fringed tunic and overstuffed leggings, takes us on a guided tour of Merrie England. There are dioramas of evil Norman barons and terrified Saxon serfs, lashings of gore all around. We are asked repeatedly to be brave. We do our best.[2]

Even Cohn is not immune to the allure of the pseudo past, however, since he resides in an archetypal English village with its parish church, wishing well, duck pond, lych gate, village green, traditional pub and propinquitous manor house. Indeed, it was there that he came up with the idea for his book, after back-to-back encounters with the old and new lords of the manor. The newcomer, naturally, is a marketing man, a musical maestro who made his fortune from that *Eroica* of the ad industry, the hands-that-do-dishes jingle for Fairy washing-up liquid. But it was only when Cohn ran into the old lord, a dispossessed blue-blood, that the title of his retro text sprang to mind ('On my way back to the cottage I passed [the old lord]. He was driving home from the pub in his ancient Ford, barely outspeeding a strolling pheasant. As we crossed, he doffed his sola topi, and out of nowhere, for no conscious reason, I started humming "Yes, We Have No Bananas"'.)[3]

Retro, of course, is epitomized by the interpenetration of old and new, and it is entirely appropriate that a creative artist, like Cohn, would respond at some subconscious level to this serendipitous clash of past and present, high and low, title and trade. The really interesting thing, however, is that no further explanation or rationale for his text is provided. Nor, for that matter, is it necessary.[4] *Yes We Have No* perfectly captures the nostalgia-larded tone of his text by means of an old song, once used as an advertising jingle, about an aristocratic product that has fallen on hard times.

Bear with me while I explain.

If one examines the extant literature, it is easy to conclude that the banana business is obsessed with production.[5] The bananarchives are replete with publications on meteorological requirements, growing season figures, plantation cultivation statistics, import-export tonnages, distribution facility locations, banana boat displacements, laugh-a-minute minutiae of national and international trade agreements, and surely-not, well-I-never, step-back-in-amazement factoids. Did you know, for example, that they're not called 'bunches' but 'hands' of bananas, or that they're herbs and hence don't grow on trees? I could go on.

Tiresome as it is, this preoccupation with production is eminently understandable, not least because the banana is such a sensitive creature.

Robust enough in its own backyard – south-east Asia to start, though some authorities subscribe to the idea of a separate American evolutionary strain – the wus doesn't travel particularly well (or at least not very far, due to its rapid ripening cycle). In the subtropics, admittedly, the banana is a ubiquitous staple crop, with more than 500 different varieties – we westerners tend to make do with the Cavendish, the Lacatan and the Gros Michel – but what it lacks in latter-day exclusiveness it makes up for in illustrious lineage. It was cultivated by the neolithic civilizations of the Indian sub-continent; known to the Ancient Greeks, thanks to Alexander's great adventures in the fertile crescent; introduced to central America and the Caribbean by seventeenth-century Spanish missionaries; and, indeed, derives its botanical name, *Musa sapientum*, from the legend that the Three Wise Men rested, ruminated and refreshed themselves under its agreeably shady canopy.[6] Yet, despite bananas' subtropical omnipresence and occasional appearance in the premodern marketplaces of western Europe – the high prices they commanded made *sapientum* an attractive, if spoilage-prone, cargo – formal trading arrangements didn't really develop until the mid-nineteenth century. Steamships, refrigeration facilities, customized railway cars and, above all, a vast network of retail outlets, were necessary before the banana business really took off.[7] By 1890, nonetheless, 13 million bananas per annum were being imported into the United States and, after an organizational shake-out at the start of the twentieth century, a small number of large, labour- and capital-intensive companies came to dominate the industry (United Fruit Company, Dole, Fyffes, Geest, etc.).

They still do.

Important though the production side of the banana equation undoubtedly is, it can be contended that marketing is just as important, possibly more so. At this remove in time, it is easy to forget that consumers in the western world had to be taught how to eat the banana. When Thomas Johnson first brought the fruit to Britain in 1633, his attempts to sell it met with considerable consumer resistance, not to say hilarity. This historical moment of bawdy bafflement is brilliantly recreated by Jeanette Winterson in *Sexing the Cherry*:

> When Jordan was three I took him to see a great rarity and that was my undoing. There was news that one Thomas Johnson had got himself an edible fruit of the like never seen in England . . . I took Jordan on a hound lead and pushed my way through the gawpers and sinners until we got to the front and there was Johnson himself trying to charge money for a glimpse of the thing . . .
>
> But I would have none of it and whipped off the cover myself, and I swear that what he had resembled nothing more than the private parts of an Oriental. It was yellow and livid and long.

'It is a banana, madam,' said the rogue.

A banana? What on God's good earth was a banana?

'Such a thing never grew in Paradise,' I said.

'Indeed it did, madam,' says he, all puffed up like a poison adder. 'This fruit is from the land of Bermuda, which is closer to Paradise than you'll ever be.'

He lifted it above his head, and the crowd, seeing it for the first time, roared and nudged each other and demanded to know what poor fool had been so reduced as to sell his vitality.

'It's either painted or infected,' said I, 'for there's none such a colour that I know.'

Johnson shouted above the din as best he could . . .

'THIS IS NOT SOME UNFORTUNATE'S RAKE. IT IS THE FRUIT OF A TREE. IT IS TO BE PEELED AND EATEN.'

At this there was unanimous retching. There was no good woman could put that in her mouth, and for a man it was the practice of cannibals. We had not gone to church all these years and been washed in the blood of Jesus only to eat ourselves up the way the Heathen do.[8]

Notwithstanding the pioneering endeavours of Thomas you-need-hands Johnson, bananamarketing only really began when the fruit was popularized at the 1876 Philadelphia Centennial Exhibition.[9] Individually wrapped in tinfoil and sold for the then princely sum of 10 cents, they were the talking point of the show, along with the Bell telephone, the Carlyss engine, an enormous sculpture of Iolanthe cast in butter by an artistically inclined Arkansas farmer, and the carnivalesque delights of Century City, a contiguous shanty town of beer halls, bawdy shows and bootleg banana sellers. In order to further stimulate consumption, therefore, the big banana companies instituted long-term promotional programmes, both individually and collectively. The emphasis, at least initially, was on information rather than imagination, as the consuming public had to be apprised of banana-eating etiquette, as well as the alternative ways in which *Musas* could be prepared. Promotional posters, postcards, pamphlets, placards and periodicals poured from the presses of the banana barons and, by the early 1880s the tropical tubers were being described (in United Fruit Company's page-turner, *Points about Bananas*) as: 'wholesome, cheap, nutritious, delicious, easily digested, always in season, available everywhere, no waste, convenient for the dinner pail, good food when cooked, good food when not cooked, the poor man's food, the children's delight, endorsed by physicians, put up and sealed by nature in a germ-proof package and produced without drawing on the Nation's resources'.[10] Bananas, what is more, could be consumed at any time – sliced on cornflakes for breakfast, eaten in salads at lunchtime and fried with meat at dinner.

Mmmmmmm*musa*.

Perhaps the most significant factor in the growth of the banana business, however, was the fact that it provided nourishment for a marketing practitioner of genius. The industry, to be sure, produced many memorable marketers down the years. The anonymous advertising creative who came up with the 1960s 'unzip a banana' slogan certainly deserves an honourable mention, as does the equally anonymous Edison of banana boxes, whose inter-war invention of the flat-pack container transformed the handling process. No less illustrious is the unknown product placement officer behind bananas' not infrequent appearance in television ads for PG Tips, the *Musa* muso responsible for the celebrated Chiquita Banana jingle of the 1940s,[11] the redoubtable Ayer advertising executive who persuaded Georgia O'Keeffe to paint a series of tropical fruit posters for the Dole company (a lifelong opponent of crass commercialism, O'Keeffe took the money and the all-expenses trip to foreign climes but refused to paint the posters)[12] and, not least, the lateral thinking de Bonos of the banana business who promoted *sapientum* skins as shoe-polishing stand-bys, a homeopathic cure for warts and – hey, man – a mild hallucinogenic.[13]

Nevertheless, in the annals of *musa*-marketing there is nothing, or no one, to compare with the bananantics of Roger Ackerley.[14] In his early 1900s heyday, Ackerley (1863–1929) was known as the Banana King, though he has not gone down in history as such. Thanks to an outrageous biography published posthumously by his louche second son, J.R. Ackerley (1896–1967), he is variously remembered as a flamboyantly Gay Hussar, who instituted a scandalous court case against his lover, the Count de Gallatin; a notorious bigamist, who sired and sponsored a second family unbeknown to the first; and, not least, a monstrous sexual predator, who cut a syphilitic swathe through British street-walkers and banana plantation workers alike, and who died of the dread disease for his transgressions. Yet despite his spotted private life, Roger Ackerley was a banana marketer extraordinary. Along with Arthur Stockley, a distant cousin of Fletcher Christian, the *Bounty* mutineer, he built up Elders and Fyffes as the foremost fruit and vegetable empire in western Europe. In many ways, indeed, Ackerley and Stockley were the Barnum and Bailey of the banana business. Stockley was a technocrat, who focused on production, transportation and the complex logistics of getting the temperamental tuber to Britain in tip-top physical condition. Ackerley's aim, on the other hand, was akin to that of P.T. Barnum prior to 'The Greatest Show on Earth': namely to put a banana on the tip of every Britisher's tongue.[15] And, like the Great Showman, the Banana King succeeded brilliantly.

Viewed in retrospect, Ackerley's task might seem simplicity itself, given the immediate and immense popularity of the fruit with consumers. Set against this, however, Ackerley was faced with a consuming public who regarded the banana as a luxury, an exotic, a special treat that was eaten only at certain times of the year, Christmas in particular. Added to the issue of seasonality, the *Musa* maestro was required to dispel unfounded rumours that Fyffes-brand bananas had to be cooked before eating and that their skins were especially slippery, a clear and present danger to housewives, horses and hackney cab drivers. The rumours, as one might imagine, were fomented by the company's competitors, who dealt in the smaller, darker-hued, decidedly delicate Canary Island variety that then dominated the banana business (rather than the larger, yellowier, most robust Gros Michel strain from Jamaica that was Fyffes' principal stock in trade). But, such short-sighted spoiling tactics – which only served to bruise the banana market as a whole – were a trivial matter compared to Ackerley's *real* dilemma. Namely, creating a market for the vast quantity of fruit that Stockley's side of the operation was supplying. The plantations, steamships, port facilities, distribution warehouses, storage depots and suchlike were all extremely expensive investments that had to be operated at very high levels of throughput, in order to make a reasonable return on capital. Ackerley's task, therefore, wasn't so much about *establishing* a market for the banana as *expanding* it substantially.

The Banana King, suffice it to say, rose effortlessly to the challenge. In less than five short years, he turned the banana into the most popular fruit in Britain, ahead of apples, oranges, pears, peaches and all the rest. Although Ackerley's incredible achievement was ultimately predicated on his belief that the market for bananas was infinite (sod the environment!), it was primarily achieved by his adoption of a single, constantly reiterated message – that bananas were healthy, natural and an essential part of everyone's everyday diet. This bananas-equals-health equation was reinforced by a constant round of promotional activities at carnivals, festivals and parades. He hired nutritionists to stomp the lecture circuit, proselytizing on the banana's behalf; he supplied banana propaganda to magazines; he organized 'banana parties' amongst the Bloomsbury set; he educated the trade about best banana behaviour; he produced pamphlets and banana recipes by the gross; he invented the banana sandwich and initiated the slice or squash debate (middle classes slice, working classes squash); he circulated believe-it-or-not stories about banana diets, such as the eighty-nine-year-old who attributed his longevity to 4 pounds of whiskey-marinated bananas per day, or the shipwrecked seafarer who not only survived for a month on bananas alone but was rescued in the rudest of health; and he variously emphasized the fruit's low calorific content or high nutritional value, depending on the precise needs of the market segments concerned (invalids, OAPs, children, fashion plates and adherents of the then popular 'simple life' philosophy of biologist, dietician and Nobel Prize winner, Ilya Metchnikoff).

Most importantly of all, Ackerley made sure that the fruit was unfailingly affordable. This was initially achieved by avoiding traditional, high-cost greengrocers, who were committed to the Canary banana, in favour of channelling Gros Michels through low-cost coster-mongers. Yet, even when the Gros Michel was firmly established, hidebound middlemen had fallen into line and Fyffes had a virtual monopoly on the European banana business, Ackerley ensured that efficiencies in distribution were passed on to the consumer. The 'penny banana' was not simply his stated ambition but, once achieved, it was ruthlessly policed. Any attempted profiteering by wholesalers or distri-butors during occasional times of shortage – due to hurricanes, disease, political disputes or whatever – incurred the incandescent ire of Ackerley, as did any fruiterer foolish enough to sell the prodigious plantain in less than perfect condition. Immediate expulsion from Fyffes' family circle was the price of disobedience. Philandering with the fruit was forbidden in the Empire of the Banana King.[16]

Ackerley's achievements would be remarkable by any standards, but what places him amongst the marketing immortals is the fact that he did it twice. Just as P.T. Barnum, the Clown Prince of premodern marketing, was prematurely dethroned and fought his way back from the brink, so too the Banana King rebuilt the business in the 1920s. In fact, Ackerley's triumph in the aftermath of the First World War – in effect, an enforced four-year break in supply – was even greater than in the banana's salad days at the start of the century. The penny banana was restored; a new slogan, 'the all food fruit', was coined and reproduced on every available surface (shop fascias, window displays, delivery vans, etc.); a Retail Contact Service of quick-response, in-store merchandisers was estab-lished, as a sort of shelf-stacking SWAT team; a specific trade-targeted slogan – 'remember, they must be ripe' – was repeated *ad nauseam*; the findings of company-sponsored nutritionists, fibre-rich diets of food faddists and the 'banana therapies' of alternative medicinemen were publicized with semi-religious fervour; a Nike-style stable of sportsmen and women was recruited as celebrity spokespersons; biplanes towing banana dirigibles, or embellished with banana wing-walkers, flew in formation over towns, cities and holiday resorts; banana floats were supplied for civic processions; elaborate stands were erected at exhibi-tions and fancy dress competitions; bizarre banana-besuited barkers patrolled the country's high streets on Saturday afternoons – as did banana sandwich boarders – doling out free samples of the fruit; mass cook-ins were conducted, featuring famous chefs and restaurateurs, whose culinary tips were circulated in a tie-in glossy-magazine-cum-newsletter, *The Banana Budget*; and, naturally enough, unlimited supplies of *sapientum* were made available to the immortal Florrie Ford when 'Yes, we have no bananas' became a big hit in 1923.[17] Indeed, the promotional value of the song was brilliantly exploited by the *Musa* master, who delivered 10,000 cardboard hands of bananas to music shops emblazoned with 'Yes, we have no bananas. On sale here!'.

Similar arrangements were made for the ensuing spate of me-too banana songs, such as 'Bye, bye Banana', 'The Banana Foxtrot' and 'I've Never Seen a Straight Banana'. (Ackerley offered a £1000 reward for the first straight banana to be found in captivity.)

The crowning glory of Ackerley's marketing career, however, occurred just prior to his death in 1929, when he introduced the famous sticky blue label, which still adorns every bunch of Fyffes bananas. In a single gesture, subsequently imitated by every self-regarding fruit and vegetable from artichokes to zucchini, he transformed an undifferentiated commodity into a blue-labelled superbrand. As the company's biographer rightly recorded, 'They were the first to brand-name bananas and it was Fyffes who, in the 1920s, engineered a banana sales campaign which was so successful that in Europe the words Fyffes and bananas became almost synonymous, thus suggesting that, like the chicken and the egg, there was some doubt about which came first'.[18]

Despite his grossly distorted posthumous reputation, few would deny that Roger Ackerley was a brilliant bananamarketer. He succeeded in making *Musa* part of people's daily dietary regimen; he ensured that bananas formed part of the fruit bowl display on almost every kitchen table; and, in the rough and tumble world of the fruit and vegetable kingdom, he firmly established the banana as – well – top banana, a position it holds to this very day. Despite stiff competition from apples, oranges, grapes and latter-day interlopers like lychees, uglis and mangoes, bananas are the biggest-selling fruit in the world. Bar none.[19] Cheap, cheerful and constantly available, the banana is easier to eat than many of its competitors, its packaging is superlative and it has its own built-in best-before system.[20] At just 90 calories per 100 grams, with high levels of vitamin and mineral content (serotonin in particular), it is the happy fruit, the nutritional fruit, the perfect fruit, no less. Banana marketers of Ackerley's generation boasted that it was 'as good as steak', though our twenty-first-century tuber touts would doubtless be deeply offended by the comparison. Until such times, of course, as mad banana disease breaks out . . .

If anything, in fact, the banana has been spoiled by success. It may be a top seller but it has lost its allure. It may be practically perfect but perfection gets boring after a while. It may be a staple of every self-respecting fruit bowl but it is now bog-standard, unremarkable, invisible, a nonentity beside the exotics of the supermarket produce section – papayas, passion fruit, pomegranates, sweet potato, prickly pears. Where once it signified cornucopia, today it signifies commodification. As Willis astutely observes in her essay 'Learning From the Banana':

Of all the fruits marketed in today's supermarkets, the banana is the least interesting. Always available and cheap, it is now taken for granted. While we might linger over the apples and oranges in an attempt to choose between different sizes and varieties (do we want Florida or California; Washington State or Appalachia?), the banana fails to stimulate such questions. First of all, while there are countless varieties of native bananas, distinguished by their taste, texture and colour, the North American palate has been trained to accept only one: the Lacatan. Plantains and small red bananas are sometimes marketed along with the more recognisable yellow variety. But these seem of a different class altogether. The choice does not seem one of choosing between a Granny Smith and a Red Delicious, but between a banana and something else. While a supermarket can hardly consider itself 'super' without bananas, the status of its produce department depends upon the availability and appearance of everything besides bananas. No longer the exotic commodity . . . the banana is commonplace and bought out of habit. There it is – green or yellow; winter, spring, summer, or fall – about the only thing that distinguishes one banana from another is its sticker.[21]

For Willis, the sticker is symbolic of the mendacious manoeuvrings of multinational capital, a semiotic sleight-of-hand that transforms use value into exchange value. The label thus epitomizes the rapacious relationship between fat cat fruit executives in their air-conditioned skyscrapers and put-upon plantation workers in the shanty towns of South America. Much the same point is made by Enloe, who takes a feminist tack on the sticker issue by showing how the Chiquita banana label – based on 1930s song-and-dance sensation, Carmen Miranda – encapsulates the pernicious plight of women workers on banana plantations (wages, sexploitation, etc).[22] Although no right-thinking individual would challenge this post-colonial critique – United Fruit Company executives possibly excepted – it is also true to say that banana labels stand for much more than exploitation. Where once the luscious blue label symbolized decadence, excitement, exoticism and delight, today it carries connotations of parsimony. In a world where every single apple, orange or egg comes stamped with an individual seal of approval, the banana's one-label-per-hand policy is redolent of rationing, want, corner-cutting and couldn't-care-less marketing. In many cases, the labels have disappeared completely, leading one to suspect that generic, retailer-brand bananas are wreaking havoc behind the scenes. Yellow packs are back with a vengeance. The banana's best years are behind it. The decline stage of the banana life cycle has commenced. Bananas are the Prell, the Omo, the Crosse & Blackwell, the Ferrero Rocher of the fruit and vegetable department. Can the 'Ambassador's Banana' be far away?

Indeed, the torpor into which the tuber has latterly sunk is exemplified by BT's use of the banana in its current ad for cheap telephone calls; by First Direct's appropriation of *Musa sapientum* to symbolize reduced bank charges; by Jungle.com's claim to be the best of the bunch for cut-price computer equipment; by the BBC's ruse of a banana-suited fool to promote a TV-licence discount scheme; by Bananalotto, a dubiously downmarket, no-stake-necessary cyberlottery; and by the Royal Festival

Hall's banana-emblazoned brochure for a series of lectures on the banality of contemporary literary criticism, where leading authorities are unable, or unwilling, to distinguish good from bad, high from low, chalk from cheese, Ps from Qs or apples from pears.[23] Be that as it may, the latter-day abjection of the banana is perhaps best illustrated by the recent case of Phil Calcutt, who couldn't give them away.[24]

A nothing if not canny shopper, Mr Calcutt calculated that he could literally make a killing on the banana promotion in his local Tesco superstore. The plantains were priced at a modest £1.17 for 3 pounds but, more pertinently perhaps, they also carried 25 loyalty card points, worth £1.25 when redeemed. The store, in effect, was paying its customers 8p to take away 3 pounds of mellow yellows. Never one to look a gift banana in the mouth, Phil promptly purchased 942 pounds for the princely sum of £367.38. Unfortunately, he couldn't fit all of his Windward Islands windfall into the back of his Peugeot 208 and, after several trips to the superstore, he succeeded in squeezing twenty-five cases into the living room of his semi-, where they were stacked from floor to ceiling. Giving them away, however, was even more of a problem, because many banana beneficiaries were suspicious of his motives or assumed that there was something wrong with the fruit. Their suspicions, admittedly, were understandable since Phil is an employee of the Ministry of Defence and might well have been working on a top secret project involving exploding bananas. Nevertheless, there was no call for the reaction of one irascible recipient who responded to Mr Calcutt's largesse with the words, 'It's money we want, not bananas.' On the other hand, his Dunkirk-spirited colleagues at the MoD took 70 pounds off his hands and anointed him – of all things – 'The Banana King'. Local schoolkids, likewise, shouted 'Bananaman' whenever Phil the Philanthropist passed by. And, notwithstanding the penny-pinching calculations of one misanthropic newspaper editor, which showed that Mr Calcutt lost out on the deal when time, trouble and transport costs were taken into account, the fact of the matter is that Phil's big banana feat attracted an enormous amount of favourable publicity, to say nothing of the 7850 bonus points on his Tesco loyalty card. Roger Ackerley would have been proud of him.

The great banana give-away of January 1997 appears to have been prompted by mild English eccentricity, though such was the volume of press coverage that one suspects the existence of an aspirant Ackerley in the bowels of Tesco's banana-buying department. The episode, nevertheless, has interesting implications for products in the late-maturity/early-decline stage of their life cycle (where commodity status holds sway and price promotions are the principal means of differentiation). It reminds us of the wider cultural dimension, that there is more to the banana than its lowly standing as a supermarket staple. It forces us to reflect on the fact that the fruit is capable of escaping its produce department confines to float free in public relations hyperspace. It informs us that *Musa* may be mouldering – one foot in the grave, the other on a banana skin, as it were – but its soul goes marching on.

As a free-floating signifier, in fact, the banana reigns supreme. The merest glance across the cultural landscape reveals a veritable cornucopia of bananartefacts. The Body Shop, for example, sells banana soap, scrub, shampoo, bath oil, lip gloss and hair putty, plus macho-masculine lines based on hemp, the banana's closest living relative. Banana brooches, badges, bookmarks, toothbrushes, tiepins, hair clips, combs, clocks, rings, pipes, paperweights, fridge magnets, lucky charms, mugs, cups, cookie jars, glasses, knives, lamps, lights, furniture, musical instruments, motorbikes and soft toys, are readily available. Banana ornaments made of brass, glass, lead, wood, plastic, pewter, ceramics, silver and gold can be purchased, as can the ceremonial Bali Banana, a best-selling item of Made-in-Taiwan tourist tat. Banana-embellished ties, T-shirts, trousers, tuxedos, tank-tops, tights, turbans, trainers, sneakers, sweaters, slippers, slacks, skirts, scarves, sarongs, smocks, swimsuits, ski pants and Bermuda shorts are being sported by taste-free fashion victims near you. Banana books are two-a-penny; banana suits are available from theatrical costumiers; and inflatable bananas are all the rage on football terraces (and, let's be honest, there's no shortage of rage thereon). There's even a big market, believe it or not, for sticky banana labels.[25] First edition Fyffes Blues of July 1929 are particularly highly prized, apparently. These people call themselves collectors. I reckon they're bananoraks.

The fruit, furthermore, is meat and drink to many people. Or so it seems. Certainly, there's no shortage of banana line-extensions. Banana bread, banana cakes, banana chutney, banana croquettes, banana cutlets, banana donuts, banana dumplings, banana flambé, banana frosting, banana jelly, banana muffins, banana omelette, banana pancakes, banana parfait, banana pie, banana popcorn, banana relish, banana soup, banana stuffing and banana toast are just some of the better known forms of banana fodder. Banana-flavoured comestibles are no less common, whether it be alcoholic beverages, baby food, breakfast cereals, confectionery, chocolate, ice lollies, milk shakes, slurpees, sorbets, sodas, yoghurts or, that special something you can eat between meals without ruining your appetite, condoms. Banana is best, however, when combined with something sticky, runny or deliciously messy. My brother-in-law owns a coffee bar in Cardiff and by far his biggest-selling side-dish is banoffee, a glutinous amalgam of banana and toffee. Elvis's declining years amply demonstrated the calorie-packed punch of banana, jello and deep-fat fried peanut butter sandwiches. And it is a scientific fact that the single greatest triumph of the ice-cream makers' art is the Banana Split. Ben and Jerry's Chunky Monkey, a knock-em-dead combination of banana, chocolate chip and walnuts, undoubtedly comes close, as does Delmonico's original Baked Alaska of 1887, which was based on banana-flavoured ice cream.[26] Nevertheless, there is nothing to compare with the Banana Split in all its three-scoops, syrup-steeped, whipped-cream, cherry-surmounted glory. As Philippe Delerm evocatively describes it in *The Small Pleasures of Life*:

> It's never easy to order this mountain of simple pleasure. The waiter notes your request with professional deference, but you can't help feeling sheepish. There's nothing childish in the whim, something which resists both dietary and aesthetic objections. Banana splits are all about basic appetite, about puerile and provocative gluttony. As the waiter brings it to you, neighbouring tables cast incredulous glances at your plate. A banana split is served either on a dinner plate or in an enormous boat-like dish, neither of which is remotely discreet. At other tables diners are eating out of slender dishes made for storks, nibbling at thin slices of chocolate cake on dainty saucers. But banana splits like to spread themselves. It's all part of their earthy appeal . . . There are millions of people in this world dying of hunger. You can just about entertain such a sobering thought in front of a slab of dark chocolate. But confronted with a banana split? As the apparition spreads before your eyes, you suddenly realise you're no longer hungry.
>
> Fortunately, remorse sets in, and you soldier on with your decadent choice. A healthy sense of defiance comes to the rescue of your waning appetite. You're breaking the rules again, like the naughty child who used to steal jars of jam from the larder, only this time you've managed to flaunt a forbidden pleasure before the world of grown-ups. Right through to the last spoonful, it's a sin.[27]

Above and beyond the ingestible and ornamental, there's the weird and wonderful world of bananascapes, bananabrands and banana art. To mention but a few examples of each: the Banana Bookshop in London specializes in remaindered books (Cleo Rocos's *Bananas Forever* figured prominently in the window display when I paid it a visit); the Banana Café in Paris provides the usual provender for its largely gay clientele (bananabaguettes a speciality, presumably); the Banana Tree in Dublin sells all sorts of kitsch kitchenware (including the eponymous device that keeps fruit bowls safe from banana-induced over-ripening); and Banana Bondage in New York stocks the kind of requisites your parents warned you about (and I'm much to inhibited to investigate, even for scholarly purposes). When it comes to bananabrands, moreover, a short short-list might include the Banana Boat range of sun protection creams; the Blue Banana transportation company in Western Australia; Bananajack, an exclusive collection of retro Aloha shirts and banana bandanas; Banana Republic, the massively successful mail order operation and 350-store subsidiary of the Gap; and ABC's syndicated television series, *Bananas in Pyjamas*, which comes equipped with a judicious selection of tasteful tie-in merchandise – videos, CDs, T-shirts, soft toys, torches, sunglasses, backpacks, glow-in-the-dark beach balls and, naturally, a natty line of blue and white striped pyjamas. *Bananas in Pyjamas*, to be sure, are only the latest in a long line of bananartistes. According to Marina Warner's brilliant overview of banana art, *sapientum* is a staple of television shows (*The Banana Bunch*, especially), popular music (Harry Belafonte's 'Banana Boat Song', Tori Amos's 'Ode to the Banana King'), film (Woody Allen's *Bananas* and the sublime scene in *Sleeper*), song and dance (Carmen 'tutti-frutti' Miranda, in particular), high art (de Chirico's *The Uncertainty of the Poet*, Cindy Sherman's *Untitled 1992*), low art (Warhol's Velvet Underground album cover, Freddy Mercury's banana busby in the video for 'I'm going slightly mad'), popular expressions ('going bananas', 'top banana', 'banana republics'), urban myth (the EC's rumoured ban on bent bananas, the Berlin Wall brought down by Ossis' bananas shortage), and, above all, banana skits, sketches and comedy routines (slippery-skin-precipitated pratfalls, Billy Connolly's big banana feet, etc).[28]

The banana, then, seems to have transcended the product life cycle. It has escaped its culinary confines, slipped its comestible moorings and colonized the wider cultural sphere. Like Monkey Kong, the superhuman cybersimian, whose powers derive from magic *Musas*, the banana is taking over the world. Bananarchy in the UK is upon us. Cry 'yes we have no' and let slip the bananas of war. The really interesting thing, however, is that nobody seems to mind. Bananomie prevails in our present postmodern world. Whereas the globalizing endeavours, not to say marketplace megalomania, of Nike, Disney, McDonald's and suchlike have latterly given rise to ad-busting guerrilla tactics, popular protests and street violence on occasion, the banana has got off fairly lightly hitherto.[29] There is no academic hand-wringing about Fyffefication the way there is about Disneyization, McDonaldization, Cocacolonization and all the rest.[30] The human rights record of banana growers is no better – considerably worse, in fact – than the barbarities that are alleged to occur in the name of Nike, Starbucks, Disney and what have you. What's more, the twenty-first-century banana business is just as big, if not bigger, than the sneakers, sodas and soft toy trade. Indeed, banana 'culture', all things considered, is almost as pervasive as Burger Kultur. Yet, compared to the naked hostility that Nike, McDonald's and the Gap have recently endured, the bananacrats are leading charmed lives.

There are, one suspects, any number of historical, cultural, economic and product-specific reasons for this state of affairs. The consumerist tumbrels, furthermore, may yet find room for the bananakings, bananaristos and bananabobs, honest or otherwise. Nevertheless, it is not unreasonable to suggest that marketing – once again – has something to do with it. Nike, Disney, Coke, Starbucks and McDonald's are acknowledged masters of modern marketing. They rank among the biggest brand

names in the world, their marketing resources are infinite and systematically deployed. They are lionized in marketing, advertising and communications textbooks (I defy you to find a discussion of bananas in
mainstream marketing texts). They have divested themselves of superfluous distractions, such as production and distribution, to concentrate
their efforts on brand-building. Their marketing *supplement* – that is, the
difference between the cost of the product or service and the price for
which it sells – is astronomical. And, as anyone who has ever accidentally
infringed upon their trademarks will readily testify, they operate brand
protection policies that are ruthlessly efficient, verging on Stalinesque.
They are, in short, the organizational embodiment of modern marketing.
When sociologists enumerate the distinguishing characteristics of
Disneyization, they are recounting the component parts of the APIC
paradigm.[31] When Coca-colonization is lambasted by bleeding-heart
liberals, it is an implicit critique of the Coca-Kotlerization process.[32]
When cultural commentators bemoan McDonaldization – and note its
offensive infiltration of every seemingly sacrosanct institution from
education to the arts – they are merely maligning the modern marketing
concept.[33]

Fyffefication, by contrast, elicits no such animosity.[34]

What, then, can marketers learn from the bananaburghers? Well, it
seems to me that there is a lesson here for the marketing brand, the
nothing if not extensive product line that trades under the Marketing
label. For those of us who toil in the malarial marketing plantations,
especially those operated by the UFCs of higher education, it is easy to
forget that marketing is a product, a commodity, a brand. It is a conceptual comestible that competes in the agora of academic life and sits
on the societal supermarket's well-stocked shelves. Marketing is
marketed like any other cultural SKU and, as one might expect, it has
to earn its keep in the DPP model of existential space allocation.

In this regard, Marketing is manifestly the *Musa* of business and
management, the banana in the socio-economic fruit bowl, the *sapientum*
of scholarship. Like the banana, Marketing hails from a specific natural
habitat – land of the free gift, home of the brand name – and it has
been transplanted with gusto (often to inhospitable or inappropriate
milieux).[35] Like the banana, Marketing is ubiquitous, since there is
hardly a corporate or institutional household in the world that doesn't
contain a bunch of marketers, at various stages of ripeness (and, as with
bananas, they are best kept separate). Like the banana, Marketing is
distributed by a small number of large middlemen, who harvest, tranship
and deliver the hands of knowledge (KFC, the Kotler Fruit Company, is
perhaps best known). Like the banana, Marketing comes in a host of
varieties, albeit very few are normally found hanging on the display

hooks of the profession (Levitt's Lacatan, Gros Michel Baker and Hunt the Cavendish are our principal principles plantains).[36] Like bananas, Marketing has broken out of the business school larder and colonized the wider cultural sphere (priests, politicians, media pundits, arts spokespersons and all the rest have something to say about marketing-cum-consumption, as does almost every academic discipline from sociology to literary criticism).[37] Like the banana, Marketing is profoundly political, whether it be in the subordination of women (for female plantation workers, read housewives), its megalomaniac desire to be the organizational top banana (ahead of the apples of accounts, the pears of personnel, the oranges of operations and the strawberries of strategy), or indeed in its recent precipitation of a transatlantic trade war, where the Relationship Marketers of the EU challenged the Coca-Kotlerization techniques of US-style transaction marketers (only to have their theories appropriated and retransmitted by Uncle Sam, in a marketing mini-Marshall Plan).[38]

Like the banana, moreover, Marketing burgeoned during the late nineteenth century, reached its pinnacle in the Bartonesque spiritual-side-of-trade 1920s, largely disappeared from view during the Second World War, re-emerged stronger and fitter in the 1950s and, of late, has become increasingly retrospective in ethos. Once the epitome of exoticism, an alluring rarity, the fruit of the wise – Simon Nelson Patten, no less, held bananas up as a symbol of the good life[39] – the banana is now familiar, steadfast, trustworthy, mundane, its wistful blue labels bespeaking heritage, tradition and remembrance. *A la recherche de la banane perdue*. Analogously, marketing used to be considered the secret of corporate success, a powerful magic wand wielded by hidden persuaders and other high priests, which transformed penurious organizational frogs into profitable corporate princes. Nowadays, marketing is nothing special, nothing secret, nothing magical, nothing out of the ordinary. Marketing is everywhere, marketing is unavoidable, marketing is ubiquitous, marketing is boring, marketing is bereft. It has lost its lustre, it is lacking in allure, it can't be given away, as the Phil Calcutts of our field are finding. The corporate cornucopia contains more captivating conceptual consumables, the couscous of Competencies, the kumquats of TQM, the kiwi fruit of Knowledge Management. Marketing *Musas* are still there, of course, but mainly for decoration, for show, for completeness (since a fruit bowl isn't a fruit bowl without a marketer or two). All that remains for our conceptual costermongers is to relive the glory days when marketing was the pick of the bunch, an exclusive premium-priced brand, a logo to die for, a product line that occupied pride of place in the display windows of thought.

However, when we look back over our product's life cycle, it is clear that, even though marketing is the *Musa* of management, it has taken its cue from the burger rather than the banana.[40] Modern marketing is the apotheosis of McDonaldization – rational, rigorous, efficient, effective, ubiquitous, unstoppable – indeed, the two are synonymous, as noted earlier. While most would agree that McDonaldized marketing has been brilliantly successful, to the extent that it is an organizational staple, a pedagogic necessity, the convenience food of corporate life, many maintain that it is completely devoid of taste, of personality, of intellectual nutrition. Modern marketing, in many ways, is the sweaty cheeseburger of business and management and, although its sales figures cannot be gainsaid, the people that produce it remain deeply unloved. For all marketing's smiley-faced, family values, have a nice one, happy mealy-mouthed, pseudo-bonhomie, consumers remain suspicious, chary and reluctant beneficiaries of our fries-with-that largesse. Just as today's anti-capitalist protesters unfailingly choose to trash the nearest McDonald's, so too marketing is considered unspeakable by legions of commentators on popular culture, be they sociologists, anthropologists or newspaper columnists. Even fully paid-up marketing professionals are joining in the chorus of disapproval. Can you imagine Burger King's employees turning up their noses at a Whopper?

I can.

It seems to me that if marketing wishes to make amends and endear itself to its long-suffering customers – practitioners, pedagogues and postgraduates alike[41] – it is time to abandon the McDonaldized model. After all, there's only so much marketing MSG, academic additives and intellectual E-numbers a body can take. Marketing needs to revert to a serotonin-rich diet; it needs to get in touch with its *sapientum* side; it needs a *Musa* muse; it needs to get back to its big banana roots. Lest there is any misunderstanding, I am not suggesting that marketing seek inspiration from the wan bananas found in the fruit containers of contemporary commercial life. They too have lost their allure, thanks to McDonaldized marketing. I'm recommending, rather, that we look beyond the fruit bowl to free-floating banana signifiers and that we turn to the past, the good old days when bananas made their bawdy arrival in the western marketplace. Bananas, lest we forget, are sexy, bananas are fun, bananas are carnivalesque.[42] From the music hall ribaldries of Marie Lloyd, though the erotic banana dance of 1920s superstar Josephine Baker, to the Bananaman skits on *Eurotrash*, *sapientum* has constantly been associated with salaciousness, suggestiveness, smuttiness, particularly the humorous impropriety of the cheeky-chappie, oh-er-missus, bit-near-the-knuckle-but-no-real-harm-in-it variety.[43] The Internet, admittedly, contains all sorts of eye-averting banantics – or so they tell me – but the amusing *Musa* aspect (banana skins, banana jokes, Bananarama, etc.) ensures that the fruit is regarded as comic rather than crude, saucy rather than sleazy, burlesque rather than blue.

Marketing too is sexy, funny and carnivalesque. Sex sells, or so we are repeatedly informed, and the billboards daily remind us ('Hello Boys', 'Size Matters', Lara 'Lucozade' Croft, Häagen-Dazs, Obsession, Magnum, Opium). Humour pervades the contemporary marketscape, as each and every commercial break makes abundantly clear (think Budweiser frogs, think Carling Black Label, think Tango). The carnival-esque combination of transgression, inversion and good old-fashioned vulgarity has been associated throughout history with the marketplace. Of course, you would never know any of this from the academic marketing literature, which has studiously avoided all carnal, comedic and carnivalesque thoughts in its chimerical pursuit of scientific status – Prim, Proper, Prude, Puritan are the real 4Ps, don't you know – but just because marketing researchers want to avoid getting their hands dirty doesn't mean that grubby paws don't exist or that people aren't having fun with them.[44] It is entirely appropriate, is it not, that the front cover of Saunders's *Humour in Advertising*, an anthology of best promotional practice, should feature a banana skin and that the companion volume, *Sex in Advertising*, contains several examples of bananas being used to hawk condoms.[45] Get your bananarubbers here, folks.

The carnivalesque, then, is one way of circumventing the decline stage of marketing's Product Life Cycle. There is, however, another bawdy banana benefit, insofar as it turns the cycle into a circle by taking us back to the very beginning, to paradise, to Adam and Eve. Although apples have shamelessly taken the credit for centuries, the historical facts are incontrovertible – the 'forbidden fruit' in the Garden of Eden was a banana.[46] Sixteenth-century theologians debated this matter at length (presumably after a hard day's fitting angels on to the head of a pin), and the general consensus was that the Tree of Knowledge was our tumescent tuber. Now, some of the sophisticates amongst you might surmise that the deciding factor was the fruit's undeniably phallic shape. But the ecclesiastic adjudicators, in fact, were swayed by the fibrous leaves of the banana plant, which could be woven into modesty-preserving loincloths when Adam and Eve became aware of their nakedness. Be that as it may, the premodern belief in arcadian bananas was so strong that the botanical name for the plantain – next branch down from *Musa sapientum* on the Tree of Life – is *Musa paradisiaca*. Actually, the two terms are often mistakenly transposed in the banana-pocrypha.

Irrespective of such minor nomenclatural misdemeanours, the crucial point is that, if the banana was the forbidden fruit of the Garden of Eden, then the Serpent was the first marketing man! This theory, it must be stressed, is by no means untenable, since temptation, titillation and titivation are essential aspects – arguably the essence – of marketing.[47] Marketing, moreover, has always been imbued with an arcadian, utopian, paradisal cast, whether it be the products and services that promise us a perfect smile, hair, family, holiday or, for that matter, the tools, techniques and theories that make up the marketing concept and which promise to deliver a perennially profitable, customer-orientated organization.[48] Marketing paradise is always around the next bend in the banana. You may laugh, but sceptics should recall George Orwell's encounter with an opium addict who claimed to have discovered the secret of the universe in his nightly dreams. Only he kept forgetting to write it down. Well, one night he remembered to put pen to paper and, on waking the next day, discovered that he had written the deathless words: 'The banana is big but its skin is bigger'.[49]

Big Mac marketing is big but banana skin marketing is bigger.

10

Revolting Marketing: Gross is Good!

The TV ad for AM-PM convenience stores opens with a motorist munching contentedly on his mustard-covered, 59-cent hot dog. Face smeared in excess condiment, he realizes he's forgotten the napkins but can't go back inside looking like Bart Simpson's body-double. Ever resourceful, he reaches for the pine-tree air freshener dangling from his rear-view mirror and *wipes his mouth with it*.

Gross!

A bikini-clad *Baywatch*-babe runs towards the camera, her generous embonpoint exaggerated by sexploitative slow-motion. The gravel-toned voiceover announces, 'If this is your idea of quality television, then we've got the perfect product for you . . . Big Fat Tacos!' Three huge slobbering comestibles are thrown on to a groaning counter and, after extolling their suppurating virtues in odious close-up, the advertisement for Del Taco restaurants closes with the Orwellian invocation, 'We know who you are and we know what you want.'

Grosser!!

Stranded in the desert with only a broken-down flatbed for company, an unshaven, roughneck Romeo bites into his Carl's Junior hamburger. The ketchup spurts uncontrollably, narrowly missing his blue jeans and scuffed work-boots. From out of nowhere a silver Porsche appears and adroitly pulls over. The window slides down to reveal a stunningly beautiful female driver. She looks suggestively at the abandoned epicure, only to wince noticeably when his disgusting burger drips on to the gleaming metalwork. He flings the offending object over his shoulder and they speed off to the advertiser's words of nutritional wisdom, 'If you can get something hotter and juicier than a Carl's Junior hamburger, go for it!'

Grossest!!!

As the twenty-first-century dawns, it seems that advertising is immired in a pit of profanity, a bottomless pit of profanity.[1] Far from turning over a new and improved leaf, today's advertisers are engaged in an offensive offensive, a full-frontal attack, an enfilade of effluent. Although we live in a brave new world of relationship marketers, green consumers and socially conscious custodians of brand spirit, it looks as though advertising's top minds are on lower things. Much lower. Positively Palaeozoic. These days, advertisers don't so much wear their hearts on their sleeves as wipe their noses on them. Differentiation is giving way to defecation. Positioning is mutating into propositioning. Purulence is advertisers' argot of choice, and blasphemy their byword.

In Britain, a clothing retailer, French Connection UK, makes waves with its almost-but-not-quite offensive acronym. Billboards emblazoned with 'fcuk fashion' and 'fcuk me' stop traffic, stimulate a flood of complaints and lead to eventual censure by the official advertising watchdog. The company replies with the billboard, 'fcuk advertising.' And pre-tax profits double.[2]

Jerusalem, the holy city, is similarly affronted by an advertising campaign for Chacko, a local fast-food restaurant. 'Who the fuck is Chacko?' may well be an intertextual allusion to the best-selling album by rock star Gumpy, but many religious leaders and tourists are mortified by such an egregiously offensive slogan. For David Clayman, director of the American Jewish Council, the Chacko ad represents 'a new depth of vulgarity in a society with a long, painful record of tastelessness'. Yet sales of the company's kosher burgers soar.[3]

Diesel apparel, meantime, features four young, rosary-reciting nuns wearing blue jeans made of 'pure virginal 100 per cent cotton'. The British Safety Association, a quasi-government body, promotes safe sex with a leaflet depicting the Pope alongside the strapline, 'Eleventh Commandment, thou shalt wear a condom.' Virgin Megastore employs images of Mary, mother of God, to help move a few more CDs and computer games. Carlsberg reminds drinkers of its famous Danish lager that 'There's no room at the inn'. And even stolid stationery companies like International Paper muscle in on the irreligious act with indecent variants on a 'Jesus loves me' theme.[4]

Above and beyond blasphemy, bad language and gastronomic abomination, advertising's shock troops are not averse to sexism, lewdness and libidinal overkill.[5] A Europe-wide campaign for Gossard lingerie announces, 'Who said a woman can't get pleasure from something soft?' Tour operator Club 18–30 promises 'Beaver España', alongside photographs of bulging male crotches and the less than subtle strapline, 'Ladies, can we interest you in a package holiday?' Levi's relaunches its 'twisted seam' jeans with an appropriately warped campaign featuring disembodied denims frolicking, fondling and fornicating in public places. Bol.com, an online bookstore, follows suit with naked bibliophiles wrapped up in a hard cover, whilst wrapped around each other. Organics Shampoo shows a stunning redhead peering down the front of her bikini bottoms, in order to prove that it 'keeps hair colour so long, you'll forget your natural one'. Sure anti-perspirant depicts a dishevelled, gently glowing, presumably post-coital *femme fatale*, whose 'visible quickie' is insufficient to trouble the company's invisible underarm deodorant. And who can forget Calvin Klein's infamous 'kiddie pornography' campaign of 1995, which courted free publicity through questionable allusions to underage sex, only to incur the incandescent wrath of concerned parents worldwide? Benetton, of all companies, purported to be outraged by the tastelessness of CK's 'cheesy eight-millimetre porn film'.

Happy though advertisers are to wallow in the malodorous marketing mire, it is evident that several different offensive dimensions are being exploited.[6] A typology of tastelessness is called for and, hesitant as I am to impose order on ordure, a 4Cs classification can be tentatively identified. *Carnal* pertains to sexually explicit or sexploitative campaigns, such as Renault's claim that 'size matters', Wonderbra's welcome on the 'Hello Boyos' hillsides and shirt-maker Van Heusen's contention that a man is not a man without fifteen and a half inches to play with. *Corporeal* refers to bodily fluids, fecal matter and analogous unmentionable natural functions. These range from Marks & Spencer's distasteful depictions of half-eaten left-overs, through Supernoodles' suggestion that plates should be licked clean rather than washed, to the Red Bull drinker's shit-for-shat response to an avian incontinence incident. *Creedal* comprises offences against religious beliefs, broadly defined, or widely accepted societal norms. Benetton's notorious nun-kissing-priest poster epitomizes the former and their 'condemned to die' montage of death row incumbents is an interesting example of the latter (inasmuch as many Americans believe in capital punishment and are affronted by the company's ill-considered support for convicted killers). *Cultural*, finally, offends against the canons of aesthetic taste, as in a recent 'Reassuringly Expensive' campaign by Stella Artois. This portrays beer bottles being opened on top-of-the-range consumer durables – BMW Roadster, Sony Digital Betacam, Saladino glass table, Gibson semi-acoustic – though the resultant scratches are more deeply offensive than reassuringly expensive. Unless, that is, an appetite for destruction is the taste of our times.

Taste, to be sure, is a moveable feast. The bad taste of today is the good taste of tomorrow. Yesterday's shock-horror is today's so-what shrug, as the history of the artistic avant-garde reminds us.[7] When Whistler famously 'flung a pot of paint in the public's face', he engaged in a *culturally* offensive act, even though *Nocturne in Blue and Gold* is now regarded as a proto-Impressionist masterpiece. When Salman Rushdie published *The Satanic Verses* in 1988, the *creedal* consequences were catastrophic – fatwas, riots, assassinations, diplomatic incidents, round-the-clock protection, etc. – and rumbled on for the best part of a decade. When Manzoni canned his own excrement in the early 1960s, it seemed that the depths of *corporeal* degradation had finally been plumbed, although signed tins of Manzoni Merde are now worth £30,000 apiece. When *The Playboy of the Western World* was first performed in 1907, the playwright's reference to female underwear caused a slash-the-seats, wreck-the-theatre, lynch-the-author riot, though few now appreciate that the word 'shift' was then considered *carnal* rather than coy. These days, we are more offended by the Japanese anarcho-artists, Cai and Xi, who adopted a strictly functional approach to Duchamp's 'Fountain' when they actually pissed in the Surrealist's priceless urinal.[8] Cultural, creedal, corporeal and carnal thus combine into an offensive imbroglio. With effrontery like that, who needs advertising?

Although it is hard to beat a pair of revolting aesthetes – Gilbert and George, come on down – the commercial shock tactics of look-ma-no-image dotcom companies are certainly within spitting distance.[9] To be perfectly honest, however, I'd rather not wallow in the E-ffluent E-ndeavours of our E-minent E-missaries. Suffice it to say that their disgusting dotcommercials range from sniffing dogs' bottoms and proctology lessons for butthole surfing wannabes, to straightforward braggadocio about the size of their packages. So instead, I'll try to do the decent thing – for once in my life – and attempt to account for the rise of malodorous advertising.[10]

Naturally, I'm hesitant to offend the offensives (as creatives are known nowadays), but it seems to me that there are four main reasons for this latter-day turn-off turn-on. First, offensiveness is effective. At a time when consumers are bombarded day and daily by countless commercial messages – most of them safe, sanitized and deadly serious – blasphemy, ribaldry and scatology stand out from the crowd in all their gory glory. In the words of new wave advertising gurus, Jonathan Bond and Richard Kirshenbaum, outrageousness gets 'under the radar', the mental screen that today's sated shoppers use to filter unwanted marketing communications.[11]

For instance, the in-your-face advertising of Carl's Junior – euphemistically termed the 'messy burger' campaign – has led to unprecedented increases in traffic and transactions, reversing the Anaheim-based company's five-year slide in sales.[12] 'We could hardly believe it,' said Neil Naruff, brand manager at the time: 'the campaign had an immediate effect on our business, perhaps the most positive in years'. Likewise, Calvin Klein's kiddie pornography prompted a sixfold increase in jeans sales among the target market segment, who rebelliously revelled, as teenagers are wont to do, in their guardians' moral outrage.[13] The campaign, according to Marian Salzman, corporate director at Chiat/Day, New York, proved 'pretty effective' among its intended audience, 'the fashion buyer who's looking for relatively safe ways to rebel'.

Second, offensiveness is efficient. Abominable ads not only stand out from the compliant commercial crowd but almost always stimulate a (horrified) second look, a (disgusted) double-take that sends 'frequency' figures skyrocketing, for starters (to say nothing of 'gross rating points').[14] Granted, the second glance is often reluctant, the double-take virtually involuntary, but this merely confirms offensive advertising's remarkable ability to stop 'em in their tracks. Its impact, in effect, rests upon the admittedly paradoxical psychology of disgust, which comprises a strange combination of repulsion and attraction. William Miller, a leading academic authority on distasteful behaviour, contends that we are mesmerized by the mephitic, fascinated by the fetid, hopelessly drawn to the distasteful.[15] We can't bear to look, yet can't bear not to look at, say, horror movies, auto accidents, fist fights or bodily waste, especially our own. 'Even as the disgusting repels,' he says, 'it rarely does so without capturing our attention. It imposes itself upon us.'[16]

A striking example of this repulsion–attraction quality is found in a Singaporean magazine advertisement for Spin washing powder, which portrays a pair of soiled underpants alongside an invitation to scratch 'n' sniff.[17] One's total revulsion at the very idea is immediately followed by a spontaneous sense of curiosity, a mental race through the moral and mechanical possibilities ('Surely they haven't gone that far, have they?' 'If they can reproduce eau-de-Cologne, can they replicate the repugnant?' 'Dare I test it?') No less magnetic in its repulsiveness is the much-cited 'disembowelled shark' shocker of Kadu, an Australian clothing manufacturer.[18] The ad's *infamy* is largely attributable to its timing, since it appeared at the same time as two fatal shark attacks – to a predictable torrent of mass media outrage – but its *impact* is almost entirely due to the arrestingly revolting imagery. A great white shark's technicolor innards ooze across a wooden quayside. The masticated contents include a semi-digested human corpse and immaculately indigestible Kadu beachwear. Tough clothes, indeed!

Third, offensiveness is cheap (as well as nasty). As the Kadu controversy indicates, there's nothing quite like provocative advertising to attract the attention of news-hungry media. Sensationalism, alas, sells newspapers, attracts audiences and provides endless opportunities for sanctimonious, space-filling op-eds. A product or service can thus be publicized for next to nothing. When salaciousness is on offer, so it seems, minuscule advertising budgets can stretch a very long way indeed. 'The bang per buck is beyond thermonuclear,' claims one gross-out marketing authority, 'we're talking Big Bang per buck'.[19]

Take Benetton, perhaps the most infamous exponent of unexpurgated advertising.[20] The company grabbed headline after headline, generated affronted editorial after affronted editorial, and garnered sale after sale – at least initially – with its wilfully offensive images of human immiseration, tastefully interspersed with collages of multicoloured condoms, a rogues' gallery of male genitalia, the stark naked posturing of Luciano Benetton and, lest we forget, scandalous shots of a shot soldier, a car bombing and a dying AIDS victim. All on a Lilliputian advertising spend of $5.6 million.[21] French Connection, similarly, shocked a nation for less than £1.5 million, most of which was recouped through the sale of 150,000 'fcuk me' T-shirts, and Calvin's kiddie campaign captured the front pages of both the *Washington Post* Style section and the Business section of the *New York Times*. Most advertisers would cut off their right arm for that kind of media exposure, though dismemberment might not be sufficiently newsworthy these degenerate days.

Fourth, like it or loathe it, offensiveness is easily emulated. A copy-cat element is clearly at work. Many corporations, so it seems, are content to follow Benetton's feculent lead. When the sewer's the place to be, there's no shortage of wannabe sewer-rats determined to out-plumb each others' depths of degradation.[22] Anything you can doo, I can doo better, so to speak. Astonishing though it is to think of diarrhoea or disease or death or detumescence, or debauchery, or depravity or good old-fashioned *double entendre* as the latest management fad, yet that's where the advertising action's at, sad to say, that's what PR people are packaging, pure and simple, that's the nature of the Benetton-inspired beast, don't you know.

Thus, sheets of extra-soft toilet tissue are attached to magazine ads for a Citroën sports car, which guarantees a 'positively sphincter twitching 0–60 in 7.2 seconds'; a child relieves itself in the street to remind British dog-owners of their rectal responsibilities; a dead horse hangs from a hook, thereby promoting animal welfare; a single raised digit, the international sign language of obscenity, helps sell cheap cigars; a naked woman is tied to a chair with items of clothing from the 'slightly twisted' Full Circle range; the Vegetarian Society articulates its 'much easier not to eat meat' message with photographs of operation scars labelled 'stomach cancer', 'throat cancer', 'bowel cancer'; a man is kicked viciously in the crotch for borrowing his girlfriend's Nissan without permission; the naked model in a life-drawing class is smitten by an Impulse body-sprayed art student, only to be embarrassed by his ensuing erection; a dead man's body complete with engorged member advertises Sky Broadcasting's movie channel (meanwhile the Playboy Channel promises 'Morgasms'); an Italian ISP employs a bare-breasted Amazon to pose the provocative question, 'Why pay for it when you can get it for free?'; Ogilvy and Mather concocts completely phoney facts about the incidence of underage sex – 61% of twelve-year-olds are sexually active, no less – only to disingenuously claim that they represent 'the statistics of the future'; a British political association, Conservative Futures, emulates French Connection with a CFUK campaign, only to be sued for its exploitative attempt to cash in on FC's proprietary profanity; and, not to be outdone, a cinema ad for London's Great Frog jewellery store ends with that celebrated commercial show-stopper, the fabled magic bullet of marketing communications: 'If you don't like it . . . fuck off.'

They make Jerry Della Famina's 'from those wonderful folks who gave you Pearl Harbor' seem positively angelic by comparison.[23]

Marketing's moral majority might wonder, possibly despair, about this bathroom humour bandwagon and hope against hope that there'll be a revolt against revulsion, ideally sooner rather than later. Gross-out advertising, however, cannot be separated from developments in the wider social and cultural sphere. At a time of supposed national dumbing-down, when shock-jocks rule the airwaves, pornography pervades the Internet, television channels are chock-a-block with 'shockumentaries', and prominent talk-show hosts, such as Conan O'Brien, openly boast of gas-passing, sniffing and kindling competitions,[24] it is hardly surprising that today's advertisers are bending with the wind, as it were. When Young British Artists like Damien dissected-sheep Hirst, Tracey dirty-bed Emin, Chris elephant-dung Ophili and Ron dead-dad Mueck adopt a I-see-no-shit attitude, is it any wonder that English advertisers endeavour to outdoo whatever YBAs throw at them?[25] Indeed, when cult cartoon series like *South Park* embrace Christmas poo, foetal millinery and chocolate salty balls, amongst others too mephitic to mention, and each summer unfailingly excretes a top grossing gross-out movie – *Dumb and Dumber* (Vesuvius of diarrhoea erupts in Dolby stereo), *There's Something about Mary* (extra-hold, bodily-fluid-enhanced hair gel), *American Pie* (making out with Granny Smith's shortcrust), *Scary Movie* (all of the above, with an increased sperm count)[26] – is it fair to condemn today's advertisers for grabbing a slice of the repellent action, for tapping this vein of venality, for trying to catch a fragrant whiff of celebrity phero-mone?

Likewise, the late, lamented Lewinsky scandal, with all its sordid revelations concerning oral sex, semen stains, coitus humidor, penile malformations and general presidential philandering surely proves – as if proof were needed – that an excremental ethic has penetrated virtually every social stratum in America from the sophisticates on Jerry Springer to the hypocrites on Capitol Hill. Monica-marketing[27] was big business for a while, as the fading T-shirts, blurred videotapes, stalled movie deals, broken sex toys and remaindered joke books about the 'state of the nation undress' continue to remind us. The Starr Report, one suspects, will be remembered less for its inventory of the president's peccadilloes than for its lurid celebration of the flotsam, jetsam and general detritus of contemporary consumer culture – the Gap, Banana Republic, Hugs and Kisses, Gingko Biloba, Revlon, American Express, Altoids *et alia*. As that fount of the postmodern marketing Zeitgeist,

Entertainment Weekly, wryly observed at the time, 'its artful weaving of brand names into the narrative . . . offers an unparalleled lesson in product placement'.[28]

'Greed is good' was bad enough, but 'gross is good' simply beggars belief. Come back Gordon Gekko, *Wall Street* is forgiven.

Above and beyond developments in the cultural sphere, there is an important demographic dimension to advertising's headlong plunge into postmodern putrescence. In this respect, perhaps it is time to acknowledge what has been evident for some considerable time: the baby boom generation is bust. Although boomers remain the driving force of western economies, in terms of sheer numbers, spending power and marketer orientation (that is, the principal focus of marketing activity), the cutting edge of consumer cool is firmly in the hands of post-boom cohorts. Slackers call the shots. Gen-X sets the agenda. The blank generation rules the roost.[29]

Slackers, admittedly, may not aspire to anything, or so the tiresome stereotype suggests, but it seems that many now aspire to be slackers. Aspiring to anti-aspiration is the order of the day. The shock of discovery and initial denigration of this post-1960 generation has rapidly given way to the realization, among ever-youthful baby boomers, that they *really are* getting old, that there *really is* a newer, younger, second-generation Pepsi Generation of adults whose mores, values, beliefs and behaviours are different, distinctive and, to some extent at least, desirable. Boomers have thus gone from top dogs to smelly cats in less time than it takes to catch a rerun of *Friends*, the archetypal X-rated sitcom.

Generation Next, by contrast, now counts key opinion formers, political movers and shakers, television producers, network schedulers, movie stars, top musicians, literary luminaries, legal eagles, hi-rolling stockbrokers, leading fashion designers, computer programmers, cultural commentators and cutting-edge intellectuals amongst its number. Supposed slacker traits such as streetwise cynicism, scepticism, self-reliance, slothfulness, solipsism and a sophomoric sense of *Saturday Night Live*-nurtured, gross-out humour are in the ascendant, albeit far from ubiquitous. And if Generation-Ex doesn't like it, they can . . . Great Frog themselves.

More to the point, there is an important managerial and marketing dimension to the valorization of prototypical X-er attributes. As leading-edge, forty-year-old slackers enter early middle age, with all its attendant anxieties and crises, they also find themselves in positions of very great power and responsibility.[30] Many of today's much-vaunted CEOs hail from Generation X (almost all of the dotcommandants, for starters). Marketing departments, advertising agencies and research houses are increasingly staffed and run by post-baby-boom people (the postmodern advertising authorities, Bond and Kirshenbaum, are in their late thirties, as is Beverly Day, the marketing manager of Carl's Junior). And, not least, a new cohort of management gurus is stepping into the (still-warm) shoes of Drucker, Handy, McKenna, Kotler, Levitt and so on Bruce Tulgan, author of *Managing Generation X*, is in his early thirties; the anti-guru management gurus, Michelwait and Thorpe, are in their mid-thirties; Ridderstrale and Nordstrom, authors of the hip-n-happenin *Funky Business*, have yet to hit the big four 0; much-lauded corporate fools, Firth and Leigh, have hardly a grey hair between them; and today's hot-shot marketing scholars – Craig Thompson and Susan Fournier in the States, Susan Hart and Mark Ritson in the UK, Mark Gabbott and Richard Speed in Australia, Suzanne Beckmann and Patrick Hetzel in continental Europe, to name but a few – are all on the right side of the mid-life divide.[31]

When a new generation, with new ideas, with new spokespersons and with new ways of seeing, doing and making sense of things finds itself holding the levers of pragmatic and paradigmatic power, it is almost inevitable that management generally and marketing in particular should find itself manhandled into a whole new mindset. Indeed, one of the most striking things about the, no longer derogatory but increasingly dull and derivative, discussions of Generation X is the enormous emphasis placed upon marketing and advertising. Not only did Copeland's eponymous novel coin the much-chanted postmodern marketing mantra, 'I am not a target market', but it was also advertising agencies who first latched on to the X-er moniker and did much to create, circulate and commercialize the construct.

In certain respects, marketing consciousness is *the* defining feature of post-boom cohorts. Children of the hydra-headed telecommunications revolution – cable, VCRs, MTV, CDs, shopping channels, the web etc., etc. – X-ers have been hammered by the hard sell since their formative years. They have endured literally decades of advertisers' emollient entreaties and have been blitzed by commercial breaks from the cradle to, well, middle life or thereabouts. Unsurprisingly, then, they are wise to the wiles of marketing practitioners, fluent in the idiom of advertising and fully cognizant of the concepts, strategies, objectives and intended outcomes of commercial activity. Focus groups repeatedly reveal that Gen-X consumers are capable of efficiently and expertly filleting advertising campaigns, brand extensions, new product developments or whatever, often employing the appropriate marketing argot in the course of their deconstructive endeavours. So attuned are they that advertising illiteracy may well be less prevalent than literary illiteracy these days, though many traditional marketers, frustrated in their inability to get through to X-ers, might respond that advertising dyslexia is the *real* problem.

This advertising Xpertise is or should be unremarkable, given that approximately half of all college students now take marketing courses

and those that don't are exposed to an enormous amount of marketing-
and advertising-related discourse in magazines, newspapers, television
shows and so on. The essential point, however, is not that contemporary
consumers are *au fait* with marketing or advertising, nor indeed that
they are sophisticated, sceptical and, when they feel like it, subversive
shoppers. The key issue is that they are not impressed by much of what
advertisers offer. What's more, they know that advertisers know they are
not impressed by much of what advertisers offer. That doesn't impress
them either. Many of them, in fact, genuinely like and admire advertising. They just don't think advertisers are very good at it. As the
advertising savants Bond and Kirshenbaum observe, 'Shooting down the
advertising has become a kind of sport, designed to show that [con-
sumers] are not stupid enough to be manipulated, particularly by those
without enough respect for their intelligence to at least make the sport
interesting'. They have a saying in their agency that perfectly illustrates
this point: 'Your strategy is showing.'[32]

Modern marketing is thus hoist by its own petard. It has spawned,
suckled and supplied an advertising-savvy generation of consumers. And
they, in classic Freudian fashion, are biting the hand that feeds them,
fouling the marketing nest and, as the recent anti-capitalist riots in
Davos, Seattle and London clearly demonstrate, endeavouring to
destroy the very lifestyle delivery system that helped create their own
sense of self-identity. They'll be complaining about bananaburgers next.

The emergence of marketing-communications-conversant consumers
may help account for the reflexive, knowing, self-referential turn in
contemporary commercial life, which is replete with advertisements
about advertising, spot the product puzzles and intertextual allusions to
other ads, movies, television programmes and so on. However, it does
not explain the latter-day propensity for impropriety. After all, it is
perfectly possible to play postmodern marketing charades without
recourse to rude gestures or risqué referents. Granted, Generation X
grew up in the permissive society, courtesy of make love not war,
contraceptive pill-popping, *Valley of the Dolls*-reading baby boomers.
They endured adolescence when Mel Brooks was breaking wind in
Blazing Saddles, Divine was dining out on ordure in *Pink Flamingos* and
President Nixon was deleting expletives amongst other less salubrious
activities. What's more, they reached full maturity when the ironic smirk
of David Letterman was endearing rather than irritating, Bret Easton
Ellis touched the nadir of rat-wrangling degeneracy in *American Psycho*
and Jerry Seinfeld handled masturbation in a prime-time sitcom.
Pornography is thus par for the course, obscenity seems normal, grossness is no big deal for today's cadre of consumers. Leading Gen-X
spokesperson, Geoffrey Holtz goes so far as to suggest that his peers'
fondness for offensiveness is a reflection of, and commentary on, 'the
banality and vapid commercialism omnipresent in our culture'.[33]

Holtz's explanation may well hold water, even if it is hard to swallow (Gen-X as offenders of the faith?), but perhaps something deeper than demographics is at work. For example, one oft-cited cause of our ostensible descent into degradation is the aforementioned *fin-de-siècle* effect (see Chapter 1).[34] Just as the turn of the twentieth century was characterized by depravity, decadence, despondency, sexually trans-mitted diseases, economic-cum-technological dislocation and an extra-ordinary preoccupation with divination, necromancy and matters paranormal, so too the twenty-first-century cusp seems obsessed with analogous concerns. Only nowadays UFOs have superseded ouija boards, AIDS occupies the syphilis slot, cyber barons are reconfigured robber barons, genetic defects have replaced 'bad blood' in the chamber of scientific horrors and child sex abuse is to today's moral guardians what homosexuality was to Oscar Wilde's contemporaries.[35] Indeed, these parallels are so marked that some prominent theorists of post-modernity, principally the incomparable Jean Baudrillard, maintain that the western world is engaged in a massive process of rewinding, replaying, reviewing and re-presenting the long march of history in order to salve our collective consciences concerning the complete mess we made of the century just past. Naturally, he employs arrestingly revolting imagery to illustrate his thesis:

> When ice freezes, all the excrement rises to the surface. And so, when the dialectic was frozen, all the sacred excrement of the dialectic came to the surface. When the future is deep-frozen – and, indeed, even the present – we shall see all the excrement come up from the past. The problem then becomes one of waste. It is not just material substances, including nuclear ones, which pose a waste problem but also the defunct ideologies, bygone utopias, dead concepts and fossilized ideas which continue to pollute our mental space. Historical and intellectual refuse pose an even more serious problem than industrial waste. Who will rid us of the sedimentation of centuries of stupidity? As for history – that living lump of waste, that dying monster which, like the corpse in Ionesco, continues to swell after it has died – how are we to be rid of it?[36]

Repugnance is a strange sort of repentance, to be sure, and an alterna-tive explanation of our present putrescent propensities is provided by the so-called 'arrested development thesis'. According to its foremost exponent, Andrew Calcutt, post-war western society (as a whole, not just the individual demographic cohorts of Generations W, X, Y or what-ever) is characterized by *aspirations to adolescence*.[37] Whereas adulthood was once deemed an admirable state, a right and proper place of maturity, solidity, seriousness and societal responsibilities, these days no one wants to grow up, let alone grow old. We live in a world of middle-aged teenage rebels, who were weaned during the post-war boom – the television age – and whose worldview was shaped, in its entirety, by the jeans-wearing, rock 'n' rolling, Tolkien-reading, drugs-taking, anti-establishment ethos of pop culture. In this society of perpetual Peter Pans and Lost Boys, where even the establishment is anti-establishment and there is nothing left to rebel against (except rebelliousness), everyone aims to remain, in the words of middle-aged rocker Bryan Adams, 'Eighteen Til I Die'. Slick Willy Clinton plays sax, amongst other teenage pursuits; Tony 'Bambi' Blair boasts of his long-haired, bell-bottomed, rock band past; fortysomething CEOs rollerblade to the office with a copy of *The Face* tucked inside *The Financial Times*; and Homer Simpson, Springfield's father of the year, is our adult role model of choice. Almost inevitably, therefore, the culture of our times reflects this adolescent sensibility. Sex, smut, snot, flatulence, foul language, bodily functions, bad manners, new-laddism, narcissism, superciliousness, scatology, secretions, sarcasm, cynicism, irony, ribaldry, offensiveness, truculence and an overwhelming desire to shock, subvert, revolt are par for our course. Or should that be coarse?

Suffice it to say, marketers and advertisers have not been slow to exploit this permanent teenager propensity. As Summerskill records, recent years have seen a slew of products and services aimed at 'kidults', thirty-five going on fifteen-year-olds. Sony Playstations, pavement scooters, pro-wrestling, cyberpuppies, the Chrysler PT Cruiser and top-of-the-range trainers are all proving popular with 'middlescents' (mainly fully grown men who live with their parents and have the wherewithal to indulge their expensive teenage fantasies).[38] Mutton dressed as lamb marketing is no less evident amongst Pepe-wearing, Porsche-driving, ponytail-sporting fiftysomethings, who assume that age shall not wither them nor custom stale their infallible Viagra.[39] In these fountain-of-youth circumstances, where there is a direct correlation between HRT and the short skirt/stilettos/sequins/cosmetic surgery combo, it is entirely appropriate that advertisers should formulate campaigns based on archetypal adolescent emotions and thereby assist with the product's forever young positioning.

Plausible though such explanations undoubtedly are, the basic problem with both the arrested development thesis and the *fin-de-siècle* effect is that they avoid the basic offensive issue. They effectively displace gross-out advertising to a transcendent, all but incontestable domain, where cyclical theories of time obtain or the wheel of life can be stopped at age seventeen (or thereabouts). Likewise, X-planations predicated on Generation X-cess's X-crementalism are just a convenient X-cuse for those wedded to modern marketing ideology, insofar as environmental influences can always be called upon to account for everything.[40] Analogously, the cultural sphere hypothesis, whereby every creative artist is a shit-shoveller of sorts, overlooks the important fact that contemporary advertising *leads* rather than follows artistic endeavour. Revolting artists are rank amateurs beside offensive advertisers. The ad industry has donned the shock-horror mantle of the aesthetic avant-garde. Conversely, it is no accident that today's cutting-edge artists are routinely described as marketing executives in paint-splattered mufti. Art for mart's sake is the order of the day.[41]

Instead of contending that marketing *reflects* the surrounding socio-economic environment – 'society gets the advertising it deserves', etc. – perhaps it is time to be upfront about our fondness for feculence. In saying this, I don't mean that marketing and advertising should acknowledge that they *contribute* to the purulence that pervades twenty-first-century life. We already know that. The reflect or affect debate, remember, is almost as old as the history of marketing itself. I, for one, accept that, say, the television ad for Six Flags theme park, which features a satisfied customer vomiting into a trashcan, serves to perpetuate today's 'anything goes' ethos. I recognize that the industry awards showered on the Benetton campaign and Calvin Klein's kiddie pornopticon – the former featured in 'best of the twentieth century' lists and the latter was nominated for top honours at the first VH-1 music and fashion awards ceremony – help legitimize and indeed encourage additional advertising outrages. I too am amazed that New Labour chose to boast of the UK's offensive marketing capability, when it displayed Benetton, French Connection and Gossard lingerie ads in a recent 'Cool Britannia' exhibition at the Victoria and Albert Museum.[42] So much for 'tough on grime, tough on the causes of grime'.

My point, rather, is much more straightforward. It seems to me that (a) there is nothing wrong with offensiveness; (b) that advertising has always been offensive; and (c) that advertising should aim to offend. By its very nature, I grant you, grossness is disgusting, revolting, unpleasant. It's meant to be. It wouldn't be gross if it weren't. However, the fact that we find certain things repugnant doesn't necessarily make them wrong, or bad or morally suspect. Offensiveness may not be nice, but it is part and parcel of life.

Indeed, according to Georges Bataille, a much-maligned French theorist of the inter-war era, whose work has latterly been resurrected and widely acclaimed, the western world has been deluding itself with the Enlightenment-inspired notion that reason, order, rationality and rectitude comprise the mainsprings of civilization.[43] The meaning of life is predicated just as much upon death, disorder, deviance, destruction, derangement, disrespect and disgust, he maintains. Irrationality, waste, excess, transgression, madness, mysticism, extravagance, absurdity, putrescence, promiscuity, concupiscence and suchlike are an essential aspect of the human condition. They are not aberrant, improper or, indeed, unmentionable. Frogs and snails and puppy dogs' tails are no less important than sugar and spice and all things nice. In many ways more so.

Concomitantly, the cultural anthropologist Mary Douglas maintains that disgust is triggered at typological interfaces, by things that are unclassifiable, ambiguous, betwixt and between, neither one nor the other, neither here nor there.[44] Marketing and advertising are many things, admittedly, but they are classic commercial instantiations of in-betweenness, with production on one side and consumption on the other, with practice to the left and theory to the right, with abstruse economics-cum-psychology above and real world managers-cum-practitioners below. Marketing boasts of its intermediate, bridge-building ability – its co-ordinating role in the firm – and the history of the field is riven with either/or antagonisms. Is it an art or a science, sacred or profane, idiographic or nomothetic, qualitative or quantitative, concept generating or concept testing, romantic or neo-classical? Does it reflect or create consumer demand? Which half of advertising works? Is it in crisis or on the cusp of greatness? When is a price cut better than a sales promotion? Is marketing a function or a philosophy, a place or a process, a force for the good or a pernicious means of exploiting human credulity, cupidity, carnality? Irrespective of the answers, it is the industry's inherent ambivalence, liminality and equivocation that makes it the perfect breeding ground for disgust, depravity, degeneracy and defilement.

Advertisers, however, do not need cultural anthropologists or obscurantist Gallic erotomanes to place offensiveness in its proper perspective. The history of advertising and promotion is replete with repulsion, whether it be in the animal welfare commercials of the 1980s, David Ogilvy's shock-sells advice of the 1960s, the keep-death-off-the-roads campaigns of the 1940s, the litany of odious bodily ailments invented in the 1920s – BO, halitosis, athlete's foot, housemaid's knee, wrinkled elbows (!) – or Edward Bernays's Progressive Era promotional stunts for syphilis awareness and analogous unspeakables.[45] The putative packaged-goods promoters of the late nineteenth century warned of the insectoid horrors that infested the dry-goods grocer's cracker barrel or oat bin; they emphasized the serious health risks run by users of other people's combs, toothbrushes or razor blades; and they repeatedly stressed the adulterated dangers that inhered in competitors' products, which were unfailingly manufactured in insalubrious conditions by flagrantly irresponsible processes.[46]

As we noted in our study of the American medicine show, furthermore, advertising's heritage of gross-out excesses, of egregious outrageousness, of snake-oil selling charlatanism, is second to none. True, practitioners in general and academics in particular have repeatedly tried to distance themselves from such dubious activities. Prominent examples of attempted exculpation include: the 'truth in advertising' movement prior to the First World War; the 'marketing science' mindset of the great society 1960s; and today's relationship marketers who promise to love, honour and obey their customers, 'til death them do part. However, as advertising historian Jackson Lears cogently demonstrates,[47] there has always been a transgressive side to commerce; a rude, crude, rambunctious, end-of-the-pier dimension to advertising endeavour. For most people, in fact, the carnivalesque side of salesmanship *is* salesmanship. Everyone 'knows' that selling, marketing and advertising types are hucksters, shysters and outright cheats, whose claims to care for their customers are just another con, another three-card marketing monte, another attempt to pull the wool over credulous consumers' eyes. No matter how much marketing communicants may protest their innocence, the profession is, and always will be, associated with patent medicine showmen, snake-oil spin doctors and the itinerant peddlers, Yankee traders and commercial pitchers of yore. And there's nothing offensive about that.

What I'm suggesting, in other words, is that the contemporary crudities of Carl's Junior, Del Taco and Luciano Benetton are part of a dishonourable tradition that stretches back to the founding father of our field, P.T. Barnum, whose success was based on transgression, offensiveness, egregious exploitation and ethical turpitude.[48] People, remember, rolled up in their millions to stare at his dwarfs, giants, freaks, mutants, bearded ladies, Siamese twins, Circassian beauties and missing links, all of whom served as promotional 'skyrockets' for the main event, be it a circus, a theatrical performance or a retroscape like the American Museum. Stupendously nauseating though today's noisome marketers are, or aspire to be, they simply do not compare with P.T. Barnum, the grandee of grossness, the virtuoso of vulgarity, the savant of saprogenicity, the connoisseur of conduct unbecoming. Barnum was the original offensive marketer, the forebear of FCUK, the ancestor of AM-PM, the precursor of Calvin Klein's kiddie porn side-show. When it comes to rank rankings, PTB pulls rank on everyone.

Although many might be revolted by the thought of marketers resurrecting (and boasting of) their offensive advertising forebears, there's another way to look at it. If marketing has always had an unmentionable and well-hidden offensive dimension, the fact that our field is getting in touch with its fetid side should surely be welcomed rather than condemned. The AM-PM, Carl's Junior and Del Taco television ads suggest that advertising is coming out of the gross-out closet. Strange though it sounds, gross-out is actually an indication of growing maturity and professional self-confidence, a recognition, recuperation and, to some extent, reclamation of marketing's hucksterish heritage. Many academics, admittedly, with their intellectual overinvestment in customer orientation, social responsibility, moral propriety and ethical rectitude may be incapable of appreciating the importance of customer disorientation, anti-social irresponsibility, immoral impropriety and unethical turpitude. But as today's aspiration to abomination indicates, advertising practitioners are already ahead of the academicians, as is so often the case.

This, of course, is not to suggest that *all* advertising should be offensive or that grossness is appropriate to every product, service or situation. While it is all pervasive at present amongst desperate-for-an-image dotcom companies, anything-to-attract-attention charities, and eat-my-soiled-shorts fashion-forwarders, it doesn't follow that feculence is right for, say, financial services, fast food or home furnishings (though their time will doubtless come). Nor, for that matter, does offensiveness appeal to, or meet the approval of, all and sundry. As might be expected, the splatter treatment appears to be particularly attractive to nerds and nose-pickers of all ages, whereas many women, especially those with young children, are often upset by the ostensibly offensive. Indeed, the growth of grossness mustn't obscure the ever-present possibility of excessive excess. That is to say, excess is effective when non-excess is normal but when excess is everywhere, excessiveness somehow palls beside non-excess and normality (even though the norms of normality will have shifted in the interim).

Until such times as New Puritanism kicks in, however, perhaps we should sit back and enjoy advertising's egregious offensiveness. Not only is it in keeping with society's adolescent mindset, not only is it in tune with Generation X-cess, not only is it advertising's principal claim to artistic fame, not only is it a retro reminder of a distinguished (if disagreeable) marketing tradition, not only does it release us from the oppressive shackles of customer care, whiter than whiteness, moral probity and honesty-is-the-best-policy hypocrisy, but it acknowledges that advertising is a commercial embodiment of the grotesque.[49] Exemplified by the works of Hieronymous Bosch, Pieter Brueghel, Goya and, latterly, Francis Bacon, the grotesque is a mode of aesthetic discourse that rejoices in the misshapen, the mutant, the mephitic, the malodorous. As the bestiary of trade characters bears witness – the Tango monster, the Honey monster, the Hofmeister Bear, Joe Camel, Boddington's Bull, Bibendum, the Budweiser frogs and many more besides – advertising is the contemporary repository of the monstrous, the fantastic, the gruesome, the grotesque.[50]

If, indeed, the grotesque serves 'to pierce the veil of familiarity, to stab us up from the drowse of the accustomed, to make us aware of the perilous paradoxicality of life',[51] then it is time to recognize that the really repugnant aspect of our specialism is not the occasional shock-horror commercial or sniggering reference to bodily waste. The real offensiveness, rather, inheres in our customer-worshipping ideology, in our tired and tiresome APIC paradigm, in our modern marketing mindset. As Goya's famous etching *The Sleep of Reason Produces Monsters* reminds us, the pursuit of reason, rationality, rectitude and realism inevitably calls forth the repugnant, the repellent, the revolting, the retrogressive.

Today's marketing monstrosities are a *consequence* of excessive customer orientation. Marketing science has created a Frankensteinian throwback. Gross-out advertising represents the return of the marketing repressed.

And if you don't like it, you can . . . erm . . . make out elsewhere.

CONCLUSION

TRAPPING THE SUBSTANCE

11

Rejuvenating Marketing: The Big Tease

Close-up of pearly-white picket fence, topped by dollops of full-bodied fuchsias. A heavily laden bumblebee ambles from pistil to stamen and sluggishly ascends through passing showers of apple blossom. Pull back to reveal a pristine front yard, its emerald carpet carefully fitted around the recesses of a clinkered clapboard house. Three steps rise to a wisteria-fringed veranda, dressed with double settee, swing seat, aged rocker and low-slung Shaker table. A checkerboard lies open, the game unfinished from the night before. Sound effects from within. The fleur-de-lys front door bursts open, three backpacked, lunchboxed, spring-heeled third-graders spill forth and tumble down the path. A yellow school bus awaits. Tracking shot traces its regular route, down lime-lined boulevards of complementary clapboards and perfect pickets; past the wood-slat water tower, brownstone fire station, Iconic-entablatured town hall and reassuringly redbrick doctor's surgery; through the diner-, deli- and bank-bedecked Main Street, with its hanging-basket-garlanded street lamps, like floral scales of justice; to the empty but expectant school yard, the local seat of learning, the heart of the community.

Voiceover: *There once was a place where neighbours greeted neighbours in the quiet of the summer twilight. Where children chased fireflies. And porch swings provided easy refuge from the cares of the day. The movie house showed cartoons on Saturday. The grocery store delivered. And there was one teacher who always knew you had that special something. Remember that place? Perhaps from your childhood. Or maybe just from stories. It held a magic all its own. The special magic of an American home town. Remember that place? That place is here again, in a new town called Celebration. Celebration is a place that takes you back to that time of innocence. A place where the biggest decision is whether to play kick-the-can or king-of-the-hill. A place of caramel apples and cotton candy, secret forts and hopscotch on the streets. Celebration. A new American town of block parties and Fourth of July parades. Of spaghetti dinners and school bake sales, lollipops and flies in a jar. Celebration. A town that's bringing back a good idea and making it better. A whole new kind of lifestyle that's not new at all – just lost for a while. That fellow who said you can't go home again? He was wrong. Now you can come home. To Celebration. Your new hometown.*

Thus spake the video brochure for Disney Corporation's Celebration, a new town in central Florida, which opened for business on 18 November 1995, Mickey Mouse's birthday.[1] The Experimental Prototype Community of Tomorrow finally arrived, approximately thirty years after Walt envisioned it, and of all things it turned out to be a thing of the past, a retro suburb of Main Street, USA. This is a proper community, however, imagineered to the n-th degree. Building controls are strictly enforced. Carefully screened residents are required to choose from a menu of six basic house types – Classical, Victorian, Coastal, Mediterranean, Colonial Revival, French Farmhouse – and are limited to one yard sale per year, for fear of lowering the tone of the neighbourhood. Lawns must be properly tended, washing cannot be hung out to dry, the precise hue of external paintwork is vetted beforehand and only white or off-white window coverings are permitted. Incredibly, Celebration is the only place on earth devoid of Disney artefacts and crass commercialism. It is, in fact, 'a new, old-fashioned hometown, perhaps like the one you grew up in – or maybe just wish that you had'.

Pass the barf bag.

Celebration may be the epitome of ersatz, the mutant love-child of Minnie Mouse and Louis Mumford, but it is not unique. The Olde Towne movement is the latest thing in the United States.[2] Seaside (Florida), Kentlands (Maryland) and Congeniality (California), to cite but three of these Potemkin Villages for the Viagra-Prozac Generation, are tasteful evocations of the past that never was, pseudo-small-town idylls of welcoming front porches, unfailingly friendly neighbours and God-fearing patriots, who salute the flag, support the local sheriff and subscribe to the American Dream. As it was, so shall it be. Equally evocative, albeit at the opposite end of the taste spectrum, are the gated communities of elephantine McMansions that dot the ex-urban landscape.[3] A monument to new money, the self-made men of Clinton's economic miracle, these mega-structures comprise Rabelaisian mismatches of pretend Palladian pilasters, Rapunzelesque towers, crenellated battlements, Gothic double garages and Neo-Colonial, alfresco jacuzzis with surround-sound and matching loungers. They are the plaid blazers, baseball caps and polyester pants of US real estate.

Great Britain is no different. Today's Cool Britannics like to think of themselves as above such grotesquery, vulgarity and ostentation. We are, are we not, a self-effacing nation of exquisite taste, effortless discernment and, the occasional outbreak of new money-inspired naffness notwithstanding, *Antiques Roadshow*-induced sagacity. Sadly, the available evidence suggests otherwise. The UK equivalent of Celebration is Poundbury in Dorset, an old-fashioned new town predicated on the fogeyish architectural principles of HRH the Prince of Wales.[4] Derided and dismissed in equal measure when it was first mooted in the late eighties, Poundbury is now considered a model community, the half-timbered template for the twenty-first-century. A retro-Ruritania it may well be – all cobbled streets, thatched roofs, fieldstone cladding, cast-iron railings and decorative horse troughs – but few would deny that it works.

And, once again, it is not alone. South Woodham Ferrers, a new olde towne in Essex, epitomizes contemporary attempts to sculpt the soul of Albion in stone.[5] Some hoity-toity architectural critics have been quick to condemn its vernacularized car park, Georgian-roofed filling station and grocery superstore masquerading as a traditional Essex barn. But others rejoice in its *genius loci*, they take pride in its conservation-minded closeness to the soil, they relish its respect for time-steeped British tradition, for people who know their place, for old acquaintance not forgot, for this sceptr'd isle set in the silver sea, for (swelling chords, join hands, all together now) England's green and pleasant land.

The past has also been pressed into service by Richard Rogers, newly ennobled urban guru and late-modernist architect extraordinary. Charged with envisioning the future of Britain's cities, in light of the estimated four million new houses needed by 2020 (due to smaller family sizes and increased household numbers), Lord Rogers' Urban Task Force recommends recolonizing the inner cities, reimagining public transport and refurbishing the country's stock of old but beautiful buildings.[6] Or, to be more precise, the UTF is attempting to accelerate an already existing trend. Such is the desire to do up derelict buildings, especially in the south-east, that developers are complaining of a shortage of rehab opportunities. Victorian factories, churches, schools, hospitals, warehouses, workhouses, asylums and, in one celebrated case, public toilets have been transformed into great British abodes.[7] Cleaned up, spit-n-polished, and all-mod-conned, these new-look old buildings combine triple glazing, central heating and communal fitness suites with stucco coving, wooden flooring and wrought-iron spandrels, to offer today's well-heeled residents a retrofitted home fit for heroes.

The suburbs, similarly, are suffused with brand new period homes, twenty-first-century Garden Cities, where neo-Georgian, mock-Tudor, demi-Gothic and all-purpose Edwardian co-exist quite happily. Provided you're not an architectural purist, that is. Barratt, Bovis, Bryant and a host of bespoke builders offer a wide range of revival-ish house styles – Mondeo man gets medieval – on their portfolios of prestigious estates for parvenus.[8] Instantly aged, courtesy of mature tree planting, antique-effect garden fencing and quick-growing varieties of Virginia creeper,

Russian vine or Beanstalkus Leylandii, these des reses for the demi-
monde obviate the need to wait for heritage by accelerating the ravages
of time. And just in case we don't get the message, the developments are
unfailingly anointed with a suitably bucolic moniker – The Brambles,
The Sheddings, The Dove Cote, The Harvest Home. I speak from
personal experience, since the Brown barracks resides on one such estate,
a Baroque-Bauhaus hybrid with mansard roofs, flint block facings,
cobbled car ports and Art Deco satellite dishes. Its name? Whitethorn.

Some residents of Regency town houses, Victorian redbricks, inter-
war semis, thatched Cotswold cottages or Kentish oasthouses may be
appalled by the likes of Whitethorn (hey, it must be exclusive, definite
article-less developments always are). But, as the latter-day DIY boom,
burgeoning 'House Beautiful' magazine market and manifold MDF-off
television programmes bear witness, there's hardly a house in the
country – room, one suspects – that isn't a repository of *Repro de Luxe*.
Aside from stick-on ceiling roses, chipboard banister assembly kits,
plastic strips of cut-to-size leaded lights and electric-candle-effect chan-
deliers, all sorts of interior design anachronisms, solecisms and mala-
propisms are on ostentatious display. Faux antique tables, chairs,
carpets and mirrors; almost-old davenports, fireplaces, lampstands and
CD racks; and nearly-neo display cabinets, stuffed with reproduction
Rockwood vases, cod Clarice Cliff ceramics and Lalique-alike crystal-
wares, stand sentinel in the nation's unused lounges. Our country's
kitchens come equipped with ancient Agas or rehab Rayburns, bogus
austerity cupboards or pantries, oak-veneer, lime-laminate or pseudo-
mahogany Welsh dressers, and unglazed, rough-cast or, for all I know,
pre-chipped earthenware crockery. Britain's bedrooms boast brand new
Jacobean four-posters, hint-of-Gothic headboards, built-in Beaux Arts
wardrobes, Pre-Raphaelite pillowcases, Book of Kells inspired duvet
covers, Arts & Crafts alarm clocks, touch-tone bakelite telephones
and en-suite bathrooms that look like the store cupboard of an
Edwardian apothecary. Even our studies come complete with self-
assembly captain's chairs, vintage roll-topped, claw-footed, computer-
ready escritoires and I-remember-the-sixties i-Macs, on which we cruise
the Retronet or play the latest version of Tomb Raider, Retro Helix or
Age of Empires II.

Needless to say, a vast army of retropreneurs has emerged to service
this market. Enumeration is impossible and pointless. A glance at the
small ads in any 'weekend', 'living' or 'how to spend it' newspaper
supplement, let alone leafing through the designer-porn pages of House
'n' Garden-led glossies, is sufficient to convince anyone that retro rules
the home front. In interior speak, admittedly, the word 'retro' refers to a
specific style or look – kitsch Americana, mainly[9] – but if a broader
past-meets-present interpretation is permitted, then *le mode retro* is
unarguably the universal language of western domesticity. This ersatz

Esperanto is spoken by innumerable opinion leaders, fashion plates and lifestyle gurus, ranging from Ralph Lauren to Blockley's of Telford. The latter manufactures 'heritage' bricks for the building industry. A complex, computer-aided process of 'tumbling' and 'distressing' – akin to stonewashed jeans technology – is used to simulate the colour, texture and broken surfaces of old bricks. Mildewed, pock-marked and soot-stained models are also available from Blockley's impressive new brick range.[10] Lauren, likewise, purveys an imaginary English, aspirant upper crust, polo- and croquet-playing, pre-Great-War, *Brideshead Revisited*, honey-still-for-tea lifestyle. Brilliantly, it has to be said. The Lauren look is all and endlessly applicable to whatever product category the former tie salesman deems appropriate – bed linen, restroom requisites, designer paint, aged oak tables, distressed leather chairs, tearful tea services and slightly upset sideboards, to say nothing of fashion, footwear, fragrances, spectacles, socks, suitcases and the flagship store to end all flagship stores, on 72nd and Madison.[11]

Although Lauren and Blockley's epitomize the big and small, B2C and B2B, American and British, high- and low-profile extremities of contemporary retrochic, there are any number of in-betweenies. Masterframe, for example, sells a 'bygone collection' range of double-glazed, uPVC replacement windows which replicate the traditional box sash design found in most pre-war houses. Not only are they indistinguishable from original timber windows, but they offer all the modern conveniences of heat retention, noise insulation, low maintenance and state-of-the-art security features, whilst avoiding the perennial problems of damp, draughts, rattles, flaking paint, rotting wood and sticking cords. How can anyone resist the company's amazing buy-four-get-one-free offer?

Whilst waiting for Masterframe's window dressers to arrive, there's just enough time to peruse the House of Bath mail order catalogue. An exclusive chaise-longue in Wedgwood blue, inspired by the nineteenth-century French original, perhaps? Or, what about a pair of polyresin corbels, available in Grecian, Roman or Medieval mouldings? How does a delicately proportioned, rosewood veneer, two-seater Regency settee, covered in studded beading and striped velveteen, sound? If Victoriana is preferred, look no further than HoB's hand-painted, solid pine, seven-drawer tallboys, three-panel cotton tapestry screens (with brass-effect hinges) and four matching watercolours of enamel bathtubs (in two-inch, wood-finish, crackle-gold frames). Doubters, cynics and hands-on enthusiasts are respectfully invited to examine the collection at House of Bath's flagship store in Barrett Street, a fully restored recreation of the 'former glory' of this one-time international emporium.

Martha Stewart, however, doesn't need a flagship store to vouchsafe her retro bona fides.[12] As America's leading lifestyle expert, her books, magazines, website, television programmes, radio shows, syndicated advice columns, mail order business and exclusive licensing deal with

K-Mart and paint manufacturer, Steubin Williams, are sufficient to ensure that Martha Stewart Living Omnimedia is in a league of its own. Like Lauren, for whom she once worked as a catering consultant, Stewart sells a complete package predicated on a judicious mix of tradition, simplicity, self-sufficiency and stitch-in-time nostalgique. Home cooking, house restoration, garden maintenance, wedding party planning, holiday season decoration, hand-made gifts, gallant table settings, immemorial flower arrangements and all manner of do-it-yourself domestic duties are grist to the Martha Stewart mill. Her recipes, recommendations and it's-a-good-thing titbits are unfailingly interlarded with time-was anecdotes, when the neophyte homemaker sat in her mother's noisy but welcoming New Jersey kitchen; or exchanged gustatory secrets with the Russian immigrants who lived next door; or picked wild cherries, strawberries and peaches at her grandma's iceboxed, brass-utensiled, pot-bellied-stoved country cabin; or acquired her skills as a seamstress in between modelling assignments for *Marie Claire*, selling stock for top Wall Street brokerage, Monness, Williams & Sidel, and bringing up her only daughter in time-honoured, middle-class, love-thy-neighbour-as-thyself fashion. Not even the proliferation of Martha Stewart skits, jokes and parodies, widespread scepticism about her impossibly perfect lifestyle package, and a best-selling, no-holds barred unauthorized biography, which alleged that she bullied her ex-husband, exploited her spineless employees, maltreated her estranged daughter and invented most of her claims to fame, seem capable of denting Stewart's reputation or dislodging her from her position as America's foremost retro-trafficker.[13] As the marketing director of K-Mart observed at the commencement of their $25 million licensing deal, Martha Stewart *is* America.[14]

Well, almost. Another contender for America's retro-meister in chief is Thomas Kinkade.[15] The only artist to be quoted on the New York Stock Exchange, his Media Arts Group posted a turnover of $128 million in 1999. A self-styled 'romantic realist', who wears his small-town heart on his homespun sleeve, Kinkade's paintings portray a profoundly nostalgic milieu of thatched cottages, efflorescent gardens, hallucinogenic hedgerows, lighted windows, vine-clad gazebos, steaming waterfalls, smoking chimney pots, winding country lanes, invitingly open gateways, steeply arched footbridges and gently glowing Victorian street lamps. Indeed, most of his luminescent landscapes, seascapes, snow-scapes and cityscapes are set in an entirely imaginary yesteryear, when close-knit families strolled arm in arm to church, horses and traps were the major means of transport, and God-fearing, love-thy-neighbour community spirit was the order of the day. This retro message is reinforced by accompanying mini-narratives, which explain the provenance of, and inspiration behind, each painting. For example, his 'Hometown Memories' collection represents an attempt to tap into the rich seam of associations that the words convey:

As we stroll down the tree-shrouded lane, you'll notice the landmarks that are familiar to every hometown – neighbourhood houses aglow with lights, the people of the village, well-worn sidewalks, and even a family or two – the Dalmatian in a front yard, the cat darting across the rain-slicked street. These are the places where families thrive, children grow up and memories are made. In the distance you will see the steeple of the village church – the spiritual foundation of every hometown. One can imagine that the Sunday service is about to commence on this rainy spring evening.[16]

Saccharine-covered schmaltz with extra helpings of sentimentality, I grant you, but it is disconcerting to think that one in twenty US households actually owns one of Kinkade's radiant artworks. Although it is easy to dismiss his *oeuvre* as a manifestation of middle American mawkishness, or attribute his success to the in-built intrigue of the canvases (they all contain hidden Where's Wally-style references to his ever-loving wife, N), what cannot be denied is that Kinkade runs a brilliant retromarketing operation. In addition to his mass-produced canvases, which are sold on QVC, via a highly successful website and through 150 signature retail stores known as Redemption Centers, his images are reproduced as place mats, pillows, sheets, towels, rugs, mugs, coasters, calendars, jigsaws, cookie jars, fridge magnets, lamps, La-Z-Boy recliners, screen savers, mouse mats and many more. Indeed, if the recently announced deal with US Home Corporation comes to fruition, the Houston-based property development company will construct entire communities based on Kinkade's arcadian vision.[17]

Um . . . let me guess . . . Kinkadia?

Thomas Kinkade's ambition, then, is to turn the world of his imagination into an attractive lifestyle option. Ralph Lauren and Martha Stewart, as might be expected, are the stated corporate role models, although his claim to have posterity in mind suggests a Barnumesque flair for self-promotion. Kinkade purports to be on a direct line of descent from Norman Rockwell, another retro artist adored by the general public, detested by the critics and who circulated his work through innovative distribution channels, namely magazine covers. Rockwell actually features in many of Kinkade's paintings; he claims to have worked in Rockwell's New England studio; and he considers the latter-day recuperation of America's leading inter-war artist (a huge Rockwell retrospective is touring the States at present), as a vindication of his much-maligned artistic vision. Aesthetically speaking, Kinkade's work is much closer to Maxfield Parrish, a brilliantly successful commercial artist, whose radiant paintings of fanciful retroscapes – fairy tale castles, mythical figures, comely maidens – were enormously popular in the first quarter of the twentieth century.[18] They too were used to sell a wide variety of goods and services – tyres, typewriters, lightbulbs, cigars, books by L. Frank Baum, etc. – and distributed by unorthodox means, calendars and chocolate boxes in the main. Like Rockwell, Parrish is back in fashion, as innumerable album covers, advertising treatments and movie story-boards bear witness.

Regardless of Kinkade's aspirations to lasting fame or his disingenuous assertions that the art establishment's disdain is due to Media Art Group's innovative channels of distribution, which conspicuously circumvent the art gallery circuit, the essential point is that his retrorientation is not new. Just as Martha Stewart is the latest in a long line of lifestyle-cum-etiquette gurus (Nancy Mitford, Brownie Wise, Miss Manners, Emily Post, Betty Crocker et al.); just as Ralph Lauren retails a romanticized version of Anglo-Saxon squiredom, itself an invented tradition of the mid-nineteenth century, which was revived in the 1930s and at various times since; and just as the House of Bath, Blockley's, Masterframe and so on are doing what generations of retro merchants have done before them (Laura Ashley, Liberty's, Roycroft, Omega Workshops, William Morris, Wedgwood, religious relic manufacturers in the Middle Ages, etc.), so too Thomas Kinkade is using tomorrow's technology to sell his unctuous images of yesteryear.

Even Celebration is not particularly new, as Ebenezer Howard's 'Garden City' movement and Louis Mumford's manifold American equivalents remind us.[19] In west London, for instance, the House Hill Garden Estate, an extensive development of half-timbered, neo-Tudor dwellings dating from the 1930s, was *and is* as strictly controlled as Mickeyville, Minnieton, Mousewich-in-Arden (call it what you will). From the outset, the House Hill Garden Estate was scrupulously supervised and paternalistically policed. Houses were painted in regulation black and white; hedges and lawns regularly trimmed; tradesmen were required to call at back doors only; and washing could only be hung out to dry on Mondays and Tuesdays. Contemporary planning regulations, moreover, ensure that unsightly extensions, conservatories and car ports are outlawed.[20] Levittown, likewise, is widely regarded as the epitome of American post-war progressivism, a production line of clapboard boxes. This is true, to some extent, but Levitt's initial range of house types – Colonial, Rancher, Cape Cod – not only combined period styling with state of the art production methods, but were based on Frank Lloyd Wright's famous prairie house of the 1930s, itself a pastiche of prior architectural styles.[21] These retro-residential tracts, what is more, were as rigorously regulated as House Hill Garden Estate or Celebration, at least initially. Fences were forbidden, lawn cutting carefully monitored and outside clothes-drying prohibited, except on a specially designed rack.

Celebration, in short, is simply the latest in a long line of retrovilles and it is unlikely to be the last of the breed. Several para-Poundbury 'villages' are already on the DoE drawing board, subject to planning permission, eco-warrior protests and 'despoiling the Garden of England' appeals process. Some pundits, to be sure, contend that the dawning of a new millennium will be accompanied by a look-to-the-future, turn-over-a-new-leaf, tomorrow-is-another-day mindset. And, in fairness, it is easy to assemble a Sharper-Imaged argument. After all, many leading FMCG manufacturers, such as Unilever, Procter & Gamble, Sarah Lee and Heinz, are ruthlessly pruning their old brand portfolios.[22] Influential newspapers are printing lists of pensionable brand names – Harrods, Hallmark, Vesta, Rolex – that have not only passed retirement age but are prime candidates for commercial euthanasia.[23] Increasingly exasperated complaints are being made about Britain's Ruritanian respect for the past, its obsession with old buildings, historic preservation and the superannuated trappings of Empire. Several high-profile, much-publicized, Lottery-funded new museums, such as the Royal Armouries (Leeds), the Earth Centre (Doncaster) and the National Popular Music Centre (Sheffield), have failed to attract the paying public in sufficient numbers, which is read as a harbinger of history's end.[24] And the new generation of dot.com nabobs is deemed indicative of all our hi-tech tomorrows and the need to shed the trappings of the past.

However, for every long-established product deleted by Unilever or Sarah Lee, another old favourite steps into the retro breach by celebrating its illustrious heritage, or inventing one to go (Ovaltine, Scots Porridge Oats, Hewlett Packard). For every list of non-U brands, a campaign is mounted, or possibly engineered, to save an old favourite from destruction (Subbuteo, Meccano, Heinz Salad Cream). For every newspaper article bemoaning Britain's past times obsession, another celebrates an against-the-odds triumph of preservationists (signal boxes, stately homes, stands of trees or whatever). For every new museum struggling to make ends meet, several others are opening their doors to clamouring hordes of heritage lovers (Tate Modern, the revamped Pompidou Centre, Jewish Museum, Berlin, MOMA extension). For every contention that the Internet is the future incarnate, another commentator compares MP3 pirates to information superhighwaymen, the Dick Turpins of our digital age.[25] And so the temporal tit-for-tat continues.

Now, this is not to suggest that today's retro fixation will continue unabated. Predicting the future is impossible enough without calculating the need for nostalgia in times to come. However, even if some kind of forward-thinking, new times aesthetic makes its presence felt in the very near future, as it did at the start of the twentieth century, backward glances are unlikely to be abandoned completely. After all, even the most go-getting, onward and upward epochs of recent Anglo-American history – the 1980s and the 1950s – exhibited a retro undertow. Both Reagan and Thatcher considered themselves upholders of the great tradition, Victorian values and the pioneering spirit; Levi's and Coca-Cola, as we noted in the preface, adopted a retro orientation in the middle of the decade that aspired to aspiration; *The Country Diary of an Edwardian Lady* not only dominated the best-sellers list for several years but spawned all sorts of twee tie-in merchandise, from tea towels to place mats; and the so-called Great Crash of 1987 led to a litany of 'lessons from 1929'.[26] The 1950s, likewise, were inspired as much by the American past as by its illimitable future. Thus, the *locus classicus* of contemporary retroscapes, Disneyland, was opened in 1955, at the height of the Eisenhower era; some of the most successful fifties sitcoms – *Mama, Amos 'n' Andy, The Honeymooners* – were predicated on profoundly nostalgic premises; suburban tract homes typically combined futuristic kitchens with ante-bellum drawing rooms; the moon shot was regarded as a continuation of the rootin-tootin, frontier tradition; and, as we have seen, marketing was completely reinvented by several retro-minded intellectuals.[27] As Hine perceptively notes, the advertising of the fifties 'embraced the rocket and the covered wagon with equal fervor, really as manifestations of the same spirit'.[28]

Hesitant as I am to introduce hot and heavy theorizing at this late stage in the proceedings, I'm going to make an exception for weird and wonderful Walter Benjamin (1892–1940), the presiding spirit of the present book, a retromarketing scholar *avant la lettre* and, sad to say, a born loser. He failed his PhD thesis; found himself unable to secure an academic appointment; had his work repeatedly rejected by the then influential Frankfurt Institute; was forced to make ends meet by producing children's radio programmes; and, spent fourteen years of his life gathering material for a book on Parisian shopping arcades, only to commit suicide before the opus was published.[29] Walt's rough notes for the *Passagen-Werk* (Arcades Project) are extant, however, and they reveal that he was fascinated by retro, by marketing, by old objects, abandoned possessions, superseded technologies, long-forgotten fads and the general flotsam and jetsam of the commercial system, all of which eventually washed up on the windswept, weatherbeaten shores of the shopping arcades.[30]

The *Passagen-Werk*, in effect, was based on the interpenetration of past and present. This propensity, for Benjamin, was epitomized by the remarkable fact that new ideas often come wrapped in old packaging. Thus, the first factories, railroad cars, electric lightbulbs and wrought-iron works were designed to look like country villas, stagecoaches, gas flames and carved woodworkings respectively. The first mechanical looms produced 'hand-woven shawls' from the Orient. The first steam engines had two mechanical feet that were raised and lowered alternately, like a horse. Early aeroplanes flapped their wings. Prototype photographs imitated paintings. Mass-produced cooking utensils were initially decorated with mythic motifs. Structural steel was covered in stone cladding, with classical carvings, fretwork and ornamentation. The

French Revolution modelled itself on Ancient Greece; social reformers invariably offered utopian prescriptions premised on small-scale, neo-feudal agricultural systems; and early advertising posters for new products frequently harked back to prehistoric times (Caxton's heavily promoted Bible, 'traditional' patent medicines, Salome selling cigarettes etc.). The arcades themselves, moreover, were built with state-of the-art technology – steel frame, sheet glass, skylights – yet their interiors were a riot of Romanesque columns, arches, pediments, marbled shop-fronts and archaic detailing. The nineteenth-century Parisian arcades, in fact, were retro through and through. 'Just as there are places in the stones of the Miocene or Eocene Age that bear the impression of huge monsters out of these geological epochs, so today the Passages [Arcades] lie in the great cities like caves containing fossils of an ur-animal presumed extinct: The consumers from the pre-imperial epoch of capitalism, the last dinosaurs of Europe.'[31]

Benjamin's key point, however, is not that retro represents the last gasp of the past, an unhealthy obsession with yesteryear, an indication that impetus has been lost, that degeneration is setting in, that imagination has fled, that the present has run out of ideas. Quite the reverse. Retro is a harbinger of revolution. It is an integral part of the development process. It is a pre-figuration, an 'anticipatory illumination' of the future.[32] As the present can't be transcended, or the future predicted, the past is the only place available to anticipate the 'not yet'. Retro doesn't repeat the past, it redeems it. And, in so doing, it provides a fleeting revelation of tomorrow's possibilities, of things to come, of paradise regained and rejuvenated. The angel of history, according to Benjamin, has its face turned to the past, as it is blown into the future by ever-strengthening winds of change. Meanwhile, the wreckage of technological, political and economic development piles up inexorably at its feet.[33]

Now, few would deny that there is a monumental pile of retro wreckage in marketing's neck of the woods. As this book has sought to convey, the contemporary marketing scene is knee-deep in retro products, retro goods, retro services. Consider wrist watches. Once marketed as the apogee of modernity – ever more precise, ever more functions, ever more submersible, ever more fashionable, ever more improved – watches are now retro ever after. Old-style styling is *de rigueur*; watchmakers promote their illustrious pedigree; and nostalgic advertising treatments are the norm. Rotary, established in Switzerland, 1895. Tag Heuer, Swiss-made since 1860. Breguet, *depuis* 1775. Breitling, 1884. Maurice Lacroix, tomorrow's classics. Piaget, true values never change. You don't own a Philippe Patek, just keep it for the next generation. Dunhill's heritage collection of 1930s watches, lighters and cigarette cases are 'recreated in the spirit of the originals'.

Going on holiday, likewise, is a resolutely retro experience, a constant round of museums, galleries, ruins, sights, excursions, old towns, walled cities, quaint quarters, traditional markets, historic hotels, repainted piers, revitalized pleasure beaches, refurbished festival malls, authentic restaurants, rattling trams and wall-to-wall heritage. Cunard invites well-heeled mariners to relive the Golden Age of Cruising on board its bang-up-to-date liner, *Cariona*. Brittany offers a taste of the fourteenth century as an alternative to the twenty-first. A few days of *fin-de-siècle* luxury can be had on one of many retro railroads – the Venice Simplon-Orient-Express, South Africa's Blue Train or Australia's Great South Pacific Express. The newly refurbished George V Hotel in Paris asks us to 'imagine a turn of the century ambience enhanced by all of tomorrow's amenities'. Heritage Hotels recommends that 'if you want to go back into history, make sure you travel first class'. Even Club Med, one-time exemplar of Euro cool, now persuades its patrons to re-treat, re-acquaint, re-discover, re-attach, re-involve, re-unite, re-new.

The music industry, moreover, is retro a-go-go. The Bay City Rollers are back. Crosby, Stills, Nash and Young are packing 'em in Stateside. Bruce Springsteen reconvenes the E-Street Band and releases a four-CD retrospective. Diamond Dave Lee Roth is rumoured to be rejoining Van Halen, with an album and tour to follow. *Yellow Submarine* is digitally remastered and re-released on CD, DVD and mini-disk; Pink Floyd reconstruct *The Wall*; Woodstock '99 is held on an ex-airforce base, of all places, with a replica B52 bomber at the main entrance. Ricky Martin reinvents the Latino crooner; boy and girl bands are all the rage (whither David Cassidy and Donny Osmond?); Marilyn Manson does Alice Cooper impersonations; Lenny Kravitz is this week's Hendrix; Macy Gray is Billie Holiday reborn; The Black Crowes get back to their roots, as Faces imitators (who imitated the Stones, in turn) and go on tour with Jimmy Page, recycling Led Zeppelin's greatest hits. Tribute bands, tribute albums, neo-easy listening, retro AOR, so-and-so sings standards and sepia-hued movie soundtracks are all around us. Every other television advertisement, so it seems, boasts a golden-oldie backing track. Slade sells Ford trucks, Hawkwind hawks silver machines for Mazda, Status Quo boogie on down to Argos, Thunderclap Newman flies British Airways, Cream crank out 'White Room' for Apple computers, Hot Chocolate perform miracles for Pantene shampoo, Earth Wind and Fire are playing at a Burger King near you and James Brown feels good about laxatives.

Quite.

If forced to select a single product category that encapsulates today's retro-fixation, my choice would probably be washing powder. For what seems like a month of Sundays – for what, in fact, was a month of Mondays – Ariel, Persil, Surf, Tide, Bold and all the rest represented the very apotheosis of progress. Aided and abetted by pristine laboratory workers and periodic pseudo-scientific innovations, they resolutely pursued the grand narrative of ever-increasing whiteness, an ablutopia where rings around the collar are no more and underwear is sufficiently grime free to risk being run down by a bus. Of late, however, there has been a dramatic shift in this long-standing spin-cycle grail of whiter than whiteness. Soap powder manufacturers have come to realize that they reside in a multicultural, eco-friendly, united-colours-of-Benetton universe of non-Caucasian clothes. Epitomized by New Ariel Colour and Persil Colour Protection, this acknowledgement of washday diversity comprises nothing less than a realignment of laundry's elemental philosophical stance. White is no longer right. Retro attempts to forestall the ageing process – to protect, preserve and perpetuate the colour of old clothes – are the order of the day. New-and-improved has finally been superseded by as-good-as-always.[34]

Retro, of course, is not confined to products, places, promotions and pricing policies, such as Tower Records' recent offer of five 'classic videos' for the 'retro price' of £5.49. It is also about principles, precepts, philosophies and paradigms, such as they are. This book has contended that the future of marketing lies in its past; that by examining the prehistory of modern marketing we may better understand the essential character of our field; that it is high time marketers learnt to appreciate its BKH, its Before Kotler Heritage. Granted, this means abandoning customer orientation, which has been the *sine qua non* of our discipline since Levitt did his Copernican thing and placed consumers at the centre of marketing's universe. But, is that such a bad thing? Surely it's time to recognize that every attempt to better satisfy the needs of customers is doomed to failure, insofar as it only serves to further alienate them. We don't like to admit this to ourselves but the basic fact of the matter is that people en masse *distrust* marketing and marketers. They act on the assumption that marketing types are out to rip them off – with good reason in many cases – or out to make money from them at the very least. It follows that our ostentatious attempts to declare undying love, to get ever closer to the customer, to satisfy their every desire, are immediately discounted or treated with suspicion and contempt. We seem to work from the premise that consumers can't see through us, that they are taken in by our promises, however sincerely meant or indeed kept. The complete opposite is the case. Customers start from a position akin to, 'who is this lying, thieving bastard and why is he pretending to care for me?' and no amount of counter-argument will alter that fact. Counter-argument, in fact, merely reinforces consumers' distrust. You know, if we were *really* customer orientated, we would rejoice in their hostility (instead of moaning that nobody understands us) and try to build on consumers' rambunctious, roistering, renegade, roguish perceptions.[35]

I appreciate, of course, that I'm not saying anything especially new. The erasure of customer focus has been advocated by a number of prominent marketing academics and, analogously, the anthropologist

Mary Douglas explains all buyer behaviour in terms of choices that are *not* made.[36] Consumers don't know what they want but are absolutely certain about what they don't want ('I wouldn't be seen dead in that!'). Marketing, therefore, should be devoted, not to fulfilling customers' unexpressed and inexpressible needs, but to finding out what they don't want and giving them less unacceptable alternatives. Or, since consumers will continue to suspect our motives, it might be better to find out what they don't want and not give it to them. Sado-masochistic marketing is the next big thing. Trust me!

Abandoning customer orientation, it must be stressed, is not the same as saying that consumers are unimportant or that marketers aren't interested in their needs, wants and desires. Nothing could be further from the truth. Business organizations need customers in order to survive and prosper. End of story. What it does imply, however, is that customers are not the be all and end all of marketing, that they are not the field's central focus, that they are not even the point of departure. Many marketers, one suspects, would accept the first of these assertions, and possibly the second, since all sorts of non-consumer marketing foci have been posited at one time or another (resources, profitability, competition, exchange, etc.).[37] Most, nevertheless, might balk at the third, because it is a fundamental tenet of modern marketing that customers are the starting point of all business activity. As everyone knows, a long list of maxims, aphorisms and sayings can be cited in support of this premise – 'the customer is . . . always right/king/#1/tops/everything/ knows best' (delete as applicable) – and, anyway, what's the alternative? Indeed, *what's the alternative is the nub of the matter*. When all is said and done, the principal reason that the APIC paradigm has held on so long is the lack of an acceptable alternative. Any number of pseudo-replacements have been suggested, admittedly, but these rarely challenge the post-Levitt precept of customer-centricity or, if they do, are instantly dismissed as 'not marketing'. The consumer is not simply marketing's starting point; this idea comprises the *hard core* of our 'scientific research programme' (in a Lakatosian sense), the indisputable assumption at the heart of the discipline's belief system.[38]

At the same time, we shouldn't conclude that change is impossible or assume that marketing is permanently immured in the APIC paradigm, locked in an imitation iron cage of customer-centredness from which there is no escape. Again, this is not the case. The copious 'mid-life crisis' literature indicates that the Kotlerite paradigm is becoming increasingly unacceptable.[39] The alacrity with which the RM bandwagon was boarded, even though it only offered a turbo-charged version of the customer-orientated same, is testimony to the growing desire for reinvention.[40] The traditional explanation of marketing failings – that the organization is 'production orientated', 'sales orientated' or, *in extremis*, 'not doing it properly' – no longer passes muster, because marketing is ubiquitous.

There can't be an organization in the developed world that isn't fully *au fait* with the marketing concept, possesses a strategic marketing plan or two, or conducts all manner of market research studies into its customers motives, attitudes, preferences and behaviours. Many marketers continue to see themselves as evangelists for the cause, proselytizers amongst the heathens, but they're living in the past, retro evangelists one and all. If modern marketing is failing these days, it is because there is something wrong with modern marketing itself. Although this uncomfortable fact can be sidestepped, excused or deferred – increasingly recalcitrant consumers, the ferocity of global competition, the pace of technological change, blah, blah, blah – the rise of retro suggests that marketers have had enough of jam tomorrow. Indeed, perhaps the single most important lesson of the retro revolution is that marketing existed before customer-orientation was its defining feature and, despite mainstream textbooks' continuing disdain for 'sales era' or 'production era' practices, they weren't inferior to the present day. On the contrary, pre- 'marketing era' marketing was extremely sophisticated and extremely successful. The golden age of marketing was the 1920s, not the 1960s.[41]

What, then, is the essence of marketing, if it is not customer orientation? The answer, as this text has sought to show, is summarized in the acronym TEASE. Marketing, to put it in appropriately mythopoetic idiom, is a *Trickster* figure. It is the clown, the fool, the joker, the dissembler, akin to Loki of Norse myth (and Spiderman comics), the wily Coyote beloved by Native Americans (and Warner Brothers cartoons), Mark Twain's timeless Tom Sawyer and Lorelei Lee of *Gentlemen Prefer Blondes*. Trickster figures are an embodiment of the carnivalesque.[42] They disseminate disruption, promote playfulness, incite pomposity-pricking laughter and, ultimately, engender much-needed enlightenment. It is no accident that trickster figures are often associated with marketing (Hermes is the god of markets, after all). It is no accident that marketing practitioners have often employed trickster figures in their merchandise-moving machinations (Joe Izuzu, Tony the Tiger, the Tango monster, the Typhoo chimps, Joe Camel, Louis, the Budweiser chameleon, etc.).[43] It is no accident that tricksters occupy a liminal, interstitial, betwixt and between position, much the way marketing spans the divide between producer and consumer, between want and need, between I-wish and what-now. Marketing is Lucille Ball, Sergeant Bilko, Bugs Bunny, the peerless Painless Potter, the sublime Sequah, the wonderful Wizard of Oz and the one and only P.T. Barnum. Combined.

Marketing could be the Top Cat of the academy. Instead it is Officer Dibble.

Alongside its tricksterish credentials, marketing is characterized by *Exaggeration*, by excess, by extremity, by exuberance, by extra, extra,

extra. Traditionalists try to portray marketing as truthful, as honest, as straight talking, as an essentially realist endeavour. It is nothing of the kind. Marketing means more, *more*, MORE! Marketing refreshes the parts that other management functions can't reach. Marketing is shop-til-you-drop, live-life-to-the-max, the-ultimate-driving-machine, the-best-a-man-can-get, the-crumbliest-flakiest-milk-chocolate, the-world's-favour-ite-airline, the-best-lager-in-the-world. Probably. It is the Whopper, the Monster Burger, the Big Kahuna burger, the New Double Rodeo Cheeseburger, the mega-mall, the hypermarket, the category killer, the superduper-giant size, the 7-11 Super Big Gulp, the acme, the apogee, the ultimate, the XXL, the double-ply, the triple-strength, the blockbuster, the colossus, the extravaganza, the cheapest, the largest, the mostest, the greatest show on earth. Size matters. Less is more. Marketing is every-thing. The list, at the risk of exaggeration, is endless. Marketing dis-course, in short, is hopelessly hyperbolic and it is both accepted and discounted as such by consumers.[44] That is why shoppers remain sceptical when marketers claim to love them, care for them and have their interests at heart. Marketing's promises – however well meant or indeed adhered to – are ordinarily taken with a pinch or two of salt. *And rightly so*. It follows, therefore, that there is no point in telling consumers the unvar-nished truth, because they will assume that it is the varnished unvarnished truth and act accordingly. Despite the protests of straight-talking, customer-hugging, honesty-is-the-best-policy do-gooders, the simple fact of the matter is that marketing is exaggerated, it always has been exag-gerated, it always will be exaggerated. Marketing needs more exaggera-tion, not less. As the master self-marketer and workshy evangelist of the drinking classes, Oscar Wilde, once artfully observed, 'Moderation is a fatal thing. Nothing succeeds like excess.'

Marketing, furthermore, is *Adolescent*. Like teenagers and young adults of legend, it is sex mad, it is smutty, it is gross, it is disgusting, it is hyperactive, it is irrepressible, it is irresponsible, it is inarticulate, it is clumsy, it is disjointed, it is egotistical, it is megalomaniacal, it is unim-pressed by its elders and betters. It thinks of itself as an adult but acts like a child. It is sullen and narcissistic by turns. It wants to save the world, when it's not self-preoccupied. It is condescended to and claims to be misunderstood. It is prone to pretensions, tantrums, overstatements and moodswings of all kinds. It is interstitial, neither one thing nor the other. It is in love with being in love, as the Relationship Marketing paradigm indicates. Adolescence, admittedly, is not a state one normally associates with marketing, despite the obvious parallels, and the fact that so much selling effort is targeted at this particular demographic cohort (movies, music, MTV, sodas, sneakers, sportswear, cigarettes, clothes, computer games).[45] The typical academic, rather, regards marketing as a crisis-stricken adult in middle life, though this is to confuse biological age (fortysomething years of the APIC paradigm) with psychological age (teenage angst) and thus constitutes an anthropomorphic step too far. Non-academic commentators, on the other hand, tend to portray marketing as a means of interpellating the inner child – Disney is not just for children, it brings out the child in all of us, etc. – or exploiting the not-so-inner child through pester power and tweenie-oriented advertising. Marketing, appropriately, lies somewhere between the two, not quite an anxious adult nor an innocent child, but a little bit of both. The important point is not where marketing lies on the chronological scale or whether marketing will eventually become a responsible member of the community. The key point is that marketing should *aspire* to adolescence and *resist* growing up. There are too many adults in the world. Marketing doesn't need to become one of them. It should seek to remain a teenage rebel. It hopes to die before it gets old.

Spirituality is another important aspect of marketing. As noted at several junctures in this book, marketing is a belief system, no more, no less. The benefits that marketing can bring to organizations, whether profit-making or not-for-profit, have less to do with marketing technology, marketing plans, marketing information systems and all the rest – useful though these are – than the *belief* that marketing orientation can make a difference, a real difference, a demonstrable difference. And it does. Marketing works. But only if people believe that it works. In this regard, the biggest single cause of marketing's latter-day existential crisis is the simple fact that no one really believes in modern, Kotlerite marketing any more. The crisis has nothing to do with the failings of marketing science – the spurious hypothesis tests, the meaningless mathematical models, the chimerical search for general laws, universal principles and all-singing-all-dancing theories of the marketplace – because science is a belief system in itself. Nor is it attributable to the recent, rapid rise of the relationships paradigm, since its 'triumph' has more to do with the belief that relationship-building is the key to success than any substantial difference between it and the previous paradigm. (RM's inevitable failure, furthermore, will occur when the agnostics eventually prevail.) Nor, for that matter, will the crisis be resolved now that we know marketing is a belief system, now that its spiritual side has been recuperated and we can discuss, without embarrassment, the magical, the supernatural, the otherworldly aspects of marketing endeavour. Knowing something is a belief system is not the same as believing in it, though believing that it is a belief system is at least a start. Perhaps the best we can hope for, in such sceptical circumstances, is a temporary suspension of disbelief, which as Samuel Taylor Coleridge reminds us, is the domain of storytelling, aesthetics and the imagination. Remember, 'once faith is lost, then the land and its broken myths can only be reclaimed by turning inward, by escape to a world of fictions'.[46]

Entertainment is an equally integral part of the marketing mindset. P.T. Barnum, as Chapter 4 explained, was a self-confessed humbug. He ripped consumers off. He made no bones about it. He did it again and again. He did it in such an entertaining way, however, that people felt they got more than their money's worth. The same is true of Sequah, Painless Potter, L. Frank Baum, Roger Ackerley and the rest of the rapscallions described herein. Cheating, to state the blindingly obvious, is wrong and customers won't stand for it. But charlatanry is not the same as cheating.[47] It adds an extra dimension of panache, of exaggeration, of enjoyment, of sheer chutzpah – and that's what renders the unacceptable acceptable. Think about it. Every movie, novel, play, painting, stage show, theme pub, television programme and professional wrestling bout is a fake, strictly speaking. However, that doesn't make them meaningless, or unworthy, or beneath contempt (well, maybe the wrestling).[48] Modern marketers set great store by the truth, by trust, by honesty, by probity and one can understand why this is so, given marketing's Del-Boyish, back-of-a-lorry, nod-and-a-wink, know-wot-I-mean-mate reputation. The truth, however, is that people don't want the truth, the whole truth and nothing but the truth. Nor, in our postmodern world, is there any Truth to tell. Truth effects, of course, can be staged; the discourse of truth is regularly deployed; but if one is seeking the unvarnished truth, the unalloyed truth, the unadulterated truth, then marketing is not the place to look. Nor should it be. Modern marketers have spent so much time attending to the steak that they have forgotten how to sizzle. Modern marketing is so obsessed with substance that its trappings are in tatters. Modern marketing is so determined to explain the 'working' half of advertising that the 'wasted' half – the half that actually does the work – has been neglected. Marketing is fun. Marketing is diverting. Marketing is engaging. Marketing is playful. Marketing is glitz. Marketing is glamour. Marketing is spectacular. Marketing is razzmatazz.

And I mean that most sincerely, folks.

There is more to TEASE than Tricksterism, Exaggeration, Adolescence, Spirituality and Entertainment, however. TEASE exceeds the sum of its parts. In many ways, indeed, it is the add-on, the garnish, the free gift, the magic dust, the little bit extra that makes all the difference. It is the difference that makes a difference. It is the difference between the sum of the parts and the final tally. There are many parts to the marketing paradigm, admittedly, but I believe that the *con*cept is quintessentially about jesting, japing, joshing and you-know-when-you've-been-Tango'd tomfoolery. Teasing, in short. Marketing is about untangling knots, smoothing out difficulties, making things happen and steering goods from A to B, via C. Teasing, that is. Marketing is about getting in people's hair, about being annoying, about back-combing like billy-o and making things stand up on end. Teasing, in other words. Marketing is about flirtation, about tantalizing, about coquetry, about insatiable desire, about love at first sight, about eyes meeting across a crowded room.[49] Teasing, to be sure. Myopia doesn't come into it.

Why do marketers insist on telling the truth when people want to hear little white lies? It seems to me that we should be whispering sweet nothings in their shell-likes. We need to make extravagant promises, the wilder the better. It's time to titillate, titivate, tantalize, turn on the charm. We ought to chat up our customers, not get down on one knee to them. There's no need to abandon APIC, or at least not completely. But always remember that it's only a start. Marketing is more than the 4Ps, the 7Ss, the 30Rs or whatever the latest alliterative mnemonic happens to be. Marketing is the extra roll of a Baker's dozen. Marketing is something for nothing. Marketing is more for your money. Marketing is the big tease. Marketers should seek to develop marke*tease*, expor*tease*, produc*tease*, adver*tease*, segmen*tease*, targe*tease*, techno*tease*, TEASE-*tease*. Any *tease* you want, really. Tease for two. Tease up Mother Brown. Tease puns are killing me.

Only teasing.

Rewriting Marketing: Pedagogic Appendix

'Oh yeah, you're the postmodern guy. Tell me, how do you teach that stuff?' You know, if I've heard that question once, I've heard it a thousand times. The funny thing is, however, I have never had a problem when I present 'that stuff' to students, be they post- or under-graduate. On the contrary, I find that they get it right away, that they know where I'm coming from, that 'that stuff' makes a semblance of sense to them. Now, I wouldn't for a moment claim to be more in touch with today's students than the scientifically minded marketing majority. It seems to me, nevertheless, that if we live in a postmodern world, as many maintain, then postmodern marketing perspectives may be more pertinent than the 'modern' paradigm that continues to hold sway in our field. If, moreover, contemporary marketing is characterized by a retrospective orientation, as the present book has sought to show, then the new-and-improved, onward-and-upward ethos that dominates traditional Kotlerite textbooks is completely out of kilter with twenty-first-century commercial practice.

As *Marketing – The Retro Revolution* has been written for a general audience – titter ye not! – I feel obliged to include some appropriately pedagogic material or approximations thereof. Instead of resorting to a carefully chosen collation of case studies (their narratological appeal notwithstanding), I'd like to reflect on the preceding eleven chapters, plus preface. Not only is this more in keeping with postmodern reflexivity, but it also gives me a chance to address some of the issues (deliberately) omitted from the foregoing essay. The hope, therefore, is that my reflexive ruminations might provide the starting point for class or seminar discussion. In this regard, please bear in mind that *Marketing – The Retro Revolution* is a fairly broad-brush treatment. I'm well aware that the topics I raise are more nuanced than the present volume pretends. I appreciate, furthermore, that there's a world of difference between the modern marketing paradigm, as it is ordinarily portrayed in BFBAMs, and how marketers behave on a day-to-day basis. APIC, nonetheless, is presented as the marketing ideal, the way marketing should be, the condition that marketing practice must aspire to. The aim of this book is to challenge the Kotlerite ideal and to posit an equally idealized replacement. TEASE, in other words, is a normative alternative to APIC and thus portrays marketing, not as it is, but as it ought to be.

To begin at the beginning, I suspect that the preface will have offended quite a few readers. The majority of these will doubtless be affronted by the thought of my air guitar antics (albeit the double-necked tennis racket was my actual adolescent axe of choice). But for those who persevered, the key academic issue is Americanization. My contention that marketing is quintessentially American is sure to be contested. We are regularly informed, are we not, that all sorts of marketing practices went on prior to the emergence of modern marketing in the Eisenhower era.[1] Long, in fact, before the colonization of the United States of America. Josiah Wedgwood, the medieval guilds, the ancient Greeks, neolithic flint-knappers and the lapis lazuli tradespersons of pre-cuneiformed Mesopotamia, have all been plausibly posited as proto-marketing pioneers. Modern marketing, moreover, is not exclusively North American, as the Relationship Marketing paradigm (Scandinavia), the Postmodern Marketing paradigm (France), and several other nationally inflected variants remind us (British pragmatics, Irish poetics, German isolationism, Japanese indifference, etc.). Indeed, it can be convincingly contended that each and every organization possesses its own idiosyncratic marketing modality or, if one really wants to take it to the limit, that every individual commercial decision comprises a unique instantiation of marketing mores.

I'm not disputing either of these temporal (premodern marketing) or spatial (different Ps for different places) arguments. At the same time, however, I think there is something special about the Barnumesque marketing that emerged in the late nineteenth century and the customer-orientated paradigm that erupted in the post-war epoch. I suspect that most non-marketing people associate marketing with the United States of America.[2] I believe that the sheer ubiquity of marketing nowadays has blinded us to the fact that it comes from America. Yes, marketing has *become* universalized, in much the same way as the movie industry is now Hollywoodized, fast food is McDonaldized, theme parks and heritage centres are Disneyfied and the soft drinks business is Coca-Colonized. Such is its omnipresence, that we even project it backwards in time in order to convince ourselves that marketing has always been with us and thus represents some kind of innate human trait. Personally, I very much doubt that Josiah Wedgwood considered himself a marketing man – the concept simply didn't exist – let alone our friendly neighbourhood flint-knapping Neanderthal. Indeed, even when allowances are made for academic anachronism and twenty-first-century ubiquity, I would submit that marketing still retains a distinctively American cast.

Discussion Questions. Can American marketing imperialism be stopped? Should it be stopped? What's the most effective way of stopping it? Why hasn't it been stopped before now?

Chapter 1 is an attempted *tour d'horizon* of retromarketing. It identifies three different types of retro, seeks to account for the recent retro outbreak and suggests that a retro stance can be taken on marketing theory and thought. Each of these assertions is debatable in itself (are there any other forms of retro? have important explanatory factors been omitted? is it legitimate to infer that the rise of retro has implications for marketing thought?). But the issue that I want to focus on is *definitional*. In Chapter 1, I avoid giving a definition of retromarketing, arguing that it is pointless.[3] Now, I won't deny that an agreed definition of retro – like an agreed definition of 'brands', 'internationalization', 'involvement', 'marketing' etc. – would be convenient, but marketing's record in this area suggests that it's unlikely to happen, unless all manner of arbitrary decisions concerning retro/not-retro are imposed upon the material. Where, for example, does retro begin? The seventies, the sixties, the nineteenth century, the day before yesterday? How many parts of the marketing mix – assuming it is possible to agree on the make-up of the mix – must be included before the retro designation is officially bestowed on a product or service? Does a completely new product with ye-olde advertising count? What about ye-olde services with a contemporary promotional twist?

That said, I suspect most people see retro in decadal terms – the seventies, the fifties, the twenties, etc. – and, indeed, decadal temporal schemata are very popular in our field.[4] Decades, to be sure, are somewhat arbitrary cultural constructs in themselves (when did the sixties *really* begin?) and are subject to the sorts of gross stereotyping we noted in our discussion of retroscapes in Chapter 8. What's more, they too come complete with definitional imponderables. How much of a 'cooling off' period is necessary before a decade is revivable? Are we ready for a nineties comeback, for yet another round of retro? Will the pick 'n' mix decade be back before we have finished picking it clean?

Discussion Questions. What is the function of marketing definitions? As none has ever been agreed upon, except on a short-term basis, why do we continue to pursue the definitional chimera? Is it purely a pragmatic matter or, as Foucault would have us believe, are there important political dimensions to inclusion and exclusion? Discuss the suggestion that there have been so many seventies revivals since the seventies that they have lasted longer than the original decade.

In Chapter 2, we returned to the primal scene of the 'modern' marketing paradigm. Theodore Levitt, to be sure, wasn't solely responsible for the post-war marketing revolution. The pioneering contributions of Drucker, Keith and McKitterick played an important part in the transformation, as many commentators have observed. One suspects, however, that the canonization of the latter three has more to do with marketing's desire to manufacture heroic antecedents – the rhetoric of mainstream texts requires a cadre of champions, great men, free thinkers and misunderstood geniuses – than with the impact their publications had at the time (Drucker's was a throw-away remark, for example, and McKitterick's paper appeared in an obscure volume of conference proceedings). The same cannot be said for 'Marketing Myopia', an award-winning paper that appeared in a highly regarded journal and proved controversial from the outset. It is surely no exaggeration to state that 'Marketing Myopia' was an intellectual watershed and, given its enduring influence, that a deconstructive critique is long overdue. Pulling a classic paper apart doesn't mean the end of marketing civilization as we know it, nor is it a traitorous act. Quite the opposite, in fact. It is only by reading against the grain and turning conventional wisdom on its head, as Levitt himself was wont to do, that we can better appreciate a classic's importance.

Aside from its close reading of a marketing classic, Chapter 2 makes a couple of debatable points. The first of these is that the 1950s was an anti-marketing decade, an era when marketers and advertisers were held in fairly low esteem. Although there is plenty of anecdotal evidence to this effect, there is no way of proving the point, or of categorically refuting it. In a situation where interpretation is all and the evidence is ambivalent, much depends on what the investigator seeks to find. Ambivalence, I believe, is the operative word here, because the standing of marketing is always somewhat ambivalent, a paradoxical combination of attraction and repulsion. With this in mind, it can be contended that an attraction–rejection dialectic exists, where marketing's social standing waxes and wanes with the passage of time. Certainly, it helps account for the situation in the 1920s, whereby Barton strove valiantly to render marketing respectable, and the latter-day plunge in marketing's esteem, on account of the vociferous critiques of the no-logo contingent.

A rhythmic reading is also relevant to the other main point at issue in Chapter 2. It was argued that Levitt's great achievement involved repositioning the consumer in marketing's cosmology. By situating the consumer at the centre of our conceptual universe, he effectively redefined what it means to be marketing orientated, what qualifies as marketing, the activities that warrant the appellation 'marketing'. If it's not consumer-centric, then it's not marketing. QED. This is as close to a proper paradigm shift (in the Kuhnian sense) as a pre-paradigmatic discipline like marketing gets. However, it is important to appreciate that highly sophisticated marketing activities went on before Levitt's modern marketing revolution. What's more, the customer still figured prominently in this pre-Copernican epoch, albeit not at the centre, not as the point of departure, not as the supreme court of marketing appeal (pardon my mongrel metaphors). The issue, therefore, is where *exactly* does the consumer/customer stand relative to the marketing system? Purely for the purposes of discussion, I would submit that a cyclical process is again at work. In the inter-war era, as Marchand shows, marketers portrayed themselves as the consumer's partner, a dependable friend who could always be turned to for honest advice. They were equals, in other words, rather than the consumer-master/marketer-slave posture posited by Levitt. At the start of the twentieth century, however, marketing ruled the roost, marketers called the shots, a marketer-master/ consumer-slave situation obtained. *Caveat emptor* and *si populus vult deciperi, decipatur* (if the people want to be deceived, let them) were the marketing maxims of the time.[5] The first half of the cycle, then, swings from marketing on top, through equal standing, to consumer on top. In the post 'Marketing Myopia' epoch, furthermore, we have witnessed a gradual reinstatement of consumer-marketer equality (most notably in the rapidly fading Relationship Marketing paradigm) and the closing of the circle at the very end of the century, when cries of 'forget the customer' and 'ignore the customer' are increasingly heard. *Caveat emptor*, once again, is our retro motto of choice.

> *Discussion Questions. Consider the Consumer Situation Cycle. Does it withstand close scrutiny? Identify the causes of the cycle, if any. What is its driving force? How does it relate to the waxing and waning of marketing's social standing?*

The main matters arising in Chapter 3 are belief systems in general and magic in particular. The latter, to be sure, erupts at several points in the book, Chapter 6 especially, but it's best to consider it within the broader context of spirituality. Outsiders, neutral observers and the great marketing unwashed – that is, the precious few who have not been indoctrinated into the APIC mindset – cannot help but be struck by the prevalence of 'magical' appeals in marketing and advertising. Our critics, moreover, often employ magically inflected terms of derision: witch doctors, hocus pocus, jiggery pokery, mumbo jumbo and so forth. In fact, one of the most celebrated Marxist critiques of marketing, by Raymond Williams, memorably described it as 'the magic system'.[6] Yet marketers themselves are strangely reluctant to mention the M word in polite company and, although there are one or two published papers on magical marketing, the supernatural is conspicuous by its absence from mainstream marketing discourse. Why should this be?

Well, the obvious answer relates to the negative connotations that the term 'magic' conveys (from an academic marketing perspective, I hasten to add). For good or ill, magic is irredeemably associated with conjuring, card tricks, sleight of hand, sword-swallowing, sawing scantily clad assistants in half, top hats infested with doves, rabbits or silk scarves, and the applause-inducing abracadabras of Paul Daniels, David Copperfield, David Blaine and so on. Worse, the term is tainted with irrationality, anarchy, new ageism and the whole west coast, slightly flaky, bad acid, berry-eating, tree-hugging, Age of Aquarius, give peace a chance, remember (not remembering) the sixties, anti-marketing, anti-nomian, anti-authoritarian, alternative lifestyle thing.

Modern marketing, then, can't admit to being magical, because to do so automatically undermines what little credibility it has. And herein lies the real problem. It is this desperate desire to be taken seriously, to prove that we are fully paid up scientists – rigorous, objective, white-coated laboratory workers – that is the major cause of our discipline's low standing (fluctuations in esteem notwithstanding). If marketing really wants to raise its status, it should be boasting of its magical capability, alluding to its secret, customer-compelling powers (*pace* Packard), and dropping cryptic hints about ancient sources of commercial wisdom. The irony, indeed, is that magic contains a very rich corpus of concepts. There are several schools of magical thought, ranging from the pioneering mentalistic analyses of Taylor and Fraser, through functional, contextual, structuralist, psychoanalytical and semiotic perspectives, to the recent phenomenological account of magical experience persuasively posited by Glucklich.[7] The nature, purpose and efficacy of magic have been much debated and it is variously considered to be a form of pre-scientific science, a force for group solidarity or something that 'works' by suggestion and/or PNI (psychoneuroimmunology). Nevertheless, the key point is that marketing *is* magic and our field would be much better off if we acknowledged the fact and got to grips – belatedly – with our natural conceptual constituency.

Discussion Questions. Assemble a selection of glossy magazines and examine the advertisements for 'magical' appeals or 'supernatural' treatments of any kind. Are such appeals fairly evenly spread or are some product-markets more magical than others? Can you account for this? Is the 4Ps, the 'hey presto' of marketing thought? Why, for that matter, should marketers believe anyone who doesn't believe in marketing?

Without question, P.T. Barnum is the personification of the present book. He epitomizes the spirit of TEASE. He is retromarketing incarnate. He is, in my humble opinion, the greatest marketing man who ever lived. So pervasive is the peerless Prince of Humbugs that the subtitle of this text should be 'Six Degrees of P.T. Barnum', though three degrees is closer to the mark. Almost everyone mentioned herein is connected in some way to the great showman: William James and his brother's childhood visits to the American Museum; L. Frank Baum being taken to see the Cardiff Giant; Sequah as an alumnus of Kickapoo, Healy and Bigelow's homage to the humbugger in chief. Even Joe Camel, American Tobacco's timeless trade character, was based on one of Barnum and Bailey's bactrians. Barnum, what is more, went buffalo hunting with General George Custer, attended the gala performance of Oscar Wilde's American tour, planned to write a book with Mark Twain and actually has an (appropriately ostentatious) typeface named after him.

Barnum, in many ways, transcends discussion, but his story is pertinent to an egregious absence from the present book; namely, the fourth P of price. My critics will doubtless take me to task for failing to examine pricing considerations. There is, as I point out in a couple of places, a retro dimension to contemporary pricing behaviours. Internet auctions, web-based buying groups, cyberhaggling and suchlike are undoubtedly a throwback to the bazaar, the forum, the agora. *The Cluetrain Manifesto* in particular makes much of this analogy.[8] However, I chose not to give pricing a chapter to itself.

And why?

Because I don't believe that pricing is a marketing matter. It doesn't form part of the TEASE framework. Once again, I would stress that this does not mean pricing is unimportant or that it can be safely ignored. As with environmental considerations and customer preferences, pricing still registers on the corporate radar and emits a very strong signal. But the problem with pricing under the APIC paradigm is that it features too strongly, it looms too large. The inevitable upshot is that marketers spend much of their time justifying advertising expenditure, measuring marketing's contribution or calculating brand equity to the n-th degree. There's nothing wrong with that, *but it is not marketing*. Marketers have become penny wise and pound foolish. They are, as Barnum observes in his 'money getting' lecture, saving at the spigot and wasting at the bung-hole.[9] It is impossible, according to the great showman, to spend too much on marketing. False economy in marketing matters is much worse than excess expenditure. Marketing is inherently excessive, or it was when Barnum ruled the waves.

> *Discussion Questions. If, as Barnum suggests, there's one born every minute, why should marketers bother with customer care? Is, however, Barnumarketing past its sell-by date? Who are the Barnums of our time? Richard Branson? Max Clifford? Damien Hirst? Anita Roddick? Tom Peters? Examine their achievements in Barnumesque terms.*

Barnum may have been retromarketing incarnate and his autobiography, *Struggles and Triumphs*, was one of the most widely read books of the nineteenth century (second only to the Bible, according to many literary authorities). But the admittedly inspirational story of his life is of little practical use to aspiring marketeasers, those who intend to implement the TEASE framework. A how-to-do-it text is sorely needed and, fortunately, one is ready to hand. It was written by 'Professor' Harry Helms, the mentor of Harry Reichenbach, who figured prominently in Chapter 5. Entitled *Schemes and Tricks*, it comprises an inventory of 'how to' marketing maxims, suggestions and anecdotes. In short, a sort of *High Visibility*-cum-*Marketing the Arts* for premodern managers and aspirant impresarios.[10]

According to this Philip Kotler of the Progressive Era, promotion is of paramount importance and every opportunity should be taken to advertise one's wares. Thus, 'Shipping tags make a good ad. Have your attraction printed on same, tie a string through the hole and you can tie them on any old thing.' Or, 'If you got a dog, put a lettered blanket on him. Advertise your business on the blanket.' Product development is no less noteworthy and a constant stream of new ideas is vital, especially if the show lingers for more than a few days in lucrative localities. To this end, the learned one lists various NPD possibilities including 'how to start a carnival geek show', 'how to make turkeys dance' (put them on a heated iron floor) and 'the barbed-wire fence sale' (an early version of the infamous aluminium siding schemes of the 1950s). Place, likewise, needs careful thought, both at the micro and macro levels. The best location, apparently, is adjacent to a saloon, which generates additional spin-off trade and thereby benefits both businesses, though the precise site is less significant than the territory itself. Prior market research to 'find out what class of people live in the neighbourhood' is the key to success, as is the characteristic ethnic mix, since 'Germans, Bohemians, Polish and Swedes are the best medicine buyers'. Price, however, is not particularly salient, as the purpose of the show is to sell patent medicine rather than make a profit on the door. In this regard, the professor recommended a counter-skimming policy. The first performance should be completely free, the second one paid, but with reduced charges for children, and subsequent shows progressively more expensive, culminating in the grand finale, where free gifts are distributed, prizewinners rewarded and, naturally, top dollar paid by nostrum-hungry hypochondriacs.

Important though the 4Ps were, therapeutic promises were the *raison d'être* of the operation and Helms recommended majoring on the medicines' magical properties. His product line included Wonder Working Blood Purifier, Mystic Cough Medicine, Spirit-Oil Liniment, Necromantic Salve, Magic Tooth Powder and Wizard's Soap. Although such supernatural items were easily obtained – 'go to any wholesale drug house and they will put the goods up for you' – it was imperative to present them in a suitably spiritual manner. This involved standard occult sales ploys ranging from simple sleight of hand, through illusions and mind reading, to a full spirit-cabinet act, all judiciously interlarded with pitches for the magic potions. 'The whole point,' Professor Helms judiciously observes, 'is to press on their minds that your remedies have the same mysterious powers as you have while performing your tricks.'

As with many scholars, the good professor was stronger on marketing theory than marketing practice. *Schemes and Tricks* didn't sell particularly well, possibly because he couldn't quite decide on a recommended retail price (it is variously listed at $1, 50 cents and a quarter). And so, in a desperate attempt to increase sales, he resorted to offering free gifts with every purchase. These included a 'complete system of hypnotism', 'sweet sixteen love perfume, greatly admired by the ladies' and 'the greatest tape worm secret in the world, guaranteed to remove worm with head and all'.

You don't get that from Kotler.

> *Discussion Questions. Take a selection of introductory marketing textbooks and treat them as a literary genre. What are the principal components of the principles package? What, if anything, is excluded? Examine the 'environment' chapter in detail and identify any differences in coverage. Itemize the key environmental influences on the market for marketing texts.*

Chapter 6 comprises the mid-point of the book and, in many ways, it represents the most ambitious and least successful essay in *Marketing – The Retro Revolution*. On the one hand, it attempts a form of cultural criticism, inasmuch as it adopts an unusually catholic interpretation of the 'boxes' concept. It thus places a strategic marketing commonplace within a much wider context. On the other hand, any such exercise is doomed to failure, since the subject of boxes is so vast that it can't possibly be captured in such an overview. The textual receptacle that is Chapter 6 is unable to contain the phenomena it claims to accommodate. It is thus certain to be dismissed as trite and superficial. There is no mention, for example, of boxes in the sphere of games and sport. One immediately thinks of penalty boxes, boxing rings, cricket squares, tennis courts, bowling greens (to say nothing of players' protective 'boxes'), chessboards, checkers, crosswords and board games generally. Warfare, what is more, is replete with defensive squares, box formations, strategic grids, square-bashing, cross-fire patterns, enfilades and all the rest. The same is true of the quack medicine business, described in Chapter 5, which is stuffed with therapeutic black boxes of one kind or another.[11]

Such is the wealth of receptacles, in short, that breaking out of the box of marketing representations is a strategic mistake, a classic case of opening the proverbial can of conceptual worms. This in itself, however, contains an important lesson for marketing, in that it parallels the broadening debate of the 1960s. As everyone knows, the upshot of this controversy was that marketing was deemed applicable to just about everything – every organization, every situation, every domain, every person. Marketing is the be all and end all. Superficiality is the inevitable consequence, as is the disdain of the specialists in the spheres it happily tramples over. Indeed, it can be contended that marketing's preoccupation with matrices, boxes and grid squares is a *direct consequence* of its universalist ambitions. As Susan Stewart observes in *On Longing*, her superb study of collections, the basic problem faced by many collectors is that their chosen field – postcards, porcelain, pewter, Picasso – is so enormous that the task is impossible. Accordingly, this threat of infinity is counterbalanced by the articulation or imposition of boundaries. It is this need for containment, Stewart suggests, that explains the popularity of 'collecting objects that are themselves containers: cruets, pitchers, salt-and-pepper shakers, vases, teapots, and boxes, to name a few'.[12] Marketing's fondness for matrices, in short, represents an unconscious attempt to impose control on the infinite of commercial life.

There is, however, an important caveat. The matrices that marketers usually engage with are two-dimensional, whereas the boxes brought into our discussion from the wider cultural sphere are predominantly three-dimensional. The surprise and secrecy that Chapter 6 champions are a consequence of this third dimension and, hence, a defender of the APIC faith might reasonably contend that it is unfair to criticize marketing's strategic squares on these grounds. Although this defender of the faith argument is eminently plausible, it doesn't withstand close scrutiny. Many of the boxes in the wider cultural sphere – on television, on film, in books, in fairy stories – are themselves two-dimensional. Their intrigue arises from the storyteller's art, the author's ability to make us believe the unbelievable, to suspend our disbelief, *à la* Coleridge. The problem with strategic marketing matrices doesn't lie with the matrix as a mode of representation. It rests with the box-builder's inability to arouse our curiosity, to tickle our fancy. It is a failure of imagination, not illustration.

Discussion Questions. If marketing's matrix mania is a consequence of the late 1960s decision to broaden its domain, then the textbooks of the pre-broadening era should be devoid of grid squares. Compare a mainstream textbook of the mid-1960s with one of today – first and current editions of Kotler are ideal – and calculate the proportion of squares in each (relative to all illustrations). Examine editions from intervening decades to see if there is any evidence of a secular trend. What factors might account for the rise in boxology?

In 1835, Hans Christian Andersen published a pamphlet, *Eventyr, fortalte for Born*, containing his first four fairy stories, one of which was 'The Princess on the Pea'. As children of all ages know, this tells the tale of a scientific test, designed to verify the truth claims of the nobility, princesses in particular. A single pea is placed under twenty mattresses, on top of which are piled a further twenty feather beds. Impostors invariably spend a comfortable night, luxuriating in the mountain of bedding. But such is the sensitivity of true princesses that they complain of an irritant, something hard under the bedclothes disturbing their peaceful repose.[13]

It is a moot point whether marketing is a blue blood of the academy (and scientific truth is established by slightly different procedures these days), but there is no doubt that our discipline's dogmatic slumber is being disrupted by an errant P. That P is Planning. For more than a generation, planning has been regarded as the bedrock of modern marketing, the hard core of the Kotlerite concept, the P in APIC, no less. In recent years, however, it has been subject to mounting criticism and, while planning is still widely practised, it is more like a meaningless, if well-meaning ritual than a forecast of meaningful marketing possibilities. Marketing planning is a magical rite for managers. And there's nothing wrong with that.

The principal problem with marketing planning is not that it's a magical rite but that planners refuse to acknowledge its magical qualities. Planners persist in believing that plans are of paramount importance and, while their conviction is touching (indeed, necessary, as noted in Chapter 3), wishing will not make marketing plans rigorous, rational, reliable or robust. It is only in fairy stories that wishes come true, frogs turn into princes, pigs can fly, sows' ears make silk purses and marketing plans come to fruition exactly as anticipated. Fairy stories, in fact, are what marketing plans really are and, again, there's nothing wrong with that. As Chapter 7 argues, marketing planners are in the tale-telling business, the happily-ever-after business, the somewhere-over-the-rainbow business, the L. Frank Baum business.

To be sure, the writers of marketing texts are also in the tale-telling business, after a fashion. Chapter 7, for example, comprises a simple morality tale, where an unfortunate situation (marketing plans are pointless) is made better (planners should become storytellers) and everyone lives happily after (sort of). *Marketing – The Retro Revolution*, incidentally, is also based on an overarching narrative structure . . .

Discussion Questions. Work out the underpinning structure of Marketing – The Retro Revolution. *Hint: concentrate on the principal protagonist of each chapter. Extra Hint: the original protagonist of Chapter 5 was Anton Mesmer, not Sequah; the first draft of Chapter 7 used Hans Christian Andersen as the storytelling exemplar; and Chapter 8 once contained a lengthy section on Karl Marx, marketing man. A free coconut to the first person who can tell me what the structure is (someone enlighten me, please!).*

Suspense, so they say, is the secret of successful storytelling. In an attempt to add an element of surprise to Chapter 8, I suggested that marketing is inherently spatial and chose not to develop the argument. The more cynical amongst you may conclude that it's a bit much to condemn mainstream marketing for ignoring place and then proceed to ignore it myself. But, hey, that's TEASE for you! And anyway, the spatial side of marketing is a recurring theme throughout the book. In the preface I contend that marketing is quintessentially American; the focus of Chapter 5 is the itinerant medicine show; and at various points I intimate that marketing is not merely American *tout court*, but primarily a Yankee phenomenon, a child of New England and the north-eastern United States generally. The boasting, barking, bunkum and ballyhoo that is considered characteristic of marketing (by the general public, as opposed to sophisticated scholars like ourselves) was propagated, polished, perfected and popularized by pedlars, picaroons and patent medicine purveyors of predominantly Puritan descent. It is surely no accident that many of the pioneers of puffery described in this book – Barton, Barnum, Baum, etc. – hail from the north-east corner of the American continent. Or is it?

While you're thinking about that one, let me put another spatial possibility to you. If the premodern marketing of Barnumesque stripe is a child of New England, then the modern marketing paradigm of the post-war era is pre-eminently *suburban*. At this remove in time, it is easy to forget that the rise of modern marketing, and the very rapid crystallization of its key constructs, coincided with the burgeoning of the 'burbs. Between 1950 and 1970, the suburban population of the United States grew from 35 million to 84 million people, a 144% increase.[14] It was in this era, moreover, that many of the delivery mechanisms of modern marketing – television, shopping centres, supermarkets, interstate highway, fast food restaurants – came to the fore and much of marketing's early post-war energy was devoted to what could be considered 'suburban' product categories: cars, furnishings, kitchen equipment, washing powder, pet food, toys, yard goods and the like. True, the *Ozzie-and-Harriet, Leave-it-to-Beaver*, wife-dog-and-2.4-children stereotype may be somewhat at odds with the parochial, xenophobic, A-bomb-anxiety-ridden *actualité* of the 1950s. Likewise, metropolitan opinion leaders' disdain for suburbia, and all that it stands for, tends to obscure the utopian impulse that stimulated this ex-urban exodus in the first place. Nevertheless, the whole fifties, Formica, tailfins, happy families era is now widely regarded as America's golden age, a time of picket-fenced, barbecue-pitted, chrome-plated perfection, when pre-PC, pre-feminist and pre-multicultural mores held sway. It is entirely appropriate, is it not, that the prime mover of suburbanization was called Levitt. In 1946, the Levitt brothers Bill and Alfred built the first of their vast housing estates, later immortalized in the Pete Seeger song, 'Little

Boxes', and although the brothers' later developments included variations on the original, 800 square foot, four-room, Cape Cod design, Levittowns were the absolute epitome of the mass-production, mass-marketing, mass-consumption mindset. In many ways, they are the perfect metaphor for modern marketing: bland, boring, boxy, banal, ubiquitous, uninspiring and, while not unappealing in a pink flamingo, family-station-wagon, three ducks on the wall kind of way, they are hopelessly stereotyped, egregiously kitsch, irredeemably ersatz.

> *Discussion Questions. Is marketing the retroscape of scholarship? To what extent does marketing come from the wrong side of the tracks and is this the reason that the better class of scholar – sociologists, anthropologists and historians who study consumption, for example – consistently ignore the work of business school types? Account, if you can, for marketing's roots in the north-eastern United States.*

In Chapter 9, *Musa* was mooted as a metaphor for the marketing brand. Our specialism, according to some, is entering the decline stage of its product life cycle and the banana was held up as a symbol of both its present parlous state and carnivalesque hope for the future. Certainly, the banana/marketing parallels are striking and nowhere is this better illustrated than in their mutual retro bent. The present book contains numerous examples of retromarketing in action, but the banana's retro credentials need to be confirmed (just in case you reckon I'm bluffing).

In this regard, one immediately thinks of the recent rise in retro cuisine, the kitsch dishes of the past that are eaten ironically (Prawn Cocktail? Black Forest Gâteau? Chicken Maryland? Love those deep fried bananas!). Equally evocative are the EU's proposals to dispose of the banana surplus by distributing them free to schoolkids, like the eleven o'clock milk-breaks of yore. What's more, Marks & Spencer's policy of selling mini-bananas – perfect for kiddies' lunch boxes – represents a retailing throwback to the early days of the trade, when *Musas* were much smaller than they are at present. The same is true of grocery superstores' growing penchant for exotic, high-profit-margin, para-Lacatanian varieties of *sapientum*, such as the Hawaiian Red, Blue Java, Praying Hands and Rhino Horn. Sainsbury's analogous acquisition of an entire Caribbean island, to grow organic bananas, is tantamount to retro colonialism, as protesters have already made clear.

Indeed, it seems to me that Sainsbury's actions are indicative of perhaps the most profound parallel between the prodigious plantain and the marketing 'product'. Namely, the political dimension. Bananas look innocent enough in the supermarket or on the kitchen table. Yet hiding behind the hands is a labyrinthine political system that makes the Stasi look like bungling amateurs. The recent banana trade war between the EU and the USA was ostensibly fought on behalf of indigent producers in Central America and former colonial protectorates seeking access to ring-fenced European markets. In practice it had just as much to do with presidential pork-barrelling – the United Fruit Company was one of Clinton's biggest backers – and the market power of big banana companies than the problems of banana producers in the developing world. One doesn't need to dig up the CIA-backed Guatemalan coup of 1954, engineered by marketing spin-*meister* nonpareil Edward L. Bernays, to know that *Musas* are just about as political as they come.[15]

Marketing too looks innocent enough in the corporate fruit bowl. Proponents present it as neutral, as normal, as natural, as a reasonably honest reflection of consumer preferences, competitive strategies and the general state of the market. An unbiased stance on how things really are. Although this particular perspective is regurgitated in almost every mainstream marketing textbook, it is utterly preposterous. Marketing is inherently, incorrigibly, irredeemably political, all the way from the intra-organizational politics of marketing planning to the training programmes of marketing's professional bodies. McDonaldized market-ing may seek to sell innocence, but the marketing product is anything but. This is exemplified by the recent round of anti-capitalist protests – Seattle, London, Davos, Prague – which invariably culminate in ritual-istic trashing of McDonald's. The interesting thing is that these protests are a *consequence* of customer orientation. For decades, marketers have been telling their customers that the customer is king and, now that customers are exercising their marketer-given rights, marketers are in no position to complain. By presenting themselves as caring, sharing, customer-orientated organizations (rather than, say, profit orientated) and having betrayed consumer confidence (by means of third world exploitation) marketers have created a rod for their own backs. It is striking, is it not, that the anti-capitalist protests are conducted in a carnivalesque manner, the rambunctious side of marketing that was abandoned by the APIC, customer-orientated paradigm of the 1960s. The protesters aren't opposed to marketing as such, they are opposed to the hypocritical, hug-a-customer marketing of the 'modern' era.

Discussion Questions. There has been much talk of political marketing – the application of marketing principles to political parties – but much less consideration of marketing politics, the political side of marketing practice. Itemize the intra-organizational (marketing trumps accounts) and international (marketing as a front for Americanization) aspects of marketing politics and apply your insights to the consumer (pester-power) and cerebral (politics of publications) spheres. To what extent is the TEASE framework political?

My father was a welder and I'm a welder too. Except that, in keeping with academics' status as the proletariat of post-industrial society, I weld together tissues of texts instead of sheets of metal. As much as anything else, this book is about other books. Many of the chapters take publications as their point of departure, whether they be much-loved classics like Baum's *Wizard of Oz* and Levitt's 'Marketing Myopia', or best-selling tracts like Barton's *The Man Nobody Knows* and Packard's *Hidden Persuaders*, or, indeed, commercial detritus like the *Innovations* catalogue and Fyffes' sticky blue labels. Most importantly perhaps, *Marketing – The Retro Revolution* has been written to counterbalance traditional marketing textbooks. It does not attempt to complement the modern marketing paradigm. It offers an alternative to APIC. It is a counter-Kotler critique. It hopes to depose the model of marketing that has dominated our field for fortysomething years and replace it with TEASE-based marketing principles.

Regardless of its revolutionary aspirations, the present text is primarily a work of literary criticism and the methods it has employed are appropriately literary. Despite appearances to the contrary, *Marketing – The Retro Revolution* is not an historical investigation, nor does it pretend to be. This book, rather, adopts and adapts the research methods of the New Historicists, a leading school of contemporary literary criticism. Although there are several versions of New Historicism, they are all characterized by a belief in the essential textuality of historical knowledge; by fondness for historical accidents, incongruous juxtapositions, speculative inversions, telling anecdotes and flights of historical fancy; and by a discursive mode of discourse that eschews detailed textual analysis for narrative sweep and judicious digressions. Above all, however, the New Historicists refuse to privilege any single data source. Playbills, chapbooks, adverts and analogous textual ephemera are considered just as insightful as the traditional literary canon (hence the eclectic mix of sources in the present text).[16]

New Historicism, to be sure, is one among many latter-day schools of literary theory, almost all of which are applicable to marketing 'texts', broadly defined. It is no exaggeration to state that the entire contents of the present volume could be 'read' in a radically different manner, depending on the theoretical stance adopted. This point is perfectly illustrated in Chapter 10, where revolting aspects of twenty-first-century advertising are interpreted as a revival of Barnumesque freak shows and the grotesque tradition within western art. Although such retro readings are in keeping with New Historicist method, there are other ways to look at it. From a psychoanalytical perspective, it could be contended that contemporary gross-out advertising illustrates the 'anxiety of effluence'. Just as aspirant poets are weighed down with the weight of prior aesthetic achievements and are driven by an Oedipal desire to supersede their literary forebears, so too today's band of offensive advertisers are beset by the saprogenic accomplishments of the promotional piss artists of times past, P.T. Barnum in particular. Indeed, it seems to me that marketing *per se* is stricken by the 'anxiety of impudence'. The low esteem in which it has traditionally been held has forced the field to overcompensate for its purported transgressions. Hence, the post-war emphasis on science, measurement, probity, professionalism, trust, rectitude and what have you. The upshot is that marketing's innate insouciance, irreverence and downright indecency have been obliterated by do-gooding, well-meaning, customer-stroking, nothing-if-not-nauseating inoffensiveness.

I'm backing Barnum.

Discussion Questions. Is advertising vulgar? Should advertising aspire to vulgarity? Are advertisers ashamed of their vulgar heritage? If vulgarity is good enough for Rabelais, Cervantes, Swift, Sterne, Dickens, Wilde, Joyce and Boccaccio, to name but a few, why should advertisers worry about propriety? Indeed, if marketing is customer orientated, as Kotler contends, what have marketers to gain from disgusting their customers?

Inoffensiveness may have mainstream marketing in its vice-like grip, but vice-lite litters the contemporary commercial landscape. As the advent of gross-out advertising attests, our field is witnessing the return of the marketing repressed. Retro regression therapy is called for and, in the final chapter, a tantalizing, titillating, titivating alternative is posited. Summarized in the acronym TEASE, this replaces abjection with flirtation, prefers scurrility to sincerity, recommends ribaldry rather than rigour and elevates exaggeration over exactitude. It maintains that Marketing is a Trickster, marketing is Excessive, Marketing is Adolescent, Marketing is Spirited, marketing is Entertaining. Marketing is something for nothing. Marketing is more than your money's worth. Marketing is never knowingly understated. Marketing is magic realism for managers.

Some readers, admittedly, might conclude that TEASE is an add-on, an aspect of marketing that can be accommodated within the existing APIC paradigm. Surely, they'll surmise, it is just another version of the old argument that marketing is artistic, marketing is creative, marketing is right-brained. Everyone knows that already and, while it is necessary to be reminded of the fact from time to time, there's no need to make a song and dance about it, let alone a paradigm shift. Although I can appreciate why many might lean towards such an interpretation (enough already, no threat, business as usual) and although I recognize that readers' readings are beyond authorial control (as latter-day literary theory reminds us), I'd like to stress the radical alterity that TEASE represents.

Perhaps the best way to appreciate its implications is to refer to the so-called 'broadening' debate, mentioned earlier. Thirty years ago, Kotler and Levy extended the customer-oriented APIC paradigm far beyond its for-profit focus and, in so doing, effectively transformed it into a universal verity, applicable in all circumstances, to all phenomena, at all times.[17] True, some scholarly Cassandras warned of adverse long-term consequences, but the Kotler–Levy marketing philosophy carried the day and has since been applied to every conceivable domain, from continents to celebrities.

If the Kotler–Levy protocols are the equivalent of marketing's Big Bang, TEASE comprises the Big Crunch. It is not something that is sprinkled on top of APIC, irrespective of the setting. It is a replacement for APIC. It insists that the term 'marketing' be reserved for teasing activities, and teasing activities alone. Marketing is the something special, the hyperbolic hoopla, the charismatic catalyst that is added to commercial situations, be they advertising campaigns, new product launches, sales promotion incentives or hold-the-front-page publicity stunts. *And that is all it is.* Customers, according to the TEASE framework, are not marketing's concern, nor are profits, nor are prices, nor is planning, nor is strategy, nor is the environment, nor is research, nor is anything else that is conventionally considered to be marketing's 'property'. To repeat, this does not mean that market research, or customer care or profit margins or corporate strategies are unimportant. Quite the opposite. It simply means that they no longer qualify as marketing. APIC activities can still go on. Indeed, it is imperative that they do. But let's not pretend that in performing these activities we are 'doing' marketing. Marketing starts where APIC stops.

Discussion Questions. Unlike APIC, TEASE is very unevenly spread throughout marketing at present. Certain advertising campaigns and promotional stunts exhibit expertease but other areas are bereft. Identify the prime movers of TEASE – practitioners, professionals, philosophers, pedagogues – and discuss whether it is applicable to every marketing situation.

Reciting Marketing: Notes and References

Recuperating Marketing: On Commencing a Course of Retro Shock Treatment

1. Pathetic, I know, but at least I'm not alone. In the course of his travels-through-darkest-England, journalist Nik Cohn discusses the case of Les, another (equally sad) advertising wannabe, who worked on all sorts of imaginary campaigns before Her Majesty's Pleasure intervened (*Yes We Have No*, London, Secker and Warburg, 1999, p. 37).

2. Naturally, I was hoping for a tie-in double album, *Tales from Topographic Bananas*, emblazoned with Roger Dean artwork and a gatefold sleeve. Ah, the innocence of the pre-punk epoch!

3. In retrospect, I realize that I should have approached an ad agency, rather than a market research company, but then I've never been the sharpest suit in the marketing wardrobe.

4. Copious examples of today's retromarketing mindset are contained in, K. Naughton and B. Vlasic, 'The nostalgia boom', *Business Week*, 23 March, 1998, pp. 58–64; B. Menkamp, 'Boomerang branding', *Brandweek*, 10 November 1997, pp. 24–26, 31–36; D. Redhead, *Products of Our Time*, Basel, Birkhauser, 2000; R. Seymour, 'The 90s: erase and unwind', *The Best of British: 1960–1999, Four Decades of Design*, Manchester, The Observer, 1999, pp. 22–30.

5. See for example: R. Samuel, *Theatres of Memory Volume I: Past and Present in Contemporary Culture*, London, Verso, 1994; B.B. Stern, 'Historical and personal nostalgia in advertising text: the fin de siècle effect', *Journal of Advertising*, 21 (4), 1992, pp. 11–22; M.B. Holbrook and R.M. Schindler, 'Market segmentation based on age and attitude toward the past: concepts, methods and findings concerning nostalgic influences on consumer tastes', *Journal of Business Research*, 37 (1), 1996, pp. 27–39; R. Tredre, 'The shock of the old', *The Observer Life*, Sunday 24 October, 1993, pp. 24–25.

6. Always! Check out that typography on the can. It looks as though it's just been torn from the return carriage of a battered Remington.

7. The debate is summarized in S. Brown, 'Life begins at 40? Further thoughts on marketing's mid-life crisis', *Marketing Intelligence and Planning*, 13 (1), 1995, pp 4–17. However, if there is one thing that symbolizes this loss of intellectual confidence, it is the Special Millennium Edition of Kotler's *Marketing Management*. Its principal selling point – I kid you not – is that it has 'fewer pages' than previous versions!

8. K. Marx, 'The Eighteenth Brumaire of Louis Bonaparte', in *The Marx–Engels Reader, Second Edition*, edited by R.C. Tucker, New York, Norton, 1978 [1852], pp. 594–617.

9. Although for many marketing and consumer researchers, 'historicism' remains a dirty word – thanks to Karl Popper's forty-year-old polemic – the fact of the matter is that New Historicism has taken over from Deconstruction as the cutting edge of the liberal arts. The methodology employed in the present text is loosely New Historicist, insofar as it focuses on marginalia, ephemera and intriguing historical accidents, rather than traditional canonical texts. The marketing canon is not ignored, of course, but it is examined from an unusual and hopefully interesting angle. Excellent overviews of New Historicism are available in J. Brannigan, *New Historicism and Cultural Materialism*, Basingstoke, Macmillan, 1998; P. Hamilton, *Historicism*, London, Routledge, 1997; and C. Gallagher and S. Greenblatt, *Practicing New Historicism*, Chicago, University of Chicago Press, 2000.

10. This is discussed in detail by R.R. Locke, *The Collapse of the American Management Mystique*, Oxford, Oxford University Press, 1996; S. Furusten, *Popular Management Books*, London, Routledge, 1999; and M. Kipping and O. Bjarnar (eds), *The Americanisation of European Business: The Marshall Plan and the Transfer of US Management Models*, London, Routledge, 1998. Popular versions of the Americanization argument are available in: R. Reeves, 'Your country needs US', *The Observer*, Sunday 23 January, 2000, p. 18; S. Marling and G. Kittel, *American Affair: The Americanisation of Britain*, London, Boxtree, 1993; M. Prowse, 'Consumption, consumption, consumption', *The Financial Times Weekend*, Saturday 16 September, 2000, p. xxiv.

11. In keeping with retrospective precept, 1960s media guru Marshall McLuhan is also back in intellectual fashion (see P. Benedetti and N. DeHart, *Forward Through the Rearview Mirror: Reflections on and by Marshall McLuhan*, Scarborough, Prentice-Hall, 1997).

12. I'll be considering Walter Benjamin in due course. In the *Passagen-Werk*, he notes that *la révolution* had come to mean 'clearance sale' by the mid-nineteenth century (S. Buck-Morss, *The Dialectics of Seeing: Walter Benjamin and the Arcades Project*, Cambridge, MA, MIT Press, 1991, p. 284).

1   Remembering Marketing: The Future is History

1. H. Pearman, 'Curiouser and curiouser', *The Sunday Times*, Culture, 16 May, 1999, pp. 14–15.

2. Anon., 'Aroma therapy', *Marketing Week*, 8 April, 1999, pp. 28–29; L. Killgren, 'Joe Lyons makes comeback', *Marketing Week*, 17 June, 1999, p. 5; P. Haynes, 'Nostalgia', *Forbes*, 26 January, 1998, p. 47.

3. J. Carnter-Morley, 'Showing their age', *The Guardian*, Style 2, Friday 25 June, 1999, pp. 10–11.

4. P. Buxton, 'C-T begins £10m XXXX relaunch', *Marketing Week*, 1 July, 1999, p. 6.

5. T. Blanchard, 'Natural Habitat', *The Observer Magazine*, Sunday 13 June, 1999, pp. 16–21.

6. A. Patterson, S. Brown, L. Stevens and P. Maclaran, 'Casting a critical "I" over Caffrey's Irish Ale: soft words, strongly spoken', *Journal of Marketing Management*, 14 (7), 1998, pp. 733–748; L. Stevens, S. Brown and P. Maclaran, 'Through the past darkly: the case of Caffrey's Irish Ale', in C. Gilligan (ed.), *Proceedings of the 1998 Annual Conference of the Academy of Marketing*, Sheffield, Sheffield Business School, 1998, pp. 494–499.

7. B. Gannaway, 'Back to the future', *The Grocer*, 10 October, 1998, pp. 36–39; R. Stodghill, 'VW's new Bug: cute but . . .', *Time*, 19 January, 1998, pp. 44–46; A. Mitchell, 'Retrospective branding', in M. Evans and L. Moutinho (eds), *Contemporary Issues in Marketing*, Basingstoke, Macmillan, 1999, pp. 90–91.

8. S.L. Holack and W.J. Havlina, 'Nostalgia: an exploratory study of themes and

emotions in the nostalgic experience', in J.F. Sherry and B. Sternthal (eds), *Advances in Consumer Research, Vol. XIX*, Provo, UT, Association for Consumer Research, 1992, pp. 380–387; M.B. Holbrook and R.M. Schindler, op. cit.; B.B. Stern, op. cit.; R. Goldman and S. Papson, *Sign Wars: The Cluttered Landscape of Advertising*, New York, Guilford, 1996; J. Hannigan, *Fantasy City: Pleasure and Profit in the Postmodern Metropolis*, London, Routledge, 1998; S. Tannock, 'Nostalgia critique', *Cultural Studies*, 9 (3), 1995, pp. 453–464.

9. Granted, an agreed definition of 'retro' (like an agreed definition of 'brands', 'internationalization', 'involvement', 'marketing', etc.) would be convenient, but marketing's record in this area suggests that it's unlikely to happen, unless all manner of absurdly arbitrary decisions concerning retro/not-retro are imposed upon the phenomenon.

10. Past Times, *Past Times Company History*, Oxford, Historical Collections Group PLC, 1998.

11. P. Haynes, op. cit., p. 47.

12. D. Hillman and D. Gibbs, *Century Makers: One Hundred Clever Things We Take for Granted Which Have Changed Our Lives over the Last One Hundred Years*, London, Weidenfeld and Nicolson, 1998.

13. Anon., 'Return of the Beetle', *The Economist*, 10 January, 1998, p. 80; R. Stodghill, op. cit.

14. The postmodern theorists amongst you will recognize this as a twist on Fredric Jameson's contention that postmodernism is primarily characterized by *pastiche* and *schizophrenia*. Pastiche pertains to the PoMo notion that stylistic innovation is impossible and all that remains is to combine, recycle or playfully evoke extant forms, modes and genres. Schizophrenia refers to postmodernism's purported loss of historical depth, the fact that temporal epochs are infinitely recyclable as distinctive aesthetic styles – 1970s-ness, Edwardian-ness, or whatever – which can be piled on top of each other, as it were, in a kaleidoscopic, hallucinogenic, but ultimately depthless, 'perpetual present'. In this respect, I think it is fair to say that Jameson provides the principal theoretical underpinnings to the present volume – it is concerned with the perpetual present and comprises a pastiche/parody of mainstream marketing textbooks – though I have attempted to keep his convoluted concepts out of the body of the text.

15. Anon., 'Sunshine love affair: "sexiest car" is ten years old', *Financial Mail on Sunday*, 27 June, 1999, p. 44.

16. G. Adair, *Surfing the Zeitgeist*, London, Faber and Faber, 1999, p. 211.

17. L. Bouzereau and J. Duncan, *Star Wars Episode I: The Making of The Phantom Menace*, London, Ebury Press, 1999; Anon. '*Star Wars*: the ride starts here', *Empire*, Star Wars *Special Edition*, August 1999, pp. 10–161.

18. F. Jameson, 'Postmodernism and consumer society', in H. Foster (ed.), *Postmodern Culture*, London, Pluto, 1985, pp. 111–125.

19. A. Lorenz, 'Reitzle maps out Jaguar's route into the future', *The Sunday Times Business*, 4 July, 1999, p. 7.

20. R. Hutton, 'Time machines', *The Sunday Times Sport*, 7 March, 1999, p. 23.

21. Anon., 'Losing its cool', *Marketing Week*, 15 April, 1999, pp. 26–27.

22. Shades of the New Coke débâcle and subsequent launch of Coca-Cola Classic, though the one-hundredth anniversary of the glass bottle might also have had something to with this particular promotion!

23. P. Buxton, 'Sainsbury's makes AMV pay for "Value" failure', *Marketing Week*, 1 April, 1999, p. 12; G. Alexander, 'Kellogg faces crunch as rival overtakes it', *The Sunday Times Business*, 10 January, 1999, p. 8.

24. R. Samuel, op. cit.

25. B. Gannaway op. cit.; B.B. Stern, op. cit.; D. Lowenthal, *The Heritage Crusade and the Spoils of History*, Cambridge, Cambridge University Press, 1998.

26. Nostalgic advertising interpellates the inner child, according to Goldman and Papson, op. cit.

27. S. Brown, E.C. Hirschman and P. Maclaran, 'Presenting the past: on marketing's

reproduction orientation', in S. Brown and A. Patterson (eds) *Imagining Marketing: Art, Aesthetics and the Avant-Garde*, London, Routledge, pp. 145–191.

28. D. McCrone, A. Morris and R. Kiely, *Scotland the Brand: The Making of Scottish Heritage*, Edinburgh, Edinburgh University Press, 1995.

29. S. Macdonald and G. Fyfe (eds), *Theorizing Museums: Representing Identity and Diversity in a Changing World*, Oxford, Blackwell, 1996; N. Merriman, *Beyond the Glass Case: The Past, the Heritage and the Public in Britain*, Leicester, Leicester University Press, 1989; R.W. Belk, *Collecting in a Consumer Society*, London, Routledge, 1995.

30. M.B. Holbrook, 'Nostalgia proneness and consumer tastes', in J.A. Howard (ed.), *Buyer Behavior in Marketing Strategy*, Englewood Cliffs, NJ: Prentice-Hall, 1994, pp. 348–364.

31. P. Ward, *Kitsch in Sync: A Consumer's Guide to Bad Taste*, London, Plexus, 1991.

32. R. Samuel, op. cit.

33. L. Stevens et al., op. cit.

34. F. Davis, *Yearning for Yesterday: A Sociology of Nostalgia*, New York, Free Press, 1979.

35. B.R. Barber, *Jihad vs. McWorld: How Globalism and Tribalism are Reshaping the World*, New York, Ballantine Books, 1995.

36. The literature on globalization is so vast that citation is virtually pointless. Useful overviews are available in F.J. Lechner and J. Boli, *The Globalisation Reader*, Oxford, Blackwell, 2000; D. Held, A. McGrew, D. Goldblatt and J. Perraton, *Global Transformations: Politics, Economics and Culture*, Cambridge, Polity, 1999; J. Tomlinson, *Globalisation and Culture*, Cambridge, Polity, 1999.

37. S. Brown, *Postmodern Marketing*, London, Routledge, 1995; S. Brown, *Postmodern Marketing Two: Telling Tales*, London, ITBP, 1998.

38. S. Hilton, 'The subtle making of a new McNation', *The Observer*, Business, Sunday 13 June, 1999, p. 9; A.A. Gill, 'Not taken by his surprises', *The Sunday Times Culture*, 6 June, 1999, pp. 26–27; R. McLuhan, 'McDonald's curries favour with 70s parody for new line', *Marketing*, 24 June, 1999, p. 20.

39. S. Elliott, 'Lukewarm Skywalker', *Q Magazine*, August 1999, p. 140.

40. B. Gannaway, op. cit.

41. S. Brown, 'Premonitions of Paradiso: millennial madness, *fin de siècle* fever and the end of the end of marketing', in S. Brown and A. Patterson (eds), *Proceedings of the Marketing Paradiso Conclave*, Belfast: University of Ulster, 1999, pp. 1–13.

42. S. Brown, J. Bell and D. Carson, 'Apocaholics anonymous: looking back on the end of marketing', in S. Brown, J. Bell and D. Carson (eds), *Marketing Apocalypse: Eschatology, Escapology and the Illusion of the End*, London: Routledge, 1996, pp. 1–20.

43. R. Goldman and S. Papson, op. cit.

44. R. Venturi, D.S. Brown and S. Izenour, *Learning from Las Vegas*, Cambridge, MA, MIT Press, 1972.

45. Indeed, it's still being alluded to. A recent 'Raised the Hovis Way' advertisement depicts a thirtysomething preparing a traditional crispy bacon and brown sauce sandwich – like she did as a child – to the strains of Dvořák, Hovis's timeless theme tune.

46. J. Lears, *Fables of Abundance: A Cultural History of Advertising in America*, New York, Basic Books, 1994, p. 383.

47. D. Lowenthal, *The Past is a Foreign Country*, Cambridge, Cambridge University Press, 1985; D. Lowenthal, 'Nostalgia tells it like it wasn't', in C. Shaw and M. Chase (eds), *The Imagined Past: History and Nostalgia*, Manchester, Manchester University Press, 1989, pp. 18–32.

48. J. Barzun, *From Dawn to Decadence. 500 Years of Western Cultural Life: 1500 to the Present*, New York, HarperCollins, 2000.

49. R.W. Belk, op. cit. The classic reference, however, is N. McKendrick, 'Josiah Wedgwood and the commercialisation of the Potteries', in N. McKendrick, J. Brewer and J.H. Plumb, *Birth of a Consumer Society*, London, Europa, 1982, pp. 100–145.

50. F. MacCarthy, *William Morris: A Life for Our Time*, London, Faber and Faber, 1995.

51. M. Pendergrast, *For God, Country and Coca-Cola: The Unauthorized History of the World's Most Popular Soft Drink*, London, Weidenfeld and Nicolson, 1993.

52. F. Jameson, *Postmodernism, or, The Cultural Logic of Late Capitalism*, London, Verso, 1991; J-F. Lyotard, *The Postmodern Condition: A Report on Knowledge*, trans. G. Bennington and B. Massumi, Manchester, Manchester University Press, 1984 [1979].

53. A. Bryman, *Disney and his Worlds*, London, Routledge, 1995.

54. The 'I have seen the future and it works' adage was coined by the celebrated American muckraking journalist Lincoln Steffens in the immediate aftermath of the Russian Revolution. However, it was also used as a slogan for the New York World's Fair of 1939.

55. S. Brown, 'The three Rs of relationship marketing: retroactive, retrospective, retrogressive', in T. Hennig-Thurau and U. Hansen (eds) *Relationship Marketing: Gaining Competitive Advantage through Customer Satisfaction and Customer Retention*, Berlin, Springer, 2000, pp. 393–413.

56. For example, S. Brown, 1995, op. cit.; A. O'Driscoll and J.A. Murray, 'The changing nature of theory and practice in marketing: on the value of synchrony', *Journal of Marketing Management*, 14 (5), 1998, pp. 391–416; L. O'Malley and M. Patterson, 'Vanishing point: the mix management paradigm reviewed', *Journal of Marketing Management*, 14 (8), 1998, pp. 829–851; D. Brownlie, M. Saren, R. Wensley and R. Whittington (eds), *Rethinking Marketing: Towards Critical Marketing Accountings*, London, Sage, 1999.

57. P. Kotler, *Kotler on Marketing: How to Create, Win and Dominate Markets*, New York, Free Press, 1999.

58. A. Smithee, 'Kotler is dead!', *European Journal of Marketing*, 31 (3/4), 1997, pp. 315–325; M.B. Holbrook, 'Feline consumption: ethography, felologies and unobtrusive participation in the life of a cat', *European Journal of Marketing*, 31 (3/4), 1997, pp. 214–233; R.W. Belk, 'Three coins in Caesar's Palace fountain: interpreting Las Vegas', in J.W. Alba and J.W. Hutchinson (eds), *Advances in Consumer Research, Vol. XXV*, Provo, UT: Association for Consumer Research, 1998, pp. 7–9; N. Piercy, *Market-led Strategic Change: Transforming the Process of Going to Market*, Oxford, Butterworth-Heinemann, 1997; N. Piercy, *Tales from the Marketplace: Stories of Revolution, Reinvention and Renewal*, Oxford, Butterworth-Heinemann, 1999.

59. A. Herman, *The Idea of Decline in Western History*, New York, The Free Press, 1997.

60. L. McT. Anderson, 'Marketing science: where's the beef?', *Business Horizons*, 37 (1), 1994, pp. 8–16; S. Blair, 'Market research is dead, RIP (Real Innovation Please!)', *Marketing Business*, June 2000, pp. 20–22; S. Armstrong, 'What's on the agenda: the focus group', *The Business*, Saturday 29 July, 2000, p. 9. See also E. Shorris, *A Nation of Salesmen: The Tyranny of the Market and the Subversion of Culture*, New York, Avon, 1994.

2 Reviewing Marketing: The Defective Vision of Theodore Levitt

1. 'Once upon a time' also resonates, as do 'Marley was dead', 'Miss Brooke had that kind of beauty which seems to be thrown into relief by poor dress', 'When Gregor Samsa awoke one morning from troubled dreams he found himself transformed in his bed into a monstrous insect' and, lest we forget, 'In the beginning God created the heaven and the earth'. First lines are cogently discussed by D. Lodge, *The Art of Fiction*, Harmondsworth, Penguin, 1992; A. Oz, *The Story Begins: Essays on Literature*, London, Chatto and Windus, 1999; E.W. Said, *Beginnings: Intention and Method*, London, Granta, 1985; and P. Norman, 'I've started so you'll finish', *The Sunday Times Culture*, 9 January, 2000, p. 16.

2. As Norman (op. cit.) notes, 'In almost every paper and magazine I pick up, I find

pieces whose headlines and pictures demand that I read them, but whose ghastly, clunky, clichéfied intros stop me in my tracks. Most have been used countless times before. "Such and such is alive and well and . . ." "I have seen the future and it . . ." "Just when you thought it was safe to . . ." "It is a truth universally acknowledged . . .". Faced with such sentiments, what else is there to say except, "I am that soldier".'

3. Texts targeted at undergraduates are yet another happy hunting ground of hackneyed introductions. The basic assumption seems to be that today's students are slothful, sub-normal so-and-sos, with minimal attention spans. Therefore, the sheer pervasiveness of the marketing system has to be patiently explained to the lazy sods. Surely not!

4. T. Levitt, 'Marketing myopia', *Harvard Business Review*, 38 (4), 1960, pp. 45–56.

5. S. Brown, 'Marketing and literature: the anxiety of academic influence', *Journal of Marketing*, 63 (1), 1999, pp. 1–15.

6. T. Levitt, 'Retrospective commentary', in B.M. Enis and K.K. Cox (eds), *Marketing Classics: A Selection of Influential Articles*, Boston, Allyn and Bacon, 1975, pp. 20–23.

7. E.C. Bursk, 'Marketing myopia', *Harvard Business Review*, 38 (4), 1960, p. 2.

8. Drucker is another candidate, of course, though I'm not sure that he qualifies as a *marketing* guru, since his contributions pertain to much more than mere marketing. See S. Crainer, *The Ultimate Business Guru Book: Fifty Thinkers Who Made Management*, Oxford, Capstone, 1998; J. Micklethwait and A. Wooldridge, *The Witch Doctors: Making Sense of the Management Gurus*, New York, Times Books, 1996.

9. T. Levitt, *The Marketing Imagination*, New York, Free Press, 1986.

10. T. Levitt, *Innovation in Marketing*, New York: McGraw-Hill, 1962.

11. Mind you, *HBR* is notoriously nepotistic. Levitt edited the journal for several years and did his stint as chair of Harvard's marketing department (far be it for me to imply that these factors influenced the *HBR* review process . . .).

12. Lest you conclude that I'm being unnecessarily critical, I should point out that when 'Marketing Myopia' was first republished in 1962 (in *Innovation in Marketing*, note 10 above), it included an enormous, self-justifying footnote on the railroads industry, a footnote that was not in the original version and was never seen again. Presumably, the author had been taken to task in the interim by representatives of the railroads business. On the rhetoric of 'Marketing Myopia' generally see, G. Marion, 'The marketing management discourse: what's new since the 1960s?' in M.J. Baker, *Perspectives on Marketing Management, Volume 3*, Chichester, Wiley, 1993, pp. 143–168.

13. T. Levitt, 1975, op. cit.

14. The anti-Levitt argument is summarized in H. Mintzberg, *The Rise and Fall of Strategic Planning*, New York, Free Press, 1994 (especially the section '"Marketing Myopia" Myopia', pp. 279–281).

15. S. Brown, *Postmodern Marketing*, op. cit., p. 104.

16. T. Brennan and M. Jay, *Vision in Context: Historical and Contemporary Perspectives on Sight*, New York, Routledge, 1996; M. Jay, *Downcast Eyes: The Denigration of Vision in Twentieth-century French Thought*, Berkeley, University of California Press, 1994; D.M. Levin, *Modernity and the Hegemony of Vision*, Berkeley, University of California Press, 1993; D.M. Levin, *Sites of Vision: The Discursive Construction of Sight in the History of Philosophy*, Boston, MA, MIT Press, 1997.

17. R. Jakobson, *Fundamentals of Language*, Paris, Mouton, 1975. Jakobson's framework is examined and extended in D. Lodge, *The Modes of Modern Writing: Metaphor, Metonymy and the Typology of Modern Literature*, London, Arnold, 1977.

18. As the oil industry was (and remains) a national icon, inasmuch as it symbolizes American know-how, Levitt's exemplar proved particularly powerful. The iconic status of the 1950s oil industry is discussed in D. Halberstam, *The Fifties*, New York, Ballantine Books, 1993 (Chapter 8, especially).

19. T. Levitt, 1960, op. cit., p. 56. Emphasis in original.

20. P. Kotler and R. Singh, 'Marketing warfare in the 1980s', *Journal of Business Strategy*, 1, Winter, 1981, pp. 30–41.

21. T. Peters and R.H. Waterman, Jr., *In Search of Excellence*, New York, Harper and Row, 1982.

22. A dyspeptic to the last, I have denounced entertainment venues elsewhere (S. Brown, *Songs of the Humpback Shopper (and Other Bazaar Ballads)*, 1998, available as a free download from www.sfxbrown.com).

23. P. de Man, *Blindness and Insight: Essays in the Rhetoric of Contemporary Criticism*, London, Routledge, 1983.

24. S. Brown, *Postmodern Marketing*, op. cit. See also S. Brown and P. Maclaran, 'The future is past: marketing, apocalypse and the retreat from utopia', in S. Brown et al., *Marketing Apocalypse*, op. cit., pp. 260–277.

25. A case for the place of intellectual conflict is convincingly made by R. Collins, 'On the sociology of intellectual stagnation: the late twentieth century in perspective', in M. Featherstone (ed.), *Cultural Theory and Cultural Change*, London, Sage, 1992, pp. 73–96.

26. The impact of Wakeman's portrayal is considered in T. Frank, *The Conquest of Cool: Business Culture, Counterculture and the Rise of Hip Consumerism*, Chicago, University of Chicago Press, 1997. A more general overview of the era is available in J. Sivulka, *Soap, Sex and Cigarettes: A Cultural History of American Advertising*, Belmont, CA, Wadsworth, 1998.

27. On the relationship between management and literature, see R.A. Brawer, *Fictions of Business: Insights on Management from Great Literature*, New York, John Wiley, 1998. *Mad* magazine, incidentally, was first published in 1952, though Alfred E. Nueman (the mag's simple-minded mascot) wasn't introduced until 1956.

28. P. Murray, *Reflections on Commercial Life: An Anthology of Classic Texts from Plato to the Present*, New York, Routledge, 1997; J.B. Twitchell, *Lead Us Into Temptation: The Triumph of American Materialism*, New York, Columbia University Press, 1999.

29. T. Frank, op. cit.; D. Halberstam, op. cit.

30. J. Miller, *Almost Grown: The Rise of Rock*, London, Heinemann, 1999 (especially pp. 163–168). Also, G. Lipsitz, *Time Passages: Collective Memory and Popular Culture*, Minneapolis, University of Minnesota Press, 1990 (Chapter 5 in particular).

31. The 1994 movie, *Quiz Show*, captures the controversy perfectly. See also D. Halberstam, op. cit.

32. On fads generally, see F.W. Hoffmann and W.G. Bailey, *Mind and Society Fads*, New York, Haworth, 1992; and T. Thorne, *Fads, Fashions and Cults: From Acid House to Zoot Suit*, London, Bloomsbury, 1993. For American popular culture, an excellent year-by-year account is available in D. Epstein, *Twentieth Century Pop Culture*, London, Carlton Books, 1999.

33. See, for example, M.F. Rogers, *Barbie Culture*, London, Sage, 1999.

34. G. Tibbals, *Business Blunders: Dirty Dealing and Financial Failure in the World of Big Business*, London, Robinson, 1999; R.F. Hartley, *Marketing Mistakes: Fourth Edition*, New York, John Wiley, 1989 (especially Chapter 6); R. Rothenberg, *Where the Suckers Moon: The Life and Death of an Advertising Campaign*, New York, Vintage, 1994; T. Hine, *Populuxe: From Tailfins and TV Dinners to Barbie Dolls and Fallout Shelters*, New York, MJF Books, 1999; D. Epstein, op. cit.

35. 'Almost overnight Congress set up the National Aeronautics and Space Administration (NASA) to plan and execute space exploration. Congress also passed the National Defense Education Act, which shifted the focus of education to strengthen curricula with advanced programs in science, advanced mathematics and languages' (J. Sivulka, op. cit., p. 253). On the Conant report, see T. Hine, *The Rise and Fall of the American Teenager*, New York, Avon Books, 1999. Marketing, needless to say, fared particularly badly in the Ford and Carnegie reports on business education (R.A. Gordon and J.E. Howell, *Higher Education for Business*, New York, Columbia University Press, 1959; F.C. Pierson et al., *The Education of American Businessmen: A Study of University-College Programs in Business Administration*, New York, McGraw-Hill, 1959).

36. Far from being a local British difficulty, the 'Two Cultures' controversy of May 1959 chimed perfectly with the post-Sputnik, science-orientated concerns then extant in the US. Snow's dichotomy had a major influence on the thinking of John F. Kennedy, amongst others. See S. Collini, 'Introduction', in C.P. Snow, *The Two Cultures*, Cambridge, Canto, 1993, pp. vii–lxxiii.

37. B. Levenson, *Bill Bernbach's Book*, New York, Villiard, 1987, pp. xvi–xvii. On Bernbach see T. Frank, op. cit.; D. Higgins, *The Art of Writing Advertising: Conversations with Masters of the Craft*, Chicago, NTC Books, 1965; J.B. Twitchell, *Adcult USA: The Triumph of Advertising in American Culture*, New York, Columbia University Press, 1996.

38. S. Fox, *The Mirror Makers: A History of American Advertising and its Creators*, Urbana, University of Illinois Press, 1997.

39. J.K. Galbraith, *The Affluent Society*, new edition, Harmondsworth, Penguin, 1999.

40. Regression therapy, regrettably, had already been repressed due to *The Search for Bridey Murphy* scam of 1956. *The Search* was written by amateur hypnotist, Morey Bernstein. He claimed to have age-regressed a Colorado housewife, Virginia Tinge, whose former lives included that of a nineteenth-century Irish farm girl, Bridey Murphy. The book triggered a nationwide fad for reincarnation – 'come as you were' parties were particularly popular, as was the Reincarnation Cocktail – until such time as Tinge was exposed as a sufferer of False Memory Syndrome, fifties-style. See D. Epstein, op. cit., p. 65.

41. V. Packard, *The Hidden Persuaders*, New York, David McKay, 1957.

42. V. Packard, *The Status Seekers*, New York, David McKay, 1959; V. Packard, *The Waste Makers*, New York, David McKay, 1960.

43. D. Horowitz, *Vance Packard and American Social Criticism*, Chapel Hill, University of North Carolina Press, 1994, p. 185. On the advertising industry's response, see M. Mayer, *Madison Avenue, U.S.A.*, New York, Harper and Bros, 1958. This laid great stress on the scientific, rational credo of most agencies, JWT in particular.

44. D. Horowitz, op. cit., p. 108.

45. Ibid., p. 162. Dichter also responded at length to Packard's charges in *The Strategy of Desire*, New York, Doubleday, 1960.

46. The shock-horror, appalling yet appealing aspect of *The Hidden Persuaders* is cogently described in T. Hine (1999, op. cit., p. 28), 'Vance Packard's best-selling book on the psychological dimensions of advertising came as a shock to many consumers when it appeared in 1957 . . . At the same time, it couldn't help but evoke admiration for the cleverness of the industry, how much it had learned about people and the wit with which it used the information. People enjoy being fooled creatively, never more so than during the Populuxe era'.

47. S. Rogers, 'How a publicity blitz created the myth of subliminal advertising', *Public Relations Quarterly*, 37 (Winter), 1992–3, pp. 12–17. An excellent summary of the subliminal 'scare' is contained in M. Rogers, 'Subliminal advertising: the battle of popular versus the scholarly views', in S.C. Hollander and T. Nevett (eds), *Marketing in the Long Run: Proceedings of the Second Workshop on Historical Research in Marketing*, East Lansing, Michigan State University Press, 1985, pp. 69–82.

48. J.B. Twitchell (1996, op. cit., pp. 111–116). See also W. Poundstone, *Big Secrets: The Uncensored Truth About All Sorts of Stuff You Are Never Supposed to Know*, New York, Quill, 1983 (especially pp. 214–218); W. Poundstone, *Biggest Secrets: More Uncensored Truth About All Sorts of Stuff You Are Never Supposed to Know*, New York, Quill, 1993 (especially pp. 231–236); B. Archer, 'Blink and you'll miss it', *The Guardian*, Friday 4 February, 2000, p. 13. With regard to the effects of embedding, we need look no further than David Letterman's recent talk-show confession, 'I don't believe in subliminal advertising. Then again, I went shopping yesterday and bought a combine harvester'!

49. W.B. Key, *The Age of Manipulation: The Con in Confidence, the Sin in Sincere*, Lanham, Madison Books, 1989.

50. V. Packard, *The Hidden Persuaders: A New Edition for the 1980s*, Harmondsworth, Penguin, 1981, p. 36.

51. Ibid., pp. 15, 24, 33.

52. T. Levitt, 1960, op. cit., p. 56.

53. S. Brown, 1999, 'Marketing and literature', op. cit. Again, you might conclude I'm being hard on marketing's foremost spokesperson, but that is not my intention. I, for one, think it is noteworthy that Levitt's 'other' *HBR* paper in 1960 – the one everybody's forgotten about – comprised an unprovoked attack on the snake-oil sellers of Motivation Research ('The M-R snake dance', *Harvard Business Review*, 38 (6), 1960, pp. 76–84). Clearly, Levitt needed a scapegoat for his customer-centred reinterpretation of marketing – people who weren't doing it properly! – and the snake dancers of motivation research fitted the hate-figure bill. As everyone knows, however, love and hate are less polar opposites than two sides of the same coin.

54. He is liberally endowed, for example, with what is now termed the 'Teflon factor', the fact that nothing untoward seems to stick. Despite his failed predictions in 'Marketing Myopia' and consistent inconsistency in conceptual matters (he variously stresses and dismisses the importance of packaging, pricing, differentiation, change, stability, youth, experience, small companies, large companies, information technology, globalization and the like), the good ship Levitt sails serenely on, seemingly unperturbed by the scholarly turmoil in its wake. What a guy!

55. Consider the evidence: Theodore Levitt is a leading academic authority in a leading academic institution, yet he manages convincingly to portray himself as a practical man, an ordinary Joe, one of the guys. His carefully crafted textual persona is that of a cracker-barrel management philosopher, a purveyor of wry, homespun, horny-handed, no-nonsense, seat-of-the-pants, eminently implementable pearls of marketing wisdom. This portrayal, paradoxically, is reinforced by the cerebral milieu from which he hails, thanks to his periodic denigration of woolly-headed academics, as well as his own immensely engaging sense of (often self-deprecatory) humour.

56. I have examined this at length elsewhere (see S. Brown 1999, 'Marketing and literature', op. cit.).

57. At the time of 'Marketing Myopia', Ted Levitt was a little-known German-Jewish immigrant, without a PhD, who had recently been made a lecturer in Harvard Business School, that bastion of WASP-ish sensibility. But rather than rail against the establishment, Levitt valorized the role of the outsider as an architect of change in organizations and industries alike. Mesmerized by its seemingly immortal message, we tend to forget that 'Marketing Myopia' was written at the very start of Levitt's career, before he could afford to indulge in magisterial magnanimity and ironic self-deprecation. Hence his disparagement of motivation research, whilst making use of their epigrams and stressing the need to comprehend consumers' deepest desires!

58. J.N. Sheth, D.M. Gardner and D.E. Garrett, *Marketing Theory: Evolution and Evaluation*, New York, John Wiley, 1988.

59. For example: M. Klein, *No-Logo: Taking Aim at the Brand Bullies*, London, HarperCollins, 2000; R. Levine, C. Locke, D. Searls and D. Weinberger, *The Cluetrain Manifesto: The End of Business as Usual*, London, FT.com, 2000; R. Thomson, *Soft*, London, Bloomsbury, 1998; B. Fowler, *Scepticism Inc.*, London, Vintage, 1999; S. Millhauser, *Martin Dressler: The Tale of an American Dreamer*, London, Phoenix, 1996; B. Bryson, *Notes from a Big Country*, London, Doubleday, 1998; D. Brooks, *Bobos in Paradise: The New Upper Class and How They Got There*, New York, Simon and Schuster, 2000; D. Butler et al., 'Cover story: attention all shoppers', *Time*, 2 August, 1999, pp. 38–43; J. Robinson, *The Manipulators: A Conspiracy to Make us Buy*, London, Simon and Schuster, 1998; A.L. Benson, *I Shop, Therefore I Am: Compulsive Buying and the Search for Self*, Northvale, Jason Aronson, 2000; P. Underhill, *Why We Buy: The Science of Shopping*, London, Orion, 1999.

3   Redeeming Marketing: The Spiritual Side of Trade

1. B. Barton, *The Man Nobody Knows: A Discovery of the Real Jesus*, Indianapolis, Bobbs-Merrill, 1925.

2. Accounts of Barton's life and works are contained in: S. Fox, op cit; T.J.J. Lears, 'From salvation to self-realization: advertising and the therapeutic roots of the consumer culture, 1880–1930', in R.W. Fox and T.J.J. Lears (eds), *The Culture of Consumption: Critical Essays in American History, 1880–1980*, New York: Pantheon Books, 1983, pp. 1–38; L.P. Ribuffo, 'Jesus Christ as business statesman: Bruce Barton and the selling of American capitalism', *American Quarterly*, Summer, 1981, pp. 206–231; R. Marchand, 'The corporation nobody knew: Bruce Barton, Alfred Sloan and the founding of the General Motors "Family"', *Business History Review*, 65 (Winter), 1991, pp. 825–875; J.G. Vitale, *The Seven Lost Secrets of Success*, Ashland, VistaTron, 1992; J.B. Twitchell, 1996, op. cit.

3. R. Marchand, *Advertising the American Dream: Making Way for Modernity, 1920–1940*, Berkeley, University of California Press, 1985; R. Marchand, *Creating the Corporate Soul: The Rise of Public Relations and Corporate Imagery in American Big Business*, Berkeley, University of California Press, 1998; D. Pope, *The Making of Modern Advertising*, New York, Basic Books, 1983; F. Presbrey, *The History and Development of Advertising*, New York: Greenwood Press, 1968.

4. Coolidge's entire speech, delivered on 27 October 1926, is reproduced as an appendix in Presbrey (op. cit., pp. 619–625).

5. I discuss this inclination in 'Trinitarianism, the Eternal Evangel and the three eras schema', in S. Brown et al., *Marketing Apocalypse*, op. cit., pp. 23–43.

6. See for example: R. Marchand (1985, op cit); J. Lears (1994, op. cit.); S. Strasser, *Satisfaction Guaranteed: The Making of the American Mass Market*, New York, Pantheon, 1989; M.H. Bogart, *Artists, Advertising and the Borders of Art*, Chicago, University of Chicago Press, 1995; P.W. Laird, *Advertising Progress: American Business and the Rise of Consumer Marketing*, Baltimore, MD, Johns Hopkins University Press, 1998; R.S. Tedlow, *New and Improved: The Story of Mass Marketing in America*, Oxford, Heinemann, 1990; S.C. Hollander and R. Germain, *Was There a Pepsi Generation Before Pepsi Discovered It?*, Lincolnwood, Illinois, NTC Books, 1992; J. Sivulka, op. cit.

7. S. Lewis, *Babbitt*, New York, Harcourt Brace, 1922. Needless to say, Lewis's condemnation of catchphraseology ensured that 'Babbitt' and its cognates entered the language as catchphrases for catchphrasers. The ambivalence of advertising's status during the inter-war era is neatly summarized by Marchand (1985, op. cit.).

8. B. Barton, op. cit., p. 143.

9. Ibid., p. 153.

10. R.L. Moore, *Selling God: American Religion in the Marketplace of Culture*, Oxford, Oxford University Press, 1994, p. 213; D. Mayer, *The Positive Thinkers: Religion as Pop Psychology from Mary Baker Eddy to Oral Roberts*, New York, Pantheon, 1980, pp. 178–179; L.P. Ribuffo, op. cit., p. 221.

11. Such a doctrine, to be sure, was hardly original. The Protestant work ethic, which held that one best served God by best using one's talents in one's particular calling, had long been a staple of Puritan fare and, for Weber at least, a key factor in the rise of the industrialized west. In fairness, however, Barton's position was much more sophisticated than this big-business-boosting, apologist-for-capitalism caricature suggests. Far from maintaining that the marketplace was the measure of all things, Barton believed that contemporary business life was seriously deficient in several spiritual respects. Something had been lost. The lambs had gone astray on the road to market. Interestingly, these are almost exactly the same complaints made by Vance Packard, another WASP, in the late 1950s, albeit shorn of the attendant evangelical apparatus. See J. Lears, 'Review of *Vance*

Packard and American Social Criticism, by D. Horowitz', *The New Republic*, 10 March, 1994, pp. 32–37.

12. For the theological backgrounds of first generation Madison Avenue madmen see J.B. Twitchell, 1996, op. cit., pp. 32–39; D. Pope, op. cit., pp. 178–179; M. Mayer, 1958, op. cit.

13. On 28 October 1940, President Franklin D. Roosevelt castigated Representative Barton and two fellow non-interventionists, Representatives Martin and Fish, with the deathless words, 'Great Britain would never have received an ounce of help from us if the decision had been left to Martin, Barton and Fish' (quoted in L.P. Ribuffo, op. cit., p. 206).

14. C.V.R. George, *God's Salesman: Norman Vincent Peale and the Power of Positive Thinking*, New York: Oxford University Press, 1993; M. Mayer, 1980, op. cit.

15. Aside from the excisions in the body of the text, the 1960 reprint removed the original epigraph ('Wist ye not that I must be about my father's *business*'), and toned down the chapter titles, to boot (Chapter 5, 'His Advertisements' became 'His Work and Words', and Chapter 6 'The Founder of Modern Business' turned into 'His Way in Our World').

16. Quoted in J. Vitale, 1992, op. cit., p. 94.

17. As the 'universal' quote indicates, Barton had broadened – to put it mildly – the marketing concept some forty years before Kotler and Levy.

18. Excellent overviews of the mind cure movement are contained in M. Mayer (1980, op. cit.), T.J.J. Lears, (1983, op. cit.) and W. Leach, *Land of Desire: Merchants, Power and the Rise of a New American Culture*, New York, Pantheon, 1993 (especially Chapter 8).

19. I have discussed Theophrastus Bombastus and his descendants in S. Brown, 'Tore down *à la* Rimbaud', in S. Brown, A.M. Doherty and B. Clarke (eds), *Romancing the Market*, London, Routledge, 1998, pp. 22–40.

20. Strictly speaking, this was the 'Second Great Awakening'. The first occurred in August 1801, at Cane Ridge, Kentucky, when Barton Stone organized an inter-denominational meeting and triggered a national religious revival (see H. Bloom, *The American Religion: The Emergence of the Post Christian Nation*, New York, Simon and Schuster, 1992).

21. M. Mayer, 1980, op. cit., pp. 32–45.

22. C. Fraser, *God's Perfect Child: Living and Dying in the Christian Science Church*, New York, Metropolitan, 1999; G. Gill, *Mary Baker Eddy*, Reading, Perseus, 1998; H. Bloom, op. cit. (Chapter 7, in particular); M. Mayer, 1980, op. cit.

23. S. Cranston, *H.P.B.: The Extraordinary Life and Influence of Helena Blavatsky*, New York, Putnam, 1993; P. Washington, *Madame Blavatsky's Baboon: Theosophy and the Emergence of the Western Guru*, London, Secker and Warburg, 1993; J. Godwin, *The Theosophical Enlightenment*, Albany, State University of New York Press, 1994.

24. W. Leach, 1993, op. cit.

25. The turn-of-the-century doll craze is examined in A.M. Colbert, K.M. Rassuli and L. Dix, 'Marketers, dolls and the democratisation of fashion', in D.G.B. Jones and P. Cunningham (eds), *Marketing History Knows No Boundaries*, Proceedings of the 8th Conference on Historical Research in Marketing and Marketing Thought, Kingston, Queen's University, 1997, pp. 113–122. For a broader cultural perspective on dolls and mannequins generally see H. Schwartz, *The Culture of the Copy: Striking Likenesses, Unreasonable Facsimiles*, New York, Zone Books, 1996. Miniatures are also cogently covered in S. Stewart, *On Longing: Narratives of the Miniature, the Gigantic, the Souvenir, the Collection*, Durham, NC, Duke University Press, 1993.

26. L. Simon, *Genuine Reality: A Life of William James*, New York, Harcourt Brace, 1998.

27. W. James, *The Will to Believe and Other Essays in Popular Philosophy*, New York, Dover, 1956 [1897]; S.C. Rowe, *The Vision of James*, Rockport, Element, 1996.

28. W. James, *The Varieties of Religious Experience*, New York: Touchstone, 1997, p. 91.

29. As libidinal mid-life yearnings for an attractive twentysomething. See L. Simon, op. cit., p. 282.

30. Patten's life and work is summarized in W. Leach, 1993, op. cit., pp. 231–244; J. Lears, *Fables of Abundance*, 1994, op. cit., pp. 113–117; D. Fox, *The Discovery of Abundance: Simon N. Patten and the Transformation of Social Theory*, Ithaca, NY, Cornell University Press, 1986; R. Tugwell, 'Notes on the life and work of Simon Nelson Patten', *Journal of Political Economy*, 31 (April), 1923, pp. 153–208; D.B. Schluter, 'Economics and the sociology of consumption: Simon Patten and early academic sociology in America, 1894–1904', *Journal of the History of Sociology*, 1 (Fall-Winter), 1979–80, pp. 132–162.

31. You see, it really does make you go blind (or myopic, at least)!

32. J. Lears, *Fables*, 1994, op. cit., p. 113.

33. Patten's widely scattered writings are gathered together in R. Tugwell, *Essays in Economic Theory*, New York, Knopf, 1924.

34. M. Mayer, 1980, op. cit., p. 171.

35. Dale Carnegie's life and continuing impact are ably dissected in G. Kemp and E. Claflin, *Dale Carnegie: The Man Who Influenced Millions*, New York, St Martin's Press, 1989; see also S. Crainer, 'Dale Carnegie' in *The Ultimate Business Guru Book*, Oxford, Capstone, 1998, pp. 27–29; and L. Thomas, 'A shortcut to distinction', in D. Carnegie, *How to Win Friends and Influence People*, New York, Pocket Books, 1981, pp. 237–248. For Norman Vincent Peale, the best source is C.V.R. George, op. cit. M. Mayer (1980, op. cit.) is also excellent, as is Peale's 1984 autobiography, *The True Joy of Positive Thinking*, New York, Quill. The current crop is covered in S. Pattison, *The Faith of the Managers: When Management Becomes Religion*, London, Cassell, 1997; A.A. Huczynski, *Management Gurus: What Makes Them and How to Become One*, London, Routledge, 1993; J. Micklethwait and A. Wooldridge, op. cit.

36. I.I. Mitroff and E.A. Denton, *A Spiritual Audit of Corporate America: A Hard Look at Spirituality, Religion and Values in the Workplace*, San Francisco, Jossey-Bass, 1999.

37. C. Reed, 'With God as my co-worker', *The Observer Business*, Sunday 28 November, 2000, p. 11.

38. S. Tam, *God Owns my Business*, New York, Horizon House, 1991; D. Baron and L. Padwa, *Moses on Management: Fifty Leadership Lessons from the Greatest Manager of All Time*, New York, Pocket Books, 1999; L.B. Jones, *Jesus CEO: Using Ancient Wisdom for Visionary Leadership*, New York, Hyperion, 1995.

39. B. Summerskill, 'Clutter to be swept off streets', *The Observer*, Sunday 23 July, 2000, p. 10; S. Brown, 1998, *Songs of the Humpback Shopper*, op. cit. (available from www.sfxbrown.com); D. Goss, 'A Hell of a vision: marketing the human resource dream', in S. Brown, A.M. Doherty and B. Clarke (eds), *Proceedings of the Marketing Illuminations Spectacular*, Belfast: University of Ulster, 1997, pp. 264–271; B.L. Beyerstein and D.F. Beyerstein, *The Write Stuff: Evaluations of Graphology – The Study of Handwriting Analysis*, Buffalo, Prometheus Books, 1992.

40. Condimantics, I guess, must be the technical term for soothsaying with the aid of ketchup or brown sauce splashes. An analogous technique, condomantics, also springs to mind, though I hesitate to speculate on the details of the process, other than to say it presumably involves nine-month forecasts.

41. D. Chopra, *The Seven Spiritual Laws of Success*, New York, Bantam, 1996 (see also Chopra's *Creating Affluence: The A to Z Guide to a Richer Life*, 1999); C. Handy, *The New Alchemists: How Visionary People Make Something Out of Nothing*, London, Hutchinson, 1999; J. Kunde, *Corporate Religion: Building a Strong Company through Personality and Corporate Soul*, London, Pearson Education, 2000; M.C. Scott, *Reinspiring the Corporation: The Seven Seminal Paths to Corporate Greatness*, Chichester, Wiley, 2000; D. Firth and H. Campbell, *Sacred Business: Resurrecting the Spirit of Work*, Oxford, Capstone, 1997; L. Weinreich, *Eleven Steps to Brand Heaven: The Ultimate Guide to Buying an Advertising Campaign*, London, Kogan Page, 1999; H. Pringle and M. Thompson, *Brand Spirit: How Cause Related Marketing Builds Brands*, Chichester, Wiley, 1999; B. Cohen and J. Greenfield, *Ben & Jerry's Double Dip: How to Run a Values-Led Business and Make Money, Too*, New York, Fireside, 1997; M. Wertheim, *The Pearly Gates of Cyberspace*,

New York, Norton, 1999; E. Davis, *TechGnosis: Myth, Magic and Mysticism in the Age of Information*, London, Serpent's Tail, 1998.

42. P. Wilson, *The Little Book of Calm*, Harmondsworth, Penguin, 1999.

43. A good example of this is Kimberly Lau's recent root-and-branch critique, which denounces the west's commodification of eastern belief systems, such as aromatherapy, yoga and T'ai Chi (K.J. Lau, *New Age Capitalism: Making Money East of Eden*, Philadelphia, University of Pennsylvania Press, 2000).

44. I summarize this literature in S. Brown, 'Devaluing value: the apophatic ethic and the spirit of postmodern consumption', in M. Holbrook (ed.), *Consumer Value: A Framework for Analysis and Research*, London, Routledge, 1999, pp. 159–182.

45. See R.W. Belk, 'Studies in the new consumer behaviour', in D. Miller (ed.), *Acknowledging Consumption: A Review of New Studies*, London: Routledge, 1995, pp. 58–95.

46. The fullest expression of this thesis is found in D. Miller, *A Theory of Shopping*, Cambridge, Polity, 1998.

47. As C. McDannell (*Material Christianity: Religion and Popular Culture in America*, New Haven, Yale University Press, 1995) convincingly demonstrates, however, consumption and Christianity have always been very closely intertwined. With regard to the spirituality of consumption, the classic references are: R.W. Belk, M. Wallendorf and J.F. Sherry, Jr., 'The sacred and profane in consumer behaviour: theodicy on the Odyssey', *Journal of Consumer Research*, 16 (June), 1989, pp. 1–38; R.W. Belk, *Highways and Buyways: Naturalistic Research from the Consumer Behavior Odyssey*, Provo, UT, Association for Consumer Research, 1991; R.W. Belk, 'Hyperreality and globalisation: culture in the age of Ronald McDonald', *Journal of International Consumer Marketing*, 8 (3/4), 1996, pp. 23–37.

48. The management-as-religion analogy is carefully dissected by S. Pattison, op. cit.

49. R.A. Kent, 'Faith in four Ps: an alternative', *Journal of Marketing Management*, 2 (2), 1986, pp. 145–154; R.A. Kent, 'The Protestant ethic and the spirit of marketing: visions of the end', in S. Brown et al., *Marketing Apocalypse*, op. cit., pp. 133–144.

50. S. Brown, *Postmodern Marketing*, 1995, op. cit.

51. P. Maclaran and M. Catterall, 'Bridging the knowledge divide: issues on the feminisation of marketing practice', *Journal of Marketing Management*, 16 (6), 2000, pp. 635–646; M. Catterall, P. Maclaran and L. Stevens, *Marketing and Feminism: Current Issues and Research*, London, Routledge, 2000.

52. W. James, 1997, op. cit., p. 91.

53. S. Brown, *Postmodern Marketing*, 1995, op. cit.

54. S. Brown, 'Art or science? Fifty years of marketing debate', *Journal of Marketing Management*, 12 (4), 1996, pp. 243–267.

55. R. Firth, *Religion: A Humanist Interpretation*, London: Routledge, 1996, p. 15.

56. E.C. Hirschman, 'Ideology in consumer research: 1890 and 1990: a Marxist and feminist critique', *Journal of Consumer Research*, 19 (March), 1993, pp. 537–555; W.P. Hetrick and H.R. Lozada, 'Theory, ethical exchange and the experience of marketing', in D. Brownlie, M. Saren, R. Wensley and R. Whittington (eds), op. cit., pp. 162–176; R. Elliott and M. Ritson, 'Post-structuralism and the dialectics of advertising: discourse, ideology, resistance', in S. Brown and D. Turley (eds), *Consumer Research: Postcards from the Edge*, London, Routledge, 1997, pp. 190–219; H. Willmott, 'On the idolisation of markets and the denigration of marketers: some critical reflections on a professional paradox', in D. Brownlie et al. (eds), op. cit., pp. 205–222.

57. One of the most convincing articulations of this position is found in J. O'Shaughnessy, *Competitive Marketing: A Strategic Approach*, London, Routledge, 1995.

58. The literature on segmentation is, well, vast. You hardly need citations from me.

59. A. Harrington, *The Placebo Effect: An Interdisciplinary Exploration*, Cambridge, MA, Harvard University Press, 1997; S.E. Taylor, *Positive Illusions: Creative Self-Deception and the Healthy Mind*, New York, Basic Books, 1989; L. White, B. Tursky and

G.E. Schwartz, *Placebo: Theory, Research and Mechanisms*, New York, Guilford, 1985; P. Reiff, *The Triumph of the Therapeutic: Uses of Faith after Freud*, London, Chatto and Windus, 1966; M. Mayer, 1980, op. cit.; C. Fraser, op. cit.

60. D. Carson and S. Brown, 'Marketing: unity in diversity', *Journal of Marketing Management*, 10 (7), 1994, pp. 549–552.

61. You may think I'm being unfair on Philip Kotler here (in Chapter 7, what's more, I refer to him as St Philip). However, this is not so. I'm simply representing him in his own terms. In Kellogg Graduate School of Management at Northwestern University, there's a mural depicting the great and good of the past and present Marketing Department – Sid Levy, Louis Stern, Gerry Zaltman, et al. Above them all, sitting on a cloud, with a beatific expression on his face, is none other than Saint Philip himself. Need I say more?

4 Reconfiguring Marketing: The Greatest Sham on Earth

1. W.W. Porter and C.L. Thaddeus, *P.T. Barnum Presents Jenny Lind: The American Tour of the Swedish Nightingale*, Baton Rouge, Louisiana State University Press, 1980.

2. The study, admittedly, was less than scientific, since it involved checking the indices of the principal principles textbooks on display at the Academy of Marketing Annual Conference (July 2000). The only reference I could find was in Frank Bradley's *Marketing Management: Providing, Communicating and Delivering Value* (Hemel Hempstead, Prentice-Hall, 1995), and even then it was an allusion to the 'one born every minute' aphorism.

3. See for example, P. Kotler and G. Armstrong, *Principles of Marketing*, Upper Saddle River, NJ, Prentice-Hall, 1996, seventh edition; R.P. Bagozzi, J.A. Rosa, K.S. Celly and F. Coronel, *Marketing Management*, Upper Saddle River, NJ, Prentice-Hall, 1998.

4. The relationships metaphor is skilfully dissected in L. O'Mally and C. Tynan, 'The utility of the relationship metaphor in consumer markets: a critical examination', *Journal of Marketing Management*, 15, 1999, pp. 587–602. See also S. Fournier, S. Dobscha and D.G. Mick, 'Preventing the premature death of relationship marketing', *Harvard Business Review*, 76 (January–February), 1998, pp. 42–51.

5. B. Adams, *E Pluribus Barnum: The Great Showman and the Making of U.S. Popular Culture*, Minneapolis, University of Minnesota Press, 1997; N. Harris, *Humbug: The Art of P.T. Barnum*, Chicago, University of Chicago Press, 1973; A.H. Saxon, *P.T. Barnum: The Legend and the Man*, New York, Columbia University Press, 1989; D.J. Boorstin, *The Image: A Guide to Pseudo-Events in America*, New York, Atheneum, 1973 [1961].

6. Examples include, J. Lears, 1994, op. cit.; R. Marchand, 1985, op. cit.; P.W. Laird, op. cit.; and J. Wicke, *Advertising Fictions*, New York, Columbia University Press, 1988.

7. These range from *Barnum, the Broadway Musical* (1980), through children's books like C.M. Andronik, *Prince of Humbugs: A Life of P.T. Barnum* (New York, Atheneum, 1994) and short story collections such as S. Millhauser, *The Barnum Museum: Stories* (Normal, IL, Dalkey Archive Press, 1997) to the 1999 made-for-television movie, *P.T. Barnum* (with Beau Bridges in the title role), as well as the famous routine by former world ice dance champions, Jayne Torvill and Christopher Dean.

8. There are many noteworthy biographies of Barnum including M.R. Werner, *Barnum*, New York, Harcourt Brace, 1923; I. Wallace, *The Fabulous Showman*, New York, Knopf, 1959; and P.B. Kundhardt, P.B. Kundhardt III and P.W. Kundhardt, *P.T. Barnum: America's Greatest Showman*, New York, Knopf, 1995. The last of these was based on a PBS television series of the same name.

9. P.T. Barnum, *The Life of P.T. Barnum, Written by Himself*, New York, Redfield, 1855.

10. From the *Washington Post* obituary of 8 April 1891, quoted in B. Adams, op. cit., p. 1.

11. As *The Times* of London recorded, 'Barnum is gone. That fine flower of Western civilisation, that *arbiter elegantiarum* to Demos gave, in the eyes of the seekers after amusement, a lustre to America. He created the metier of showman on a grandiose scale, worthy to be professed by a man of genius . . . His name is a proverb already, and a proverb it will continue'. Quoted in I. Wallace, op. cit., p. 254.

12. *Printer's Ink*, 4, (16), 1891, p. 548. Quoted in P.W. Laird, op. cit., p. 44.

13. J. Vitale, *There's a Customer Born Every Minute: P.T. Barnum's Secrets to Business Success*, New York, Amacom, 1998.

14. 'Phineas Taylor Barnum is acknowledged by nearly all the major historians of advertising as the indubitable creator of American advertising' (J. Wicke, op. cit., p. 55). Likewise, in his monumental history of advertising, Frank Presbrey (op. cit., p. 211) observes that he was 'the first great advertising genius and the greatest publicity exploiter the world has ever known'.

15. See J.B. Twitchell, *Carnival Culture; The Trashing of Taste in America*, New York, Columbia University Press, 1992; and D.D. Yuan, 'The celebrity freak: Michael Jackson's "grotesque glory"', in R.G. Thomson (ed.), *Freakery: Cultural Spectacles of the Extraordinary Body*, New York, New York University Press, 1996, pp. 368–384. Lolo Ferrari, incidentally, was an Italian porn star who had eighteen operations to enhance her breasts – they ballooned, believe it or not, to 54G – and who died in tragic circumstances. See T. Blanchard, 'Plastic fantastic', *The Observer Life*, Sunday 6 August, 2000, pp. 26–33.

16. Barnum's principles of marketing are summarized in S. Brown, 'The unbearable lightness of marketing: a neo-romantic, counter-revolutionary recapitulation', in S. Brown et al. (eds), *Romancing the Market*, op. cit., pp. 255–277.

17. Quoted in I. Wallace, op. cit. p. 63.

18. Many other examples of Barnum's retro-marketing mindset could be cited, but I think you've got the picture.

19. Such was PTB's interest in new technology and the latest scientific advances that he was officially lauded by the Smithsonian Institution in the mid-1880s (see P.B. Kunhardt et al., 1995, op. cit., pp. viii–ix).

20. Interestingly, Barnum's very first ad was for a patent medicine that purported to prevent baldness. The pertinence of this point will become apparent in Chapter 5. Try to control yourself in the meantime.

21. P.T. Barnum, *Struggles and Triumphs; or, Forty Years' Recollections of P.T. Barnum, Written by Himself* (Hartford, J.B. Burr, 1869). The book about humbuggery, *Humbugs of the World*, appeared in 1866 (Detroit, Singing Tree Press, 1970).

22. One of the reviews of his autobiography (see note 21, above) stated, 'Compared to Barnum, Cagliostro himself was a blundering novice, or perhaps it would be more just to say that he had the misfortune to be endowed with a more tender conscience' (quoted in I. Wallace, op. cit., p. 22). The escapades of Count Alessandro Cagliostro are recounted in S. Brown, 'Tore Down *à la* Rimbaud', 1998, op. cit.

23. Quoted in I. Wallace, op. cit, pp. 177–178. The public reaction to Barnum's autobiography is discussed at length in T. Whalen, 'Introduction: P.T. Barnum and the birth of capitalist irony', in P.T. Barnum, *The Life of P.T. Barnum, Written by Himself*, Urbana, University of Illinois Press, 2000, pp. vii–xxxvii.

24. R. Blumberg, *Jumbo*, New York, Bradbury, 1992. The Jumbo soap opera is covered in Barnum's manifold biographies.

25. In 1834, the year Barnum arrived in the city, *The New York Sun* mischievously announced that life had been discovered on the moon. Millions fell for the hoax, which turned the *Sun* into the best-selling newspaper in the country. The *National Enquirer* of its day!

26. See N. Harris, op. cit. The American nineteenth-century confidence man is ably discussed in W. Wadlington, *The Confidence Game in American Literature*, Princeton, Princeton University Press, 1975; W.E. Lenz, *Fast Talk and Flush Times: The Confidence Man as a Literary Convention*, Columbia, University of Missouri Press, 1985; and K.

236   Notes and references

Halttunen, *Confidence Men and Painted Women: A Study of Middle-Class Culture in America, 1830–1870*, New Haven, Yale University Press, 1982.

27. There have been many studies of hoaxes and hoaxers, for example, C.D. MacDougall, *Hoaxes*, New York, Dover, 1958; C. Sifakis, *Hoaxes and Scams*, New York, Facts on File, 1993; Reader's Digest, *Scoundrels and Scalawags: Fifty-One Stories of the Most Famous Characters of Hoax and Fraud*, Pleasantville, Reader's Digest Association, 1968; G. Stein and M.J. MacNee, *Hoaxes! Dupes, Dodges and Other Dastardly Deceptions*, Detroit, Visible Ink, 1995; S. Burton, *Impostors: Six Kinds of Liar*, London, Viking, 2000.

28. Scholarly propriety compels me to point out that the phenomenal appeal of the Cardiff Giant also had something to do with . . . ahem . . . the size of its petrified appendage. Prurience is the fifth 'P' of marketing, don't you know. Well, okay, the sixth, after placebo (see Chapter 3).

29. P. Kotler and J. Scheff, *Standing Room Only: Strategies for Marketing the Performing Arts*, Cambridge, MA, Harvard Business School Press, 1997; F. McLean, *Marketing the Museum*, London, Routledge, 1997; E. Hill, C. O'Sullivan and T. O'Sullivan, *Creative Arts Marketing*, Oxford, Butterworth-Heinemann, 1995.

30. R. Bogdan, *Freak Show: Presenting Human Oddities for Amusement and Profit*, Chicago, University of Chicago Press, 1988.

31. The literature on creativity is almost as extensive as that on consciousness. I summarize some of the principal contributions in S. Brown, *Postmodern Marketing Two*, 1998, op. cit. Barnum's remarkable ability to exploit existing ideas is examined by L. Braudy, *The Frenzy of Renown: Fame and its History*, New York, Oxford University Press, 1986.

32. The wonderful 'woolly horse' episode is well worth recounting. Another time . . .

33. P.B. Kunhardt et al., op. cit., p. 337.

34. J. Locke, *An Essay Concerning Human Understanding, Vol 2*, Oxford, Clarendon Press, 1894, p. 146.

35. G. Hartman, 'Preface' in H. Bloom et al., *Deconstruction and Criticism*, New York, Seabury Press, 1979, pp. vii–ix.

36. Doubtless, it is also possible to explain Barnum's consumer-baiting business principles in psychoanalytical terms. Sadly, I have neither the space nor the expertise to do so.

37. Note, Bruce Barton did not claim that customers were the be all and end all of marketing. He merely maintained that marketers should be straight, ideally honest, with consumers. The positioning of marketing *vis-à-vis* its markets will be examined in the Pedagogic Appendix.

38. Analogously, the very idea of customer satisfaction is absurd, teetering on tautological. Think about it. Marketers don't want satisfied customers because satisfied customers are no longer in the market. They're satisfied, after all! Marketing, if anything, is about customer *dissatisfaction*, about keeping them coming back for more, about creating, stimulating and exploiting customer needs, wants and desires. There's a world of difference between dissatisfaction, the state of not being satisfied, and outright hostility (which is how marketers traditionally interpret the concept of dissatisfied customers).

39. The 'truth in advertising' movement predates the First World War (see D. Pope, op. cit.).

40. C.V. Ford, *Lies! Lies!! Lies!!! The Psychology of Deceit*, Washington, American Psychiatric Press, 1996; J.A. Barnes, *A Pack of Lies: Towards a Sociology of Lying*, Cambridge, Cambridge University Press, 1994; E. Giannetti, *Lies We Live By: The Art of Self-Deception*, London, Bloomsbury, 2000; D. Goleman, *Vital Lies, Simple Truths: The Psychology of Self-Deception*, London, Bloomsbury, 1997.

41. P. Kerr, 'Introduction', in P. Kerr (ed.), *The Penguin Book of Lies*, Harmondsworth, Penguin, 1990, pp. 1–8. 'Advertising', as Kerr (op. cit., p.5) observes, 'is full of people who will lie as fast as a dog will lick a dish'. See also A. Garfinkel, 'Truths, half-truths and deception in advertising', *Papers in Linguistics*, 10, 1997, pp. 135–149.

42. C.V. Ford, op. cit., pp. 7–10.

43. Ibid., p. 8.

44. I consider some of this literature in S. Brown, *Postmodern Marketing Two*, 1998, op. cit. See also J.N. Sheth, D.M. Gardner and D.E. Garrett, *Marketing Theory: Evolution and Evaluation*, New York, Wiley, 1988.

45. R. Rothenberg, op. cit.

46. S. Brown, 'Premonitions of Paradiso', 1999, op. cit.

47. Not everyone, admittedly, subscribes to this believe-the-unbelievable explanation of Barnumesquery. Beardsworth and Bryman, for instance, have recently contended that his audiences adopted an ironic posture, akin to that found among fans of all-in-wrestling. That is to say, everyone knows it's a fake and revels in the fakery (A. Beardsworth and A. Bryman, 'Late modernity and the dynamics of quasification: the case of the themed restaurant', *Sociological Review*, 47 (2), 1999, pp. 228–257). This is true to some extent, but Barnum's appeal is slightly more subtle, insofar as the fakery is upfront but the mechanisms are hidden. Everyone knows that they're going to be conned at some stage in the proceedings. However, they don't know what form the fakery will take, how he's going to do it or indeed the precise timing of the trickery. Barnum's bamboozling is closer to that of the card sharp than the groaning grappler.

48. C. Koelb, *The Incredulous Reader: Literature and the Function of Disbelief*, Ithaca, NY, Cornell University Press, 1984.

49. J. Greenwald, 'Herbal healing', *Time*, 23 November, 1998, pp. 58–68.

50. L. Braudy, op. cit., p. 501.

51. The term was coined by P.E. Meale, president of the Midwestern Psychological Association, in 1956.

52. For reviews of the Barnum Effect phenomenon see P.A. Marks and W. Seeman, 'On the Barnum Effect', *The Psychological Record*, 12, 1962, pp. 203–208; D.H. Dickson and I.W. Kelly, 'The Barnum Effect in personality assessment: a review of the literature', *Psychological Reports*, 57, 1985, pp. 367–382; and A. Furnam and S. Schofield, 'Accepting personality test feedback: a review of the Barnum Effect', *Current Psychological Research and Reviews*, 6, 1987, pp. 162–178. Papers are still regularly published on the topic; for example, M.L. Piper-Terry and J.L. Downey, 'Sex, gullibility and the Barnum Effect', *Psychological Reports*, 82 (2), 1998, pp. 571–576.

5 Repositioning Marketing: Ballyhoo's Who

1. See, for example B. Appleyard, 'Real Will hunting', *The Sunday Times, Culture*, 7 February, 1999, pp. 2–3; J. Thompson, 'At last – the list to end all lists: a bluffer's guide through the blizzard of Millennium polls', *The Independent on Sunday*, 28 November, 1999, p. 10; P. McCann, 'Welcome to the world's greatest hits', *The Times*, Saturday 1 January, 2000, p. 14.

2. Who dares d'oh more is none! S. Caulkin, 'Shakespeare in the black', *The Observer Business*, Sunday, 7 February, 1999, p. 16; H. Bloom, *Shakespeare: The Invention of the Human*, London, Fourth Estate, 1999; E. Potton, 'Do the Bard, man', *The Times Metro*, Saturday 29 July, 2000, pp. 20–21.

3. P. Corrigan, *Shakespeare on Management: Leadership Lessons for Today's Managers*, London, Kogan Page, 1999; J.O. Whitney and T. Packer, *Power Plays: Shakespeare's Lessons in Leadership and Management*, New York, Simon and Schuster, 2000; V. McKee, 'Henry V becomes an eye-opener for today's leaders', *The Times*, Saturday 6 February, 1999, p. 27; M. Campbell, 'Cry God for sales as the Bard goes centre stage in US boardrooms', *The Sunday Times*, 9 January, 2000, p. 9.

4. J. Ashworth, 'Dramatic change to art of team building', *The Times*, Saturday 6 February, 1999, pp. 26–27.

5. W.B. Burruss, *Shakespeare the Salesman*, Chicago, Dartnell, 1942.

6. D. Rushe, 'How McDonald's bit off more than it could chew', *The Sunday Times Business*, 10 January, 1999, p. 6.

7. J. Vidal, *McLibel: Burger Culture on Trial*, London, Pan, 1997.

8. N.Z. McLeod (dir.), *The Paleface*, Hollywood, Paramount Pictures, 1948.

9. F. Tashlin (dir.), *Son of Paleface*, Hollywood, Paramount Pictures, 1952. Okay, okay, I've cheated a little here. Potter didn't actually try to sell snake oil in *The Paleface*, though he did have trouble pulling teeth painlessly. However, the medicine show theme reappeared in the sequel, in the form of Dr Lovejoy and his 'Wonder Tonic'.

10. S. Brown, 'Art or science?', 1996, op. cit.

11. A.S. Hynd, 'The great tooth tycoon', in *Professors of Perfidy*, New York, A.S. Barnes, 1963, pp. 181–197. See also D. Armstrong and E.M. Armstrong, 'Medicine shows: pitch doctors take to the road', in *The Great American Medicine Show: Being an Illustrated History of Hucksters, Healers, Health Evangelists and Heroes, from Plymouth Rock to the Present*, New York, Prentice-Hall, 1991, pp. 173–184.

12. M.T. McGee, *Beyond Ballyhoo: Motion Picture Promotion and Gimmicks*, Jefferson, McFarland, 1989; C.J. Furhman, *Publicity Stunt! Great Staged Events that Made the News*, San Francisco, Chronicle, 1989; M. Borkowski, *Improperganda: The Art of the Publicity Stunt*, London, Vision On, 2000.

13. J. Lears, 1994, op. cit.; R. Marchand, 1985, op. cit.; M. Klein, op. cit.

14. A.S. Hynd, 'Reichenbach – master of ballyhoo', in *Professors of Perfidy*, 1963, op. cit., pp. 40–88.

15. P.B. Kundhardt et al., op. cit. Many variations on this silence-is-golden, curiosity-killed-the-cat stunt were utilized by nineteenth-century medicine show operators and stand-alone pitchpersons (cf. note 18 below).

16. On hypnotism see: D. Pick, *Svengali's Web: The Alien Enchanter in Modern Culture*, New Haven, Yale University Press, 2000; A. Winter, *Mesmerized: Powers of Mind in Victorian Britain*, Chicago, University of Chicago Press, 1998; D. Forrest, *The Evolution of Hypnotism*, Forfar, Black Ace, 1999.

17. A.S. Hynd, op. cit.

18. The single best study of the American medicine show is B. McNamara, *Step Right Up*, Jackson, University Press of Mississippi, 1995. Also useful are D. Armstrong and E.M. Armstrong, op. cit.; V. McNeil, *Two White Horses and a Brass Band*, Garden City, Doubleday, 1947; S.H. Holbrook, *The Golden Age of Quackery*, Macmillan, New York, 1959; J.H. Young, *The Toadstool Millionaires: A Social History of Patent Medicines in America before Federal Legislation*, Princeton, Princeton University Press, 1961.

19. F. Presbrey, op. cit.

20. B. McNamara, op. cit., p. 104.

21. Ibid., p. 32.

22. Out-and-out con-men, known as 'jamb' or 'jam' artists, were ostracized by showpersons as a rule, because their chicanery damaged everyone's reputation.

23. B. McNamara, op. cit., p. 55.

24. W. Schupbach, 'Sequah: an English-American medicine man in 1890', *Medical History*, 29, 1985, pp. 272–317.

25. R. Porter, *Quacks: Fakers and Charlatans in English Medicine*, Stroud, Tempus, 2000, p. 65.

26. Albeit understandable, Kickapoo's litigiousness was a bit rich, since they stole most of their ideas from P.T. Barnum (as did the entire medicine show tradition).

27. As Young (op. cit.) demonstrates, the medicine show concept long predated the itinerant impresarios of the *fin-de-siècle*. The American Colonies were awash with faux apothecaries-cum-lay-preachers, who combined saving souls with saving lives, and a vigorous transatlantic trade in British patent medicines existed until the War of

Independence encouraged Yankee entrepreneurs to do their own thing. Long before the Colonies were colonized, however, quacks and mountebanks roamed the highways and byways of western Europe. Quackery is considered at length in R. Porter (op. cit.) and S.H. Holbrook, 1959, op. cit. See also E. Jameson, *The Natural History of Quackery*, London, Michael Joseph, 1961; E. Maple, *Magic, Medicine and Quackery*, London, Robert Hale, 1968; J. Camp, *Magic Myth and Medicine*, London, Priory Press, 1973.

28. An informative historical overview of US citizens' penchant for Native American cross-dressing is available in P.J. Deloria, *Playing Indian*, New Haven, Yale University Press, 1998.

29. The Wild West shows of Buffalo Bill are cogently summarized in R.L. Wilson and G. Martin, *Buffalo Bill's Wild West: An American Legend*, New York, Random House, 1998. The 'extinct tribes' remark is attributed to Mark Twain by D. Armstrong and E.M. Armstrong, op. cit., p. 179.

30. J.H. Young, op. cit., pp. 175–176.

31. J. Greenwald, op. cit.

32. K.T. Greenfeld, 'New health drinks or old-style snake-oil elixirs?', *Time*, 23 November, 1998, p. 61.

33. R. McKie, 'Watchdog to police Chinese cures', *The Observer*, Sunday 23 July, 2000, p. 7; J. Burns, 'Irish mail order ban on popular herb', *The Sunday Times*, 5 March, 2000, p. 4; C. Gorman, 'Is it good medicine? Herbs have been used for centuries to help the sick in countries like China. They can heal, but they can hurt you too', *Time*, 23 November, 1998, p. 69.

34. H. Foster, 'Beauty report, the age of ayurveda', *The Observer Magazine*, Sunday 30 January, 2000, p. 53.

35. D. Armstrong and E.M. Armstrong, op. cit.; G. Sutton, 'Electric medicine and mesmerism', *Isis*, 72 (263), 1981, pp. 375–392; J.D. Livingstone, *Driving Force: The Natural Magic of Magnets*, Cambridge, MA, Harvard University Press, 1996 (especially Chapter 13, 'Mesmerism and magnetic therapy', pp. 202–217).

36. I don't want to labour the medical parallels, since I've alluded to the placebo effect in Chapter 3. Suffice it to say that marketing cures all known ills!

37. J. Micklethwait and A. Wooldridge, op. cit. (especially Chapter 1 'The fad in progress', pp. 23–42).

38. M.J. Wolf, *The Entertainment Economy: How Mega-media Forces are Transforming our Lives*, London, Penguin, 1999.

39. J. Micklethwait and A. Wooldridge, op. cit., pp. 23–25.

40. S.H. Holbrook, 1959, op. cit. (especially Chapter 1, 'The high noon', pp. 3–13).

41. J.H. Young, op. cit. (Chapters 13 and 14 in particular, pp. 205–244).

42. D. Armstrong and E.M. Armstrong, op. cit.

43. A detailed study of the inter-war legislation, including an in-depth assessment of Tugwell's contribution, is contained in J.H. Young, *The Medical Messiahs: A Social History of Health Quackery in Twentieth Century America*, Princeton, Princeton University Press, 1967. The post-war situation is covered in J.H. Young, *American Health Quackery*, Princeton, Princeton University Press, 1992.

44. As early as 1773, for example, the Puritans of Connecticut were legislating against travelling apothecaries (J.H. Young, 1961, op. cit.).

45. For the Hadacol extravaganza, see J.H. Young, 1967, op. cit.; B. McNamara, op. cit.; and D. Armstrong and E.M. Armstrong, op. cit.

46. John R. Brinkley's celebrated 'monkey glands' scam is summarized in Reader's Digest, op. cit., pp. 560–578.

47. B. McNamara, op. cit., p. 152.

48. 'All sold out, professor' was an expression used by snake-oil salespersons in the course of the medicine shows. During the 'commercial breaks', scores of snake-oil sales assistants ran up and down the aisles disbursing the magical elixir to excited customers.

Their accompanying shouts of 'all sold out, professor' apparently added to the buying frenzy. So, now you know.

49. Only joking, but it's a nice thought, isn't it?!

50. Yeah, I made this up too. Allow me some poetic licence, will you? Hadacol may be gone but it is not forgotten. On the contrary, in a tour de force of retro HBA marketing, Johnson & Johnson has recently launched Benecol, a nutritional supplement based on pine tree essence. Can the Benecol Caravan be far behind?

51. The 'enacted' character of the strategic marketing environment is expertly dissected by L. Smircich and C. Stubbart ('Strategic management in an enacted world', *Academy of Management Review*, 10 (4), 1985, pp. 724–736).

52. A lengthy discussion of the marketing environment is contained in A. Palmer, *The Business and Marketing Environment*, London, McGraw-Hill, 1996. See also, D. Mercer, *Marketing Strategy: The Challenge of the External Environment*, London, Sage, 1998.

6   Representing Marketing: The Secret of the Black Magic Box

1. S.J. Gould, 'A special fondness for beetles', in S.J. Gould, *Dinosaur in a Haystack: Reflections in Natural History*, London, Jonathan Cape, 1996, pp. 377–387.

2. Ibid., p. 385.

3. H.I. Ansoff, 'Strategies for diversification', *Harvard Business Review*, 35 (5), 1957, pp. 113–124.

4. The 'build a better mousetrap' saying is usually attributed to the titanic marketing man, Elbert Hubbard (sorry, maybe next time). With this in mind, I wonder where the 'break out of box' cliché came from. Whoever it was, retract it forthwith!

5. These matrices are described and discussed in most standard strategy textbooks; see for example R.M. Grant, *Contemporary Strategy Analysis: Concepts, Techniques, Applications*, Oxford, Blackwell, 1998; G. Johnson and K. Scholes, *Exploring Corporate Strategy*, Hemel Hempstead, Prentice-Hall, 1998.

6. P. Kotler, G. Armstrong, J. Saunders and V. Wong, *Principles of Marketing: The European Edition*, Hemel Hempstead: Prentice-Hall, 1996, p. 231.

7. M. McDonald and J.W. Leppard, *Marketing by Matrix: 100 Practical Ways to Improve Your Strategic and Tactical Marketing*, Oxford, Butterworth-Heinemann, 1992.

8. G. Harding and P. Walton, *Bluff Your Way in Marketing*, Horsham, Ravette Books, 1987.

9. M.E. Porter, *Competitive Advantage*, New York, Free Press, 1985.

10. H. Mintzberg, *The Rise and Fall of Strategic Planning: Reconceiving Roles for Planning, Plans, Planners*, New York, Free Press, 1994.

11. H. Mintzberg, B. Ahlstrand and J. Lampel, *Strategy Safari: A Guided Tour through the World of Strategic Management*, London, Prentice-Hall, 1998.

12. S. Brown, *Postmodern Marketing Two*, op. cit.

13. Morris Holbrook frequently makes use of matrices, but the fullest expression of this tendency is found in his edited book, *Consumer Value*, 1999, op. cit.

14. See S. Brown, 'Devaluing value', op. cit., pp. 159–182.

15. P. Lukas, 'Brannock device', in *Inconspicuous Consumption: An Obsessive Look at the Stuff We Take for Granted, from the Everyday to the Obscure*, New York, Crown, 1997, pp. 16–17.

16. Some of these are referred to in S. Brown, *Postmodern Marketing*, 1995, op. cit.

17. The social history of shoes is brilliantly recounted by C. McDowell, *Shoes: Fashion and Fantasy*, London, Thames and Hudson, 1994.

18. This reluctance to buy shoes contaminated by other people's feet might seem surprising, given that most off-the-peg clothes buyers are cognizant that several others may

have tried them on. However, it could well be related to the fact that footwear, like gloves, moulds itself to the wearer's body and is thus imprinted with their presence, as it were. There are few sights sadder than piles of second-hand shoes, unmatched, unboxed, unwanted.

19. T. Hine, *The Total Package: The Secret History and Hidden Meanings of Boxes, Bottles, Cans and Other Persuasive Containers*, Boston, Back Bay Books, 1995.

20. In addition to my shoe box experiences, I had another striking encounter with the enormous store people place by boxes when investigating the Japanese market for Irish full-lead crystal. There hangs a tale . . .

21. P. Lukas, op. cit.

22. B. Cornfeld and O. Edwards, *Quintessence: The Quality of Having It*, New York, Crown, 1983. For Tupperware see A.J. Clarke, *Tupperware: The Plastic Promise in 1950s America*, Washington, Smithsonian Institution Press, 1999.

23. R. Kovel and T. Kovel, *The Label Made Me Buy It! From Aunt Jemima to Zonkers – The Best-Dressed Boxes, Bottles and Cans from the Past*, New York, Crown, 1998.

24. D. Sudjic, *Cult Objects: The Complete Guide to Having it All*, London, Paladin, 1985, pp. 111–112.

25. T. Hine, op. cit.

26. S. Jeffries, *Mrs Slocombe's Pussy: Growing Up in Front of the Telly*, London, Flamingo, 2000.

27. H. Kingsley and G. Tibbals, *Box of Delights: The Golden Years of Television*, Basingstoke, Macmillan, 1989.

28. S. Armstrong, 'The gospel according to Keanu', *Sunday Times Culture*, 13 February, 2000, p. 22.

29. M. Collings, *This is Modern Art*, London, Weidenfeld and Nicolson, 1999; J. Fineberg, *Art since 1940: Strategies of Being*, London, Laurence King, 2000; R. Hughes, *American Visions: The Epic History of Art in America*, London, Harvill, 1997.

30. Boxes in literature are beautifully described by V. Cunningham, *In the Reading Gaol: Postmodernity, Texts and History*, Oxford, Blackwell, 1994. In case you're wondering about Vonnegut's marketing background, he variously worked in the public relations department of General Electric and as a salesman for Saab, before becoming a full-time writer. Several of his early short stories, incidentally, deal with the marketing-saturated suburban environment of 1950s America.

31. T. Bulfinch, *The Illustrated Age of Fable: The Classic Retelling of Greek and Roman Myths Accompanied by the World's Greatest Paintings*, New York, Stewart, Tabori and Chang, 1998.

32. H.C. Andersen, 'The Tinder-box', in *The Complete Fairy Tales*, Ware, Wordsworth Editions, 1997, pp. 1–8.

33. W. Moore, *Schrödinger: Life and Thought*, Cambridge, Cambridge University Press, 1989.

34. T.H. Leahey, *A History of Modern Psychology*, Englewood Cliffs, NJ, Prentice-Hall, 1991; D.N. Robinson, *An Intellectual History of Psychology*, Madison, University of Wisconsin Press, 1986; J.K. Galbraith, *A History of Economics: The Past as the Present*, London, Hamish Hamilton, 1987; E. Screpanti and S. Zamagni, *An Outline of the History of Economic Thought*, Oxford, Oxford University Press, 1993.

35. T.A. Bass, *The Predictors*, London, Allen Lane, 1999.

36. A bit of a strained segue, admittedly, but bear with me.

37. J. Randi, 'Conjuring in the new world: the Brothers Davenport and their spirit cabinet', in *Conjuring*, New York, St Martin's Press, 1992, pp. 52–56.

38. S. Skinner, 'Pregnant with the Messiah', in *Millennium Prophecies: Predictions for the Year 2000 and Beyond*, London, Virgin, 1994, pp. 108–109.

39. S. Freud, *The Interpretation of Dreams*, trans. J. Strachey, Harmondsworth, Penguin, 1991 [1900].

40. The literature on gift-giving is vast. A useful summary is found in C. Otnes and R.F.

Beltramini, *Gift Giving: A Research Anthology*, Bowling Green, Ohio, Bowling Green State University Popular Press, 1996.

41. C.G. Jung, *The Archetypes and the Collective Unconscious*, trans. R.F.C. Hull, London, Routledge, 1990; C.G. Jung, *Psychology and Alchemy*, trans. R.F.C. Hull, Princeton, Princeton University Press, 1993; R.A. Segal, *Jung on Mythology*, Princeton, Princeton University Press, 1998.

42. F.X. King, *The Encyclopaedia of Mind, Magic and Mysteries*, London, Dorling Kindersley, 1991.

43. U. Becker, 'Magic squares', in *The Element Encyclopaedia of Symbols*, Shaftesbury, Element, 1994, pp. 184–187.

44. See S. Skinner, op. cit.; F.X. King, op. cit.; A. Aveni, *Behind the Crystal Ball: Magic and Science from Antiquity to the New Age*, London, Newleaf, 1996; P. Roland, *Revelations: Wisdom of the Ages*, Berkeley, CA, Ulysses Press, 1995; C. Wilson, *The Occult: A History*, New York, Barnes and Noble Books, 1995.

45. S. Brown, 'The unbearable lightness of marketing', 1998, op. cit.

46. J.B. Twitchell, 1996, op. cit., p. 31.

47. It is no accident, as T. Hine (1995, op. cit.) observes, that many of the world's great religions organize worship around containers of sanctity – from chrismal to cathedral – since they encourage congregations' belief in the efficacy of their contents.

48. M.K. Shanley, *The Memory Box: Gathering the Keepsakes of the Heart*, Marshalltown, Sta-Kris, 1996; S. Athorne, 'Memory boxes', *The Sunday Times Magazine*, 12 September, 1999, pp. 34–37; B. Hillier, 'Take two time capsules', *The Times Weekend*, Saturday 18 December, 1999, pp. 1–2; see also the novel *The Memory Box* by M. Foster (London, Chatto and Windus, 1999).

49. H. Mintzberg et al., 1998, op. cit.; C. Hackley, 'Towards a post-structuralist marketing pedagogy – or from irony to despair', in R. Mayer (ed.), *AM2000 Conference Proceedings*, Derby: University of Derby, 2000, pp. 732–743; N. Piercy, 'A polemic. In search of excellence among business school professors: cowboys, chameleons, question-marks and quislings', *European Journal of Marketing*, 33 (7/8), 1999, pp. 698–706.

50. Actually, postmodernists' disdain for boxes is, in many respects, misplaced. The pantheon of postmodern philosophers is replete with intellectuals who have constructed cerebrality squares. Check it out!

51. T. Bulfinch, op. cit.

52. W. Poundstone, 1983, op. cit; W. Poundstone, 1993, op. cit.; W. Poundstone, *Bigger Secrets: More Than 125 Things They Prayed You'd Never Find Out*, Boston, Houghton Mifflin, 1986.

53. For example: P. Hughes, 'Left, then right, then left again', *The Observer Review*, Sunday 6 August, 2000, p. 6; S. Singh, *The Code Book: The Science of Secrecy from Ancient Egypt to Quantum Cryptography*, London, Fourth Estate, 1999; R. Ingpen and P. Wilkinson, *Encyclopaedia of Mysterious Places*, London, Guild Publishing, 1999.

54. This is an important point and I'll be addressing it in the Pedagogic Appendix.

55. Quoted in S. Singh, op. cit., p. vi.

7   Re-planning Marketing: If Ever a Whiz of a Swiz There Was

1. Innovations, *Innovations Millennium Collection*, Preston, Innovations, 2000.

2. The *Innovations* phenomenon is discussed in I. Robson and J. Rowe, 'Marketing – the whore of Babylon?', *European Journal of Marketing*, 31 (9/10), 1997, pp. 654–666.

3. How quickly marketing fads and postmodern panics pass! Who now remembers the maleficent millennium bug?

4. See for example: J. Westwood, *30 Minutes to Write a Marketing Plan*, London,

Kogan Page, 1997; S. Dibb, L. Simpkin and J. Bradley, *The Marketing Planning Workbook: Effective Marketing for Marketing Managers*, London, Routledge, 1996; A. Hatton, *The Definitive Guide to Marketing Planning*, London, Financial Times, 2000.

5. S. Dibb et al., op. cit., p. 162.

6. M. McDonald, *Marketing Plans: How to Prepare Them, How to Use Them*, London, Heinemann, 1984; M. McDonald, *Marketing Plans: How to Prepare Them, How to Use Them*, fourth edition, Oxford, Butterworth-Heinemann, 1999.

7. M. McDonald, 'Strategic marketing planning: theory and practice', in M.J. Baker (ed.), *The Marketing Book*, fourth edition, Oxford, Butterworth-Heinemann, 1999, p. 60.

8. J.J. Corn and B. Horrigan, *Yesterday's Tomorrows: Past Visions of the American Future*, Baltimore, MD, Johns Hopkins University Press, 1996; W.A. Sherden, *The Fortune Sellers: The Big Business of Buying and Selling Predictions*, New York, Wiley, 1998; C. Canto and O. Failu, *The History of the Future: Images of the 21st Century*, trans. F. Cowper, Paris, Flammarion, 1993; S.P. Schnaars, *Megamistakes: Forecasting and the Myth of Rapid Technological Change*, New York, Free Press, 1989.

9. H. Kahn and A.J. Wiener, *The Year 2000: A Framework for Speculation on the Next Thirty-Three Years*, New York, Macmillan, 1967.

10. S.P. Schnaars, op. cit., pp. 20–21.

11. J.J. Corn and B. Horrigan, op. cit., pp. x–xv.

12. W.A. Sherden, op. cit.

13. F. Popcorn, *The Popcorn Report: Faith Popcorn on the Future of Your Company, Your World and Your Life*, Garden City, Doubleday, 1991; R. Shalit, 'The business of Faith', *The New Republic*, 18 April, 1994, pp. 23–29; W.A. Sherden, op. cit., pp. 220–224.

14. R. Shalit, op. cit., p. 23.

15. W.A. Sherden, op. cit., p. 224.

16. See for example: B.K. Boyd, 'Strategic planning and financial performance: a meta-analytic review', *Journal of Management Studies*, 28 (4), 1991, pp. 353–374; J. Leppard and M. McDonald, 'A re-appraisal of the role of marketing planning', *Journal of Marketing Management*, 3 (2), 1987, pp. 159–171; M. McDonald, 'Strategic marketing planning: theory, practice and research agendas', *Journal of Marketing Management*, 12 (1), 1996, pp. 5–27.

17. This criticism is a bit much, to put it politely. After fortysomething years, planners can hardly continue to blame bozo managers for failing to give it a fair shot. Formal planning *has* been properly tried and found sorely wanting.

18. Malcolm McDonald 'Strategic Marketing Planning' (1999, op. cit., pp. 70–76) lists ten barriers to successful marketing planning, ranging from lack of CEO support to a reluctance to plan for planning.

19. H. Mintzberg, op. cit.; H. Mintzberg et al., op. cit.

20. S. Brown, *Postmodern Marketing*, 1995, op. cit.

21. H. Mintzberg et al., op. cit.

22. 'Environmental turbulence' is yet another common justification for formal planning. The gist of this argument is that business conditions are so fast-moving, so mutable, so uncontrollable nowadays that careful planning is more necessary than ever before. Failure to plan in turbulent times spells disaster, invites failure, is tantamount to incompetence and the like. Granted, 'environmental turmoil' has been used as a rallying cry since the earliest days of strategic planning and careful planning may not be the most appropriate response to socio-economic turbulence, in any event. Nevertheless, the fact of the matter is that business conditions are no more complex, faster-moving or whatever than they have been at various times in the past. It only seems that way; the passage of time smoothes out minor perturbations; and, not least, the things-have-never-been-tougher claim is patently self-serving, since it demonstrates how much better, smarter and more astute today's marketers are than the amateurs back then, who obviously didn't know how lucky they were.

23. Indeed, the recent millennial transition has stimulated an orgy of prognostication. See for instance: S. Griffiths, *Predictions: 30 Great Minds on the Future*, Oxford, Oxford

University Press, 1999; Y. Blumenfeld, *Scanning the Future: 20 Eminent Thinkers on the World of Tomorrow*, London, Thames and Hudson, 1999; S. Chowdhury, *Management 21C*, London, Financial Times, 2000.

24. I'm not being facetious here (well, just a little bit). The comfort-blanket aspect of planning is very important. There's no doubt that plans act as intra-organizational pacifiers, notwithstanding the political battles that may accompany their implementation. By insinuating that the future is manageable, if only in part, they function as an anxiety-reducing mechanism. In this regard, marketing plans are akin to magical rites and rituals, as Gimpl and Dakin astutely observe (M.L. Gimpl and S.R. Dakin, 'Management and magic', *California Management Review*, 1984, 27 (1), pp. 125–136).

25. Stories, needless to say, are not confined to management studies. They are everywhere. Whereas Walter Benjamin, one of the leading cultural theorists of the mid-twentieth century, famously lamented the decline of storytelling in modernity, it seems that at our millennial transition storytelling is back with a postmodern bang (see below).

26. For most commentators, the postmodern and storytelling are inseparable. According to Lyotard, the postmodern intellectual's principal function is to 'tell stories'; Jameson defines postmodernism as 'a return to storytelling'; Hutcheon regards postmodern culture as 'essentially novelistic'; Simpson diagnoses a veritable 'epidemic of storytelling' in the human sciences today; and Michel de Certeau contends that we reside in a *recited* society, one that is defined by *stories*, by *citations* of stories and by the interminable *recitation* of stories. I consider this dimension of postmodernism in S. Brown, *Postmodern Marketing Two*, 1998, op. cit.

27. Again, I've summarized much of this literature in *Postmodern Marketing Two* (ibid.). Also useful are: B.B. Stern, 'Narratological analysis of consumer voices in postmodern research accounts', in B.B. Stern (ed.), *Representing Consumers: Voices, Views and Visions*, London, Routledge, 1998, pp. 55–82; D. Brownlie, 'Beyond ethnography: towards writerly accounts of organising in marketing', *European Journal of Marketing*, 31 (3/4), 1997, pp. 264–284; J.E. Escalas, 'Advertising narratives: what are they and how do they work', in B.B. Stern (ed.), op. cit., pp. 267–289; B. Heilbrunn, 'My brand the hero? A semiotic analysis of the consumer-brand relationship', in M. Lambkin et al. (eds), *European Perspectives on Consumer Behaviour*, London, Prentice-Hall, 1998, pp. 370–401.

28. D. Brownlie and J. Desmond, 'Apocalyptus interruptus: a tale by parables, apostles and epistles', in S. Brown et al. (eds), *Marketing Apocalypse*, op. cit., pp. 66–86.

29. G. Shaw, R. Brown and P. Bromiley, 'Strategic stories: how 3M is rewriting business planning', *Harvard Business Review*, 76 (May–June), 1998, pp. 41–50.

30. To my knowledge, I hasten to add. Such is the pace of marketing scholarship that several storytelling studies will no doubt have appeared by the time this text is published.

31. A.A. Berger, *Narratives in Popular Culture, Media and Everyday Life*, Thousand Oaks, CA, Sage, 1997; S. Onega and J.A.G. Landa, *Narratology: An Introduction*, London, Longman, 1996; M. Currie, *Postmodern Narrative Theory*, Basingstoke, Macmillan, 1998; C. Nash, *Narrative in Culture: The Uses of Storytelling in the Sciences, Philosophy and Literature*, London, Routledge, 1990.

32. The literature on Baum is vast. Biographical details are provided in A.S. Carpenter and J. Shirley, *L. Frank Baum: Royal Historian of Oz*, Minneapolis, Lerner Publications, 1992; M.O. Riley, *Oz and Beyond: The Fantasy World of L. Frank Baum*, Lawrence, University Press of Kansas, 1997; W.R. Leach, 'The clown from Syracuse: the life and times of L. Frank Baum', in L. Frank Baum, *The Wonderful Wizard of Oz*, Belmont, Wadsworth, 1991, pp. 1–34; S. Rahn, *The Wizard of Oz: Shaping an Imaginary World*, New York, Twayne, 1998. (By the way, I know that it was silver slippers in the book and that ruby came courtesy of MGM. No irate letters in green ink, please. Except those with an Emerald City postmark.)

33. In light of our discussion in Chapter 2, it is noteworthy that Baum's pro-marketing books were widely banned in the anti-marketing 1950s. These days, by contrast, Oz is back in favour – reprints of the original texts, the 1939 film re-released, plans for another stage

show, etc. – largely, one suspects, on account of the centenary of Baum's landmark text. There's even a self-help spiritual cult based on the Oz books. See G.D. Morena, *The Wisdom of Oz*, San Diego, Inner Connections Press, 1998.

34. This consumption-orientated interpretation of the Oz books has become very popular in recent years. Just as consumption has become a 'legitimate' topic in lit-crit *per se*, so too Baum is getting the apologist-for-capitalism treatment. Key contributions to the debate include: W. Leach, 1993, op. cit. (especially Chapter 8, pp. 246–260); H. Schwartz, op. cit. pp. 115–117; S. Culver, 'What manikins want: *The Wonderful Wizard of Oz* and *The Art of Decorating Dry Goods Windows*', *Representations*, 21, 1988, pp. 97–116; S. Culver, 'Growing up in Oz', *American Literary History*, 4 (Winter), 1992, pp. 607–628; T.S. Gilman, '"Aunt Em: Hate you! Hate Kansas! Taking the dog. Dorothy": conscious and unconscious desire in *The Wizard of Oz*', *Children's Literature Association Quarterly*, 20 (Winter), 1995–96, pp. 161–167; M.D. Westbrook, 'Readers of Oz: young and old, old and new historicist', *Children's Literature Association Quarterly*, 21 (3), 1996, pp. 111–119; J. Zipes, 'Introduction', in L. Frank Baum, *The Wonderful World of Oz*, Harmondsworth, Penguin, 1998, pp. ix–xxix.

35. L.F. Baum, *The Wizard of Oz*, in L. Frank Baum, *The Wonderful World of Oz*, 1998, op. cit., p. 50.

36. Ibid., p. 132.

37. Like Oz, utopia is making a comeback. Recent overviews include: J. Carey, *The Faber Book of Utopias*, London, Faber and Faber, 1999; G. Claeys and L.T. Sargent, *The Utopia Reader*, New York, New York University Press, 1999; R. Jacoby, *The End of Utopia: Politics and Culture in an Age of Apathy*, New York, Basic Books, 1999; C. Kelly, *Utopias*, London, Penguin, 1999. For a marketing angle on utopia, see S. Brown and P. Maclaran, 'The future is past', in S. Brown et al. (eds), *Marketing Apocalypse*, op. cit., pp. 260–277.

38. S. Culver, 1988, op. cit.

39. The Wizard was specifically based on Barnum, not only in the original drawings by W.W. Winslow but also in Frank Morgan's portrayal of the Wizard in the 1939 MGM movie. One of the later Oz books, in fact, informs us that the Wizard was once a performer in 'Bailum and Barney's Consolidated Shows' (see Z. Papanikolas, *Trickster in the Land of Dreams*, Lincoln, University of Nebraska Press, 1995).

40. J. Zipes, op. cit., p. xxi.

41. W. Leach, 1993, op. cit., p. 254. Emphasis added.

42. The fullest discussion of Oz-as-allegory is found in P. Nathanson, *Over the Rainbow*: *The Wizard of Oz as a Secular Myth of America*, Albany, State University of New York Press, 1991. Of course, Baum's works are not unique in this regard. One only has to consider the manifold meanings 'read into' the works of George Orwell, Lewis Carroll, J.R.R. Tolkien and countless others.

43. Baum loved things. He was a total spendthrift, a shopaholic *avant la lettre*, who wrote most of the sequels whilst living in a luxurious hotel, the Del Coronado, in southern California.

44. J. Zipes, op. cit.

45. S. Brown, 'Trinitarianism, the Eternal Evangel and the Three Eras Schema', in S. Brown et al. (eds), *Marketing Apocalypse*, op. cit., pp. 23–43.

46. I explore the quest narrative in S. Brown, A.M. Doherty and B. Clarke, 'Stoning the romance: on marketing's mind forg'd manacles', in S. Brown et al. (eds), *Romancing the Market*, op. cit., pp. 1–21.

47. C. Volger, *The Writer's Journey: Mythic Structure for Writers*, Los Angeles, Michael Wiese, 1998. The twelve stages, from 'Ordinary World' to 'Return with Elixir' are contained in S. Brown, *Postmodern Marketing Two*, op. cit., p. 155. They are applied to four contrasting Hollywood movies, including *The Wizard of Oz*. Feel free to adapt it to the marketing planning process. You don't expect me to do everything for you, do you?

48. Dorothy's homesickness, however, is largely motivated by misplaced loyalty to

Uncle Henry and Aunt Em. By the fifth book, even Dorothy succumbs to Oz's charms when she finally ups sticks and relocates permanently.

49. Academic marketing is more than one hundred years old; ample time, one would have thought, to concoct a general theory or two. The 'youthful discipline' argument simply doesn't wash. *Acting* youthfully is another matter entirely, however. Sure, you're as young as you feel . . .

50. H. Eysenck, *Genius: The Natural History of Creativity*, Cambridge: Cambridge University Press, 1995; G. Morgan, *Imaginization: The Art of Creative Management*, Newbury Park, CA, Sage, 1993; J.N.T. Martin, 'Play, reality and creativity', in J. Henry (ed.), *Creative Management*, London, Sage, 1991, pp. 34–40.

51. See J. Zipes, *The Oxford Companion to Fairy Tales: The Western Fairy Tale Tradition from Medieval to Modern*, Oxford, Oxford University Press, 2000; M. Warner, *From the Beast to the Blonde: On Fairy Tales and Their Tellers*, London, Vintage, 1998; B. Bettelheim, *The Uses of Enchantment: The Meaning and Importance of Fairy Tales*, New York, Vintage, 1975; J. Zipes, *Fairy Tales and the Art of Subversion*, New York, Routledge, 1983.

52. G. Shaw et al., op. cit.; J. Peterman, 'The rise and fall of the J. Peterman Company', *Harvard Business Review*, 77 (September–October), 1999, pp. 58–64.

53. N. Piercy, *Tales from the Marketplace*, Oxford, Butterworth-Heinemann, 2000.

54. R. Jensen, *The Dream Society: How the Coming Shift from Information to Imagination will Transform your Business*, New York, McGraw Hill, 1999.

55. H. Mintzberg et al., op. cit.; S. Dunlop, *Business Heroes*, Oxford, Capstone, 1997; S. Crainer, 'Storytelling', in S. Crainer (ed.), *A Freethinker's A–Z of the New World of Business*, Oxford, Capstone, 2000, pp. 267–268.

56. Roll on *Marketing Planning the Harry Potter Way!*

8   Replacing Marketing: Reading Retroscapes

1. D. Waddle, 'Publican's suicide over Flares', *The Daily Telegraph*, 16 August, 1998, p. 10.

2. Themed environments have become a fairly hot topic in cultural studies and the sociology of consumption. Key contributions include M. Gottdiener, *The Theming of America: Dreams, Visions and Commercial Spaces*, Boulder, CO, Westview, 1997; J. Hannigan, op. cit; M. Sorkin, *Variations on a Theme Park: The New American City and the End of Public Space*, New York, Hill and Wang, 1992; G. Ritzer, *Enchanting a Disenchanted World: Revolutionising the Means of Consumption*, Thousand Oaks, CA, Pine Forge Press, 1999.

3. I.D.H. Shepherd and C.J. Thomas, 'Urban consumer behaviour', in J.A. Dawson (ed.), *Retail Geography*, London: Croom Helm, 1980, pp. 18–94.

4. A. Patterson et al., op. cit.; L. Stevens et al., 1998, op. cit.; L. Stevens, S. Brown and P. Maclaran, 'Sexing the advertising text: gender and reading Caffrey's "New York"', *Proceedings of the Academy of Marketing Annual Conference*, Derby, University of Derby, 2000, pp. 1438–1450; L. Stevens, S. Brown and P. Maclaran, 'Images of Ireland: gender, post-colonialism and the neo-Celtic Revival', in E. Fischer and D. Whitrow (eds), *Proceedings of the Fourth Gender Conference*, San Francisco, San Francisco State University Press, 1998, pp. 13–26.

5. J. Barnes, *England, England*, London, Jonathan Cape, 1998, p. 142.

6. For some examples of what I'm getting at, see A. Billen, 'Kiss of the cyber woman', *The Observer*, Sunday, 11 February, 1996, p. 8; C. Butler, 'He-mail', *Sunday Times Style*, 30 July, 2000, pp. 8–9; S. Munk, 'Playing Cupid', *The Times Metro*, 29 July, 2000, p. 23; R. Tompkins, 'Revolution? What revolution?', *The Financial Times Weekend*, Saturday 4

December, 1999, pp. I–II; M. Driscoll, 'Something stirs in the family tree', *The Sunday Times News Review*, 25 April, 1999, p. 4; D. Purgavie, 'Back to your roots: trace your family tree with the Mormons' website', *Night & Day*, Sunday 13 June, 1999, p. 36; S. Caulkin, 'Seer of cyberspace symbols', *The Observer*, 18 June, 1999, p. 9; D. Hancock, 'Malice in Wonderland', *The Times Metro*, Saturday 5 August, 2000, p. 23; S. Poole, *Trigger Happy: The Inner Life of Videogames*, London, Fourth Estate, 2000; Virgin, *The Virgin Internet Shopping Guide*, London: Virgin, 1999.

7. S. Brown, 'Institutional change in retailing: a review and synthesis', *European Journal of Marketing*, 21 (6), 1987, pp. 1–36.

8. P. Durman, 'Leschly's still running to the net', *The Times*, Saturday 6 November, 1999, p. 31; The Economist, 'Shopping around the web', *The Economist Survey*, 26 February, 2000, pp. 1–44; The Economist, 'The net imperative', *The Economist Survey*, 26 June, 1999, pp. 1–48; J. Waples, 'Net land rush', *The Sunday Times Business*, 1 August, 1999, p. 9.

9. D. Hewson, 'Harald slays the serpent', *The Sunday Times Culture*, 9 July, 2000, pp. 47–49.

10. M. Prigg and A. Williams, 'Spies behind your screen', *The Sunday Times Culture*, 6 August, 2000, pp. 47–49.

11. R. Levine et al., op. cit. For a countervailing view, see The Economist, 'What the Internet cannot do', *The Economist*, 19 August, 2000, pp. 13–14.

12. The Economist, 'Anatomy of an attack', *The Economist*, 19 February, 2000, pp. 90–91; G. Alexander, 'Hackers strike fear into net businesses', *The Sunday Times Business*, 13 February, 2000, p. 9; A. Hobsbawm, 'Hate mail', *The Business*, 4 December, 1999, p. 12.

13. T. Wright and R. Hutchison, 'Socio-spatial reproduction, marketing culture and the built environment', *Research in Urban Sociology*, 4, 1997, pp. 187–214; T. Wright, 'Marketing culture: spectacles and simulation', in T.L. Childers et al. (eds), *Marketing: Theory and Practice*, Chicago, American Marketing Association, 1989, pp. 326–328; J.A. Jakle and K.A. Sculle, *Fast Food: Roadside Restaurants in the Automobile Age*, Baltimore, MD, Johns Hopkins University Press, 1999; R. Pillsbury, *From Boarding House to Bistro: The American Restaurant Then and Now*, Boston, Unwin Hyman, 1990.

14. R. Pillsbury, op. cit., p. 5.

15. J. Krantz, *Scruples*, London, Warner Books, 1978, p. 298.

16. A compelling, characteristically thorough discussion of brand 'museums' and corporate collecting generally is available in R.W. Belk, *Collecting in a Consumer Society*, 1995, op. cit.

17. Few marketing phenomena have given rise to more raptures than Niketown. See, for example, J.F. Sherry, Jr., 'The soul of the company store: Nike Town Chicago and the emplaced brandscape', in J.F. Sherry, Jr. (ed.), *Servicescapes: The Concept of Place in Contemporary Markets*, Chicago, NTC Books, 1998, pp. 109–146; D. Katz, *Just Do It: The Nike Spirit in the Corporate World*, Holbrook, MA, Adams Media Corporation, 1994; R. Goldman and S. Papson, *Nike Culture: The Sign of the Swoosh*, London, Sage, 1998.

18. J. Hannigan, op. cit., p. 92.

19. G. Ritzer, 1999, op. cit. p. 111.

20. D. Katz, op. cit., p. 95.

21. K.A. Robertson, 'Downtown redevelopment strategies in the United States: an end-of-the-century assessment', *Journal of the American Planning Association*, 61 (4), 1995, pp. 429–437; G. Dickinson, 'Memories for sale: nostalgia and the construction of identity in Old Pasadena', *Quarterly Journal of Speech*, 83 (1), 1997, pp. 1–27.

22. S. Brown, *Retail Location: A Micro-Scale Perspective*, Aldershot, Avebury, 1992.

23. P. Maclaran and L. Stevens, 'Romancing the utopian marketplace: dallying with Bakhtin in the Powerscourt Townhouse Centre', in S. Brown et al., *Romancing the Market*, op. cit., pp. 172–186.

24. The heritage literature is summarized in S. Brown et al., 'Presenting the past', op. cit. The key source is D. Lowenthal, *The Heritage Crusade and the Spoils of History*, New

York, Cambridge University Press, 1998. Also useful, if slightly dated, is R. Hewison, *The Heritage Industry: Britain in a Climate of Decline*, London, Metheun, 1987.

25. N. Watson, 'Postmodernism and lifestyles', in S. Sim (ed.), *The Icon Critical Dictionary of Postmodern Thought*, Cambridge, Icon, 1998, pp. 53–64.

26. See K. Walsh, *The Representation of the Past: Museums and Heritage in the Postmodern World*, London, Routledge, 1992; R.W. Rydell, *All the World's a Fair: Visions of Empire at America's International Expositions 1876–1916*, Chicago, University of Chicago Press, 1984; R.W. Rydell, *World of Fairs: The Century-of-Progress Expositions*, Chicago: University of Chicago Press, 1993; S. Brown et al., 'Presenting the Past', op. cit.

27. D. Harvey, *The Condition of Postmodernity*, Oxford, Blackwell, 1989, p. 300.

28. S. Brown and A. Patterson, 'Knick-knack paddy-whack, give a pub a theme', *Journal of Marketing Management*, 16 (6), 2000, pp. 647–662.

29. M. Gottdiener, op. cit.; R.W. Belk, 'On aura, illusion, escape and hope in apocalyptic consumption: the apotheosis of Las Vegas', in S. Brown et al., *Marketing Apocalypse*, op. cit., pp. 87–107; R.W. Belk, 'Three coins in Caesar's Palace fountain', 1998, op. cit.; A.L. Huxtable, *The Unreal America: Architecture and Illusion*, New York, Free Press, 1997.

30. K. Pullinger, 'Moving sidewalks to Heaven and Hell', *The Observer Review*, Sunday 7 August, 1994, p. 3.

31. Pre-adolescent appearances to the contrary, the principal purpose of Disneyland is to provide intellectual fodder for prolix professorial folderol (been there, done that, wrote the paper, etc.). As a consequence, the academic literature on Disney almost beggars belief. Some of the better known examples include: A. Bryman, op. cit.; F.J. Fjellman, *Vinyl Leaves: Walt Disney World and America*, Boulder, CO, Westview, 1992; H.A. Giroux, *The Mouse That Roared: Disney and the End of Innocence*, Lanham, Rowman and Littlefield, 1999; The Project on Disney, *Inside the Mouse: Work and Play at Disney World*, London, Rivers Oram, 1995; A. Bryman, 'The Disneyization of society', *Sociological Review*, 47 (1), 1999, pp. 25–47; M.J. King, 'Disneyland and Walt Disney World: traditional values in a futuristic form', *Journal of Popular Culture*, 15 (Summer), 1981, pp. 116–140.

32. D. Harvey, op. cit.; S. Lash and J. Urry, *Economies of Signs and Space*, London, Sage, 1994; J. Baudrillard, *Simulations*, trans. P. Foss, P. Patton and P. Beitchman, New York, Semiotext(e), 1983.

33. J.F. Rayport and J.J. Sviokla, 'Managing in the marketspace', *Harvard Business Review*, 72 (November–December), 1994, pp. 141–150. The literature on space and place is prodigious. A useful overview is E.S. Casey, *The Fate of Place: A Philosophical History*, Berkeley, University of California Press, 1997.

34. And they all look just the same. (With apologies to Pete Seeger).

35. P. Kotler, D.H. Haider and I. Rein, *Marketing Places: Attracting Investment, Industry and Tourism to Cities, States and Nations*, New York, Free Press, 1993; P. Kotler, S. Jatusripitak, S. Maescincee and S. Jatusri, *The Marketing of Nations: A Strategic Approach to Building National Wealth*, New York, Free Press, 1997; P. Kotler and H. Kartajaya, *Repositioning Asia: From Bubble to Sustainable Economy*, Singapore, John Wiley, 2000.

36. J.N. Sheth et al., op. cit.

37. J.F. Sherry, Jr., *ServiceScapes*, op. cit.

38. The Economist, 'Frictions in cyberspace. Retailing on the Internet, it is said, is almost perfectly competitive. Really?', *The Economist*, 20 November, 1999, p. 136; The Economist, 'The failure of new media', *The Economist*, 19 August, 2000, pp. 59–61.

39. As I don't have the space to do justice to space – ahem – I'm going to leave it for now. Fear not, space cadets, I'll be coming back to it in the Pedagogic Appendix.

40. J.P. Diggins, *Thorstein Veblen: Theorist of the Leisure Class*, Princeton, Princeton University Press, 1999; J.K. Galbraith, 'A new theory of Thorstein Veblen', *American Heritage*, 24, 1973, pp. 32–40; J.A. Hobson, *Veblen*, New York, Augustus M. Kelley, 1971;

E.W. Jorgensen and H.I. Jorgensen, *Thorstein Veblen: Victorian Firebrand*, Armonk, NY, M.E. Sharpe, 1998.

41. T. Veblen, *The Theory of the Leisure Class: An Economic Study of Institutions*, London, Unwin Books, 1970 [1899].

42. C. Campbell, *The Romantic Ethic and the Spirit of Modern Consumerism*, Oxford, Blackwell, 1987; C. Campbell, 'The sociology of consumption', in D. Miller (ed.), *Acknowledging Consumption: A Review of New Studies*, London: Routledge, 1995, pp. 96–126.

43. G. Ritzer, 1999, op. cit.

44. T. Veblen, *Absentee Ownership and Business Enterprise in Recent Times: The Case of America*, New York, Augustus M. Kelley, 1964 [1923].

45. Ibid., p. 309.

46. Ibid., p. 320.

47. G. Adair, *The Postmodernist Always Rings Twice*, London, Fourth Estate, 1992.

48. G. Harding and P. Walton, op. cit.

49. J. Westwood, op. cit.

50. S. Silbiger, *10-day MBA*, London, Piatkus, 1999; M. Sobel, *The 12-Hour MBA Program*, Englewood Cliffs, NJ, Prentice-Hall, 1993.

51. Irish theme pubs, for example, have been described as: 'rubbish', 'kitsch bastardized versions of the real thing', 'hideous constructions, banal beyond all redemption'. Other commentators have been much less charitable. See S. Brown and A. Patterson, 'Knick-knack Paddy whack', op. cit., p. 648. On the excrescences of theming generally, A.L. Huxtable's (op. cit.) hilarious harangue is well worth reading, as are R. Hewison (op. cit.) and D. Lowenthal (1998, op. cit.).

52. J. Baudrillard, op. cit.; G. Ritzer, 1999, op. cit.; U. Eco, *Travels in Hyper-reality*, trans. W. Weaver, London, Picador, 1986; D. MacCannell, *The Tourist: A New Theory of the Leisure Class*, New York, Schocken, 1989; S.F. Mills, 'Disney and the promotions of synthetic worlds', *American Studies International*, 28 (2), 1990, pp. 66–79.

53. D. Sudjic, *The 100 Mile City*, London, André Deutsch, 1992, p. 172.

54. A.L. Huxtable, op. cit.; D. Lowenthal, (1998, op. cit.; D. MacCannell, op. cit.; J. Urry, *The Tourist Gaze*, London, Sage, 1990; B. Kirschenblatt-Gimblett, *Destination Culture: Tourism, Museums and Heritage*, New York, Routledge, 1998; C. Rojek, *Leisure and Culture*, Basingstoke, Macmillan, 2000.

55. S. Brown et al. 'Presenting the Past', op. cit.

56. S. Brown and A. Patterson, 'Knick-knack Paddy-whack', op. cit.

57. So much so, that those who uncritically adopt themed looks – who dress top to toe in Hard Rock, Harley-Davidson or Nike outfits, for example – are regarded as a laughing stock of the 'Man from C&A' variety.

58. T. Adorno, *The Culture Industry*, London, Routledge, 1991.

9 Rebranding Marketing: Yes We Have No Bananaburgers

1. N. Cohn, *Yes We Have No*, London, Secker and Warburg, 1999.

2. Ibid., p. 242.

3. Ibid., p. xii.

4. It is so unnecessary, in fact, that Cohn can omit the climactic noun and the all-important comma after the affirmative. Yet it still makes sense.

5. P.N. Davies, *Fyffes and the Banana: A Centenary History 1888–1988*, London, Athlone, 1990; The Economist, 'Food for thought', *The Economist*, 19 June, 1999, pp. 23–25; L.S. Grossman, *The Political Ecology of Bananas: Contract Farming, Peasants, and Agrarian*

Change in the Eastern Caribbean, Chapel Hill, University of North Carolina Press, 1998; R.H. Stover and N.W. Simmonds, *Bananas*, Basingstoke, Longman, 1987.

6. M. Warner, 'Going bananas', in M. Warner, *No Go the Bogeyman: Scaring, Lulling and Making Mock*, London: Chatto and Windus, 1998, pp. 348–373.

7. See P.N. Davies, op. cit.; P. Beaver, *Yes! We Have Some: The Story of Fyffes*, Benington, Publications for Companies, 1976.

8. J. Winterson, *Sexing the Cherry*, London, Bloomsbury, 1989, pp. 11–13.

9. D. Nasaw, 'The city as playground: the World's Fair midways', in D. Nasaw, *Going Out: The Rise and Fall of Public Amusements*, Cambridge, MA, Harvard University Press, 1993, pp. 62–79.

10. J. Lears, *Fables*, op. cit., pp. 112–113. Yes, I know they're not really tubers. Allow me some alliterative licence, will you?

11. The timeless words of the Chiquita Banana jingle are: 'I'm Chiquita Banana/And I've come to say/Bananas have to ripen/In a certain way./When they are fleck'd with brown/And have a golden hue/Bananas taste the best/And are the best for you.' They don't, as you know, write 'em like that any more.

12. M.H. Bogart, op. cit.

13. Another famous bananamarketer, who almost eclipses Ackerley in the plantain pantheon is Edward L. Bernays, the so-called 'father of spin'. I'll be mentioning him in the Pedagogic Appendix.

14. J.R. Ackerley, *My Father and Myself*, Oxford, The Bodley Head, 1968; D. Petre, *The Secret Orchard of Roger Ackerley*, London, Hamish Hamilton, 1975; P. Beaver, op. cit.; P.N. Davies, op. cit.

15. S. Brown, 'The unbearable lightness', 1998, op. cit.

16. See for example, P.N. Davies, op. cit., p. 138.

17. Ackerley's serendipitous success with 'Yes, We Have No Bananas' wasn't the only occasion when he turned a popular song into a marketing triumph. Much earlier in his career, he benefited from the entirely gratuitous insertion of 'have a banana' into the music hall, mock-cockney classic, 'Let's All Go Down the Strand' (still performed, I am reliably informed, by those Bow Bells troubadours, Chas and Dave).

18. P. Beaver, op. cit., pp. 8–9.

19. A. Davidson, 'Banana', in *The Oxford Companion to Food*, Oxford, Oxford University Press, 1999, pp. 54–55; Y. Péhaut, 'The invasion of foreign foods', in J-L. Flandrin and M. Montanari (eds) *Food: A Culinary History*, New York, Columbia University Press, 1999, pp. 457–470.

20. R. Dawkins, 'Pollen grains and magic bullets', in *Climbing Mount Improbable*, Harmondsworth, Penguin, 1996, pp. 236–253.

21. S. Willis, 'Learning from the banana', in *A Primer for Everyday Life*, New York, Routledge, 1991, p. 51.

22. C. Enloe, 'Carmen Miranda on my mind: international politics of the banana', in *Bananas, Beaches and Bases: Making Feminist Sense of International Politics*, London, Pandora, 1989, pp. 124–150.

23. An interesting academic example of the same downgrading tendency is found in Deighton's use of the banana to exemplify the Internet's profound implications for even the most mundane distribution channels (J. Deighton, 'Commentary on "Exploring the implications of the Internet for consumer marketing"', *Journal of the Academy of Marketing Science*, 25 (4), 1997, pp. 347–351).

24. The Independent, 'A bargain? No, it's a banana', *The Independent*, 15 January, 1997, p. 15; P. Slade, 'Harvest the rewards of loyalty', *The Independent*, 25 April, 1998, p. 1; R. Smith, 'Banana economics: buy 942lb of fruit, give it away – and make', *The Independent*, 15 January, 1997, p. 5.

25. S. de Bruxelles, 'Collector stuck on a bizarre new pastime', *The Times*, 17 April, 1999, p. 3.

26. P. Reinders, *Licks, Sticks and Bricks: A World History of Ice Cream*, Amsterdam, Unilever, 1999.

27. P. Delerm, *The Small Pleasures of Life*, London, Phoenix House, 1998, pp. 35–36.

28. M. Warner, 1998, op. cit.

29. M. Klein, op. cit. Make no mistake, the main banana producers have been targeted by protesters, especially environmentalists who object to the companies' liberal use of insecticide. They have escaped lightly compared, say, to the routine trashing of McDonald's by disgruntled activists and gruntled French farmers alike.

30. A. Bryman, 1999, op. cit.; G. Ritzer, *The McDonaldization of Society*, Newbury Park, CA, Pine Forge Press, 1993; G. Ritzer, *The McDonaldization Thesis*, London, Sage, 1998; B. Smart, *Resisting McDonaldization*, London, Sage, 1999.

31. A. Bryman, 1999, op. cit.

32. S. Askegaard and F.F. Csaba, 'The good, the bad and the Jolly: taste, image and the symbolic resistance to the Coca-colonization of Denmark', in S. Brown and A. Patterson (eds), *Imagining Marketing: Art, Aesthetics and the Avant-garde*, London: Routledge, 2000, pp. 124–140; R.W. Belk 'Hyperreality and globalisation', 1996, op. cit.

33. G. Ritzer, 1993, 1998, op. cit.; B. Smart, op cit.

34. S. Brown, 'Going bananas in paradise: from McDonaldization to Fyffefication', *Marketing Intelligence and Planning*, 2000, 18 (6/7), pp. 356–367.

35. Marketing, as we shall discuss in the Pedagogic Appendix, hails from the north-eastern United States.

36. Of course, they all turn Brown eventually!

37. It is impossible to summarize this para-marketing literature, since it takes in everything from Cultural Studies and newspaper columns to best-selling novels and leading schools of literary theory, New Historicism especially. I refer to some of this material in *Postmodern Marketing Two* (1998, op. cit.), but one doesn't have to look very hard to see that marketers don't have a monopoly on marketing. Some of the best marketing research nowadays emanates from these extra-marketing sources.

38. On the whole question of marketing and female subordination, see M. Catterall et al., op. cit.

39. J. Lears, *Fables*, op. cit., p. 116.

40. The banana-burger parallel is not casual. Think about it. Both are staples of the post-industrial diet. Both are cheap, cheerful and just about as fast as fast food can be. Both date from the *fin-de-siècle* and made their official début at a world's fair. Both owe their early success to a presiding promotional genius, Ackerley in the case of the banana, and the peerless Ray Kroc in the case of the burger. Both are particularly popular with children; both pioneered the use of anthropomorphic trade characters; both have a record of third world exploitation; both are characterized by complex, behind-the-scenes marketing channels; both are highly concentrated industries, with a small number of firms holding large market shares; both are multi-branded, even though the products are indistinguishable to even the most educated palates; and, both have been getting into the retroactive act of late, whether it be Chiquita's recent celebration of its hundredth anniversary or McDonald's flower-powered, happy hippies, peace, love and hold the pickle promotion for Big Mac's thirtieth birthday.

41. Undergrads can keep their Kotler Kahuna Burgers.

42. I have discussed Bakhtin's concept of the carnivalesque at length elsewhere (S. Brown, *Postmodern Marketing Two*, 1998, op. cit.).

43. M. Warner, 1998, op. cit.

44. R.W. Belk, G. Ger and S. Askegaard, 'Metaphors of consumer desire', in K.P. Corfman and J.G. Lynch (eds), *Advances in Consumer Research, Vol. XXIII*, Provo, UT, Association for Consumer Research, 1996, pp. 368–373; R. Elliott, A. Jones, A. Benfield and M. Barlow, 'Overt sexuality in advertising: a discourse analysis of gender responses', *Journal of Consumer Policy*, 18 (2), 1995, pp. 187–217; D. O'Sullivan and D. Kavanagh,

'Marketing – you must be joking', in S. Brown and A. Patterson, *Proceedings*, 1999, op. cit., pp. 186–197.

45. D. Saunders, *Humour in Advertising*, London, Batsford, 1997; D. Saunders, *Sex in Advertising*, London, Batsford, 1996.

46. P.N. Davies, op. cit.; M. Warner, 1998, op. cit.

47. J. Deighton and K. Grayson, 'Marketing and seduction: building exchange relationships by managing social consensus', *Journal of Consumer Research*, 21 (March), 1995, pp. 660–676.

48. S. Brown and P. Maclaran, op. cit.

49. I. Hamilton, *The Penguin Book of Twentieth-Century Essays*, London, Allen Lane, 1999.

10   Revolting Marketing: Gross is Good

1. B. Wheeler and J. Day, 'Shock tacticians', *Marketing Week*, 23 March, 2000, pp. 30–31.

2. J. Doward, 'Tailor's hand who fashioned a fortune with few connections', *The Observer Business*, Sunday 26 September, 1999, p. 5; A. Sherwin, 'Judge says "fcuk" is obscene and should be banned', *The Times*, Saturday 4 December, 1999, p. 3.

3. R. Miskin, 'Jerusalem in uproar over obscene ad campaign', *The Jerusalem Post*, 18 July, 1996, p. 5.

4. L. McClintock, 'Offensive weapons?: more brands are courting controversy by going for ads with shock value', *The Grocer*, 10 August, 1996, p. 15; Marketing Week, 'ASA and poster industry take over pre-vetting notorious advertisers', *Marketing Week*, 13 December, 1996, p. 12; Marketing Week, 'Clothing outfit courts controversy with ads', *Marketing Week*, 6 August, 1998, p. 7; Marketing Week, 'Jokey Jesus advertising campaign branded blasphemous', *Marketing Week*, 13 August, 1998, p. 12; Marketing Week, 'ASA slams Diesel over sexy nun ad', *Marketing Week*, 9 July, 1998, p. 12.

5. M. Chittenden and E. Saner, 'Mums in aprons are out as adland sells on sex', *The Sunday Times*, 30 July, 2000, p. 11; J. Doward, 'The flesh is weak', *The Observer Business*, 3 September, 2000, p. 10; B. Borrows, 'Too good to eat', *Night and Day*, 30 July, 2000, pp. 36–39; S. Husband, 'I'm just a simple working model', *You Magazine*, 30 July, 2000, pp. 28–31; M. Carter, 'Are you getting too much sex in your ads', *The Independent*, 31 July, 1996, pp. 2–3; Marketing Week, 'Advertisers jeopardise image in pursuit of indecent exposure', *Marketing Week*, 2 February, 1996, p. 19.

6. R. Vezina and P. Olivia, 'Provocation in advertising: a conceptualisation and an empirical assessment', *International Journal of Research in Marketing*, 14 (3), 1997, pp. 177–192; J.H. Barnes and M.J. Dotson, 'An exploratory investigation into the nature of offensive television advertising', *Journal of Advertising*, 19 (3), 1990, pp. 61–70.

7. G. Barker, 'Does art still have the capacity to shock us', *The Times*, Wednesday 23 August, 2000, p. 16; P. Wood (ed.), *The Challenge of the Avant-Garde*, New Haven, Yale University Press, 1999; M. Collings, op. cit.; P. Meecham and J. Sheldon, *Modern Art: A Critical Introduction*, London, Routledge, 2000.

8. N.P. Walsh, 'It's a new cultural revolution', *The Observer Review*, Sunday 11 June, 2000, p. 5.

9. G. Alexander, 'Advertising fever grips e-commerce', *The Sunday Times Business*, 21 November, 1999, p. 9; P. Helmore, 'Going mad on Madison Avenue', *The Observer Business*, Sunday 5 December, 1999, p. 7.

10. In this chapter I'm concentrating on advertising and promotion, but gross-out matters are relevant to marketing as a whole.

11. J. Bond and R. Kirschenbaum, *Under the Radar: Talking to Today's Cynical Consumers*, New York, John Wiley, 1998.

12. S. Stevens, 'Carl's Jr., the next generation', *Brandweek*, 3 November, 1997, pp. 32–33; R. Martin, 'Carl's Jr. shoots for big success with "messy" TV ads', *Nation's Restaurant News*, 19 June, 1995, pp. 14, 123; K. Tyrer, 'When it pays to be messy', *Adweek*, 18 September, 1995, p. 2.

13. J. Schroeder, 'Édouard Manet, Calvin Klein and the strategic use of scandal', in S. Brown and A. Patterson, *Imagining Marketing*, op. cit., pp. 36–51.

14. Frequency is a standard industry measure. It refers to the number of times an ad is seen by its intended target market during a given period.

15. W. Miller, *The Anatomy of Disgust*, Chicago, University of Chicago Press, 1997.

16. Ibid., p. x.

17. D. Saunders, *Shock in Advertising*, London, Batsford, 1996, p. 105.

18. Ibid., p. 79.

19. Self-citation makes you go blind, boys and girls. Be warned by me!

20. J. Mantle, *Benetton: The Family, the Business and the Brand*, London, Little Brown, 1999; The Economist, 'Advertising and death', *The Economist*, 19 February, 2000, p. 54; R. Carroll, 'Shock tactics that finally backfired', *The Observer*, Sunday 30 April, 2000, p. 24.

21. Compare this to the company's $100 million involvement in Formula 1 motor racing (A. Henry, 'Benetton sell team to Renault for £75m', *The Guardian*, Friday 17 March, 2000, p. 34).

22. J. Marconi, *Shock Marketing: Advertising, Influence and Family Values*, Chicago, Bonus Books, 1997.

23. J. della Famina, *From Those Wonderful Folks Who Gave You Pearl Harbor: Front-line Dispatches from the Advertising War*, ed. Charles Sopkin, New York, Simon and Schuster, 1970.

24. W. Leith, 'Off the top shelf', *The Observer Review*, Sunday 28 March, 1999, p. 5; M. Wittstock, 'How TV crossed the taste barrier', *The Observer*, Sunday 5 March, 2000, p. 19; A.J. Jacobs, 'Johnny come lately', *Entertainment Weekly*, 18 September, 1998, pp. 26–30, 33.

25. G. Barker, op. cit.; M. Collings, op cit.; B. Appleyard, 'Welcome to the freak show', *The Sunday Times Culture*, 27 August, 2000, pp. 8–9.

26. J. Dawson, 'When raspberries ripple', *The Sunday Times Culture*, 13 August, 2000, pp. 6–7; J. Patterson, 'A fanfare for filth', *The Guardian*, Friday 30 June, 2000, p. 23; M. Morris, 'Gross profits', *The Observer Screen*, Sunday 30 July, 2000, pp. 6–7.

27. Or should that be intern-al marketing?

28. A. Jacobs, 'Pop Starr', *Entertainment Weekly*, 25 September, 1998, p. 16.

29. G.T. Holtz, *Welcome to the Jungle: The Why Behind Generation X*, New York, St Martin's Griffin, 1995; J. Miller, *Voxpop: The New Generation X Speaks*, London, Virgin Books, 1995.

30. There is some debate over X-ers' 'official' year of origin. Karen Richie makes a cogent case for 1960 in *Marketing to Generation X*, New York, Lexington Books, 1995.

31. See for example M. Gwyner, 'Elite of the new economy', *Management Today*, section e, September, 2000, pp. 12–15; B. Tulgan, *Managing Generation X*, Oxford, Capstone, 1997; J. Ridderstrale and K. Nordstrom, *Funky Business: Talent Makes Capital Dance*, London, FT.com, 2000; D. Firth and A. Leigh, *The Corporate Fool*, Oxford, Capstone, 1998. The listings in Crainer's A–Z guide (2000, op. cit.) also give a sense of Gen X's growing influence in the corridors of corporate power.

32. J. Bond and R. Kirshenbaum, op. cit., p. 3.

33. G.T. Holtz, op. cit., p. 199.

34. See for example: E. Showalter, *Sexual Anarchy: Gender and Culture at the Fin de Siècle*, London, Bloomsbury, 1991; A. Briggs and D. Snowman, *Fins de Siècle: How Centuries End*, New Haven, Yale University Press, 1996; P.N. Stearns, *Millennium III, Century XXI*, Boulder, CO, Westview, 1998.

35. An excellent comparison of 'then' and 'now' is: M. Jay and M. Neve, *1900: A Fin de Siècle Reader*, Harmondsworth, Penguin, 1999.

36. J. Baudrillard, *The Illusion of the End*, trans. C. Turner, Cambridge, Polity, 1994, p. 26.

37. A. Calcutt, *Arrested Development: Pop Culture and the Erosion of Adulthood*, London, Cassell, 1998. See also note 45 (Chapter 11) below.

38. B. Summerskill, 'Playtime as kidults grow up at last', *The Observer*, Sunday 23 July, 2000, p. 20.

39. C. McDowell, 'Mutton is the new lamb', *The Sunday Times Style*, 11 June, 2000, pp. 4–5.

40. This issue is considered in Chapter 5, above.

41. S. Brown and A. Patterson, 'Figments for sale: marketing, imagination and the artistic imperative', in *Imagining Marketing*, op. cit., pp. 4–32.

42. T. Douglas, 'Poster medium has the power to survive in tomorrow's world', *Marketing Week*, 23 April, 1998, pp. 19–21.

43. For an interesting marketing-orientated treatment of Bataille, see C. Jantzen and P. Ostergaard, 'The rationality of "irrational" behaviour: Georges Bataille on consuming extremities', in S. Brown et al., *Romancing the Market*, op. cit., pp. 125–136.

44. M. Douglas, *Purity and Danger: An Analysis of the Concepts of Pollution and Taboo*, London, Routledge, 1996.

45. D. Saunders, *20th Century Advertising*, London, Carlton, 1999; D. Ogilvy, *Ogilvy on Advertising*, Chichester, Wiley, 1983; L. Tye, *The Father of Spin: Edward L. Bernays and the Birth of Public Relations*, New York, Crown, 1998; R. Marchand, 1985, op. cit.

46. S. Strasser, 1989, op. cit.

47. J. Lears, *Fables*, op. cit.

48. J.B. Twitchell, 1992, op. cit.

49. J.L. Adams and W. Yates, *The Grotesque in Art and Literature: Theological Reflections*, Grand Rapids, MI, William B. Eerdmans, 1997.

50. L. Savan, *The Sponsored Life: Ads, TV and American Culture*, Philadelphia, Temple University Press, 1994; B.B. Stern, 'Deconstructive strategy and consumer research: concepts and illustrative exemplar', *Journal of Consumer Research*, 23 (September), 1996, pp. 136–147.

51. R.P. Warren, 'The dramatic version of *Ballad of a Sweet Dream of Success: A Carol for Easter*, with the author's introduction', quoted in J.L. Adams and W. Yates, op. cit., p. 246.

11   Rejuvenating Marketing: The Big Tease

1. A. Ross, *The Celebration Chronicles: Life, Liberty and the Pursuit of Property Values in Disney's New Town*, New York, Ballantine, 1999; D. Frantz and C. Collins, *Celebration, USA: Living in Disney's Brave New Town*, New York, Holt, 1999; J. Diski, 'Thank you Disney', *London Review of Books*, 22 (16), 2000, pp. 7–9.

2. D. Sudjic, 1992, op. cit.; M.C. Boyer, *The City of Collective Memory: Its Historical Imagery and Architectural Entertainments*, Cambridge, MA, MIT Press, 1998; J. Hannigan, op. cit.; E.W. Soja, *Thirdspace: Journeys to Los Angeles and Other Real-and-Imagined Places*, Malden, Blackwell, 1996.

3. A.L. Huxtable, op. cit.

4. S. Brown, *Postmodern Marketing*, 1995, op cit. p. 118; D. Harvey, *Spaces of Hope*, Edinburgh, Edinburgh University Press, 2000 (especially Chapter 8, 'The spaces of utopia', pp. 133–181); M. Wilson, 'Comeback for the cobbled street', *The Sunday Times*, 5 March, 2000, p. 11; K. Ahmed and V. Thorpe, 'Prince's pet village gets seal of approval', *The*

Observer, Sunday 14 May, 2000, p. 5; P. Hetherington, 'Homes of the past feature in minister's vision of future', *The Guardian*, Friday 28 January, 2000, p. 12.

5. R. Samuel, op. cit.

6. S. Gardiner, 'In praise of crowded living', *The Times Weekend*, Saturday 4 March, 2000, p. 12; N. Nuttall, 'Prescott aims for greener, cheaper homes', *The Times*, Saturday 11 March, 2000, p. 7; R. Rogers, 'Richard Rogers explains his vision for a new Britain', *The Times*, Saturday 6 February, 1999, p. 4; A. Smith, 'Tales from the riverbank', *The Observer Magazine*, Sunday 21 November, 1999, pp. 12–19.

7. G. Cadogan, 'What is there left to convert?', *Financial Times Weekend*, Saturday 30 October, 1999, p. 2.

8. For example: 'Landmark architecture, contemporary apartments' (Harrods Village); 'Traditional values in a brand new home' (Crest Homes); 'Ensure your place in history' (The Imperial Apartments); 'Village life in a modern world' (Swan Hill Homes); 'Designing modern classics' (Charles Church); 'A range of stunning new homes echoing the classic styles of the past' (St James Homes).

9. M. Haslam, *Retro Style: The 50s Look for Today's Home*, London, MQ Publications, 2000; N. Marshall, *Funky Style: Creative Ideas for the Contemporary Home*, London, MQ Publications, 1999.

10. R. Samuel, op. cit.

11. S. Caminiti, 'Ralph Lauren: the emperor has clothes', *Fortune*, 11 November, 1996, pp. 80–92; J.A. Trachtenberg, *Ralph Lauren: The Man Behind the Mystique*, Boston, Little Brown, 1996.

12. S.M. Wooten, *Martha Stewart: America's Lifestyle Expert*, Woodbridge, Blackbirch Press, 1999; M. Stewart, *Good Things: The Best of Martha Stewart Living*, New York, Clarkson Potter, 1997; J. Bone, 'Home making class for Hilary', *The Times*, Saturday 11 March, 2000, p. 21; D. Whitworth, 'Lifestyle queen cleans up', *The Times*, Saturday 23 October, 1999, p. 21.

13. J. Oppenheimer, *Martha Stewart – Just Desserts*, New York, Avon, 1997.

14. Ibid., p. 299.

15. D. Cray, 'Art of selling kitsch. Don't look for these creations at your local museum. Instead, try the mall', *Time*, 30 August, 1999, pp. 62–63; S. McCormack, 'Making people feel good about themselves (the paintings of Thomas Kinkade)', *Forbes*, 2 November, 1998, p. 222; R. Rugoff, 'Who buys these paintings?', *The Business*, 12 February, 2000, pp. 30–31; P. Wollen, 'Say hello to Rodney', *London Review of Books*, 22 (4), 2000, pp. 3–7.

16. T. Kinkade and P. Reed, *Paintings of Radiant Light*, New York, Abbeville Press, 1995, p. 134.

17. A self-help, tract-publishing, seminar-running sideline, which combines material success, romantic love and born again Christianity, is also part of the Media Arts Group package. See T. Kinkade and A.C. Buchanan, *Lightposts for Living: The Art of Choosing a Joyful Life*, New York, Warner Books, 1999.

18. M.H. Bogart, op. cit.; J. Lears, *Fables*, op. cit.

19. P. Hall, *Cities of Tomorrow*, Oxford, Basil Blackwell, 1988.

20. M. Binney, 'Model village with a clean history', *The Times Weekend*, Saturday 11 December, 1999, p. 6; R. Stummer, 'Forever England', *The Guardian Weekend*, Saturday 27 November, 1999, pp. 82–83; J. Glancey, 'The hold of the old', *The Guardian Weekend*, Saturday 19 February, 2000, pp. 10–19.

21. D. Halberstam, op. cit.; T. Hine, *Populuxe*, op. cit.; J.J. Palen, *The Suburbs*, New York, McGraw-Hill, 1995; R. Silverstone, *Visions of Suburbia*, London, Routledge, 1997.

22. A. Jones, 'Twilight of the Proctoids', *The Times*, Saturday 12 June, 1999, p. 30; W. Kay, 'Tomkins slices off its bread and jam brands', *The Financial Mail on Sunday*, 11 July, 1999, p. 2; N. Bannister, 'Cooked to a turning point', *The Guardian*, Saturday 19 February, 2000, p. 24; C. Mortishead, 'US food giants thrown into the mixer', *The Times*, Saturday 18 September, 1999, p. 31; J. Doward and F. Islam, 'Household names face axe as Unilever slims down', *The Observer Business*, Sunday 26 September, 1999, p. 3;

A. Lorenz, 'Unilever crosses the Rubicon', *The Sunday Times Business*, 27 February, 2000, p. 9.

23. R. Tompkins, 'Wish you weren't here', *The Business*, 5 February, 2000, pp. 34–36.

24. To say nothing of the Millennium Doom in Greenwich. On the footfall shortfall besetting some of Britain's new museums, see R. Jenkins, 'The lost museums of ready, steady, goo', *The Times*, Saturday 23 October, 1999, p. 11; N. Mathiason, 'Cultural revolution's cul de sac: why are so many new museums in trouble?', *The Observer Business*, Sunday 31 October, 1999, p. 4.

25. R. Hudson, 'Rebels of the superhighway', *The Sunday Times Culture*, 13 August, 2000, pp. 47–49.

26. R. Samuel, op. cit.

27. A. Bryman, 1995, op. cit.; B. Bryson, *Made in America*, London, Minerva, 1994; G. Lipsitz, op. cit.; D. Halberstam, op. cit.

28. T. Hine, *Populuxe*, op. cit., p. 8. See also G.H. Marcus, *Design in the Fifties: When Everyone Went Modern*, Munich, Prestel, 1998.

29. Although a veritable Walter Benjamin industry exists within Cultural and Media Studies, marketers have been somewhat reluctant to engage with his thought, despite its clear relevance to the marketing condition.

30. W. Benjamin, *The Arcades Project*, trans. H. Eiland and K. McLaughlin, Cambridge, MA, Belknap, 1999.

31. S. Buck-Morss, op. cit., p. 65.

32. 'Anticipatory illumination' (*Vor-Schein*) is a term coined by Ernst Bloch, an exact contemporary and close friend of Benjamin. It refers to great art's ability to anticipate developments in the wider cultural sphere. The concept is discussed in E. Bloch, *The Utopian Function of Art and Literature: Selected Essays*, trans. J. Zipes and F. Mecklenburg, Cambridge, MA, MIT Press, 1988.

33. W. Benjamin, 'Theses on the philosophy of history', in W. Benjamin, *Illuminations*, London, Fontana, 1973, pp. 245–255.

34. M. Currie, *Postmodern Narrative Theory*, Basingstoke, Macmillan, 1998, pp. 101–102. It speaks volumes about our field that this striking observation is made by a literary theorist, not a marketing researcher.

35. S. Brown, 'Premonitions of Paradiso', 1999, op. cit.

36. D.J. Carson, A. Gilmore and P. Maclaran, 'To hell with the customer: where's the profit?', in S. Brown, J. Bell and D. Carson (eds), *Proceedings of the Marketing Eschatology Retreat*, Belfast, University of Ulster, 1995, pp. 72–83; J. Fairhead and M. Murphy, 'Killing the customer: service interactions as power-play and neurotic exchange', in S. Brown and A. Patterson (eds), *Proceedings of the Marketing Paradiso Conclave*, op. cit., pp. 146–158; J. Martin, 'Ignore your customer', *Fortune*, 1 May, 1995, pp. 83–86; M. Douglas, *Thought Styles: Critical Essays on Good Taste*, London, Sage, 1997.

37. I discuss many of these in S. Brown, *Postmodern Marketing*, 1995, op. cit.

38. R. Lakatos, 'Falsification and the Methodology of Scientific Research Programmes', in I. Lakatos and A. Musgrave (eds), *Criticism and the Growth of Knowledge*, Cambridge: Cambridge University Press, 1974, pp. 91–196.

39. S. Brown, 'Life begins', 1995, op. cit.

40. S. Brown, 'The three Rs', 2000, op. cit.

41. R. Marchand, 1985, op. cit. On golden ages generally, see S. Brown and P. Maclaran, 1996, op. cit.

42. M. Bakhtin, *Rabelais and his World*, trans. H. Iswolsky, Bloomington, Indiana University Press, 1984; A. Eliot, *The Universal Myths: Heroes, Gods, Tricksters and Others*, New York, Truman Tally, 1990; D. Hyde, *Trickster Makes This World: Mischief, Myth and Art*, New York, Farrar, Straus and Giroux, 1998; Z. Papanikolas, op. cit.

43. A useful discussion of the marketing dimensions of tricksterdom is contained in K. Grayson, 'The dangers and opportunities of playful consumption', in M.B. Holbrook (ed.),

Consumer Value: A Framework for Analysis and Research, London, Routledge, 1999, pp. 105–125.

44. C.V. Ford, op. cit.; J.A. Barnes, op. cit; E. Giannetti, op. cit.

45. Interestingly, this topic has recently become something of a media hobbyhorse. For example, S. Pyper, 'The tweenie boom', *You Magazine*, Sunday 14 November, 1999, pp. 42–49; A. Smith, 'Pester power', *The Observer*, Sunday 26 March, 2000, p. 20; C. McDowell, 2000, op. cit.; B. Summerskill, op. cit.

46. E.T.H. Brann, *The World of the Imagination: Sum and Substance*, Lanham, Rowman and Littlefield, 1991; R. Kearney, *Poetics of Imagining: Modern to Postmodern*, New York, Fordham University Press, 1998; R. Kearney, *The Wake of Imagination*, London, Routledge, 1994. Incidentally, the 'Once faith is lost' quotation comes from Z. Papanikolas, op. cit., p. 99

47. S. Burton, op. cit.; M.A. Henderson, *Rip Offs, Cons and Swindles*, Fortlee, NJ, Barricade Books, 1986; D.W. Maurer, *The Big Con*, Century, London, 1999.

48. The classic discussion of all-in wrestling and the importance of fakery therein is provided by R. Barthes, 'The world of wrestling', in *Mythologies*, trans. A. Lavers, London, Paladin, 1973, pp. 15–26.

49. J.E. Rogers, 'Flirting fascination', *Psychology Today*, 32 (1), 1999, pp. 36–41, 64–70; D.A. Lott, 'The new flirting game', *Psychology Today*, 32 (1), 1999, pp. 42–45, 72; E.J. Dickson, 'The eyes have it', *The Times Weekend*, Saturday 29 July, 2000, p. 4; Anon., 'How to . . . flirt successfully', *The Editor*, Friday 7 January, 2000, p. 23.

Rewriting Marketing: Pedagogic Appendix

1. The prehistory of marketing is considered in S. Brown, *Postmodern Marketing*, 1995, op. cit.

2. These days, admittedly, there can't be many who have yet to be exposed to Kotlerite marketing concepts. Think of all those short courses, television programmes, newspaper columns, marketing-for-dummies primers and suchlike. There remains, nevertheless, a marketing-is-American mindset. Check the citations in the preface, note 10.

3. The thirty-seven definitions of relationship marketing are discussed in E. Gummesson, *Total Relationship Marketing. Rethinking Marketing Management: From 4Ps to 30Rs*, Oxford, Butterworth-Heinemann, 1999. The profusion of marketing definitions is covered by M.J. Baker, 'One more time – what is marketing?', in *The Marketing Book*, fourth edition, Oxford, Butterworth-Heinemann, 1999, pp. 3–15.

4. A classic example of this propensity is R.A. Kerin, 'In pursuit of an ideal: the editorial and literary history of the *Journal of Marketing*', *Journal of Marketing*, 60 (1), 1996, pp. 1–13. On marketing periodization schemes generally see S.C. Hollander, K.M. Rassuli and L. Dix, 'Periodization schemes in marketing history: a drama in X acts', in D.G.B. Jones and P. Cunningham (eds), *Marketing History Knows No Boundaries*, Proceedings of the 8th Conference on Historical Research in Marketing and Marketing Thought, Kingston, Queen's University, 1997, pp. 85–88.

5. R. Marchand, 1985, op. cit.; R. Porter, op. cit.

6. Williams's essay on magic is reprinted in S. During, *The Cultural Studies Reader*, London, Routledge, 1993, pp. 320–336.

7. The scholarly literature on magic is judiciously reviewed in A. Glucklich, *The End of Magic*, Oxford, Oxford University Press, 1997.

8. R. Levine et al., op. cit.

9. Barnum's 'Money getting' lecture is reprinted in J. Vitale, *There's a Customer Born Every Minute*, 1998, op. cit. pp. 165–193.

10. Professor Helms's text is discussed at length in B. McNamara, op. cit.

11. I'd love to tell you the story of Dr Albert Abrams and his 'Dynamiser'. Space, sadly, doesn't permit.

12. S. Stewart, op. cit, p. 159.

13. H.C. Andersen, 'The princess on the pea', in *The Complete Fairy Tales*, Ware, Wordsworth Editions, 1997, pp. 21–22.

14. See for example, R. Silverstone, op. cit.; J.J. Palen, op. cit.; R. Fishman, *Bourgeois Utopias: The Rise and Fall of Suburbia*, New York, Basic Books, 1987.

15. Bernays' banana antics are recounted at length in L. Tye, op. cit., pp. 160–182. Incidentally, the United Fruit Company is now called Chiquita Brands International.

16. See J. Brannigan, op. cit.; P. Hamilton, op. cit.; C. Gallagher and S. Greenblatt, op. cit.

17. P. Kotler and S.J. Levy, 'Broadening the concept of marketing', *Journal of Marketing*, 33 (January), 1969, pp. 10–15.

Index